The Pianist's Bookshelf

The Pianist's Bookshelf

A Practical Guide to Books, Videos, and Other Resources

Maurice Hinson

INDIANA UNIVERSITY PRESS

Bloomington and Indianapolis

This book is a publication of

Indiana University Press
601 North Morton Street
Bloomington, Indiana 47404-3797 USA

www.indiana.edu/~iupress

Telephone orders   800-842-6796
Fax orders   812-855-7931
Orders by e-mail   iuporder@indiana.edu

Library of Congress Cataloging-in-Publication Data

Hinson, Maurice.
The pianist's bookshelf : a practical guide to books,
videos, and other resources / Maurice Hinson.
p.   cm.
Includes bibliographical references and index.
ISBN 0–253–33332–6 (alk. paper). — ISBN 0–253–
21145–X (pbk. : alk. paper)
1. Piano—Bibliography. 2. Piano music—Bibliography.   I. Title.
ML128.P3H534   1998
016.7862—dc21   97–47307
                                             MN

1 2 3 4 5 03 02 01 00 99 98

To Kendel, Lindsey, Ross, and Michelle,
our grandchildren

❧

Contents

Preface

The large amount of information related to the piano and its many aspects makes a reference source such as *The Pianist's Bookshelf* a necessity if the pianist and piano teacher wish to keep informed regarding recent developments in their constantly expanding field. This volume was written and compiled to fulfill this need.

It is very helpful for the piano teacher and pianist to know something of the origin of a particular musical work—of any literary, biographical or other details which may throw light on it, or help toward its true interpretation. The majority of pianists know very little about the works they perform. Any student in school studying English literature will be informed about the sources from which the plots of *Hamlet* or *The Merchant of Venice* are derived. Yet pianists will play Liszt's *St. Francis Preaching to the Birds* or *St. Francis Walking on the Waves* without any inkling as to the source or nature of these legends and with little opportunity given them to gain such information. It is reprehensible to not know the most elementary facts concerning the work's genesis or, as in the case of the Liszt Legends, to not know the story which the music is intended to portray.

This is only one area where *The Pianist's Bookshelf* will be of assistance. By checking the Composer Index the reader can quickly locate the books dealing with Liszt's works and find the necessary information regarding the Legends. It behooves all who teach and/or perform to know as much as possible about their field(s) of expertise.

The Pianist's Bookshelf will also be helpful for discovering what has and has not been written in English in the fields related to the piano. It can serve teachers, students, amateurs, and librarians as a guide in building their own musical literature collections.

In spite of my efforts to include all published materials relating to the piano published since 1987, items have probably been omitted. For these omissions I offer my sincere apologies. The author would greatly appreciate readers letting him know of specific items that have been overlooked.

Maurice Hinson
Louisville, Kentucky
January 1, 1998

Introduction

The contents are arranged alphabetically by author and include almost seven hundred entries. Primarily, writings in the English language are included in this book. Sixteen indexes facilitate locating works in the following areas: Accompanying and Chamber Music, Aesthetics, Analysis, Biographies, Construction and Design, Editors, Performers, Teachers and Writers, History and Criticism, Lists of Piano Music, Ornamentation, Pedagogy, Performance Anxiety: Stress and Tension, Performance Technique, Piano Duets, Transcriptions, Two or More Pianos, and Video Cassettes. A Composers Index and List of Publishers also provide assistance.

Each book entry was checked against *Books in Print* (1995/96) and/or *British Books in Print* (1995) to make certain that all books listed in this bibliography are currently available in print. A few recent books not found in the preceding titles were included if published outside the United States or the United Kingdom. Where possible, all bibliographic information has been supplied with each entry. Both the original publisher and the publisher who is currently reprinting the book are given when available. Publication dates which were unavailable are indicated with "n.d." The number of pages for each entry is usually supplied, and paperbacks are listed when known. Prices change so rapidly in the publishing world that they have been omitted in this bibliography.

The word "thesis" refers to a master's degree thesis; "dissertation" refers to a doctoral dissertation. Each thesis or dissertation entry was checked against various sources, including *Dissertation Abstracts International, Master's Abstracts,* Cecil Adkin's *Doctoral Dissertations in Musicology, RILM Abstracts, Current Musicology* listings, *Musical Quarterly* listings, Rita H. Mead's *Doctoral Dissertations in American Music,* and Roderick Gordon's *Doctoral Dissertations in Music and Education.* Most of the annotations for master's and doctoral dissertations are from *Dissertation Abstracts International* and *Master's Abstracts* and, therefore, are written by the author of the document being discussed. In a few instances, minor editing has been executed in order to create a cohesive, uniform volume.

Theses and dissertations with *M* and *UM* numbers are easy to acquire and may be ordered from University Microfilms, Ann Arbor, Michigan 48106, telephone 1-800-521-3042 (examples UM LC Card no. Mic 5894, or UM 71-15,694, or M-986.) The price for a photocopied dissertation at time of press is $36.00 for a paperback copy and $43.50 for a hardback copy. Theses and dissertations listed without numbers are usually available on interlibrary loan from the library of the listed institution.

A list of publishers and their addresses is included beginning on page 318 so that any reader may order direct from the publisher. This is often the fastest way to obtain the material. An address is provided within the entry if the document is handled through a lesser-known organization or individual.

Adams, Noah. *Piano Lessons: Music, Love and True Adventure.* New York: Delacorte Press, 1996. This book is about an adult beginner. It follows him from a computerized self-teaching system through his first teacher. A few reflections on some of the great pianists of the twentieth century add interest. The author obviously loves to play the piano, and this idea comes through loud and clear. He is now a respectable amateur pianist.

Ahn, Joel. *A Stylistic Evaluation of Charles Valentin Alkan's Piano Music: A Lecture Recital Together with Three Recitals of Selected Works of J. S. Bach, Beethoven, Brahms, Liszt, Schumann, and Villa-Lobos.* D.M.A. paper, Denton: University of North Texas, 1988, 143 p. UM 8908902. Charles Valentin Alkan (1813–1888), one of the great geniuses in music history, was widely misunderstood by his contemporaries because of his highly idiosyncratic ideas. From the perspective of the late twentieth century his innovations can be better understood, and his music is now gaining wider appreciation. Yet, today many musicians still do not know even his name, much less his achievements.

The year 1988 marked the one hundredth year since his death. In commemoration of this centennial anniversary, this thesis has been presented as a plea for a greater awareness of the achievements of this important figure in the development of piano music.

Ai, Chia-Huei. *Chopin's Concerto in E Minor, Op. 11: An Analysis for Performance.* D.M.A. paper, Columbus: Ohio State University, 1986, 83 p. UM 8618730. This analytical study provides a performance-related analysis of the *Piano Concerto in E Minor,* Op. 11 of Frédéric Chopin. The discussion is divided into three sections. Chapter One is a presentation of purpose for writing this document. Chapter Two presents the historical background of the *E Minor Concerto.* Chapter Three presents a careful analysis of each movement in order to provide the necessary background for performance.

It was found that the structure of dynamic contrasts had a close relationship with the formal structure of the concerto. Formal structural units corresponded to the composer's "dynamic arches," i.e., gradual increases or decreases in volume effected by crescendos or decrescendos. The writer offers suggestions about how to avoid memory problems in the concerto. She states that such analysis aided her own performance and that such study by all musicians could aid their subsequent performances.

Aide, William. *Starting from Porcupine.* Ottawa, Canada: Oberon Press. Fascinating memories by the head of the piano department at the University of Toronto. Mining country where the author grew up was the "Porcupine." Aide toured with some of the outstanding singers of his time. His observations on Alberto Guerrero, Glen Gould's teacher, plus other famous musicians make for insightful reading.

Albergo, Cathy, and Reid Alexander. *Intermediate Piano Repertoire.* Oakville, Canada: Frederick Harris Music Co., 1993, 104 p. Three levels of grading intermediate repertoire are discussed as well as teaching order. Characteristic elements of the four style periods are listed in chart form. This is followed by the solo literature listed in the four style periods, plus appropriate collections and anthologies. Multiperiod collections and anthologies follow; Holiday Literature, Ensemble Literature, and two appendixes (Materials for Adult Instruction and Listing of Publishers) conclude the book. This is the finest focused book on the subject and is warmly welcomed.

Albergo, Cathy, Reid Alexander, and Marvin Blickenstaff. *Celebration Series Handbook for Teachers.* Oakville, Canada: Frederick Harris Music Co., 1996, 229 p. This handbook helps teachers to progressively correlate repertoire and studies. It also provides ideas for teachers, such as tips for teaching score exploration, incorporating composition into lessons, and teaching students how to practice.

Albuquerque, Anne E. *Teresa Carreño: Pianist, Teacher, and Composer.* D.M.A. paper, University of Cincinnati, 1988, 96 p. UM 8908446. Teresa Carreño (1853–1917) was born in Caracas, Venezuela, but her family moved to the United States when she was seven years old. As an eight-year-old, Carreño made her New York debut and soon after caught the attention of Louis Moreau Gottschalk. From child prodigy, she grew into a mature artist and a beautiful woman. Carreño was affectionately known as the "Walküre of the Piano" due to her colorful and tempestuous playing and personality. Carreño's repertoire included large-scale virtuoso works and concerti by the Romantic composers, as well as several Beethoven sonatas. From the few piano rolls that she made (now reproduced on long-playing records), one finds sensitivity and clarity combined with a stunning virtuoso technique.

Amid her four marriages and five children, Carreño found the time to concertize and teach extensively both in the United States and in Europe. She taught the young Edward MacDowell, and was solely responsible for promoting his piano music in Germany. As a teacher, Carreño believed in the individuality of a student and, as such, had no fixed teaching method. The art of producing a beautiful tone quality at the keyboard was her main teaching objective. Carreño's book on pedaling was a further testament to her intimate knowledge of the piano and its repertoire.

As a composer, Carreño's output includes about forty piano pieces in various forms, a string quartet, an unpublished serenade for string orchestra, and the "Hymn to Bolívar." The piano works make tremendous technical demands on the performer. Some of her character pieces demonstrate Carreño's ability to effect a particular mood, and they display her gift for melodic lyricism. A listing of her piano works with and without opus numbers is contained in the appendix.

Alexander, Dennis. *Imagery in Piano Performance.* Video cassette. Van Nuys, Calif.: Alfred Publishing Co., 1995, 58 minutes. Alexander explores four imagery techniques that encourage artistry in piano performance: character, imagery, story imagery, and visual and color imagery. Specific examples by Alexander, Bach, Chopin, Clementi, and Mozart demonstrate how teachers may immediately use each type of imagery with their students.

Alexander, Michael John. *The Evolving Keyboard Style of Charles Ives.* New York: Garland Publishing Co., 1989, 256 p. The investigation focuses on the cultural, scientific, and philosophical bases underlying Ives's striving toward both a unique kind of keyboard writing and its musical realization. His gradual accumulation of a multiplicity of received traditions in American art and folk music of his time, together with their attendant attitudes with respect to individual performance practice and improvisation, are accounted for by a detailed examination of the major influences involved and their assimilation into the composer's innovative designs.

By inquiring into Ives's early musical environment and training, and noting his subtle modification and experimental reworking of nineteenth-century styles, discoveries made provide a groundwork for further insights into the oral and notated elements of his keyboard language. Through his experiences as an improvising vaudeville accompanist and as a more passive observer of various surviving New England vocal traditions, the revealed spiritual and acoustical manifestations exerted a strong influence on the way that the composer regarded the piano's sonority. These diverse features coalesce into an original body of solo studies representing the essence of Ives's transcendentalism: where "the evolving" is implicit in the determination of written notation and its contingent translation through live performance into musical meaning.

Alger, Brian Wayne. *Boogie-Woogie Piano Manuals.* M.A. thesis, Toronto: York University, 1985, 125 p. UM 96418. The purpose of this thesis is to provide a comparative and evaluative analysis of boogie-woogie piano manuals, and other blues manuals found to contain discussions pertaining to boogie-woogie, which were published during the early 1940s. The study of these pedagogies allows for greater insight into performance practice and the ways in which musicians and writers have thought about boogie-woogie/blues music.

In constructing a "Bibliography of Popular Piano Manuals" and a bibliography of "Boogie-Woogie/Blues Piano Solo Folios," various available piano manuals and folios were consulted for advertisements as well as pertinent books and journal articles on ragtime, blues, boogie-woogie, and jazz. Although these bibliographies are not comprehensive, they do provide a survey of sixty-two piano manuals (1897–1982) and thirty-two blues folios (1941–1977). Seven manuals published during the 1940s pertain to this topic, but only three were available for this study: Pease, Sharon. *Boogie Woogie Piano Styles.* Chicago: Forster Music Publishers, Inc., vol. 1 (1940), vol. 2 (1943); Slack, Freddie. *Boogie-Woogie: Book on 8-Beats.* New York: Robbins Music Corporation, 1942; and Paparelli, Frank. *The Blues and How to Play 'Em.* New York: Leeds Music Corporation, 1942.

The introduction develops three ideas which pertain to the study of boogie piano manuals. First, in applying idiosyncrasies gleaned from one style of music, boogie manuals continued a tradition of instruction stemming from ragtime manuals. Second, competing concepts of boogie-woogie suggest a distinction between "authentic" and "commercial" boogie. Third, these manuals may be understood as a translation of the art of the "untrained" pianist into terms familiar to "trained" pianists.

Allsop, Peter. *The Italian Trio Sonata: From Its Origin until Corelli.* New York: Clarendon Press, 1992, 334 p. Comprehensive coverage of every major composer of Italian trio sonatas during the seventeenth century. Includes two maps, music, and biographical references.

Altschuler, Eric Lewin. *Bachanalia: The Essential Listener's Guide to Bach's* Well-Tempered Clavier. Waltham, Mass.: Little, Brown & Co., 1994, 254 p. The author draws an analogy between his favorite sport (baseball) and Bach's *Well-Tempered Clavier* and gives a summary of each prelude and fugue. He defines terminology such as codettas, episodes, fugue, real and tonal answers, stretto, and counter subjects, and includes some unusual facts about each fugue. This book is an easy way to increase your knowledge about this gigantic masterpiece. Includes bibliographical references and index.

Alvarez, Yasmin. *The Development and Evaluation of a Sequential Comprehensive Keyboard Curriculum for Senior High School.* Ph.D. dissertation, University of Miami, 1992, 310 p. UM 9227184. The purpose of this study is to design and implement a curriculum for senior high school keyboard classes. The development of goals and specific objectives was the product of a survey of related literature and a summary of the implied objectives of selected keyboard textbooks.

The curriculum was implemented during one school year with eighty-six keyboard students at a senior high school in Miami, Florida. There were three classes of enrollees, two beginning and one intermediate. Students were pretested and posttested using Colwell's Music Achievement Tests 1 and 2. At the end of the year, numbers and percentages of students attaining each objective were calculated. In addition, a survey was conducted assessing the attitudes of the students toward the class. More than 80 percent of the attitude survey respondents reported that they enjoyed the class. Playing in groups and listening were liked by more than 80 percent of the students.

Amaize, Ho Pai-Hwa. *Musical Concepts for Fostering Expressivity and Interpretation in Piano Playing: A Content Analysis of Selected Written Materials (1892–1992).* D.M.A. paper, Columbia: University of South Carolina, 1993, 93 p. UM 9459973. This study objectively identifies and categorizes, through content analysis of 123 selected written materials (1892–1992), musical concepts that were emphasized by various pianists, piano teachers, and music pedagogues for fostering the creative processes of expressivity and interpretation in piano playing. Twenty-nine musical concepts are identified in the literature review, and these are subsequently ranked through content analysis procedures. Throughout the study, quotations from the literature illustrate the advice given by experts over the period of 100 years concerning expressivity and interpretation in piano performance.

Amrod, Paula J. *Rudolph Ganz: A Profile of His Life and Teaching.* D.M. paper, Bloomington: Indiana University, 1986, 210 p. Chapters include A Brief Biography, Career as Pianist, Career as Teacher, Other Contributions to Piano Pedagogy, and Appraisal as Teacher. An appendix and selected bibliography conclude the work. The Appendix is a questionnaire the author sent former Ganz students. The section in Career as Teacher dealing with Ganz's views on piano playing and teaching were of the most interest to this writer.

Anatomy of a Piano. Video cassette. Kansas City, Mo.: SH Productions, 75 minutes. John Serkin, one of New York City's most respected piano technicians, provides a detailed explanation of the basic structure and design of the grand piano. Organized into four sections for viewing in one or more sessions in the classroom or workshop setting.

Anderson, Bruce Clarke. *The Solo Piano Music of Elliott Carter: A Performance Guide.* Ph.D. dissertation, New York University, 1988, 206 p. UM 8835207. The first chapter of this study begins with an overview of the life and works of Elliot Carter. The presentation of his training, influences, musical values, and stylistic evolution provides a larger context in which to view the solo piano works.

The next three chapters each focus on analysis of one of the solo piano works: *Piano Sonata* (1945–1946), *Piano Concerto* (1965), and *Night Fantasies* (1980). Analyses of the works are based upon a modified version of Jan La Rue's method of style analysis and David Schiff's presentation of theoretical principles in Carter's music. As both approaches are based on observations of the fundamental elements of music, they are complementary and serve to enhance one another.

Schiff facilitates La Rue in his contribution of information on Carter's unique treatment of elements in a manner providing insights which would prove more elusive through La Rue's approach alone. La Rue provides a larger, all-encompassing background by providing a thorough exploration of all the musical elements and not just the aspects for which Carter has derived special approaches. The two analytical procedures have been used to identify stylistic characteristics related to performance problems rather than to develop extensive analyses of musical form and content. The use of a combination of the two approaches proved fruitful, sometimes in quite unexpected ways. Most unanticipated was the degree to which La Rue's approach proved useful when applied to Carter's later works.

In the fifth chapter, the data extrapolated in the analyses were then synthesized in the formation of a performance guide. An awareness of underlying compositional principles simplifies the task of the pianist and saves time as it facilitates and expedites the process of practice and preparation. Information gathered from personal interviews with the composer and pianists associated with his music is presented. Practical considerations and insights gained from the researcher's experience of preparation and performance of Carter's music are also included. Conclusions and suggestions for further research are presented in the final chapter.

Anderson, Christine Dow. *The Exposition and Development Sections of Schubert's Piano Sonatas.* M.A. thesis, University of Louisville, 1994, 105 p. UM 1360677. This paper contains a discussion of fifteen piano sonatas of Franz Schubert, written between 1815 and 1828. The first section offers a chronology of the sonatas. In the second section, exposition and development of the first movements are examined. The themes, transitions, connecting passages, and closing sections of the exposition are examined to determine the underlying structure and harmony. The development is viewed in relation to the exposition, with a look at the harmonic organization and thematic dependence. The final section correlates the chronology and changes in compositional technique.

Andres, Robert. *"Cherubim-Doctrine," Harmonie-Piano, and Other Innovations of Frederic Horace Clark.* D.M.A. paper, Lawrence: University of Kansas, 1993, 104 p. UM 9405710. Frederic Horace Clark (1860–1917), American pianist, pedagogue, and inventor, was, according to Rudolf Breithaupt's *Handbuch der modernen Methodik und Spielpraxis,* 3rd ed. (1912), the world pioneer in the physiological approach to piano playing. Clark's analysis is expounded in his *Lehre des einheitlichen Kunstmittels beim Klavierspiel* (The Doctrine of Unified Art of Piano Playing) (1885). Clark provided a significant link between the age of instinctive performance and the age of scientific study.

Andrews, Jane Silvey. *The Religious Element in Selected Piano Literature.* D.M.A. paper, Fort Worth: Southwestern Baptist Theological Seminary, 1986, 107 p. UM 8705895. This document examines selected piano literature which contains some religious element. The study of piano literature as a division of sacred literature has received little attention, although there are many works which have some association with religion. This association may be by a descriptive or programmatic nature, by use of a theme or tune associated with a religious text, by intentional composition for a liturgical function, or by a religious experience of inspiration on the part of the composer.

The works selected for this performer's study include the C Major Prelude and Fugue, the E-flat Major Prelude and Fugue, and the G Major Prelude and Fugue from *The Well-Tempered Clavier,* Book II, by J. S. Bach; the "Benediction de Dieu dans la Solitude" from *Harmonies Poétiques et Religieuses* by Franz Liszt; *Mosaics: Six Piano Pieces on Hebrew Folk Themes* by Denes Agay; *Icons* by Einojuhani Rautavaara; and *The Garden of Eden* by William Bolcom. They represent various periods and styles, as well as various religious associations. Formal and harmonic analyses are included in the study. The particular means of association with the religious element is discussed for each work.

Angilette, Elizabeth. *Glenn Gould (1932–1982): A Study of His Contribution to a Philosophy of Music and Music Education.* Ph.D. dissertation, New York University, 1986, 273 p. UM 8910622. Glenn Gould's writings were critically examined in order to determine their relevance to the development of a philosophy of music and music education. Gould wrote from an aesthetic position that expansively considered music in relation to other epistemological modes. His musical-philosophical thought is often embedded in writings that explore other issues. Thus, it is necessary to draw out implicit ideas and then present an interpretation.

Meta-theoretical analysis was employed in order to evaluate Gould's thought in the light of leading rationales of the philosophy of music and music education. A Gouldian model for a philosophy of music consisting of three primary parts emerged: a morality of music, a sociology of music, and an epistemology of music.

The Gouldian morality of music, which espouses a comprehensive reverence in everyday activities, functions at the apex and dominates the model. It directs music toward a subtle moral range and a goodness that is transnaturally responsible to all living and nonliving things. Gould advocates in his writings the notion that music is sociologically important to culture. He argues that music is not only a reflection of social dynamics but could potentially be a tool for the betterment of society. Gould's epistemology of music resembles phenomenological methods of inquiry in that music reveals itself (syntax), music reveals the person (semantic), and music reveals the world (semantic and ontology).

As the model shifts to a philosophy of music education, Gould's ideas assume axiological significance and are a step toward a theoretical framework (a synthetic construct) within which the musician can discover levels of personal and interpersonal meanings. The axiology stresses self and social transcendence. Gould believed that through the transformative experience of ecstasy in music, music can function as a facilitator for educational gains, e.g., accelerated learning, internal imagery, problem solving, and changing values systems. Finally, the philosophical ideas presented by Gould in his writings are highly autobiographical of his spiritual life.

―――. *Philosopher at the Keyboard: Glenn Gould.* Metuchen, N.J.: Scarecrow Press, 1992, 244 p. Based on the author's thesis, New York University, 1988. Gould argued that music is not only a reflection of social dynamics but could also be a tool for the betterment of society. Includes bibliographical references and indexes.

Apple-Monson, Linda. *The Solo Piano Music of Ross Lee Finney.* D.M.A. paper, Baltimore: Peabody Conservatory of Music, 1986, 264 p. UM 8617867. The solo piano works of American composer Ross Lee Finney (1906–1997) form an important and representative part of an *oeuvre* including music for solo voice, various solo instruments, chamber ensemble, orchestra, and chorus.

This dissertation explores Finney's musical vocabulary and traces the foundations of his development and style in his eleven published solo piano compositions to date. The first chapter contains a biography, including a discussion of his musical education, professional career, and personal philosophy. The second, third, and fourth chapters provide a comprehensive analysis of his published piano compositions.

In this study, Finney's solo piano music is categorized in three sections: the early tonal works, the serial compositions, and the children's pieces. Aspects of tonality and modality are combined in his early works: *Piano Sonata in D minor* (1933), *Fantasy* (1939), *Piano Sonata No. 3 in E Major* (1942), *Piano Sonata No. 4 in E Major* (1945), and *Nostalgic Waltzes* (1947). The incorporation of aspects of tonality within a twelve-tone framework is featured in his serial works: *Variations on a Theme by Alban Berg* (1952), *Sonata quasi una Fantasia* (1961), and *Waltz* (1977). A significant contribution to the contemporary pedagogical repertoire is made with his three sets of children's pieces for piano: *24 Inventions* (1956, rev. 1971), *32 Piano Games* (1968), and *Youth's Companion* (1981). A summary of the melodic, harmonic, rhythmic, textural, and formal characteristics of Finney's piano music is given in the fifth chaper.

Archibald, Rebecca Hart. *Understanding Beethoven's* Piano Sonata in E-Flat Major, *Opus 81A, as Program Music.* M.M. paper, California State University, Long Beach, 1990, 48 p. UM 1341760. Beethoven dedicated his *Piano Sonata in E-Flat Major,* Op. 81a, to the Archduke Rudolph, a patron and dear friend. What is distinctive about this piece is its programmatic nature. Entitled "Das Lebewohl" (The Farewell), "Die Abwesenheit" (The Absence), and "Das Wiedersehn" (The Return), the movements refer to the Archduke's departure from Vienna in May 1809, due to an invading French army, and his return nine months later.

The purpose of this study is to demonstrate that an understanding of program music—its history and development, and the effective way that it allows the composers to convey their intent to performers—is an essential element to be considered in the performance of the Op. 81a sonata. An analysis of the program and its effect on the structure of the piece will show how Beethoven preserved Classical form while conveying a programmatic message through his music.

Arnold, Janice Margaret. *The Role of Chromaticism in Chopin's Sonata Forms: A Schenkerian View.* Ph.D. dissertation, Evanston, Ill.: Northwestern University, 1992, 235 p. UM 9309337. Chromaticism is one of the driving forces that propelled changes in the harmonic language of music during the Romantic era, moving it from the solid, well-defined diatonicism of the Classical era to the new vistas of atonality offered in the twentieth century. This dissertation examines a leading Romantic composer's use of chromaticism in the context of the sonata form, the predominant representative form of the Classical era. The historical significance of the sonata form provides a particular perspective into the balance of conservative and innovative forces in the work of Frédéric Chopin, and the special status of the sonata requires an examination of the extramusical factors in Chopin's compositional choice.

The scope of this study is limited to the first movements of Chopin's two mature piano sonatas, Op. 35 in B-flat and Op. 58 in B. Schenkerian analysis of the two sonata forms reveals that the chromaticism in Op. 35 functions mostly as instances of tonicalization, fulfilling an embellishing role, whereas the chromaticism of Op. 58 plays a greater role in generating form.

Arthur Rubinstein. Video cassette. Media for the Arts, Newport, RI 02840, 74 minutes. The great pianist plays works by Mendelssohn, Liszt, and Chopin. We are then taken into Rubinstein's home where he performs five pieces by Chopin.

Ashley, Douglas. *Music Beyond Sound: Maria Curcio, a Teacher of Great Pianists.* New York: Peter Lang, 1993. American University Studies, Series XX, Fine Arts, Vol. 19. Includes bibliographical references and indexes.

Autry, Philip Earl. *The Published Solo Piano Music of Howard Hanson: An Analysis for Teaching and Performing.* D.M.A. paper, Norman: University of Oklahoma, 1996. The purpose of this document is to provide an analysis for teaching and performing the published solo piano music of Howard Hanson. His unpublished solo piano music and the ensemble works in which the piano plays an important role are beyond the paper's scope. The information presented should be helpful to teachers seeking accessible and interesting twentieth-century music to add to their students' repertoire.

Chapter One serves as an introduction, stating the purpose, need, and limitations. It also discusses related literature and outlined procedures. Chapter Two provides a short biography of Hanson, an overview of his piano works, and a discussion of general style characteristics of his music.

Chapters Three through Six present analyses for teaching and performing Hanson's solo piano works. Chapter Three analyzes the intermediate piano solos: *Clog Dance, Three Miniatures,* Op. 12, and *Two Yuletide Pieces,* Op. 19. Chapter Four examines the three pieces in *Masters of Our Day: Dance of the Warriors, Enchantment,* and *The Bell.* Chapter Five is concerned with the piano suite *For the First Time: Twelve Impressions in a Child's Day,* and Chapter Six with the three pieces in *Easy Piano Music by American Composers: The Big Bells and the Little Bells, Tricks or Treats,* and *Horn Calls in the Forest.* Each chapter provides background information for each group of pieces. A structural analysis identifies main sections, tonal areas, and compositional techniques. Suggestions for teaching and performing each work identify interpretative and technical elements.

Chapter Seven consists of a summary, conclusions, and recommendations for further study. Appendixes include a complete list of Hanson's piano works and a discography of his piano music.

Axford, Elizabeth C. *Traditional World Music Influences in Contemporary Solo Piano Literature.* Blue Ridge Summit, Pa.: Scarecrow Press, 1997, 448 p. This selected bibliographic survey and review focuses on pieces of contemporary solo piano literature which contain world music influences not normally associated with Western European art music. The annotated bibliography includes works which use or try to emulate non-Western scales, modes, folk tunes, rhythmic and/or harmonic devices, and timbres. Music cultures touched on include the Middle East and North Africa, Sub-Saharan Africa, India, the Far East, Indonesia, Oceania, ethnic North America, Russia, and Scandinavia. A unique compilation.

Ayesh, Kevin Bradley. *The Solo Piano Music of Robert Starer.* D.M.A. paper, College Park: University of Maryland, 1990, 113 p. UM 9121463. This dissertation consists of a tape recording of the complete solo piano music to date of Robert Starer (b. 1924), and a supplemental, descriptive essay that is designed to be considerably more detailed than the usual booklet that often accompanies commercial presentations of this type.

Starer's piano works range from the short to the extensive. He has contributed several genres of keyboard literature: sonatas (one traditional in form, the other unconventional); a theme and variations; fantasies; toccatas; a fugue; free forms; and preludes, caprices, and other character pieces. The large works include the two sonatas, the fantasylike *Evanescents, The Ideal Self: Fantasy, Variations and Fugue on a Song,* and *Twilight Fantasies.* Smaller character pieces, of which Starer has composed many, exist mainly in collections, such as *Five Caprices, Three Israeli Sketches,* and *At Home Alone.* Starer is perhaps best known to pianists through his instructive compositions; most popular are the two sets of *Sketches in Color.* The dissertation includes a biographical sketch of the composer and discography of Starer's solo piano works.

Backus, Joan Pauline. *Aspects of Form in the Music of Liszt: The Principle of Developing Ideas.* Ph.D. dissertation, Toronto: Victoria University, 1985. Liszt's conception of form, not fully realized until the Weimar years (1848–1860), rests on a delicate balance between the expression of thematic elements and the requirements of formal order. At the same time that Liszt's forms appear to evolve through variation and transformation, a formal organization co-exists that depends on the basic principles of sonata form for its cogency. This study is an evaluation of aspects of this dual conception of form.

The role of improvisation and variation is discussed with particular reference to the early *Harmonies poétiques et religieuses* and its revised version, *Pensée des morts.* Further to this, analyses of *Totentanz* and *Eroica* demonstrate the potential for the incorporation of sonata principles into variation form. The *Dante* sonata—a single-movement work that foreshadows many of the procedures of large-scale formal control that characterize the works of the Weimar period—is selected as an example of Liszt's mastery of sonata procedures.

The significance of Liszt's evolutionary conception of form with its gradual formation of thematic ideas and its progress toward a final apotheosis is also examined, as is the unique possibility for a new role for program music. Analyses of *Sposalizio, Hamlet,* and the *Faust* symphony illustrate these aspects of Liszt's style. This study is intended as a contribution to the understanding of Liszt's conception of form, a conception that was an innovative response to the challenge facing the post-Beethoven generation of composers. Liszt's achievement is nothing less than a reinterpretation of the essential parameters of classical form in the light of the changing musical language and aesthetic thought of the mid-nineteenth century.

Badura-Skoda, Paul. *Interpreting Bach at the Keyboard.* Trans. Alfred

Clayton. New York: Clarendon Press, 1993, 573 p., paperback. Offers many new insights. Sometimes contentious, always stimulating, this book conveys a passion for an informed interpretation of Bach's music based on a recognition and respect for Bach's actual intentions. The author becomes rather pedantic when he takes around 100 pages to prove that Bach began his short *pralltrillers* on the principal note rather than on the upper auxiliary.

Bailey, Bill. *The Piano Compositions of Ned Rorem: 1948–1954.* D.M.A. paper, Baltimore: Johns Hopkins University, 1992, 147 p. UM 9226409. Although the American composer Ned Rorem (b. 1923) has achieved considerable recognition for his vocal music and his critical and autobiographical writing, many musicians and music lovers are still unaware of his creative efforts in the realm of solo piano music. This study attempts to fill that void by its discussion of Rorem's early piano compositions, especially those composed between 1948 and 1954, and their stylistic evolution, aspects of which may be applied to other instrumental works he composed during this seven-year period.

Chapter One examines Rorem's multifaceted career, beginning with his early training prior to 1948 and continuing with an investigation of influences and events important in his life as a critic, performer, composer, and teacher. Chapter Two deals with the musical climate in which Rorem worked from 1948 to 1954 with special reference to Rorem's teachers, Aaron Copland and Virgil Thomson, and style trends prevalent in Rorem's compositions during those years. Chapters Three through Six each pertain to a specific individual work for solo piano composed between 1948 and 1954: *Sonata No. 1,* the three Barcarolles, *Seconde Sonate,* and *Sonata No. 3.* Chapter Seven offers various conclusions about Rorem's compositional style based on these piano works. The appendix contains a transcription of a lengthy interview with the composer which includes his thoughts and remembrances about circumstances surrounding these particular compositions for solo piano and other important information relevant to his musical and literary career.

Bailie, Eleanor. *Grieg: The Pianist's Repertoire: A Graded Practical Guide.* London: Valhalla Publications, 1993, 584 p. Distributed by C. F. Peters Corp. "The Pianist's Repertoire" is a series of practical guides for the solo piano. This volume is a companion to the author's earlier works on Frédéric Chopin and Joseph Haydn. The main purpose of the series "is to help pianists find pieces suitable for their own styles and capabilities" (back cover). This paperback guide provides a detailed pedagogical investigation of every piano piece by Edvard Grieg. Numerous music examples are included. "A graded list of Grieg's piano works" (pp. x–xvii) from grades 4–5 to 8+ and very advanced (VA) will be helpful to piano teachers and students.

————. *Haydn: The Pianist's Repertoire: A Graded Practical Guide.* London: Novello, 1989, 199 p. Written for teachers and students. Divided into three sections: introduction to Haydn's keyboard music, a graded list of Haydn's keyboard works, and detailed commentaries on the study and performance of every work up to a post–grade 8 standard. An index would have made the book much more useful.

Bang, Keumju. *The Study of Representative Twentieth Century Piano Compositions Appropriate for Use in Contemporary College Piano Literature Classes.* Ed.D. dissertation, New York: Columbia University Teachers College, 1987, 136 p. UM 8804204. The four representative twentieth-century composers—Béla Bartók, George Gershwin, Arnold Schoenberg, and Samuel Barber—have influenced contemporary musical thought, folk music, jazz, twelve-tone technique, and neo-Romanticism. The chosen repertoire, Bartók's *Suite* Op. 14, Gershwin's *Preludes,* Schoenberg's *Klavierstuck* Op. 33a, and Barber's *Ballade,* express these elements.

The main purposes of this study are to analyze these characteristic contemporary pieces and to demonstrate that this process of analysis enhances the abilities of students to make musical interpretations. Thus, not only do students gain insights into twentieth century piano music, but they also develop ideas about the process of analyzing piano pieces through piano literature classes.

Chapter One presents a detailed introduction which contains an explanation of the rationale, purpose of study, limitations, and procedures. The second chapter is a succinct discussion of the general characteristics of twentieth-century piano music. From Chapters Three through Five, this dissertation presents an analysis and an interpretation of four different but related pieces. The final chapter consists of conclusions and educational implications. It contains a summary of twentieth-century compositional techniques found in the four different works and piano techniques that can be developed through the study of these pieces. The study concludes that educational aspects in music learning, such as affective, cognitive, and psychomotor factors, should be balanced. Especially in piano teaching, cognitive aspects are often neglected. Teachers should help students to interpret on their own, not to imitate someone else's performance. Learning the structure can lead to better insight and, hence, can help interpret the various symbols of the composer.

Banks, Donna Whitten. *The Correlation of Selected Precollege Music Computer Programs with the "Alfred Basic Piano Library."* D.M.A. paper, Norman: University of Oklahoma, 1990, 305 p. UM 9029864. The purpose of the study is to correlate selected precollege music computer programs with the Alfred Basic Piano Library. Information in the study serves teachers in several ways. It provides a list of the musical concepts in the order that they are presented in the Alfred Basic Piano Library. It provides descriptions of twenty-five computer program disks enumerating available activities, the ability ranges of the activities, and any other distinguishing factors of pedagogy and presentation. Charts that correlate the activities of the method and the computer programs give teachers practical information on how to integrate the computer lessons into their teaching.

The chapter that reviews the literature related to the topic covers three primary areas of study. The first section of the chapter describes the many ways teachers use computer and related technology in independent studios. The second section of the chapter reviews the types of computer software available to piano teachers. The final section describes the Alfred Basic Piano Library. The computer software for this study was selected from commercially available programs designed for elementary and intermediate students which addressed the lessons in the piano method. A program was not selected if it required more hardware than a computer, a monitor, a DAC board and a 5.25-inch disk drive. Included in the study is a chart in three sections. In the left column are the concepts presented in the Alfred Basic Piano Library, Lesson Books 1A–6. In the center column are computer lessons that correlate with the Lesson Book activities. In the right column are comments to help the teacher achieve the most effective presentation.

Recommendations for further study include suggestions for additional research using other brands of computers and other leading piano methods. Suggestions also are made for studies of music computer programs for preschool children and for college music students. Other recommendations include exploring the use of MIDI in the teaching studio.

Bargmann, Theodore John. *The Solo and Instrumental Chamber Works for Piano by Roy Harris.* D.M.A. paper, Chicago: American Conservatory of Music, 1986, 158 p. UM 8616990. An overview of certain stylistic elements of Harris is first presented, including melody, rhythm, harmony, form, and texture. The following works for solo piano are then examined: *Piano Sonata, Toccata, American Ballades, Piano Suite,* and *Little Suite.* In addition, the following instrumental chamber compositions are studied: *Sonata for Violin and Piano; Soliloquy and Dance for Viola and Piano; Sonata for Violoncello and Piano; Trio for Piano, Violin and Violoncello; Quintet for Piano, Violin, and Violoncello; Quintet for Piano and Strings; Concerto for Piano, Clarinet, and String Quartet;* and *Fantasy for Woodwinds, Horn, and Piano.* Analytical discussions are provided which include consideration of the manner in which the piano is used by the composer. Certain works by other American composers of the period are considered in order to obtain a perspective of the significance of Harris's piano compositions in the context of the twentieth century. Based on the analysis, the following conclusions were drawn: 1) Harris's style in the piano works can be represented by a model which includes the elements of germ motives, modes, melody, harmony, texture, and form. A process of evolution (autogenesis) is regarded as the energy source for developing material in his compositions. The "rough-hewn" quality which is present in these works contributes to the overall style. 2) The treatment of the piano is not typically idiomatic in these compositions, perhaps because of the parameters Harris established for himself with regard to melody, harmony, and texture. Virtuosic display is well represented in some works, such as the *Piano Sonata, Toccata, Sonata for Violin and Piano,* and the *Quintet.* Mature musicianship is generally required in Harris's piano music, if not in the physical technique, then from the standpoints of intellectual understanding of form, melodic expression, and creating the desired harmonic effects. 3) Harris's piano works are part of a trend in American music.

Barr, Alison, and Elizabeth Manduca. *Successful Studio Teaching.* Portland, Maine: Manduca Music Publications, 1993, 81 p. Arranged in five sections plus bibliography with exercises and goal-setting plans in each section: Image Exercises, Organizational Exercises, Public Relations Exercises, Financial Exercises, and The Studio at Work.

Barsalou, June Eunice. *Bach's Goldberg Variations: An Historical and Self-Critical Approach.* M.M. thesis, Urbana-Champaign: University of Illinois, 1954, 108 p. The purpose of this thesis is to bring together such information about Bach's Goldberg Variations as can be found in the Bach literature that exists at the present time (1954). Includes a technical and stylistic analysis.

Barth, George. *The Pianist as Orator: Beethoven and the Transformation of Keyboard Style.* Ithaca: Cornell University Press, 1992, 192 p. Even as the ancient tradition of musical rhetoric was dying in Austria-Hungary and Germany, Beethoven was assimilating and revitalizing it; the past began to live in new ways in his music. Gustav Nottebohm's investigations, and more recent probes by Kirkendale and Kramer, have helped reveal the importance to Beethoven of ancient studies of declamation. But questions remain. How did he realize declamatory principles in performing his keyboard and chamber works? To what degree have the accretions of later nineteenth-century styles hidden those principles from us? Did he himself abandon what Carl Czerny called *der alter Style* when he became fascinated with the practices of the London school?

When Czerny recommended the metronome as a tool for achieving unity of expression in Beethoven, he was taken to task by Anton Schindler, who claimed that he misrepresented Beethoven's "rhetorical" style. The clash between the two disciples is revelatory, stemming as it does from Beethoven's having attempted a synthesis of ancient and modern ideas. But for his part Schindler had good reason to object; those who accepted Czerny's description of music and machine helped draw the curtain on the age of musical rhetoric.

Beginning with an exploration of musical time and musical character in eighteenth-century treatises Beethoven studied, this book demonstrates that Czerny's prescription for metronome use leaves the question of unity unresolved, since there are at least two radically different aspects of time at work in Beethoven's music, one of which is based on time's "knowing no equality of parts." Czerny seems to sense this, but fails in his *On the Proper Performance of All Beethoven's Works for the Piano* to provide a foundation for teaching it, at least in part because of his falsification of Beethoven's palette of articulation. "The ancients," as Beethoven knew, addressed the question of unity in a powerful way, and Schindler, despite his unscrupulous forgeries, provides the clues needed—most of them quoted from wiser contemporaries—to recover what Czerny obscured.

————. *The Pianist as Orator: Beethoven and the Transformation of Keyboard Style*. Ithaca, N.Y.: Cornell University Press, 1992, 189 p.

Baskins, Carol Ann. *The Contributions of Celia Mae Bryant to Piano Pedagogy*. Ph.D. dissertation, Norman: University of Oklahoma, 1995, 208 p. UM 9501174. Bryant's work spans three decades. This study examines Bryant's pedagogical practices and philosophy through her activities as a teacher, writer, clinician, adjudicator, and organizational leader. Throughout her life, Bryant worked at the local, state, national, and international levels to elevate the status of music.

Baytelman, Pola. *Isaac Albéniz: Chronological List and Thematic Catalog of His Piano Works*. Warren, Mich.: Harmonie Park Press, 1993, 124 p. In three parts: introduction, including a discussion of keyboard music in Spain prior to Albéniz's life, and three stylistic periods of piano works; chronological list and thematic catalog of his piano works; and appendixes: **A.** Early compositions allegedly written by Albéniz; **B.** Chronological outline of Albéniz's life and career; **C.** collections of Albéniz's piano works; **D.** Selected list of compositions for piano by Albéniz graded according to level of difficulty; and **E.** discography, bibliography, and index.

Beattie, Donald. *Guide to the Masters*. St. Louis: Edition HAS, 1992, 64 p. Contains twelve programs of literature with a selection and sequence of studies from intermediate and advanced piano music. Also includes collections from some of the great composers. The early programs (1–4) may be introduced during the middle volumes of a piano method, while later programs will extend far beyond where a method generally leaves off. Concludes with an essay on "The Great Pianists and Recording Artists."

Beauchamp, Laura Denise. *Boris Berlin's Career and Contributions to Piano Pedagogy*. D.M.A. paper, Norman: University of Oklahoma, 1994, 388 p. UM 9501164. This study contains seven chapters and several appendixes. Chapter One serves as an introduction and includes a review of related literature and a description of the procedures and sources used. Chapter Two provides an overview of piano teaching in Canada so that the reader will have a frame of reference for examining Berlin's career. Chapter Three discusses the Royal Conservatory of Music and its examination system. Chapter Four contains a biography of Berlin. Chapter Five describes his teaching in detail. Chapter Six discusses his pedagogical publications, showing how they reflect both his philosophy and the environment in which he worked. Chapter Seven summarizes Berlin's contributions and makes recommendations for further research. The appendixes provide complete lists of Berlin's publications and writings, selected reviews of his works, a selected list of public engagements, photographs and publicity, the CFMTA survey, and the letters and questions mailed to Berlin's colleagues and students.

Beck, John Michael. *Ignaz Moscheles Re-Examined: The Realization of a Full Conductor's Score for* Piano Concerto No. 1 in F Major, *opus 45.* D.A. dissertation, Greeley: University of Northern Colorado, 1986, 3 vols., 555 p. UM 8621954. This study of Ignaz Moscheles (1794–1870) begins with a biographical review of his life: his importance as a performer, teacher, conductor, composer, arranger/transcriber, editor, musicologist, and humanitarian. Moscheles's associations with several composers and performers of the nineteenth century are presented. Reviews of performances of his own compositions also appear.

The research for this study included gathering and securing required materials (books, journals, periodicals, personal interviews, personal and professional correspondence, dissertations, scores, recordings, microfilms, and pertinent information from computer data banks). Major domestic and foreign music libraries were also consulted. All extant, known, available editions of the solo and orchestral parts to Op. 45 were compared and analyzed, as were all full conductor's scores to other Moscheles piano concerti. The full conductor's score was realized, and an accompanying set of orchestral parts and a solo piano part are available from the author.

The bibliography provides documentation for the project. The appendices include **A.** Selected Pupils/Students of Ignaz Moscheles; **B.** A Complete Catalog of Compositions by Ignaz Moscheles; **C.** Variants in the Orchestral Parts; **D.** Variants in the Solo Piano Part; **E.** Variants in the Full Conductor's Scores to Moscheles's Piano Concertos; **F.**

Overview of the Holograph to the *Full Conductor's Score* to Mo-scheles's *Piano Concerto No. 4, Op. 64 in E Major*; and **G.** General Editorial Comments for the *Realized Full Conductor's Score* to Mocheles's *Piano Concerto No. 1, Op. 45 in F Major.*

Becker, Paul Jerome. *The Use of Astrology in Twentieth-Century Piano Music.* D.M.A. paper, Memphis, Tenn.: Memphis State University, 1992, 130 p. UM 9224257. The purpose of this study is to investigate the use of astrology in solo piano music of the twentieth century. An analysis of the complete settings of the signs of the zodiac for piano by four contemporary composers is the primary focus. The compos-ers and their works are as follows: George Crumb's *Makrokosmos,* Karlheinz Stockhausen's *Tierkreis,* Sherman Storr's *Zodiac Suite,* and Georges Migot's *Le Zodiaque: Douze Etudes de Concert.*
Chapter One begins with a statement of the problem in which the primary questions are posed. Chapter Two is a compilation and dis-cussion about the related literature and includes a survey of the litera-ture about astrology in general, the history of astrology, the relation-ship between astrology in art and in literature, and the relationship between astrology and music. As there is no literature that contains information specifically about astrology and piano music, Chapter Two also discusses the sources of information about the specific com-posers and/or compositions included in this study.
Chapter Three is the study itself. It has four large sections, based upon the composers and compositions studied. Each section begins with a biography of the composer. The background of the specific compositions with astrological content is discussed. An analysis of the composition follows, which is based upon a parametric analysis and biographical and autobiographical information. The extent and manner of astrological information in each composition are deter-mined through this analysis. In Chapter Four, conclusions are made based on this analysis.
An extramusical program can be either descriptive or philosophical. Generally, these four settings combine the two programmatic ideas in their incorporation of astrological information. There were primarily four different modes of incorporation of an astrological date: the com-posers tried to depict the character of the sign itself (Ram, Scorpion, etc.); they attempted to incorporate the personalities of specific people known to the composer who were born under a certain sign; they attempted to show personality traits generally associated with a per-

son born under that sign (Cancerians are supposed to be moody, for example); or they incorporated more esoteric astrological data into the compositions. Often these procedures were combined. The compositional procedures varied widely, though generally proceeding in a style already established by the composer. Often, the astrological content can be determined only through biographical or autobiographical information. It is evident that astrological content can be transferred to music and that astrology is a colorful repository from which to derive musical inspiration.

An appendix includes an annotated list of compositions by the four composers. Also in the appendix is information about a group of composers that lived in Paris in the 1940s who called themselves "Le Zodiaque." An additional appendix lists many compositions that contain astrological titles or relationships.

Beckman, Bradley John, Jr. *Ronald Stevenson's "Passacaglia on D S C H":* *Understanding the Composer's Unique Approach to Large-Scaled* *Structure.* D.M.A. paper, Denton: University of North Texas, 1994, 177 p. UM 9503914. This paper investigates Ronald Stevenson's unique treatment of large-scaled structure in his *Passacaglia on D S C H.* This analysis reveals Stevenson's approach to composing in such a large form, as well as illustrating his mastery of variation, counterpoint, and unending ingenuity for innovative piano techniques.

Bedenbaugh, Ray. *Rubato in the Chopin Mazurkas.* D.M.A. paper, Stanford, Calif.: Stanford University, 1986, 61 p. UM 8619849. The proper use of rubato in the Chopin mazurkas has long been a disputed issue among pianists. When applied with taste and understanding, it can add to the natural flow of the music, bringing it to life. Misused, it reduces the music to absurdity. This important rhythmic element stems from the dance character of the mazurka and Chopin's use of this element. Pianists of East European descent seem to have an innate comprehension of this rhythmic freedom. This aptitude may be cultural inheritance.

This topic has been explored in order to reveal some guidelines which a performer might use when studying the mazurkas. Research into the definitions of "rubato" and the overlappings of these definitions were the first steps. The author also studied the ways in which the traditional mazurkas are danced, insofar as the dance lends itself to rhythmic freedom. Firsthand accounts of Chopin's playing, Chopin's own teachings, and those of his best students have also been researched. Some of these students had students who actually made recordings of some of the mazurkas. Certain aspects of Chopin's own playing may be preserved in some of their performances. It would not be possible to give a definitive answer to such a subjective question as rubato. Still, familiarity with sources close to Chopin will help a performer in his or her musical choices.

Beethoven Piano Concerto No. 1. Video cassette. Princeton, N.J.: Films for the Humanities and Sciences, 60 minutes. ABS 4113. Alicia de Larrocha, pianist, with Michael Tilson Thomas conducting the London Symphony Orchestra. Includes rehearsal sequences and discussions between soloist and presenter (Dudley Moore) that explore the technical and creative demands of the work, and a full performance of the concerto.

Bellman, Jonathan David. *Improvisation in Chopin's Nocturnes: Some Suggested Parameters.* D.M.A. paper, Stanford University, 1990, 110 p. UM 9102212. Those who studied with Frédéric Chopin and heard his performances agree that improvisation accounted for a large part of his performance style. He improvised not only free fantasias but also ornaments to his own works (and the works of others). A substantial number of ornamental variants for his nocturnes survive in his own hand as penciled-in additions noted down for his students. In today's climate of rigorous fidelity to the printed page, it is important to remember both that Chopin's pianism was closely related to that of the Parisian School, which encouraged such decorative gestures, and that his musical taste was inclined toward Italian opera. Interpretative ornamentation was one of the opera singer's regular duties and was not seen as a liberty in any sense. Chopin's letters discussing various singers and the strengths and weaknesses of their ornamentation display much more than a passing interest in the issue. Further, his clear statements to students about the relation between piano playing and singing, and the necessity of understanding the latter in order to excel at the former, indicate that the singer's art and the pianist's were, for Chopin, nearly one and the same.

A historically informed approach to performing Chopin's nocturnes will incorporate the improvisatory tradition. Achieving this involves several preliminary tasks: identification and study of all available surviving variants by the composer, investigation of variation and ornamentation in the nocturnes as published (with regard to both style and context), and a study of Chopin's approach to constructing his ornaments and passagework in general. This last is the basis of Chopin's unique sound, and without it, ornamenting in a style appropriate to his music is impossible. His reinterpretation and reapplication of eighteenth-century compositional principles are unique in the nineteenth century.

The results of this study consist of ornaments created in accordance with the principles described above. These are presented in score form: possibilities for specific situations in three different nocturnes, and two different complete and ornamented versions of the *Nocturne in C minor,* opus posthumous.

Benestad, Finn. *Edvard Grieg, Chamber Music: Nationalism, Universiality, Individuality.* Oslo: Scandinavian University Press. Distributed by Oxford University Press, 1993, 195 p. Includes bibliographic references and index.

Berlin, Edward A. *King of Ragtime: Scott Joplin and His Era.* New York: Oxford University Press, 1994, 334 p. The finest biography of Joplin currently available. Features many illustrations, including photographs of Joplin and other ragtime writers. Also includes bibliographical references and index.

Bernstein, Seymour. *20 Lessons in Keyboard Choreography: The Basics of Physical Movement at the Piano.* New York: Seymour Bernstein Music, 1991. Distributed by Hal Leonard Corp., 176 p. Provides teachers and students with a vocabulary of choreographic movements—movements which reflect music's subtle language. Clear and concise explanations, photographs, and original musical examples.

————. *Musi-Physi-Cality: Making a Physical Connection to Musical Feeling for the Beginning Pianist.* New York: Seymour Bernstein Music, 1991. Distributed by Hal Leonard Corp., 60 p. This book is the children's version of the first seven lessons of *20 Lessons in Keyboard Choreography.* Although all aspects of the book were designed explicitly for children, many adult beginners and even advanced pianists prefer to begin their exploration of keyboard choreography with this book. Like *20 Lessons in Keyboard Choreography, Musi-Physi-Cality* contains text geared specifically for children, photographs, and original musical examples. In addition, there are attractive drawings produced in vivid color and humorous poems.

Berry, Richard Arnold. *Francis Poulenc's Settings of Poems of Paul Eluard for Solo Voice and Piano: A Reflection of French Artistic Moods from 1920 to 1960.* D.M.A. paper, Kansas City, Mo.: University of Missouri, 1985, 151 p. UM 8605286. Between 1935 and 1958, Francis Poulenc (1899–1963) composed thirty-four melodies based on poems of the French Surrealist poet, Paul Eluard (1895–1952). These "Eluard songs" include some of his finest works, probably his masterpieces in the genre of melodic. In these songs, the melodic reached its final development. Poulenc's settings of poems of Eluard for solo voice and piano reflect the prevailing artistic moods of France in the years 1920 through 1960.

Eluard was a leading figure in the Dada and Surrealist literary movements, but he moved beyond those short-lived movements to create poetic language which retained its beauty and mystery while communicating more directly with the reader. His images of light, the eyes, and the redeeming power of love appealed enormously to Francis Poulenc.

Poulenc was a twentieth-century composer in chronology and in temperament who chose to use traditional musical materials in his work. He had an uncanny ability to interpret the sometimes obscure verses of Eluard and, in fact, found himself inspired to great heights of lyricism by them. The result was a contribution to the French song literature which is almost unmatched in the history of the genre. These songs identify themselves in many ways as products of the years between the world wars.

This study examines each of the thirty-four "Eluard songs" as well as the era in which they were composed with a view toward explaining the reflection of the artistic moods by the songs during the years between 1920 and 1960.

Berthisume, Gerald Bernard. *Practice and Performance Techniques for the* Douze Etudes *of Claude Debussy.* D.M.A. paper, Seattle: University of Washington, 1989, 344 p. UM 9006933. This investigation of practice and performance techniques is directed to those etudes of Claude Debussy whose central themes were untraditional and not explored extensively by other composers. Included are the etudes for five fingers, fourths, eight fingers, ornaments, repeated notes, and opposed sonorities. This research seeks to establish further the significance of these works in the repertoire and to aid pianists, both teachers and students, in their study of them.

Each etude is investigated individually in order to examine the diversity of difficulties emanating from its central theme. Practice and performance techniques are organized under the areas of fingerings, articulations and phrasing, dynamics, rhythm and tempo, and pedaling.

Topics included in this study are establishment of a good hand position; listening habits and critical self-hearing; the attributes of slow, fast and graduated practice speeds; realization of ornaments; performance of rolled chords; fourths, balance and voicing of chords; repeated note technique; metronome usage; finger legato and substitution; and pedal techniques.

The practice and performance techniques presented here are based on pragmatic solutions to problems discovered during preparation of the twelve etudes for concert. Books on piano performance by pedagogues such as Theodor Leschetisky, Josef Lhevinne, and Guy Maier are used for reference and serve as additional sources for suggestions.

Betts, Steven Lee. *Lynn Freeman Olson's Contributions to Music Education.* D.M.A. paper, Norman: University of Oklahoma, 1995. The purpose of this study is to investigate the life of Lynn Freeman Olson and to document his contributions to the field of music education. The growth of the field of piano pedagogy in the last twenty-five years has created a need for studies of its leaders. Olson's career included work as a composer, author, editor, and clinician. He co-authored three piano courses, two early childhood music readiness series, numerous articles in music journals, and he presented over two hundred workshops throughout the world.

The study is divided into six sections. Chapter One serves as an introduction, providing statements of the problem, purpose of the study, need for the study, procedure, limitations, organization of the remainder of the study, and similar studies of other music educators and piano pedagogues. Chapter Two contains a biographical sketch of Olson's life and career. His childhood, education, career as teacher, composer, clinician, and author are among the topics discussed.

Chapter Three analyzes and critiques the three piano courses that Olson co-authored. Reviews of supplementary solos and collections that Olson composed and the compositions of other composers that he edited are also documented. Chapter Four documents the two early childhood music readiness series and briefly discusses the music that Olson composed for genres other than piano. Chapter Five discusses Olson's contributions through his writings, radio interviews, and workshops. The final chapter summarizes Olson's contributions to music education and gives recommendations for further research. Appendixes include a complete catalog of original compositions by Olson; a complete catalog of compositions edited by Olson; a list of Olson's literary works; a list of known workshops presented by Olson; a list of known presentations of "An Afternoon (or Evening) with Lynn Freeman Olson"; and criteria established by Kathleen Louise Schubert in her dissertation on Willard Palmer for evaluating piano courses.

Biller, Carolyn Virginia. *Motivating the Average Secondary Age Private Piano Students to Continue Piano Instruction.* M.A. thesis, Fullerton, Calif.: California State University, 1986, 58 p. UM 1328348. Instructional strategies were created to motivate secondary-age students in their piano study. Ten secondary-age students from the studio of Carolyn Biller evaluated piano teaching strategies. The students had used two or more of the strategies for their piano study. It was hypothesized that the students would continue studying piano during their teen years if they had a flexible plan that gave them options, immediate feedback, and allowed for their decision making. The instructional strategies met this criteria.

A questionnaire was administered to the ten students in which they evaluated the strategies. The results of the questionnaire showed that 90 percent benefited from the use of instructional strategies. On the questionnaire the students stated that they would like to take their strategies home to refresh their memories during the week. The students stated that they would like less memorization than is required on the "Play-a-thon" strategy. Also, they requested more noncompetitive strategies. The study results reflect the success of the instructional strategies in providing more success for the students at the piano and in motivating them to continue in their study.

Blair, Martha Ellen. *The Three Hindemith Piano Sonatas, 1936: A Structural Analysis.* M.M. thesis, Austin: University of Texas, 1964, 62 p. A discussion of the structure and specific style characteristics of the three sonatas.

Blevins, Ronald Stanley. *A Pianist's Analysis of Works by William Byrd, Robert Schumann, and Norman Dello Joio.* D.M.A. paper, Fort Worth: Southwestern Baptist Theological Seminary, 1990, 104 p. UM 9115294. This document is a pianist's analysis of works of William Byrd, Robert Schumann, and Norman Dello Joio. Each of the selected compositions holds some special interest for the researcher. The Byrd composition, "John Come Kisse Me Now," was selected because of an interest in the harpsichord. Schumann's *Waldszenen* were chosen because of the author's interest in the nineteenth-century character piece. *Piano Sonata No. 3,* by Dello Joio, was selected because of an interest in American composers who have been influenced by jazz.

Each of the compositions is analyzed by its form. In addition, comments are included about learning difficulties. The Byrd composition is based on a fixed harmonic pattern and, therefore, is researched from a melodic and rhythmic viewpoint. The pieces in *Waldszenen* and the Dello Joio sonata are studied from formal, melodic, and harmonic points of view.

Bloomquist, William Charles, Jr. *The "Fairy Tales" of Nikolai Medtner.* D.M.A. paper, Austin: University of Texas, 1993, 189 p. UM 9413632. The introductory portion of this study includes a biography of the composer, a discussion of *The Muse and Fashion,* a book written by Medtner which expresses his philosophy about music and its creation, and a brief overview of Russian composers who preceded him. The bulk of the paper then focuses on a detailed survey of the thirty-three *Fairy Tales.*

Bonello, Michael, ed. *The Piano Music of Charles Camilleri.* Valetta, Malta: Andrew Rupert Publishing, 1990, 73 p. A compilation of articles in seven chapters on Camilleri's piano music from 1945 to 1990. Chapter Four is devoted to *Tagsim* for two pianos. Appendix I lists selected piano works and publishers since 1948. Appendix II is a selected discography of piano works.

Bonin, Jean M. *Piano-beds and Music by Steam: An Index with Abstracts to Music-related United States Patent Records, 1790–1874.* Berkeley, Fallen Leaf Press, 1993. Includes bibliographical references and indexes.

Bowling, Irene Rüth. *British Piano Music Since 1945: A Selected Survey.* D.M.A. paper, Seattle: University of Washington, 1989, 147 p. UM 900211. Since the end of the Second World War in 1945, England has been among the leading exponents of contemporary music. The introduction of this paper outlines the many reasons leading to this postwar phenomenon. The purpose of this research is to investigate and demonstrate the great diversity and pluralism inherent in British music today. To Illustrate this point, ten composers and their selected piano works have been chosen from a list of hundreds of possibilities. Some, but not all, are world renowned. They were chosen primarily because they have written fascinating works for the piano, and their music represents important trends in British piano music of the last forty years. The composers included in this paper are Michael Tippett, Elizabeth Lutyens, Alexander Goehr, Peter Maxwell Davies, Robert Sherlaw Johnson, Richard Rodney Bennett, Jonathon Harvey, Brian Ferneyhough, Michael Finnissy, and George Benjamin. The overall stylistic divisions among these ten composers fall into three major categories: traditional-tonal, serial, and complexist. Explanations of the categories and how each composer fits within them are incorporated into the body of the paper and in the conclusion. One piano work from each composer has been chosen for detailed discussion, and twenty-nine musical examples and graphs have been included to illuminate the analyses. The conclusion attempts to tie together the major aesthetic and stylistic threads of the paper and reviews various performance problems in several of the works. A list of interviews and primary resources and a complete list of each composer's piano music and piano recordings are included in Appendixes A and B. Twenty-five additional composers and their best piano music are listed in Appendix C. Finally, Appendix D consists of four graduate recital programs that were required for the fulfillment of the doctor's degree.

Bozovich, Carey Diane. *Phrasing and Articulation in Henry Purcell's Harpsichord Suites.* M.A. thesis, Berrien Springs, Mich.: Andrews University, 1985, 218 p. UM 1328787. Little is known about Henry Purcell's application of phrasing and articulation in his harpsichord works. Therefore, an investigation of original performance practices of his harpsichord suites is needed to establish how best to phrase and articulate the harpsichord music of Purcell, especially his eight harpsichord suites.

A detailed study of Purcell's harpsichord suites, a careful review of directly related literature and Baroque performance in general, and application of Purcell's own performance and fingering practices provided the basis for conclusion. Purcells's fingering practices, evidenced by his fingered prelude and scale, yielded frequently paired articulation and rhythmic inequality. Analysis of articulation patterns of the period also indicates articulation of ornaments, and articulation over the barline and at midbar. English Baroque performance is best understood and attained through the use of certain rules and fingering, which influence rhythmic inequality and proper articulation.

Brandenburg, Octavia Leigh. *Aspects of Performance in Three Works for Piano and Tape: Larry Austin's "Sonata Concertante," Thomas Clark's "Peninsula," and Phil Winsor's "Passages."* D.M.A. paper, Denton: University of North Texas, 1993, 83 p. UM 9326617. This dissertation primarily addresses performance aspects in compositions for piano and tape, using three specific works as the basis for discussion. These compositions are representative of the medium as a whole, yet each offers its own unique set of performance problems.

Brandman, Margaret. *Contemporary Piano Method.* Video cassette. North Sydney: Warner Brothers Music Australia, 60 minutes. This series covers material for the beginning piano student through high school, university, and professional standards. Topics discussed in this video are the first approach to the piano, and elements of music through to the ability to read, feel, hear, understand, and play early-level music.

Brechemin, Louis. *The Mefisto Elements in the Piano Works of Liszt.* Thesis, Seattle: University of Washington, 1968.

Breitman, David. *The Damper Pedal and the Beethoven Piano Sonatas: A Historical Perspective.* D.M.A. paper, Ithaca: Cornell University, 1993, 134 p. UM 9318869. This work takes a "performance practice" perspective and, to the extent that performance questions are addressed, assumes the use of historical instruments or replicas.

The first portion of the study is concerned with the historical context: changes in keyboard writing associated with the emergence of the fortepiano as the dominant keyboard instrument, early pedal indications by other composers, and references to pedal in treatises.

The principal findings may be summarized as follows: 1) The two most important uses of the pedal are as a means of connection, be-tween sections of a work and at the end of movements or works (i.e., the connection of the work to the silence), and as a special register to reinforce contrasts of texture or dynamics. 2) The pedal indications in the scores are not complete; they appear where Beethoven wanted to override usual pedal practices, e.g., by pedaling through rests or harmony changes. The study includes a table which lists and analyzes each indication. 3) Based on a wide range of sources, Beethoven's "normal" (that is, annotated) use of pedal can be described with some degree of certainty.

Brendel, Alfred. *Brendel on Beethoven.* Video cassette. Philips 4400702653. Includes an introductory talk that focuses on Beethoven's style (economy, emotion, energy, character, humor). Brendel then plays the Sonata Op. 31/2 ("tempest").

Brink, Margaret Anne. *The Piano as Percussion Instrument.* D.M.A. paper, Seattle: University of Washington, 1990, 95 p. UM 9117932. The first two decades of the twentieth century witnessed several styles of piano writing, one of which emphasized motorized rhythms and detached accented sounds. This study seeks to explore the piano's role in the emergence of this style and to define the percussive quali-ties of the piano. Chapter One traces percussive instruments histori-cally; compares percussive and nonpercussive instruments; analyzes the mechanism that makes the piano a percussive instrument; and describes double escapement action which resulted in the modern in-strument as we know it. Chapter Two follows with examples of the development of percussive writing from harpsichord repertoire through virtuoso piano writing of the nineteenth century in Scarlatti's, Bee-thoven's and Liszt's usage of percussive imitation. In their music, the emergence of tremolos and fast repeated notes or chords points di-rectly to the style of twentieth century percussive piano music. Bartók, Stravinsky, and Prokofiev are investigated in Chapter Three through their thoughts from writings or interviews relating to the subject of this study. Specifically mentioned are nationalistic or folk elements as a source of their compositional style, and the potential uses of the pi-ano as a percussive instrument. Chapter Four defines the specific ele-ments of percussive writing: motor driven ostinatos, accented detached tone clusters, and percussive expression marks in musical examples from works by Bartók, Stravinsky, Prokofiev, Copland, Cowell, and Ives. In Chapter Five the role of the piano as a member of the percussion section in twentieth-century orchestral music is reviewed. The conclusion summarizes the study's findings: that the percussive elements of the piano provided great potential for early-twentieth-century percussive writing.

Brook, Alice Fuchs. *A Study of Paul Creston's "Rhythmicon" for Piano.* D.M.A. paper, Kansas City, Mo.: University of Missouri, 1992, 135 p. UM 9312260. The purpose of this study is to promote awareness and to arouse interest among both teachers and performers regarding the use of Paul Creston's *Rhythmicon* as a pedagogical source as well as recital literature. The main objectives are to present a short biographical sketch of his life; to introduce his harmonic, melodic and rhythmic ideas, including his rhythmic terminology; to discuss his *Rhythmicon*, Books 1 through 4, in terms of pedagogical sources for students; and to give a brief analysis of each piece in Books 5 through 10, in terms of technical and musical demands placed upon the student or performer.

Brooke, Dale W. *The Piano Sonatas of Serge Prokofieff.* Thesis, Seattle: University of Washington, 1958.

Brookes, Virginia. *British Keyboard Music to c. 1600: Sources and Thematic Index.* New York: Clarendon Press, 1996, 400 p. This is a reference work in two parts: Part One is an itemized list of the contents of all the manuscript and printed sources of British keyboard music to c. 1600; Part Two is a thematic index, listed alphabetically by composer, of all the pieces contained in the sources. Includes bibliographic references.

Brown, Jeanell Wise. *Amy Beach and Her Chamber Music.* Metuchen, N.J.: Scarecrow Press, 1994, 439 p. Includes a lengthy biography describing Beach's personal and professional life. Describes individually each of Beach's chamber music works, theoretically and historically. An extensive catalog contains a complete list of all published and unpublished works with performance comments. Includes bibliographic references and index.

Brown, Jonathan A. *Maurice Hinson's Pedagogical Collections for Intermediate-Level Piano Students.* D.M.A. paper, Baton Rouge: Louisiana State University, 1994, 116 p. Examines Hinson's editorial output with concentration on his collections of intermediate-level piano literature. Six chapters include a biography; an overview of pedagogical editions 1963–1974; the editorial work of Maurice Hinson; a comparison of representative scores; Hinson's Chopin collections; summary; selected bibliography; Appendix I: Music Edited by Maurice Hinson; Appendix II: Representative List of Hinson's Professional Activities.

Brown, Karen Walker. *An Analysis of the "Historical Hungarian Portraits" of Franz Liszt*. D.M.A. paper, Eugene: University of Oregon, 1990, 224 p. UM 9111094. Among the late works of Franz Liszt is a cycle of seven short piano pieces, entitled *The Historical Hungarian Portraits*. Each one was written to memorialize by describing musically the character and life of one of seven Hungarian artistic and political leaders who were involved in the Hungarian Revolution of 1848–1849. This cycle was studied to determine the individual characteristics of Liszt's compositional techniques during this last period of his life. One of the most interesting features of this music is its relationship to tonality. Other elements of music (melodic construction, use of the gypsy scale, cadences, thematic transformation, and programmatic elements) were also considered in this study of Liszt's style.

The cycle gives evidence of the dissolution of the functional harmonic system that governed nineteenth-century tonality. Each of these pieces approaches that dissolution from a slightly different perspective. "Szechenyi" and "Vorosmarty" use scales rather than chords to establish tonal relationships. "Eotvos" is focused largely on one tone, its antithesis being tritone distant. "Teleki" features three individual tones of a four-note ostinato in a shifting, progressive tonal relationship. In "Deak" tonality is centered on two chords used in the thesis-antithesis categories of functional harmony's tonic-dominant, with a reversal of function from the beginning to the end of the work. In "Mosonyi" Liszt negates tonality through chromaticism and the irregular resolution of chromatic chords. In "Petofi" and "Teleki" tonality is undermined by Liszt's treatment of traditionally unstable chords as stable. "Petofi" thus uses second inversion triads, and "Teleki," in a more radical approach, diminished triads and seventh chords. In each of these works Liszt employs new means either to negate tonal relationships, or conversely, to establish them.

One conclusion of this study is that present day trends toward giving Liszt more credit for anticipating twentieth-century compositional style not only are valid but may still fall short of the true scope of his achievement.

Brown, Naomi Noro. *Akiro Miyoshi's Didactic Works for Solo Piano.* D.M.A. paper, Baton Rouge: Louisiana State University, 1994, 109 p. Investigates mainly *Etudes en forme Sonate* (1967), *In Such Time* (1967), *Forest Echos* (1978), and *A Diary of the Sea* (1982). Also contains an appendix that discusses Miyoshi's major solo piano works *Sonate* (1958), *Chaines* (1973), and *En Vers* (1980).

Brubaker, Debra. *A History and Critical Analysis of Piano Methods Published in the United States from 1796 to 1995.* Ph.D. dissertation, Minneapolis: University of Minnesota, 1996, 650 p. Ranges from the earliest known indigenous piano tutor in 1796 to recent computer-assisted keyboard methods. Brubaker documents innovative, influential, and representative piano methods of the United States by presenting them within a historical context of interacting cultural, societal, and educational trends. The text provides a descriptive analysis of content and teaching philosophy for over one hundred instruction books or series published in the U.S., appended by a chronological, annotated bibliography of over five hundred titles. A major document.

Bruhn, Siglind. *Guidelines to Piano Interpretation.* Hong Kong: Penerbit Muzikal, 1989, 184 p. This book provides an overview of interpretation in performance. Discussed separately are the elements of shading (dynamics and agogics), articulation and touch, and ornamentation as they relate to the Baroque, Classical and Romantic piano repertoire. Another part focuses on effective practicing. If students master all of these areas, they will surely be on their way to becoming a confident and fine performer.

———. *Images and Ideas in Modern French Piano Music.* Stuyvesant, N.Y.: Pendragon Press, 1998, 420 p. Deals with extramusical influences in piano works of Debussy, Messiaen, and Ravel. The author shows how the relation between this type of influence (subtexts) and the work of music can be broadly categorized in terms of pictorialness and interiority. Each musical piece and each source text is thoroughly analyzed. A fine work that explores specific connections between music and the other arts.

———. *J. S. Bach's Well-Tempered Clavier. In-Depth Analysis and Interpretation.* Hong Kong: Mainer International Ltd., 1993, 4 vols. Available in the United States from Music Book Society, P.O. Box 339, North Andover, MA 01845–0339. The finest and most comprehensive analysis of this great work yet. Color charts for each fugue further add to the completeness of each volume.

Brunelli, Stephanie. *The Use of the Piano in the Twentieth Century Orchestra: A Study of Pulitzer Prize Compositions by Copland, Bassett, and Druckman.* D.A. dissertation, Greeley: University of Northern Colorado, 1992, 364 p. UM 9235575. This study provides the first comprehensive analysis of the use of the piano as a member of the orchestra in Copland's *Appalachian Spring* (suite version for thirteen instruments), Bassett's *Variations for Orchestra,* and Druckman's *Windows.* The piano's numerous contributions in the areas of form, melody, rhythm, harmony, texture, and color are examined in detail. The final chapter is devoted to a comparative analysis of the piano's role in the three compositions. Brunelli concludes her dissertation by addressing the issue of musical justification of the piano's orchestration within each work.

Bruno, Susan Jones. *The Published Keyboard Works of Johann Kuhnau (1660–1722).* Ph.D. dissertation, Storrs: University of Connecticut, 1986, 269 p. UM 8619100. Johann Kuhnau, creator of Lutheran church cantatas, keyboard music, a satirical novel, and other writings, is significant in the history of music as the composer of the first extensive collection of keyboard sonatas. The sonatas and two collections of partitas were printed from engraved copper plates and published between 1689 and 1700. This dissertation discusses these compositions.

Several topics are examined in this study. Material concerning social, economic, and political conditions in Germany provide background to the discussion of Kuhnau's life. A brief survey of seventeenth-century German keyboard music helps give perspective to the composer's accomplishments. Contemporary writers are cited. Each movement is examined with regard to formal structure, internal key relationships, harmony, range, texture, and rhythmic organization. The types and treatment of dances, the different introductory movements of the partitas, and the overall structure of the sonatas are examined. The role of the Baroque doctrine of affections in connection with programmatic elements in the program sonatas is discussed. One or two selections from each genre are used to illustrate important characteristics. Harmony, the fugues, and ornamentation are examined separately in more detail. The appendixes include previously untranslated writings by Kuhnau and Johann Mattheson and a solution to the algebraic puzzle from the preface to the program sonatas. The few keyboard works in manuscript are mentioned here.

This study suggests that Kuhnau bequeathed a somewhat dichotomous legacy. Immature tonality is countered by the arrangement of the partitas by key. Older forms in new settings appear with the creation of a new genre. Publication of the works for the pleasure of amateurs is accompanied by apologetic remarks about not adhering to the strict rules of counterpoint. Kuhnau's more conservative tendencies are characteristic of the middle Baroque, but his more advanced ideas came to culmination in late-eighteenth-century Classicism.

Bruser, Madeline. *The Art of Practicing: A Guide to Making Music from the Heart.* New York: Bell Tower, 1997. Bruser's approach to this perennial subject is refreshing. She gives three excellent preparatory steps for establishing physical, mental, and emotional relaxation before practicing: 1) stretching, 2) clearing the mind, and 3) opening the heart. A thorough chapter is devoted to body mechanics including photographs showing posture and hand positions for different instruments. Another chapter deals with psychological approaches to practicing. She recommends super-slow practice—focusing on one sound at a time. The final two chapters are devoted to performance.

Buchman, Andrew William. *Sonata Form in Stravinsky's Sonate (1924): An Analysis by Musical Parameters.* D.M.A. paper, Seattle: University of Washington, 1987, 187 p. UM 8713353. Stravinsky wrote only one piano sonata in his maturity. Written in 1924, it is one of a series of pieces written for his own use as a performer.

The basic structural dynamic of the first movement of the Sonate is a conceptual adaptation of the "classical" sonata-allegro model of exposition, development, and recapitulation. The development is structured as a series of confrontations between diatonic and octatonic pitch blocks, or strata, first presented in the exposition. Some conventional developmental processes (i.e., thematic and tonal ones) are also used by Stravinsky, although they are not always immediately aurally apparent. The history and sources for the Sonate are discussed. The first movement is analyzed in detail, in separate discussions of the musical parameters of form, texture, harmony, melody, and meter and rhythm. Suggestions for performance conclude the paper.

Burge, David. *Twentieth-Century Piano Music.* New York: Schirmer Books, 1990, 284 p. Covers the period between 1900 and 1990. Divided into four sections: From 1900 to the End of World War I; Between the Two World Wars; The Postwar Period; and The 1970s and 1980s. This book is not intended to be complete. Burge has discussed works that he likes and finds especially impressive and moving. The chapters on George Crumb, Frederic Rzewski, and William Albright are outstanding. Burge has a command of the piano literature of this century second to none.

Butt, John. *Bach Interpretation: Articulation Marks in Primary Sources of J. S. Bach.* New York: Cambridge University Press, 1990, 250 p. A valuable book on performance practices of Bach's music and that of his contemporaries.

Butterfield, Lorraine. *An Investigation of Rhythm in the Piano Mazurkas of Alexandre Tansman: A Guide for the Piano Instructor/Performer.* Ph.D. dissertation, New York University, 1990, 309 p. UM 9025161. Polish composer Alexander Tansman (1897–1986) received the highest awards for contribution to culture both in Poland and in France, where he lived from 1919 to 1986. He has been noted as one of the most important Polish composers of the twentieth century. Tansman composed twenty-seven mazurkas for piano during the period 1918–1949. They are considered to be among his best works for keyboard. This dissertation investigates Tansman's place in music history and the place of his mazurkas in the history of the genre as a background to the investigation of rhythm in his mazurkas.

Tansman's piano mazurkas show evidence of his cosmopolitan lifestyle. As such, the problem arises as to how these works relate to durational rhythmic and accentuation patterns that are considered to be characteristic of the genre. This study investigates these small-dimension rhythmic characteristics. Tansman did not routinely use the characteristic dotted rhythm. He favored a less diversified rhythmic pattern of eighth and quarter notes which resembles the original folk mazur and oberek durational patterns. Other stylistic features which obscure mazurka accent patterning are discussed.

The study then expands to a broader view of rhythm, based on the analytical method of Jan La Rue. The following are explored: harmonic rhythm, contour rhythm, surface articulation rhythm, dynamic rhythm, textual rhythm, and range rhythm. Coordinated articulations in these elements are discussed as they relate to larger dimension structure in these works. Harmonic, textural, and dynamic change, as well as range change, are frequent contributors in coordinated articulations in the works examined. Other rhythmic findings include ambiguity in accentuation; metric displacement; mirror rhythm; the motor element; and the stationary hypnotic effect. The linear and harmonic goal dimension is also explored, and comparisons to the rhythmic coordination analysis are made.

The researcher was the last to interview Tansman before his death. Performance guidelines based on Tansman's own comments, the historical information, and the rhythmic analyses comprise the remainder of the dissertation.

Cai, Camilla. *Brahms's Short, Late Piano Pieces—Opus Numbers 116–119: A Source Study, an Analysis and Performance Practice.* Ph.D. dissertation, Boston University, 1986, 563 p. UM 8609270. With the advent of Margit McCorkle's new *Brahms Verzeichnis,* we can see just how few sources of the many mentioned in the correspondence have indeed survived. A study of the remaining sources for the short piano pieces, *intermezzi, capricci,* rhapsodies, and others, allows us to partially reconstruct Brahms's compositional process. Remaining holographs do not usually link directly into the publishing process and, therefore, display a fascinatingly different image from that of the first edition and its publications stages. So little material from early compositional stages remains that special emphasis in this study necessarily falls on the publications stages, from engravers' copies and proof sheets to Brahms's corrections in the *Handexemplare.* The results of studying their differences provides an overview of the difficulties that face future editors of a scholarly edition and also demonstrates and details Brahms's continued active participation throughout the compositional-publishing process.

Certain pieces from the late opus numbers 116–119 provide the special analytical focus. These late pieces seem to act as studies or challenges to Brahms, to concentrate one (occasionally two) of his principles or practices of composition into a miniature form. Several specific pieces lend themselves to detailed analysis because they demonstrate such techniques especially clearly. For example, Brahms's manipulation of various elements of music to both delineate and obscure form is particularly revealing. These pieces also present knotty problems for the pianist-performer in understanding the often deliberately ambiguous rhythms or harmonies, in clarifying melodic strands buried in a contrapuntal yet pianistic texture, and in interpreting the meaning of conflicting expressive terms and symbols. Knowledge of late-nineteenth-century performance practice brings an understanding of the original context. Together, the source material, the analyses, and research concerning the piano Brahms knew suggest pathways to solutions for the rich and exciting interpretative complexities Brahms left us in these last piano solos.

Camp, Max W. *Teaching Piano.* Van Nuys, Calif.: Alfred Publishing Co., 1992, 203 p. Designed to be used as a piano pedagogy text, this book offers teachers a concise treatise on how to develop the learning and performing foundation from the beginning phases of a student's musical experience to the intermediate level of advancement. Part One proposes a pedagogical approach to developing a student's pianistic foundation. Part Two brings the pedagogical approach to life in six stages of complexity. Excellent choice of piano literature examples.

Canning, Nancy. *A Glenn Gould Catalog.* Westport, Conn.: Greenwood Press, 1992, 272 p. Looks at Gould's career as pianist, conductor, broadcaster, writer, and producer, and includes a discography of Gould's recordings. Also lists by date his CBC Archives radio and television programs, published writings, and writings about Gould.

Carden, Joy. *A Piano Teacher's Guide to Electronic Keyboards.* Milwaukee: Hal Leonard Publishing Corp., 1988, 80 p. Provides a guide for piano teachers who are interested in using electronic keyboards in weekly lessons. It shows how electronics instruments and acoustic pianos can be used as successful compliments to one another. Includes two appendixes, a glossary, and index.

Carlsen, Philip Caldwell. *The Player-Piano Music of Conlon Nancarrow: An Analysis of Selected Studies.* Ph.D. dissertation, City University of New York, 1986, 188 p. UM 8611334. The composer Conlon Nancarrow was born in Arkansas in 1912, played jazz trumpet as a young man, studied composition and counterpoint for brief periods in Cincinnati and Boston (including work with Slonimsky, Piston, and Sessions), fought in the Spanish Civil War as a member of the Abraham Lincoln Brigade, became involved in the New York new music scene on his return to the United States in 1939, and emigrated to Mexico a year later as a result of the U.S. government's refusal to issue him a passport. He has lived in Mexico ever since, working for many years in virtual isolation from other composers and musicians. Gradually, however, with the ongoing release of scores and recordings of his music, Nancarrow has gained increasing recognition and stature, exemplified by his receipt in 1982 of a MacArthur Foundation "genius" award.

Because of his isolation and his long-standing frustration at the inability of musicians to deal with even moderately difficult rhythms, Nancarrow turned in the 1940s to the player piano. He has since written nearly fifty studies for the instrument, a unique body of work that is particularly notable for its exhaustive explorations of rhythmic and temporal complexity. In this essay, Studies No. 19, 36, 8, 23, and 35 are analyzed in depth. Examples from other works are also cited. The music amply demonstrates Nancarrow's wit, inventiveness, mastery of counterpoint, preoccupation with numbers and structures, and his ability to transform the mechanical player piano into an instrument of great virtuosic and expressive power.

Carr, Cassandra Irene. *Ernest Bloch: The Piano Music.* Thesis, Seattle: University of Washington, 1978.

————. *Wit and Humor as a Dramatic Force in the Beethoven Piano Sonatas.* Ph.D. dissertation, Seattle: University of Washington, 1985, 309 p. UM 8613148. This study examines the piano sonatas of Beethoven, seeking not just to identify the musical figures, rhythms, dynamics, and harmonic movement which constitute Beethoven's vocabulary of musical humor, but, more important, to evaluate the ways in which these devices are used to further the dramatic power of the individual works.

The clear evidence is that Beethoven's youthful sense of musical humor manifested itself in rather blatant gestural humor. Deliberately simple-minded exaggeration, abrupt pauses, and sforzandi, structurally unsound phrase extensions, and overdone pathos abound in the early sonatas. Sometimes these outbursts of humor, parody, or wit are placed so as to undercut any serious drama that may have evolved; often, the explosions of humor occur in such abundance that the result is a comedy-sonata with brief moments of seriousness. Formal aspects of the sonata-allegro procedure are not often used as vehicles for wit, however, with the one exception of the preparation for the recapitulation.

In his mature works of the so-called Middle Period, many of the same devices of musical humor continue to be used. With few exceptions, though, Beethoven's extensive vocabulary of humor is used with a far more delicate touch. Fewer works that can be called comic are found; the areas of broad humor are increasingly placed so as to increase rather than undercut the serious nature of the overall work, assuming more and more the qualities of comic relief in great tragedy. Much humor here may be called ironic.

Beethoven's late sonatas suggest an ostensible return to the early concept of long stretches of low, not to say rude humor. But the meaning of the humor has shifted from those early works, largely due to the structure and style of the Beethoven sonata idea having evolved to a very different level, altering irrevocably the meaning of the humor. In many of these late sonatas, low humor is perceived as grotesque humor largely because it is juxtaposed with material of distinctly otherworldly quality; musical ideas of a transcendent nature are subjected to raucous and vulgar transformations, revealing a much heightened complexity of dramatic conception.

Carramaschi, Elizabeth. *Camargo Guarnieri, A Study of a Brazilian Composer and An Analysis of His "Sonata para piano."* D.M.A. paper, Iowa City: University of Iowa, 1987, 130 p. UM 8813109. This project is concerned with the Brazilian composer Camargo Guarnieri, especially with his "Sonata para piano," and comprises three main subjects. The first includes a detailed discussion of many aspects of Brazilian music, elements in Brazilian music (European, folkloric, and nationalistic), and an examination of nationalism in Brazilian music as manifested in three composers, Antonio Carlos Gomez, Heitor Villa-Lobos, and especially Guarnieri. The second subject, an examination of the sonata and its twentieth-century characteristics, serves as an introduction to the third subject, which is an in-depth analysis of Guarnieri's "Sonata para piano" viewed both in its nationalistic and formal aspects.

Carruthers, Glen Blaine. *Bach and the Piano: Editions, Arrangements and Transcriptions from Czerny to Rachmaninov.* Ph.D. dissertation,

Victoria, B.C.: University of Victoria, 1986. There is a tendency to
regard the pianistic reinterpretation of Bach's harpsichord, organ,
chamber, and orchestral works as an unfortunate idiosyncracy of the
Romantic perception of the music of the past. Accordingly, while much
has been written of the resurrection of the choral works, the role of
the piano in the Bach revival of the nineteenth century has received
little scholarly attention.

From the evidence in contemporary letters, diaries, concert reviews,
articles, and published versions of his music, this dissertation isolates
a number of conventions in Bach interpretation in the nineteenth century and explains the Romantic proclivity for rewriting the *Urtexte*
when transferring them to the piano. In addition, a nomenclature that
takes into account the different composition techniques employed in
the arranging and transcribing of Bach's music is defined and supported with explications and examples.

Chapter One surveys the part Bach's music played in romantic pianists' repertoires and establishes the framework for a detailed discussion, in Chapter Two, of performance practices and the various schools
of Bach interpretation in the nineteenth century. Chapter Three focuses on the rewriting of Bach's music and on the techniques used in
creating an idiomatic piano repertoire from Bach's *oeuvre*. The emendations to the Urtexte dealt with in Chapter Two have to do primarily
with piano technique, whereas those considered in Chapter Three are
related more to aesthetic and utilitarian concerns. There is a progression in the sequence of chapters from Bach piano repertoire in general, including works appropriated from other media, through piano
editions of his harpsichord and clavichord works, to arrangements
and transcriptions of his harpsichord, organ, chamber, and orchestral
compositions. The final chapter assesses the number of definitions of
"arrangements" and "transcriptions," cites their inadequacy, and sets
forth new definitions on the basis of the various factors discussed in
the preceding two chapters. An extensive biblio-discography of Bach
Bearbeitungen, the first of its kind, concludes the dissertation.

By exploring the anachronistic conjunction of Bach and the piano,
and examining the editions, arrangements, transcriptions, and paraphrases it fostered, this dissertation chronicles the course of a unique
relationship between performers and composers and the music of Bach.

Case, Angeline-Newport. *Fingering Scales.* Video cassette. Great Start,
Inc., P.O. Box 941, Mustang, OK 73064, 30 minutes. Case teaches

the major and minor scales (natural form) with some unique suggestions.

Cavett-Dumsby, Esther. *Mozart's Variations Reconsidered: Four Case Studies.* Hamden, Conn.: Garland Publishing Co., 1989. K. 613, K. 501, and the finales of K. 421 (417b) and K. 491.

Chan, Felix Chung-Chuen. *The Development of Technique for Playing the Waltzes of Frederic Chopin.* Ed.D. dissertation, Urbana: University of Illinois , 1992, 347 p. UM 9305485. The purpose of this study is to develop a practice manual designed to assist pianists in the development of the technique needed to play the Chopin waltzes. The manual consists of passages from the waltzes that require the use of György Sandor's (1981) five technical patterns described in *On Piano Playing*: five-fingers, scales, and arpeggios; staccato; free fall; thrust; and rotation. It aims at achieving the best result with the least effort by using efficient and coordinated body movements. In preparation for beginning his research, the investigator carried out an extensive review of literature on Chopin, his teaching, playing, and compositions, and of publications concerned with the views on practice and piano technique development held by noted concert pianists and pedagogues from the past and present.

Chapman, Nyaho, and William Henry. *Cyclicism in the War Sonatas of Sergei Prokofiev.* D.M.A. paper, Austin: University of Texas, 1990, 174 p. UM 9116799. Of the nine sonatas Prokofiev composed for the piano, the Sixth, Seventh, and Eighth Sonatas are among his most important compositions in any genre. The three sonatas, composed during the Second World War, were originally conceived in 1939 and completed consecutively in 1940, 1942, and 1944. As a result, they acquired the name "War Sonatas" and were considered a trilogy. The aim of the treatise is to present clearly how closely interconnected the War Sonatas are through the use of cyclicism and other unifying features.

The treatise is divided into four chapters. Chapter One gives a biographical sketch of Prokofiev and then discusses the historical context of the War Sonatas. Chapter Two offers a historical overview of cyclic techniques and then focuses on cyclicism in the War Sonatas of Prokofiev. It gives a broad view of the main cyclic and unifying features which appear across all three sonatas, identifying them as the rhythmic "Fate" motive, the pitch-related motive, and the unifying features of the interval of the third and its closely related split major/minor chord. The chapter closes with other biographical facts to further support the case for considering the sonatas a trilogy. Chapter Three presents a formal, tonal, and motivic analysis of the individual movements of the sonatas along with a more detailed consideration for the cyclic elements within the movements. Chapter Four draws together the crucial cyclic and unifying features appearing across the three sonatas, discussing each of them in much greater detail from a motivic and tonal perspective. It traces the appearance and evolution of the two main cyclic motives and the unifying features in the order in which they occur in the sonatas.

Chase, Mildred Portney. *Improvisation: Music from the Inside Out.* Berkeley: Creative Arts Book Co., 1988, 120 p. Includes bibliography.

Chay, Il-Soo. *A Stylistic and Interpretive Analysis of Selected Keyboard Works of C. P. E. Bach.* Ed.D. dissertation, New York: Columbia University Teachers College, 1989, 248 p. UM 9002515. This dissertation consists of a structural and interpretative analysis of the six sonatas from the first volume of the collection titled "Sonatas for Connoisseurs and Amateurs" by Carl Philipp Emanuel Bach. The purpose of this study is to broaden the scope of the teaching repertoire by helping students and teachers to be more aware of C. P. E. Bach's keyboard works, and to develop a better understanding of the important place these works occupy in the history of the keyboard literature.

Bach's works demonstrate the important change from the late Baroque to the early Classical styles. They show the evolution from the highly contrapuntal style of the Baroque to the more homophonic structures and designs of the Classical style. By studying the music of C. P. E. Bach, the student is given a better vision of the continuity that linked the late Baroque to the early Classical periods. In order to facilitate a clearer understanding of Bach's works, an overview of Bach's historical background is given, including the importance of Bach's treatise, *Essay on the True Art of Playing Keyboard Instruments,* and the important relationship between the characteristics of the clavichord and the formation of the German Expressive style.

The structural analysis includes the areas of form, thematic relationships and their developments, melody, harmony, and rhythm. The interpretative analysis includes a discussion of ornamentation and various performance aspects including the realization of embellishments, suggested fingerings, phrasings, and dynamics. Whenever possible, these suggestions are based on direct citations from the composer's treatise. In spite of the sixteen years that divide the first and last written sonatas included in this collection, common structural and stylistic characteristics among the six sonatas are discussed.

The study and performance of the sonatas are made more rewarding due to the existence of the composer's own interpretative directions found by a careful reading of the *Essay*. However, the better understanding that these works give to the continuity of music from the late Baroque to the early Classical periods remains the primary educational implication.

Chen, Mei-Luan. *The Variation Elements in the Piano Works of Franz Schubert.* D.M.A. paper, University of Cincinnati, 1991, 125 p. UM 9200438. In this study, the history of secular keyboard variations is first surveyed, and the different types of variation forms are discussed. Schubert's ten independent piano variation sets, including both the separate sets of variations and variations belonging to large multi-movement works, are thoroughly analyzed and discussed. The ABA and rondo movements in Schubert's piano sonatas which use the variation principle are examined, and the most representative compositions in each form are presented.

It was found that Schubert used variations in four different ways: as independent sets, as movements in piano sonatas, in works that cannot be called "variations" as such, and as a compositional procedure in ABA and rondo movements. This study confirms that Schubert was a follower of Haydn, Mozart, and Beethoven in writing mostly classical ornamental variations. Rhythm was an important element of variation technique for him. Rhythmic acceleration and rhythmic elaboration are the two devices he applied most often. His unique and most original variation technique is the use of "key variation," which is characterized by the frequent change of keys in a variation set.

Schubert's contributions to the evolution of the piano variation includes the degree of freedom used in a variation set, the writing of piano duet variations, and the use of variation as a guiding principle in compositions called "Impromptu" and "Fantasy." Schubert's piano variations are not only the completion of the classical variation style, but also the forerunner of the nineteenth-century character variation.

Cheney, Elliott Ward, III. *A Study of Contemporary Canadian Music for Violincello and Piano.* D.M.A. paper, Austin: University of Texas, DMA paper, 1994, 156 p. UM 9428430. This paper looks at selected works for violoncello and piano by seventeen significant Canadian composers. Their diverse backgrounds, as well as their works for this instrumental combination, are examined in terms of each individual composer's interpretation of Canadian musical identity. Works are also discussed regarding stylistic traits, and difficulty of the cello part. Background information is given on Canadian historical events and the emergence of several government supported organizations which have shaped the face of music in Canada.

Cherrix, Vernon. *G. Maurice Hinson: An Annotated Bibliography of His Writings.* D.M.A. paper, Louisville: Southern Baptist Theological Seminary, 1996. This study is the compilation of a systematic, classified, annotated bibliography of the articles, books, and video cassettes of G. Maurice Hinson (b. 1930) related to piano literature, piano pedagogy, and performance practice. Hinson has become internationally recognized as one of the foremost authorities on piano literature and pedagogy through his publications and pedagogical editions of piano music. His writings are rich resources of helpful information about piano literature and piano pedagogy for teachers, students, performers, scholars, and librarians. The purpose of this study is to bring all of this helpful information under bibliographic control in order to make it useful and accessible to the persons mentioned.

Chester, Nancy Claire. *The Piano Works of Wallingford Riegger.* M.M. thesis, Austin: University of Texas, 1963, 108 p. Discusses Blue Voyage, Op. 6; Scherzo, Op. 13a; Four Tone Pictures, Op. 14; Evocation, Op. 17; Finale from the "New Dance," Op. 18a; The Cry, Op. 22; Canon and Fugue, Op. 33c; New and Old, Op. 38; Variations for 2 pianos, Op. 54a; and Petite Etude, Op. 62.

Cheung, Dorothy. *Selected Piano Works of Franck, Haydn, and Chopin.* D.M.A. paper, Fort Worth: Southwestern Baptist Theological Seminary, 1992, 206 p. UM 9231655. The works selected for this study include Franck's Prelude, Chorale, and Fugue; Haydn's Andante with Variations; and Chopin's Sonata in B minor. Biographical insights and development of the historical forms are included in this study. Formal and harmonic analyses are given for each work. In addition, comments are included about performance difficulties and ways to solving these difficulties.

Chiang, Ya-Hsuan. *Pedal Technique in "La Cathédrale Engloutie" by Claude Debussy.* M.A. thesis, San Jose State University, 1992, 73 p. UM 1350075. This project has investigated systematically the piano work "La Cathédrale Engloutie" to highlight how sonority prolongation in pedal was achieved by the impressionist composer. The modern piano with its built-in sound prolonger is the ideal vehicle for expressing extended sonority. The modern music notation, however, proves to have shortcomings for indicating precisely the prolongation effects looked for by an impressionist composer.

Chou, Chien. *Variation Procedure in Rachmaninoff's Piano Works.* D.M.A. paper, Boston University, 1994, 224 p. UM 9423444. The discussion opens by examining the recently changing trend of Rachmaninoff scholarship away from the popular "life and works" variety toward that which deals directly with his music. The general characteristics of his variation procedure are outlined by examining a representative cross-section of relevant works including those works that are not formal variation sets. The third chapter is an in-depth discussion of Rachmaninoff's last work for piano and last variation set, *Rhapsody on a Theme by Paganini,* Op. 43. Its overall structure and tonal scheme are examined, and the Paganini theme and its subsequent alterations through each of the twenty-four variations and coda are analyzed in more detail.

Christensen, James. *Chamber Music Notes for Players.* Plantation, Fla: Distinctive Publishing Co., 1992, 242 p. Part One: String Quartets. Part Two: Works for Five and More Strings. Part Three: Strings with Piano: Piano Trios, Quartets, Quintets. Discusses over 200 works, sometimes including form, unusual qualities, and always with a "commentary" conclusion. More for amateurs than professional players, but includes some perceptive advice.

Chung, So-Ham Kim. *An Analysis of Rachmaninoff's Concerto No. 2 in c minor, Op. 18: Aids Towards Performance.* D.M.A. paper, Columbus: Ohio State University, 1988, 84 p. UM882446. This document presents an analysis of Sergey Rachmaninoff's Piano Concerto No. 2 from a performer's viewpoint. The aspects of this analysis include orchestration, structure, key relationships, thematic material, phrasing, harmony, and performance problems. Also included are a survey and summary of the historical and social background of Russian music and of the composer.

The era of great musical composition in Russia began on the base of nationalism in the early nineteenth century. In the late nineteenth century, however, two strong currents of ultratraditional conservatism and radical innovation coexisted. The older Romantic tradition can be represented by Rachmaninoff (1873–1943). Although national features appear also in his music, Rachmaninoff continued the tradition of Tchaikovsky (1840–1893), who was an outstanding Russian representative of the European romantic tradition. Rachmaninoff's music consists of opulent melodies, flexible rhythms, powerful sound, and rich orchestration. Like Tchaikovsky's music, Rachmaninoff's works are highly melodic and often given melancholic mood with mostly minor keys, but his writing for piano is technically as brilliant as that of Liszt.

Among Rachmaninoff's songs and piano pieces, the Second Piano Concerto in c minor, Op. 18, composed in 1900–1901, is probably one of his most popular works. The concerto consists of three movements: Moderato, Adagio sostenuto, and Allegro scherzando. The large tonal scheme of all three movements is c minor, E major, and e minor, respectively. This work contains poetic, melancholy melodies, and rich orchestrations, blending power and variety of touches with Russian coloration. It is also well balanced between piano and orchestra, requiring a careful rhythmic coordination between them.

Chung, Wan Kyu. *An Analysis and Evaluation of Beginning Piano Methods Used in Korea.* Ph.D. dissertation, Lubbock: Texas Tech University, 1992, 254 p. UM 9238991. Western music was introduced in Korea in the late nineteenth century by foreign missionaries, mostly Americans. During the thirty-six years of Japanese annexation (1910–1945), piano study began to be available for the select few who were influenced by western culture. The piano method for beginners in these times was the one by Ferdinand Beyer: *Vorschule Im Klavierspiel*, Op. 101, which was published around 1850 in Germany. This method was introduced into Korea through Japan. From the time that Korean music publishing companies began publishing this century-old German method during the 1950s, until quite recently, the Korean version was the authoritative and only piano method in Korea. When American and European piano pedagogy and piano methods were introduced in the 1970s, mostly by Korean musicians who studied abroad, the problem of the century-old Beyer method was raised among Korean piano educators. In an effort to improve and modify the Beyer method for the benefit of children, the *Beyer for Children* and the *Beyer for Young Children* were published during the 1970s. Finally, the most improved Korean piano method, the *New Se-Kwang Beyer,* was published in 1987.

As background information, this study includes a brief history of Western music, keyboard instruments, and music education in Korea.

Cisler, Valerie Clare. *The Piano Sonatas of Robert Muczynski.* D.M.A. paper, Norman: University of Oklahoma, 1993, 480 p. UM 9410272. The purpose of this study is to provide an analysis of Robert Muczynski's First Piano Sonata, Op. 9 (1956); Second Piano Sonata, Op. 22 (1965–1966); and Third Piano Sonata, Op. 35 (1974) that will promote interest, interpretative understanding, and continued performance of these works. The sonatas are Muczynski's most extensive works written for the piano; they are of high artistic value and deserve a place in the standard repertory.

Clark, Frances. *Questions and Answers.* Northfield, Ill.: Instrumentalist Co., 1992, 345 p. Clark's column from *Clavier* for twenty-six years. Would make an excellent piano pedagogy book for the inexperienced teacher. No index.

Clark, J. Bunker. *The Dawning of American Keyboard Music.* Westport, Conn.: Greenwood Press, 1988, 411 p. The finest descriptive and critical survey of American keyboard music from 1787 to 1830. Chapter titles are Sonatas, Rausch to Heinrich; Rondos, Brown to Meineke; A Variety of Variations; A Potpourri of Medleys; European and American Keyboard Battles; Organ Music, Bremner to Zeuner; Pianoforte Tutors in England and America; and The First Americanist: Anthony Philip Heinrich. Includes bibliography, name index, title index, and subject index.

Clarson-Leach, Robert. *Marguerite Wolff: Adventures of a Concert Pi-anist.* London: Artmusique Publishing Co., 1985, 137 p. Includes in-dex. Details the career of this famous English concert pianist.

Clevenger, Charles Raymond. *"Melodic Potentials" and "Real-Time A-coustics": Their Effects on the Shaping of Melodic Contours in Piano Performance.* D.M.A. paper, University of Cincinnati, 1986, 176 p. UM 8622243. This is a two-pronged study of how "melodic poten-tials" (the artistic element of piano interpretation) and "real-time acous-tics" (the cybernetic monitoring of the actual sound) work together during performance. The discussion is directed toward students and teachers of the piano.

  The study is organized into three chapters. The first contains a dis-cussion of the nature and medium of melodic communication among composer, pianist, and auditor, with some emphasis on the pianistic limitations of that communication. The second chapter addresses the challenge of reconciling artistic freedom with the composer's intent. Here the author proposes a taxonomic approach to melodic interpre-tation, beginning with the most objective data and progressing to-ward the more subjective: score, historical and theoretical context, individual's theory of performance, and cybernetic monitoring. Thus, each "screen" of the interpretative process is nested in and disciplines the next, insuring that the more subjective details of the performance do not violate the "canon of appropriateness" for a given work. The object of this exercise is for the student to begin to develop a sense of the stylistic; the author's intent is not to deny intuition or spontaneity but to call for a sense of methodology to guide them.

  In the last chapter, examples are selected from three style periods of the keyboard repertory. One or two aspects of the interpretative tax-onomy are then highlighted in each to show how a well thought-out approach can both solve a performing problem and yield a convinc-ingly stylistic result.

Cline, Eileen T. *Piano Competitions: An Analysis of Their Structure, Value, and Educational Implications.* D.Mus.Ed. dissertation, Bloom-ington: Indiana University, 1985, 779 p. UM 8610620. An increase in competition activity in communities around the United States was greeted first with enthusiasm and then gradually with concern for the ensuing effect on the personal and musical development of young pi-anists and on the art itself. Despite the scope and intensity of this activity, there was no comprehensive information available to provide guidance for students, parents, and educators in responding to resultant pressures and opportunities.

This study provides factual information regarding competition activity, along with opinions of judges, participants, organizers, and teachers. From over 250 interviews and questionnaires, summaries were made according to group characteristics, and student responses were compared with those of professional performers, teachers, and managers. A second point of departure was a study of the operations of twenty-three artist-level competitions.

Findings from these two perspectives led to the development of a historical overview of piano competitions; comparison of individual perceptions with historical realities; consideration of broader human development issues such as nature/nurture, anxiety, and motivation; and conclusions as to the impact of competitions on society and on careers and personal development, with consequent implications for education.

Conclusions were based on identification and discussion of the following key factors: 1) Major elements in organizational operation and success; 2) Societal issues: national politics and government support, business and industry, audience response, development of cultural opportunities, educational efforts, male/female career access, family response; 3) Career considerations: place in developmental sequence, age, repertoire, individual characteristics, politics, critics/press/public, counterproductivity, management, economics, rewards, alternatives, preferred careers; 4) Effect on personal growth: preparation efforts, age, attitudes, personal qualities, destructive elements, coping mechanisms, place in developmental sequence, aspirations.

The extensive bibliography is classified by competition and issue of interest.

Clinkscale, Martha Novak. *Makers of the Piano 1700–1820.* New York: Oxford University Press, 1993, 424 p. This is the first book to present details about all known extant pianos built during the earliest years of the instrument's existence.

Clinton, Mark Kennerly. *Historical and Theoretical Perspectives of Arnold Schoenberg's "Drei Klavierstücke,"* Op. 11. D.M.A. paper, Houston: Rice University, 1989, 84 p. UM 9012783. The purpose of this study is to synthesize various analytical approaches to Schoenberg's

Drei Klavierstücke, Op. 11, into a comprehensive understanding of the work. As the first complete published work in an atonal idiom, this piece has been the focus of numerous disparate analytical techniques. This document attempts to combine a variety of traditional analytical methods (historical-stylistic and formal-descriptive perspectives) with nontraditional approaches based on pitch symbolism, Schoenberg's fascination with numerology, and an underlying correlation between the Op. 11 pieces and Wagner's *Tristan* Prelude.

An examination of correspondence between Schoenberg and the pianist, conductor, and composer Ferruccio Busoni provides further insight into the aesthetic of the Op. 11 pieces. The focus of the Schoenberg-Busoni letters is Op. 11, No. 2, which Busoni arranged in a concert transcription. While both men were seeking the common goal of a new means of musical expression, Busoni's criticisms of the composition are particularly interesting in light of his roots in nineteenth-century Romanticism.

A discussion of editorial questions surrounding the *Drei Klavierstücke,* Op. 11, completes the synthesis of analytical approaches. A comparison of the manuscript, two *Handezemplare,* and the collected edition provides insight into questions of editorial responsibility and performance practice in the work.

Coffman, Don Douglas. *The Effects of Mental, Physical Practice, and Aural Knowledge of Results on Improving Piano Performance.* Ph.D. dissertation, Lawrence: University of Kansas, 1987, 175 p. UM 8813396. The purpose of this study is to examine the effects of types of practice—physical (PP), mental (MP), alternating physical/mental (PP+MP), motivational control (MC), and aural knowledge of results (RR)—on improving piano performance. The dependent variables were performance time duration, number of pitch errors, and number of rhythm errors. The subject variables were age, years of piano experience, and imaging ability as measured by the Betts *QMI Vividness of Imagery Scale.*

Forty male and forty female music education and music therapy majors at the University of Kansas for whom the piano was neither their major nor minor instrument participated in a pre- and posttest experiment with eight treatment conditions: PP/KR, PP/no KR, MP/RR, MP/no RR, PP+MP/RR, PP+MP/no RR, MC/KR, and MC/no RR. Subjects in the practice conditions rehearsed a four-measure chordal piano composition on a synthesizer six times, while control subjects read an article on sight-reading techniques. Subjects in the RR conditions either received aural KR via the synthesizer with the electrical power turned off or mentally practiced without the audio model. Three judges evaluated videotaped pre- and posttest performance independently.

An ANCOVA and subsequent Turkey test of performance time durations revealed a significant practice effect, $F(1,3)=3.34$, $p<.05$. Results showed that all three practice conditions had faster performance times than the control, and that the PP and PP+MP groups were faster than the MP group but did not significantly differ from each other. The effect of practice in reducing the number of pitch and rhythm errors was not significant. The presence or absence of aural KR did not significantly improve piano performance as measured by the three dependent variables. Piano experience and imaging ability were significantly related to performance duration times ($r=.31$, $p<.05$), but subject age was not related. The results suggest that mental practice can effectively improve the novice pianists' performance speed, especially when alternated with physical practice.

Coleman, Donna Jeanne. *A Source Study of the Fifth Movement of Charles Ives's First Piano Sonata: Toward a Critical Edition.* D.M.A. paper, University of Rochester, Eastman School of Music, 1986, 166 p. UM 8701921. This study examines the fifth movement of Charles Ives's *First Piano Sonata* in an attempt to understand its musical value and its significance within the entire sonata. These issues are addressed through analysis of the movement to determine not only its internal organization but also its thematic, structural, and aesthetic connections to the other four movements of the sonata. Exhaustive perusal of the manuscripts for the fifth movement resulted in suggested chronology of its composition, as well as listings of possible early revisions and of Ives's final corrections to the score. Taken together, these manuscript studies provide an intimate look at Ives's compositional process and at his ceaselessly active mind. Finally, the manuscript source for the printed editions contains several variants which are presented as an errata sheet for Peer International Corporation's second edition, published in 1979. The evolution of this printed edition from the original manuscript source is discussed along with the history of the sonata's first complete performance and its subsequent first recording. The important roles of Henry Cowell, Lou Harrison, William Masselos, and Paul Echols in this regard have been researched through interviews and correspondence. The result of all of the above is a shattering of misconceptions about the musical strength and aesthetic significance of the fifth movement of the *First Piano Sonata* and a new appraisal of this sonata's importance as the first half of Ives's musical autobiography.

Collaer, Paul. *Darius Milhaud; with a Definitive Catalogue of Milhaud's Works.* Trans. Jane H. Galante. San Francisco Press, 1994, 400 p. An authoritative biography of this important composer, with detailed musical analysis of most works and an excellent listing of works, including publishers.

Collester, Jeanne Colette. *Rudolph Ganz: A Musical Pioneer.* Metuchen, N.J.: Scarecrow Press, 1994. Includes bibliographical references and index. Details of this remarkable musician's life are carefully documented, especially his years as conductor of the St. Louis Symphony.

Collins, Richard. *Piano Playing: A Positive Approach.* Lanham, Md.: University Press of America, 1986, 70 p. Seven chapters aim toward producing a successful performance. Contains much practical advice. Stresses the need for a teacher to have many character words at his or her command.

Colomer, Consuelo. *On Piano Technique.* Trans. Octavio Roca. New York: Vantage Press, 1991, 59 p.

Complete Chopin Etudes. Video cassette. Chopin Video, P.O. Box 471, Radford, VA 24141. Played by David Brandon Phillips. Includes Opp. 10, 25, and *Trois Nouvelles Etudes.*

Concerto! Video cassette. Kansas City, Mo.: SH Productions. A series of three videos that show how soloist and conductor discuss the how-to's of creating a concerto performance. *Claude Frank, pianist.* Mozart's Concerto in G major, K. 453, 60 minutes. Ian Hobson, conductor, and the Sinfonia da Camera. *Lillian Kallir, pianist.* Mozart's Concerto in C major, K. 467, 60 minutes. Ian Hobson, conductor, and the Sinfonia da Camera.

Conversations with Frances Clark. Video cassette. Kansas City, Mo.: SH Productions. No. 201: Her Life and Teachings, 55 minutes. Reviews the personal history that led to Clark's ground-breaking approach, her *New School for Music Study,* and her cherished beliefs about piano education. Topics include music reading, how children learn, and the student-teacher relationship. No. 202: Her Books and Methods, 25 minutes. Discusses the relationship of Clark's method to the pianistic growth of the child and describes the purpose and structure of her teaching materials.

Cooke, Max. *Tone, Touch and Technique for the Young Pianist.* Video cassette. Melbourne, Australia: Allans Music, 67 minutes. Based on the publication by Max Cooke of the same title (Allans Music, Edition No. 958). Cooke discusses and has students demonstrate theories of posture, gesture and coordination, muscular control, finger action, role of the arms, and sense of touch. These lead to the application of the skills acquired in actual music examples.

———. *Tone, Touch and Technique for the Advanced Pianist.* Video cassette. Melbourne, Australia: Allans Music, 78 minutes. Based on the publication by Max Cooke of the same title (Allans Music, Edition No. 1203). Covers similar topics as listed above but on more advanced level. Includes exercises and pieces from the literature culminating in Brahms's *Ballade,* Op. 118, No. 3.

Cooper, Barry. *English Solo Keyboard Music of the Middle and Late Baroque.* Hamden, Conn.: Garland Publishing Co., 1989, 525 p. This is a general survey tracing chronologically the developments in English keyboard music from around the time of the Commonwealth to the middle of the eighteenth century. Looks at styles, forms, techniques, and influences, as well as problems of authorship where they exist, and the general question of ornamentation and interpretation. Includes a chapter on Purcell's harpsichord music and one on Blow's harpsichord music.

Cooper, David Cornish. *A Survey of the Solo Piano Works of Manual de Falla.* D.M.A. paper, Lexington: University of Kentucky, 1991, 199 p. UM 9129896. Spanish art music was in decline for the greater part of the late eighteenth and early nineteenth centuries. In the last quarter of the nineteenth century, a renewed vitality appeared, effected primarily by the influence of musicologist and composer Felipe Pedrell. In *Por Nuestra Música* (1891), Pedrell challenged Spanish composers to return to their roots in Spanish folksong. Manuel de Falla (1876–1946) took up the challenge and along with his contemporaries, Albéniz and Granados, returned Spanish art music to a height of excellence previously known only in the sixteenth century.

The development of Manuel de Falla as a composer is perhaps best evidenced in the solo works for piano. In these few compositions one may discern a developing facility in the use of folk elements as a basis for a compositional style. The results of de Falla's studies in Paris at the height of Impressionism are also reflected in certain piano works. It was due to his study of the works of Debussy, Ravel, and others that de Falla was able to develop into a more cosmopolitan composer. This study also discusses the basic folk elements and harmonic procedures that de Falla used in his solo piano works. Each major work is discussed from a point of view primarily designed for the performer.

Cooper, Matthew James. *Duke Ellington: The Pianist.* D.M.A. paper, University of Cincinnati, 1994, 300 p. UM 9424551. Chapter One briefly describes Ellington's piano style and summarizes his importance as a jazz pianist. Chapter Two is a biographical sketch of Ellington, with special attention to his early musical development. Chapter Three documents the early years (1899–1932), the influence of Johnson and Smith, and the earliest stride solos. Chapter Four focuses on the middle years and "typical" style, documenting Ellington's adaptation of the stride style and his contribution to swing accompaniment styles. Chapter Five covers the later years and "atypical" style, focusing especially on the recordings made in the early sixties, and discussing the possible influence of Thelonious Monk. Chapter Six summarizes the variety of Ellington's accomplishments and the evolution of his style.

Corragio, Peter. *The Art of Performance.* San Diego, Calif.: Neil A. Kjos Music Co., 1997, 3 vols. A comic-book format introduces: 1. *Pedaling—The Soul of the Piano—Introducing the Pedals and Basic Pedaling*, 40 p. 2. *The Spectrum of Expressive Touches*, 40 p. 3. *Perfect Practice*, 44 p. Basic ideas are presented using comic-book characters; clever.

Cortright, Cynthia Susan. *Gyorgy Sebok: A Profile as Revealed through Interviews with the Artist, His Colleagues and His Students.* D.M.A. paper, Norman: University of Oklahoma, 1993, 126 p. UM 9332266. The purpose of this document is to present a profile of Gyorgy Sebok, his life and work as a concert pianist, with particular emphasis on his pedagogy. The study focuses upon the artist's own philosophy and goals of teaching as revealed through personal interviews. Because Sebok does not purport a proclaimed method of teaching, discussion of him as a pedagogue must often be philosophical—even metaphysical—in nature. Specific examples of his particular teaching style and his pedagogical impact are, however, included in the form of extensive quotes from students and colleagues who responded to a formal query.

Crosby, Richard Allen. *The Piano Music of Lee Hoiby.* D.M.A. paper, University of Cincinnati, 1990, 196 p. UM 9119957. Doctoral paper dealing with solo piano works and two concertos by American composer Lee Hoiby, born in Madison, Wisconsin, on February 17, 1926. Hoiby studied piano with Gunnar Johansen at the University of Wisconsin and Egon Petri at Mills College, and his principal composition studies were with Gian-Carolo Menotti at the Curtis Institute. His numerous awards include a Fulbright Fellowship to study in Rome, a Guggenheim Fellowship, and the National Fellowship of Arts and Letters Award in 1957.
   Extensive biographical and philosophical background based on interviews of colleagues of the composer and on two personal interviews with Hoiby is included in the first two chapters. The discussion and analysis of each piano work is preceded by a brief historical background on the respective genre.

Cruz-Perez, Horacio Antonio. *The Piano Sonatas of Karol Szymanowski.* Ph.D. dissertation, Evanston, Ill.: Northwestern University, 1987, 310 p. UM 8728076. The three piano sonatas of the Polish composer Karol Szymanowski (1882–1937) are the subject of this dissertation. Through the thorough analysis of these compositions, the author attempts to trace the composer's evolution in relation to the piano sonata genre in particular, which is, by extension, a reflection of his general stylistic development, until roughly the end of World War I. Szymanowski's piano sonatas are particularly suited to the purpose stated above, for they cover his main stylistic stages within the period involved.
   The dissertation is divided into four chapters. The first three are respectively dedicated to the analysis of the three sonatas; the final chapter is devoted to the conclusions drawn from that analysis. The analysis of the First Sonata (Chapter One) investigates the origins of Szymanowski's style as the young composer tries to find his voice while working within the mainly Classical framework of his formal

training, which he complemented with the minute analysis of the works of Chopin and early Scriabin.

The Second Sonata (Chapter Two) reveals the evolution of his style into the highly chromatic manner of German late Romanticism. The Classical outlook, however, is still present in the large-scale organization of this composition. The Style of the Third Sonata (Chapter Three) represents the revolutionary changes that Szymanowski's style underwent during the World War I years. The analysis of this sonata discloses the unique blend of Impressionistic methods and Classical form achieved by the composer in his most important creative phase.

The eclecticism of Szymanowski's style and the noticeable shift of aesthetic orientation between the Second and Third Sonatas prompted the author to employ a similarly eclectic combination of analytical methods, the flexibility of which he considered essential to obtain the best possible results.

Chapter Four contains a summation of the most salient features of the composer's approach to the sonata genre, the most relevant of which are his treatment of sonata form and the fugue, which he uses in the opening and closing movements, respectively, of all the sonatas.

Culbertson, Evelyn Davis. *He Heard America Singing: Arthur Farwell, Composer and Crusading Music Educator.* Metuchen, N.J.: Scarecrow Press, 1992, 852 p. Farwell's life and musical contribution.

Cummings, Craig Campney. *Large-Scale Coherence in Selected Nineteenth Century Piano Variations.* Ph.D. dissertation, Bloomington: Indiana University, 1991, 432 p. UM 9203431. This dissertation examines strategies of large-scale form in four nineteenth-century piano variation sets: Beethoven's *Piano Sonata in E,* Op. 109, III; Schumann's *Symphonic Etudes,* Op. 13; Brahms's *Variations on a Theme by Schumann,* Op. 9; and Brahms's *Variations and Fugue on a Theme by Handel,* Op. 24. While these works contain vestiges of the rhythmic acceleration plan typical of eighteenth-century variations, analysis demonstrates that these composers employed more complicated techniques of organization.

The initial chapter establishes the historical foundation, including a brief history of variation techniques and forms, an examination of treatises by the nineteenth-century theorists Marx, d'Indy, Czerny, Riemann, and Momigny, and a summary of twentieth-century classifications of variations.

Chapter Two considers issues of analytical methodology. Schenkerian analysis proves to be valuable in that it clarifies levels of structural retention, reveals deeper-structure motivic relationships, and offers an effective tool for comparison of variations. The dissertation combines Schenkerian analysis with motivic and other approaches, resulting in an eclectic methodology which compares various musical parameters. The chapter concludes with an analysis of the Beethoven work.

Chapters Three through Five examine the compositions by Schumann and Brahms, demonstrating that although Brahms initially was enamored of Schumann's free conception of the genre, he subsequently reverted to Beethoven's structurally conservative notion. The evidence is present in Brahms's letters, teaching, and compositions.

The analyses reveal that these works are organized through the general quality of statement, departure, and return, or several cycles thereof. This overall shape is created through developments and alterations in various parameters, as well as connections between both neighboring and noncontiguous variations. Large-scale registrar plans and voice leading are important components of this process. The comparisons of different parameters and the discussion of the roles of the free variations within the entire compositions shed new light upon nineteenth-century free variation technique and form.

Curry, Michael Loren. *The Sarabande in Keyboard Music from Johann Jacob Froberger to J. S. Bach.* Thesis, Seattle: University of Washington, 1965.

Dawe, Edmund Noel. *Three Piano Sonatas by Friedrich Kuhlau.* D.M.A. paper, Vancouver: University of British Columbia, 1988. Friedrich Kuhlau (1786–1832) ranks as a minor master of the early nineteenth century. As a composer of keyboard music he is perhaps best known for his sets of sonatinas, but the twenty-two sonatas he composed from 1809 to 1831 form a significant part of his extensive output. This study examines three of his sonatas—Op. 4, Op. 46, No. 2, and Op. 127—and places them in historical context through a discussion of the importance of this genre in the repertoire of that era. A survey of contemporary keyboard performance practices is also included, as well as an introductory biographical sketch.

Kuhlau's style is undeniably conservative, with phrases of regular and predictable length in evidence throughout, and his music is often derivative of that of earlier composers from C. P. E. Bach through

Beethoven. However, his works also reflect numerous traits of early Romanticism. They are melodically rich, widely spaced sonorities are frequently employed, and textures range from delicate nuances to thickly scored passages. From a purely pianistic point of view, Kuhlau displays a fondness for scalewise and arpeggiated passages so often used to excess by lesser composers of this era, but he also clearly demonstrates that he was aware of more innovative approaches to keyboard writing.

Throughout history, countless minor composers such as Kuhlau were highly respected during their lifetimes; nevertheless, most of their compositions, including those under consideration here, have not survived on the concert stage. Consequently, there exists a vast body of literature of which little or nothing is known. It is both necessary and useful to study such works in order to gain a more complete understanding of music of their period. Moreover, a closer examination of them might well lead to a reassessment of their worth, which in turn may encourage more frequent performances.

Deahl, Lora Gay. *Principles of Organization in Robert Schumann's "Davidsbündlertänze," Opus 6 and "Kreisleriana," Opus 16.* D.M.A. paper, Austin: University of Texas, 1988, 187 p. UM 8901429. This thesis is an investigation into how unified cycles emerge from groupings of independent, contrasting works using as models two of the Schumann piano cycles, the *Davidsbündlertänze,* Op. 6, and the *Kreisleriana,* Op. 16.

On the local level, the moment-to-moment continuity of phrases, sections, and movements is seen to be pivotal. Smooth key successions (usually diatonically related thirds, fourths, or fifths) and harmonically open structures dilute the autonomy of the component parts, permitting a natural flow and interaction between and within sections and movements. Numerous unordered repetitions of distinctive motives, rhythmical patterns, harmonic progressions, and textures generate potent intra- and intermovement connections. Restrictions on the numbers of keys, textural styles, motives, and *Stimmungen* (affective states of mind) incorporated within a particular cycle give each a unified voice. In addition, the style is self-referential insofar as phrases, sections, or movements of the cycle are freely developed or transformed through traditional variation procedures from a limited number of motives and harmonic patterns.

Schumann's treatment of form has often been denigrated by music historians and theorists, but the findings of this thesis suggest that the cycles result not from instinctive juxtapositions of independent works but rather from preconceived plans which govern overall structure and control the formation of details. The framing movements (usually located at the beginning, end, and mid-point) carry the structural burden, establishing melodic or harmonic "themes," initiating patterns of *Stimmung* succession, and setting into motion coherent, unidirectional tonal plots unfolding over the entire span of the work. Symmetrical patternings of *Stimmungen* become particularly important in the lengthier cycles.

In addition, *Stimmung* arrangements and musical procedures can impart symbolic or narrative meaning to cycles. Through major-minor parallelism, motive transformation, key characterization, recall, and the use of evocative genres, Schumann's cycles recreate an unmistakable sense of historical and emotional progression, enabling the listener to make parallel connections between musical forms and life experiences.

Dennis, David McCoy. *A Guide to Practicing Selected Passages in the Piano Sonata in B Minor by Franz Liszt.* D.M.A. paper, Louisville: Southern Baptist Theological Seminary, 1986, 175p. UM 8619030. The purpose of the dissertation is to identify passages of technical difficulty in the *Sonata in B minor* for piano by Franz Liszt and to devise practice procedures which would aid both the student and the teacher in the preparation of this work for performance. Chapter Two examines various texts on piano technique, focusing on the pianistic problems as they were defined by Alfred Cortot. Chapter Three contains exercises for selected technically difficult passages found in the Liszt sonata. Several examples of each type of technical problem described by Cortot are included.

Dennis, Pamela Richardson. *A Manual for the Use of the Computer as an Instructional Tool in the Private Piano Studio.* M.C.M. thesis, Louisville: Southern Baptist Theological Seminary, 1986, 137 p. UM 1328385. The purpose of the thesis is to discover available computer materials for teaching music, to determine their applicability in the private piano studio, and to instruct the teacher on their availability and use. Chapter One includes a description of the method for achieving this purpose. In Chapter Two, general computer basics for the computer novice are described. In Chapter Three, the Apple II computer is analyzed and its applicability to music education is discussed. Chapter Four contains a short history of the use of the computer in music education. Some uses of the computer in music education are presented as well as a review of selected music programs. In Chapter Five, the information presented thus far is related to the private piano studio. In Chapter Six, the material is supported by interviews with three Kentucky piano teachers who use the computer in private teaching.

Derry, Lisa Anne. *The Pre-Classical Concerto of Johann Christian Bach: First Movement Design in the Eighteen "London" Keyboard Concertos.* Ph.D. dissertation, Bloomington: Indiana University, 1993, 261 p. UM 9404313. Johann Christian Bach's eighteen "London" keyboard concertos have a cultural and stylistic framework and thus are germane to a detailed view of the evolving formal design of the pre-Classical concerto. This study focuses on first movement formal design from its ancestry in the Baroque ritornello form successively through J. C. Bach's three sets of "London" concertos, his Opp. 1, 7, and 13.

De Souza, Elizabeth Rangel Pinheiro. *Elements of Coherence in Brahms's Opus 76.* D.M.A. paper, Boston University, 1991, 233 p. UM 9122920. Musical clues left in Op. 76 suggest that Brahms made many allusions to compositions in the previously existing repertory. Similarities between the pieces and works of other composers, already noticed by his contemporaries, are clearly detectable. Some musical traits and coincidences of dates indicate that Chopin's *Prelude* Op. 45 might have been among the pieces Brahms examined and emulated.

Motivic, thematic, and tonal materials, borrowed or not, are tightly woven to create a complex net of relationships according to a procedure that is typically Brahmsian. The contrasting character of the pieces is geared to give the set an overall symmetry around the vigorous Capriccio in C sharp minor, the fifth piece of the group. Even though each piece possesses formal characteristics marking it as an individual, codas and final cadences function also as bridges to give to the sequence of the pieces a sense of unbroken continuity.

Dettman, Gale LeRoy. *The Thirty-Two Piano Sonatas of Domenico Cimarosa.* M.M. thesis, Austin: University of Texas, 1957, 82 p.

Devuyst, Kelly Ker. *Orchestral Piano: Its Origin, Styles and Repertoire with a Stylistic Comparison and Textural Analysis of Rakhmaninov's "Symphonic Dances" and Stravinsky's "Petrushka."* D.M.A. paper, Memphis State University, 1993, 160 p. UM 9414955. The purpose of this study is to investigate the piano as an orchestral instrument in two ways. First, a brief history of the use of piano in orchestra is explored, culminating in an examination of compositional devices in several piano parts as demonstrated by some composers who most often included the piano in their orchestrations. Second, two pieces, Stravinsky's *Petrushka* and Rachmaninoff's *Symphonic Dances*, are discussed in terms of piano within the orchestral texture and in comparison with each other.

Dhuvabhark, Janida. *A Study of Chopin's Piano Sonata No. 3 in B Minor, Op. 58, with Suggestions for Performance.* D.M.A. paper, Columbus: Ohio State University, 1992, 95 p. UM 9227212. It has been in the past few decades that Chopin's compositions in large form have begun to be appreciated. The popularity of performing Chopin's large works, especially the *Sonata No. 3 in B minor,* seems to be increasing. There is a need for more knowledge about the structural and musical elements of the sonata. The purpose of this document is to provide a general study of the structural analysis and elements of the sonata, as well as a discussion of performance problems.

Chapter One contains an introduction and background of Chopin's three sonatas. Chapter Two reviews related general literature. Chapter Three provides a structural analysis of all four movements with the writer's performance suggestions, and Chapter Four contains a conclusion.

Dibble, Cameron Shawn. *John Sylvanus Thompson: Pianist, Pedagogue, Composer.* D.M.A. paper, Kansas City, Mo.: University of Missouri, 1992, 261 p. UM 9224624. To the knowledge of the author, there are no biographies of John Thompson in existence, except the short background sketches given, for example, in the 1927 Duo-Art Catalog, published by the Aeolian Company, and the profiles of Thompson printed in his published music.

Primary research was undertaken to interview relatives, former childhood acquaintances, and former students of John Thompson. A major effort in this regard was a journey to his birthplace in order to locate people who might have known him. Other destinations on this trip were New York City and Yonkers, New York, to interview former students. One source led to another and so on. Later destinations on the journey were Lyme, New Hampshire, where Thompson's niece lives, and Cincinnati, the location of the Willis Music Company, which still publishes a large number of Thompson's most famous music books. Because of the fame of the Thompson piano teaching materials, a certain mystique about Thompson existed in the author's mind and perhaps also in the perception of the public at large. John Thompson was a name without an identity. From the author's research, sufficient information about Thompson's early life was obtained to provide evidence of an early performing career, which some might have supposed did not or could not exist. Also, Thompson's asthma condition was discovered, and this difficulty certainly affected career decisions throughout his life.

The most significant discovery by the author was that Thompson appeared to have chosen teaching as a career early in life. He evidently devoted a great deal of thought to the processes of teaching and learning how to play the piano. He devised the philosophy that teaching the elements of piano technique, which are used by the concert pianist, could be applied to the child by the use of miniature forms and interesting, original melodic pieces. Thompson enlarged this idea to include reducing the melodies of many famous masterpieces, including other musical media (opera, symphonies, etc.) to the ability and capability of a small hand. This "genius" (a word used by several people) of Thompson may explain why his compositions were and are some of the most influential piano instruction materials in existence during the twentieth century.

Dicus, Kent Timothy. *A Stylistic Analysis of Selected Piano Works of Louis Moreau Gottschalk.* M.M. thesis, Tucson: University of Arizona, 1988, 120 p. UM 1333588. Although Louis Moreau Gottschalk's works are not generally recognized as being exceptionally significant in the development of musical style, they do serve as a link between the music of Frédéric Chopin and that of Charles Ives. Certain stylistic characteristics of Chopin are seen in many of Gottschalk's works, especially those which incorporate "Scherzo" and "Mazurka" passages. Simultaneously, Gottschalk's concept of using popular tunes as prominent melodies and themes was later expanded by Charles Ives. Gottschalk's works include some of America's first experimentations with form through utilization and expansion of the basic form of ABA Coda. Through his use of varied ABA form with repeated and parallel passages, Gottschalk developed his particular style of phrasing, texture, and rhythm, all of which figure prominently in his works. Four pieces are examined with these concepts as the basis for analysis.

Dieckow, Almarie. *A Stylistic Analysis of the Solo Keyboard Sonatas of Antonio Soler.* Ph.D. dissertation, St. Louis, Mo.: Washington University, 1971, 273 p. UM 72–17949. Chapter headings: Sonata-form: Expositions; Sonata-form: Excursions and Recapitulations; Dance-Types; Polyphonic Movements: Intentos; Melody, Tempo and Rhythm; Harmony; Keyboard Technique.

Ding, Xiao-Li. *Rachmaninoff Plays Rachmaninoff.* D.M.A. paper, Boston University, 1991, 179 p. UM 9125014. This document hopes to shed light not only on the interconnection between Rachmaninoff's two central spheres of activity in composition and piano performance, but also on this artist's performance ideal regarding his own music in order to arrive at a viable and informed approach through which interested interpreters, such as the present author, may gain insights into the music. The main part of the paper presents six selected works with detailed analyses. The author hopes to uncover the music's subtly shifting stylistic traits to arrive ultimately at the plausible range of interpretative possibilities for Rachmaninoff's solo piano works through copious and careful comparisons and evaluations of the following items: selected original piano music by the composer, the subsequent revisions, and the numerous recorded performance versions of the same works played by the composer.

Dorum, Eileen. *Percy Grainger: The Man Behind the Music.* White Plains, N.Y.: Pro/Am Resources, 1986, 224 p., 151 photos and other illustrations. Presents a more accurate picture of Grainger than has thus been available. The author is Australian and offers unique coverage of the Australian side of her subject. Grainger emerges in this book as humane, vital, temperate, and sane. The chronology is meticulously detailed and the social context well established.

Dossa, James Richard. *The Novelty Piano Style of Zez Confrey: A Theoretical Analysis of His Piano Solos and Their Relation to Ragtime* *and Jazz.* Ph.D. dissertation, Evanston, Ill.: Northwestern University, 1986, 273 p. UM 8621778. Zez Confrey (1895–1971), the best-known proponent of novelty piano style, composed over one hundred novelty piano solos and songs between 1918 and 1959 using techniques and figures found in ragtime, early jazz, and piano-roll arrangements. He also drew inspiration from his classical study of piano at Chicago Musical College and from his percussion background. This dissertation traces the evolution of his novelty style through musical analysis of selected compositions and discusses various novelty devices which were characteristic features of his piano solos.

As ragtime grew in popularity between 1895 and 1920, it followed two evolutionary paths; one being the development of early jazz, the other a highly commercialized form of popular music. During the 1910s, the ubiquitous player piano and flashy, full-textured piano-roll arrangements of rags and ragtime songs were largely responsible for ragtime's commercial success. Piano-roll arrangers strived constantly to create unique pianistic figures, flourishes, and ornaments to give a competitive edge to their product. Novelty piano style was created by these craftsmen when they began publishing sheet music arrangements and compositions using the same figures and devices which made their piano rolls successful.

Confrey's early-period compositions contained complex polyrhythmic passages in combination with rhythmic elements of ragtime and early jazz in a cohesive formal construction. The popularity of his pieces led him to write three method books, all of which provided instruction in novelty piano style. His middle-period works, while retaining some characteristics of his earlier pieces, were more lyrical than rhythmic, with an extensive palette of harmonic colors. His use of whole-tone scales and sonorities was influenced by harmonic practices of French impressionistic composers. His late-period pieces were intended primarily for young children.

The dissertation contains an annotated bibliography in two parts: Part One contains a list of source materials relating to Confrey and novelty piano style, and Part Two includes a list of source materials important to the study of piano ragtime and easy jazz piano styles.

Drake, Kenneth. *The Beethoven Sonatas and the Creative Experience.* Bloomington: Indiana University Press, 1994, 320 p., 485 musical examples. Instead of following the traditional chronological order of studying the Beethoven piano sonatas, Drake places them in categories that reflect certain qualities of the music. Approaching the sonatas as an interpreter's search for meaning, he begins with the Classic composers' expressive treatment of the keyboard—such as touches, articulation, line, color, silence, and the pacing of musical ideas. Drake analyzes individual Beethoven sonatas, exploring such qualities as motivic development, color, philosophies, overtones, and technical facility. A superb penetration of these masterpieces.

Dubal, David. *The Art of the Piano.* San Diego: Harcourt Brace & Co., 2nd ed., 1995, 477 p. Dubal covers the performers, literature, and recordings. Part One focuses on the diverse pianists who have made a difference in their performances. It is set up alphabetically and includes 673 pianists from Louis Adam through Nikolao Zverov. Part Two is devoted to the literature with lists of exceptional solo and concerto recordings, also alphabetically arranged from Isaac Albéniz through Stephen Wolpe. A fine index greatly adds to the book.

———. *Evenings with Horowitz: An Intimate Portrait.* Secaucus, N.J.: Carol Publishing Group, 1994. Originally published 1991, 321 p. A fascinating account of Dubal's visits with Horowitz over a period of years. The author's critical appraisals of Horowitz are of special interest.

———. *The Golden Age of the Piano.* Video cassette. Philips Classics, 80 minutes. Features performance footage from some of this century's greatest pianists, including Serkin, Horowitz, Gould, Landowksa, Hess, Rubinstein, Hofmann, Grainger, Cortot, and Cliburn. Dubal narrates and offers an exploration of the development of the piano and its role not only in the musical world but in the world at large as a symbol of democracy, self-reliance, and personal expression.

———, ed. *Remembering Horowitz—125 Pianists Recall a Legend.* New York: Schirmer Books, 1993, 400 p. Leading concert pianists describe the artistry of Horowitz—both his technical powers and his musicianship, his mastery of timbre and color, and the passion he expressed. Featuring essays by such performers as Emanuel Ax, Lazar Berman, Van Cliburn, Gary Graffman, Alicia de Larrocha, Maurizio Pollini, and Charles Rosen, this book is both a poignant reminiscence and a revelation of what great musicians hear when they listen to music.

Dubois, Thora Solveig Asgeirson. *A Performance Analysis of Selected*

Works by Barbara Pentland for Solo Piano. Ph.D. dissertation, Norman: University of Oklahoma, 1992, 223 p. UM 9311007. The purpose of this document is to present a performance analysis of three sets of solo piano pieces by Barbara Pentland. They are *Studies in Line* (1941), *Suite Borealis* (1966), and *Canticum, Burlesca and Finale* (1987). They were selected from three periods of the composer's life to illustrate the evolution of her style.

Dumm, Robert. *Pumping Ivory*. Katonah, N.Y.: Ekay Music, 1988, 220 p. This is basically a "how to practice" book. Part One deals with preparing to practice. Part Two is a plan for practicing. Part Three deals with expression. Part Four focuses on practicing for a performance. Appendix I deals with sight-reading. Appendix II deals with pedaling. Contains a large amount of practical information on the subject.

Dunoyer, Cecilia. *Marguerite Long: A Life in French Music, 1874–1966*. Bloomington: Indiana University Press, 1993, 256 p. Virtuoso performer, tireless pedagogue, and the most important French woman pianist of our century, Marguerite Long left her stamp on a whole epoch of musical life in Paris.

Dunsby, Jonathan. *Performing Music: Shared Concerns*. New York: Oxford University Press, 1995, 112 p. Includes bibliographical references and index. Focuses on the psychology of listening to the psychology of performing. Deals with a number of intriguing issues in nontechnical language. Contains vivid insights into how performers think and what they think about.

Dyal, Edith Irene Colvin. *An Examination of Factors which Associate with a Successful Outcome in Piano Lessons*. Ed.D. dissertation, New York: Columbia University Teachers College, 1991, 167 p. UM 9136379. The purpose of this research is to identify through a questionnaire those factors attributed to success in piano study. A further purpose is to determine ways to promote more rewarding lessons in the future. Major conclusions: 1) Good practice procedures are of vital importance if piano lessons are to have a successful outcome. 2) Encouragement and praise for work done well plays a strong role in the unfolding of successful piano lessons. 3) A balanced program of study, including a wide variety of music and each of the facts of music learning found to be a factor in successful lessons, provides the best probability for rewarding, successful lessons. Recommendations: 1) more attention to good practice procedures; 2) abundant positive constructive criticism; 3) extra weekly lessons in order to include all facts of music learning; 4) broader training for teachers; 5) further research with a more representative sample of the various ethnic groups.

Edel, Theodore. *Piano Music for One Hand.* Bloomington: Indiana University Press, 1994, 121 p. Includes nearly 1,000 works for the left hand plus solos for the right hand alone, and concertos and chamber works with piano parts for one, three and five hands. Part One looks at the origins of music for one hand. Part Two is an alphabetic annotated listing by composer of the repertoire in each category: solos, concertos, and chamber works.

Eide, Christina Ann. *The Solo Piano Works of Karel Husa: An Analytical Study.* D.M.A. dissertation, Tempe: Arizona State University, 1992, 350 p. UM 9237248. The four solo piano works of Karel Husa span over thirty years, from his first published work in 1943, to 1975. Husa, best known for his large ensemble works, has described himself as struggling to find the right combination of styles and techniques from both the past and the present. As a result, Husa's solo piano works convey many contrasting emotions with a limited amount of material, and each contains powerful, dramatic climaxes within classically rooted forms. Detailed analysis of the *Sonatina,* Op. 1 (1943), the *Sonata for Piano,* Op. 11 (1949), the *Elegie for Piano* (1957), and the *Sonata No. 2* for Piano (1975), reveals not only the underlying motivic connections and formal structure of each work, but also Husa's advancing compositional style.

Eigeldinger, Jean-Jacques. *Chopin: Pianist and Teacher as Seen by His Pupils.* New York: Cambridge University Press, 1989, 340 p. Based on Chopin's teaching activity and methods. Other sources include the annotated scores of pupils and associates and the statements of Chopin's students in Paris, letters, and reminiscences that were written, dictated, or conveyed by word of mouth. A major source for Chopin performance practice.

Ellsworth, Therese Marie. *The Piano Concerto in London Concert Life Between 1801 and 1850.* Ph.D. dissertation, University of Cincinnati,

1991, 383 p. UM 9200440. This study concerns the performances of solo piano concertos and Konzertstücke in London during the first half of the nineteenth century. During that period changes within the concert life of the city influenced the growth of concerto playing there. An enormous increase in the number of concerts, an extension of the concert season, and an expansion of types of concerts provided more opportunities for performance. At the beginning of the nineteenth century, benefit concerts sponsored by individual musicians, oratorio concerts, and series managed by aristocrats with conservative tastes were the chief venues for instrumental performances. By 1850 other concert organizations administered by professional musicians and members of the middle class, chamber concerts, low-cost concerts, and finally solo recitals had developed. Of particular importance was the founding of the Philharmonic Society in 1813.

The profits and performance opportunities in London attracted numerous foreign musicians to the capital. Weber, Liszt, Chopin, Thalberg, and Mendelssohn traveled there, although not all of them performed concertos. Less illustrious soloists from the Continent included Ferdinand Ries, Johann Nepomuk Hummel, and Charles Halle. Some foreigners who settled in London, either permanently or temporarily, made important contributions to the genre. Most famous among these composers were J. B. Cramer and Ignaz Moscheles.

While native soloists saw opportunities for performance increase during this period, they did not experience an equal acceptance as composers. The most gifted native-born piano concerto composers were the Irishman John Field and William Sterndale Bennett. Field spent most of the period living outside England, so it was Bennett who enjoyed a reputation as the most significant native concerto musician of the era.

Tastes in concerto repertoire shifted from a preference for such transitional composers as Hummel and Ries, Cramer and Moscheles, to early Romantic masters Weber and Mendelssohn. Interest in the concertos by Mozart and Beethoven increased especially after 1820 and received numerous performances due primarily to the efforts of native soloists. This study also includes coverage of the revival of the keyboard concertos of J. S. Bach, since their performances employed a piano as solo instrument.

Elton, Nancy Hill. *Twelve-tone Techniques as They Relate to Form in*

Selected Works of Schoenberg and Webern. D.M.A. paper, Austin: University of Texas, 1988, 194 p. UM 8901430. Arnold Schoenberg's intentions in developing the twelve-tone system were, in his own words, to "replace those structural differentiations provided by the tonal system." For him composition with twelve tones had "no other aim than comprehensibility." The purpose of this study is aimed primarily at an investigation of how formal structure in several twelve-tone works of Schoenberg and Webern is generated by local pitch constructions and linear progression. The selected works are Schoenberg's *Suite for Piano,* Op. 25; "Klavierstück," Op. 33a; *Three Songs,* Op. 48; and Webern's *Variations for Piano,* Op. 27, and *Three Songs,* Op. 23. The study of twelve-tone techniques is approached through an analysis of serial applications based on several fundamental principles including augmentation of the set, intervallic/motivic structure, and overt thematicism. While it is recognized that simultaneity and linear progression are not the only means of organizing a musical composition, the present study limits the analysis of harmony and twelve-tone techniques primarily to their role in connection with formal articulation.

Endler, Franz. *Vienna: A Guide to Its Music and Musicians.* Trans. Leo Jecny. Portland, Oreg.: Amadeus Press, 1989, 120 p. Endler, one of Vienna's foremost music critics, explores the rich history of the city's musical institutions and the illustrious composers and performers who have either called Vienna home or have had some significant connection with the "City of Music." A delight for all who admire the city and its flourishing musical life.

Englund, Virginia Allen. *Musical Idealism in Ferruccio Busoni's "Klavierübung."* D.M.A. paper, Tuscaloosa: University of Alabama, 1991, 85 p. UM 9213841. Musical idealism is a major theme in Busoni's treatise *Entwurf einer Neuen Aesthetik der Tonkunst* (Sketch of a New Aesthetic of Music). The Platonic roots of Busoni's aesthetic, the influence of Arthur Schopenhauer, and the specifics of Busoni's treatise are explained in the first section of this paper. The two main tenets of Busoni's philosophy are that 1) the purpose of art is the communication of eternal ideas, and 2) the particular pathway used in the communication of artistic ideas is irrelevant. The musical manifestation of Busoni's philosophy is examined in his ten-volume piano study, the *Klavierübung.*

Ensminger, Jonathan Dale. *An Approach for Understanding the Rhythmic Structure of Piano Compositions.* D.M.A. paper, Columbia: University of South Carolina, 1986, 131 p. UM 8704623. The goal of this study is to develop an approach for understanding the rhythmic structure of piano compositions. Principles for developing rhythmic understanding were reviewed from three disciplines: piano pedagogy, music theory, and experimental psychology. Particular attention was given to principles of rhythmic structure which apply directly to performance.

An analytical model was developed which reflects certain basic principles derived from the review of these three disciplines. This model recognizes three basic types of hierarchical rhythmic structure which have separate yet interdependent functions: motivic rhythm, metric rhythm, and linear-harmonic rhythm. Two piano compositions, the *Allemande* from the *Partita No. 1 in B-flat* by J. S. Bach, and the *Intermezzo in B-flat minor,* Op. 117, No. 2 by Johannes Brahms, are analyzed according to the model. The goal of the analyses is to examine these three types of organization and the way they interact in the compositions. An evaluation of the rhythmic structures of the compositions is made, particularly in reference to potential performance problems caused by ambiguities or conflicts among the three types of organization. Recommendations for performance are then made based on the evaluation.

Espiedra, Aviva. *A Critical Study of Four Piano Sonatas by Israeli Composers, 1950–1979.* D.M.A. paper, Baltimore: Peabody Institute of the Johns Hopkins University, 1992, 399 p. UM 9311003. Josef Tal (b. 1910), Paul Ben-Haim (1897–1983), Noam Sheriff (b. 1935), and Tzvi Avni (b. 1927) are major Israeli composers in whose works piano sonatas are significant. The four sonatas, Tal's *Sonata for Piano* (1950), Ben-Haim's *Sonata for Piano* (1954), Sheriff's *Piano-Sonata* (1961), and Avni's *Epitaph: Piano Sonata No. 2* (1979), reflect, despite their diverse and individual approaches, a trend consistently characterized by the yearning for a synthesis of East and West. East implies Middle and Near Eastern sources of the various Jewish communities' heritage, including the Bible and the Hebrew language, and the regional Arabic music; West implies the European musical language and its contemporary influences. This dissertation is a critical study and analysis of the musical parameters of these four compositions.

Faulkner, Lynn Fetzer. *Continuity in Johannes Brahms's Late Piano*

Works. D.M.A. paper, Tuscaloosa: University of Alabama, 1994, 73 p. UM 9429224. In Brahms's late piano compositions, all musical elements are employed in an effort to loosen formal constraints and provide continuity. In many of these works, Brahms produced a sense of freedom from form, composing works in which the divisional effects of cadences and other structural points have been virtually eliminated.

Fehrenbruck, Mary Jane. *The Piano in Alban Berg's Opera, "Lulu."* D.M.A. paper, Columbus: Ohio State University, 1990, 112 p. UM 9031033. This document examines various aspects of the piano in Alban Berg's opera, *Lulu.* There are two main ways in which the piano has an impact on *Lulu.* Its timbre, in the Prologue and Act III, is usually heard at cadence points and places where the style of music changes. Because Berg so strongly correlates the music to the drama, the piano therefore not only punctuates the music, but the drama as well. The other major influence of the piano on *Lulu* is that its configuration of black-keys and white-keys strongly affected the construction of the principal forms of twelve-tone series for several of the main characters. This document explores how Berg uses these black-key, white-key groupings of notes to relate the characters to each other. It also examines how these black-key, white-key groupings serve as a basis for much of the harmonic structure of the whole work. This paper also explores minor dramatic impacts of the piano on the opera. These include its use as a part of the signal motive, its being the cue for some of the performer's motions, and its reinforcing gunshots when Lulu shoots Dr. Schon.

Autobiographical aspects of *Lulu* are also investigated. The importance of the piano in Berg's life is traced. Then the piano's relationship to certain characters of the opera, who are then demonstrated to be substitutes for Berg, is explored. The importance of form in Berg's music, with particular emphasis on *Lulu,* is examined. This paper also explores Berg's general techniques of writing, and compares these to his writing in *Lulu.* Included in this is a discussion of his use of the piano in his orchestration.

Ferguson, Howard. *Keyboard Duets from the 16th to the 20th Century.* New York: Oxford University Press, 1996, 112 p. Keyboard duets, whether on one or two pianos, are great fun to play. Their technical demands range from the very simple to the extremely difficult. But with this book, every pianist, whether amateur or professional, will be able to find in the vast repertoire something to suit his or her capabilities. Ferguson traces the history of the piano duet, offers solutions to various technical problems encountered when playing, and compiles a select list of original duets with genuine musical or historical interest.

Ferguson, James Robert. *An Analytical and Comparative Study of the Three Piano Concertos of Béla Bartók.* Thesis, Seattle: University of Washington, 1962.

Fiess, Stephen C. E. *The Piano Works of Serge Prokofiev.* Metuchen, N.J.: Scarecrow Press, 1994, 252 p. The author examines the piano works stylistically and historically in relation to innovation in style in the piano music of Prokofiev's contemporaries. Includes bibliographical references, a twenty-five-page discography, and index.

Fillion, Michelle Marie. *The Accompanied Keyboard Divertimenti of Haydn and His Viennese Contemporaries (c. 1750–1780).* Ph.D. dissertation, Ithaca: Cornell University, 1982, 573 p. UM 8219388. Ten Viennese composers active before 1780, including Joseph Haydn, Georg Christoph Wagenseil, Joseph Anton Steffan, Leopold Hofmann, Jan Krtitel Vanhal, and Anton Zimmerman, wrote chamber music with obbligato keyboard. The Viennese accompanied divertimento, most frequently scored as trio or quartet, grew out of native Viennese traditions of solo sonata, concerto, trio sonata, and string trio. Consideration of the sources for ninety-three accompanied divertimenti, presumably authentic, precedes an analysis of form, texture, and style, and an evaluation of the historical significance of the genre. A complete thematic catalog accompanies full editions or excerpts of fifteen previously unedited Viennese accompanied divertimenti.

Fine, Larry. *The Piano Book: Buying and Owning a New or Used Piano.* 2nd ed., Jamaica Plain, Mass.: Brookside Press, 1987, 190 p. Candid brand reviews, how to shop for a piano, special sections on buying an older Steinway, moving or storage, servicing.

Finetti, Thomas Anthony. *An Analytic Study of the Piano Music of Giovanni Sgambati.* Ph.D. dissertation, New York University, 1985, 956 p. UM 8825337. The purpose of this dissertation is to analyze the solo piano corpus of Giovanni Sgambati and to provide a peda-

gogical guide for the interpretation and performance of selected compositions.

In the first chapter of this study, the researcher provides an overview
of the musical environment of Italy during the nineteenth century in
order to create the musical setting in which Sgambati lived and worked.
Sgambati's life and contributions and the related literature pertaining
to his solo piano works and compositional style are also presented in
this chapter. In the second and third chapters, each of Sgambati's fifty-
three piano compositions are analyzed using a modified version of La
Rue's method of style analysis developed by Walter Reinhold. Each
work is individually presented in chronological order with musical
examples to support the analytical data.

Based on the data of Chapters Two and Three, stylistic conclusions
are drawn in Chapter Four regarding Sgambati's preferences for genre
and form and his treatment of sound, harmony rhythm, and melody.
These conclusions also serve as the theoretical base for a selection
process which uses genre, formal classifications, stylistic features, and
literary citations as criteria for selecting specific compositions for further analysis and a guide for their interpretation and performance.
The eighteen works which were selected according to the criteria are
representative of Sgambati's overall solo piano corpus. The works are
the *Fugue,* Op. 6; the *Etude,* Op. 10, No. 2; "Romanze," "Canson-
etta," and "Vecchio Castello" from *Finghi Volanti,* Op. 12; the *Gavotte,* Op. 14; "Nenia" and "Toccata" from *Quattro Pezzi,* Op. 18;
Notturno, Op. 20, No. 1; "Valse" and "Air" from *Suite in B Minor,*
Op. 21; "Vox Populi," "Landler," and "Gigue" from *Pezzi Larioi,* Op.
23; "Ansista," "Marche," and "Anima appassionata" from *Melodie
Poetiche,* Op. 36; and "Melodia Campestre" from *Tre Poemi,* Op. 42.

In Chapters Five through Ten, the selected compositions undergo
further analysis in the form of time-line graphs which, together with
the data from their initial analyses in Chapters Two and Three, are
synthesized in the formation of performance guides. Utilizing many
musical examples, each performance guide consists of recommendations for the interpretation and performance of each selected work.

Fink, Seymour. *Mastering Piano Technique.* Portland, Oreg.: Amadeus
Press, 1992, 190 p. This important comprehensive book covers every
major aspect of piano technique. Excellent analyses and fine examples
are infused with easy-to-understand vocabulary and excellent illustrations.

————. *Mastering Piano Technique: A Guide for Students, Teachers and Performers.* Video cassette. Portland, Oreg.: Amadeus Press, 1994, 86 minutes. Follows the format of the book described above. All aspects of pianistic movement are clearly discussed. The video can be used alone or with the book. Fink emphasizes that movement makes the sound—if something is wrong with the sound, it is because something is wrong with the movement. A split screen is used to allow different angles to clearly demonstrate certain points.

Flaskerud-Rathmell, Susan Marie. *The Influence of Scriabin on Prokofiev's Early Piano Works: Opus 1 through Opus 29.* D.M.A. paper, Tempe: Arizona State University, 1990, 123 p. UM 9116736. The purpose of this study is to show the influence of the Russian composer-pianist, Alexander Scriabin (1872–1915), on the early piano works of his younger Russian contemporary, Sergey Prokofiev (1891–1953), specifically in pianistic figuration.

Prokofiev developed his skills as a concert pianist and composer, writing his early piano works for his own performance while a student at the St. Petersburg Conservatory (1904–1914). His student years coincided with Scriabin's fame as Russia's avant-garde composer, whose music was admired and emulated by Prokofiev and his peers. Testimonies by Prokofiev, his friends, and his teachers reveal Scriabin's significance especially during Prokofiev's years at the St. Petersburg Conservatory.

Not fully understanding Scriabin's harmonic procedures nor fully empathizing with their mystical ramifications, Prokofiev manifested his enthusiasm for Scriabin's works and their intense emotional states through pianistic means rather than harmonic ones.

Scriabin's influence in pianistic figuration is exhibited intermittently throughout Prokofiev's early piano works, Op. 1 through Op. 29. An examination of these works established that Prokofiev implemented several components of Scriabin's pianistic style (the elements of Scriabin's pianistic figuration were catalogued by Samuel Randlett in his 1966 study on Scriabin's pianistic idiom) to effect an atmosphere similar to Scriabin's music: "wide-ranging bass," "one-way arpeggios," "repeated-note arpeggios," "convoluted arpeggios," "repeated chords," "rolled chords," "trills," and "five-finger groups." Prokofiev engaged these specific pianistic elements to create the intensity of mood or stasis associated with Scriabin's works. Furthermore, like Scriabin, he used these pianistic components in tandem with one another; Prokofiev achieved an emotional intensity in his music through the textural layering of these pianistic elements.

Flemm, Eugene W. *The Solo Piano Music of Robert Helps.* D.M.A. paper, University of Cincinnati, 1990, 203 p. UM 9119960. This thesis represents the first in-depth study of Robert Helps (b. 1928), American pianist, composer, and educator. Helps was a child prodigy, winning a national piano contest at age six and having a work orchestrated and performed by Leopold Stokowski and the NBC Symphony at age thirteen. His two great teachers and influences have been Abby Whiteside in piano (1943) and Roger Sessions (1944) in composition. Hence, the dual nature of his life was well established before he graduated from high school in 1946. After a highly successful debut with the San Francisco Symphony in 1951, Helps made one of the most crucial decisions of his life—he decided to forego a career as concerto soloist with major orchestras and instead to devote himself to solo recitals, chamber music, and as a champion of serious twentieth-century music. This he has done with great success and critical acclaim for over four decades. For this he has established professional relationships with a number of distinguished artists, but the one of longest and most successful duration has been with soprano Bethany Beardslee.

The solo piano works of Helps number fourteen mature compositions, beginning with *Fantasy* (1952) to a transcription of Mendelssohn-Bartholdy's song *Schilflied* (1988). His most frequently played works are *Recollections* (1959), *Portrait* (1960), and *Nocturne* (1975). He has written a set of treacherously difficult etudes and another set of etudes for left hand. Other major works include *Quartet* (1970) and *Trois Hommages* (1972). All works are discussed at length from analytical, historical, pedagogical, pianistic, technical, and theoretical perspectives. The three stylistic genres of Helps's music, according to the composer, are neo-impressionism (influenced by late Fauré), atonal and dissonant (influenced by Sessions), and a synthesis of the two. Helps constantly intermingles these stylistic genres from work to work and rarely writes two successive compositions in the same style.

Helps began his teaching career in 1962 at Princeton University and since 1980 has been at the University of South Florida, Tampa. Two of his most renowned students are David Del Tredici and Bennett Lerner.

Forbes, Lois Thompson. *The Use of the Chopin Mazurka in the Study of Chopin's Style by Intermediate Piano Students.* Ed.D. dissertation, New York: Columbia University Teachers College, 1986, 276 p. UM 8704294. Although most of Chopin's music is technically beyond the performance capabilities of the intermediate piano student, Chopin did write some music appropriate for that student. The poetic splendor of his music should be made available to a student at this level, since the intermediate piano student is often a teenager or an adult who can understand emotionally and intellectually the complexities of Chopin's music.

The compositions by Chopin most appropriate for this level of piano performance are the mazurkas, short pieces written in the style of the nationalistic dances of Poland. The purpose of this dissertation is to facilitate the study of Chopin's style by the intermediate piano student through the use of the mazurka. Study of Chopin's mazurkas will be helpful to those teachers who might use them as models for Chopin's style but who might not be aware of all the special qualities related to the mazurka and its performance. It will also give the intermediate piano student general knowledge of Chopin's style, which will create a strong base for use in understanding and interpreting other compositions by Chopin.

This study contains five chapters. Chapter Two gives a historical background of the mazurka and the relationship between that musical form and the mazurkas of Chopin. Chapter Three discusses Chopin's style as characterized by his melody and related elements. Emphasis is given to ornamentation and rubato as two particular aspects of Chopin's style. In Chapter Four, analysis of an interpretative and structural nature is made of six mazurkas appropriate for intermediate piano students. Influence of the folk dances is also discussed. A summary is given in the final chapter as well as recommendations for study of other compositions by Chopin which have the same technical and interpretative problems as the mazurkas included in the dissertation. Numerous musical examples are included. Comparisons between various editions of Chopin mazurkas are also provided.

Forrest, David Lawrence. *The Form of the Keyboard Prelude.* M.C.A. thesis, University of Wollongong, Australia, 1987. This thesis includes a discussion of the form of the prelude, together with specific attention to the treatment of the form by J. S. Bach, Chopin, and Debussy.

The research in the paper has been limited to the works written for the modern piano and its predecessors. The repertoire of the organ was not investigated. A chronological and alphabetical listing of preludes spanning the period from 1448 to 1986 is included.

Fosheim, Karen Marie. *Similarities Between Two Dissimilar American Piano Sonatas of Robert Muczynski and Robert Starer.* D.M.A. paper, Tucson: University of Arizona, 1994, 64 p. UM 9426224. This study examines the stylistic similarities between two works that used, paradoxically, differing methods of compositional technique. These men chose different compositional languages, yet they chose the same formal structure to organize their work. This study focuses on those features that are style determinant.

Foster, Stuart David. *Tonal Methods of Cyclic Unification in Haydn's Mature Keyboard Sonatas.* Baton Rouge: D.M.A. paper, Louisiana State University, 1990, 108 p. UM 9112231. The purpose of this monograph is to explore the diverse types of harmonic relationships among movements in the mature keyboard sonatas of Joseph Haydn. The mature sonatas are defined as those written ca. 1765 and later, of which there are thirty-five. This study draws examples from seventeen of these sonatas in which intermovement harmonic relationships make significant contributions to the overall unity of the sonata.

In discussing questions of unity in Haydn's music, most scholars have concentrated on thematic or motivic similarities, which are perhaps the most obvious unifying features. This study, on the other hand, discusses examples that involve emphasis on a particular key area, use of the same or similar distinctive harmonies, or employment of similar noteworthy harmonic progressions in more than one movement of a sonata. In the body of the study, one chapter is devoted to each of these three categories.

Fouse, Kathryn Lea. *Surrealism in the Piano Music of Representative Twentieth-Century American Composers with Three Recitals of Selected Works of Ives, Cowell, Crumb, Cage, Antheil and Others.* D.M.A. dissertation, Denton: University of North Texas, 1992, 96 p. UM 9224981. This study is an examination of the Surrealist movement and its influence on the piano music of twentieth-century American composers. The first chapter explores the philosophies of the Surrealistic as well as the characteristics found in Surrealist art and literature. The characteristics discussed include the practice of automa-

tism; the juxtaposition of unrelated themes or images; and the creation of dreamlike atmospheres. The second chapter discusses these
characteristics and their appearances in the piano music of Charles
Ives, Henry Cowell, John Cage, Jane Brockman, and George Crumb.
The third chapter summarizes the life and Surrealist traits found in
their music. The fourth and final chapter examines the collage novel,
La Femme 100 Têtes, by Max Ernst, and the musical composition it
inspired, Antheil's piano preludes, *La Femme 100 Têtes*. This study
offers an interesting and wholly new synthesis of music and the related arts as it demonstrates the influence of Surrealism on much of
the American piano music of this century.

Frampton, William McLeod, III. *The Piano Music of Emmanuel Chabrier.*
D.M.A. paper, University of Cincinnati, 1986, 107 p. UM 8622282.
Alexis-Emmanuel Chabrier (1841–1894) was born in Auvergne,
France. Musical training culminated at the Lycee Saint-Louis in Paris.
He took a ministry position with the French government. His friends
included Edouard Manet, Auguste Renoir, Paul Cézanne, Paul Verlaine,
Émile Zola, Gabriel Fauré, César Franck, Camille Saint-Saëns, Henri
Duparc, and Vincent d'Indy. In 1879 he turned exclusively to composition, principally operas. His solo piano works are "Impromptu"
(1873); *Pièces pittoresques* (1881), a ten-piece suite; "Habañera"
(1885); *Cinq morceaux pour piano* (1882–1885); and "Bourrée fan-
tasque" (1891). The significant influences on his compositions are the
salon tradition, contemporary painting, Richard Wagner, Spain, and
Auvergne. Forward-looking traits in his piano music are innovative
treatment of rhythm and meter, experimentation with texture and
range, precision in diacritical markings, and the use of harmony to
introduce wit or humor. Chabrier's music bridges the gap between the
Franck–Saint-Saëns School and Impressionism.

Francis, Ouida Susie. *Guidelines for Teaching Piano Pedagogy Based on
the Developmental Teaching Philosophy of Max W. Camp.* D.M.A.
paper, Columbia: University of South Carolina, 1992, 118 p. UM
9307938. The teaching philosophy of Max W. Camp advocates a developmental approach to teaching piano which fosters independent
learning and musical comprehension. Camp advocates a holistic approach to performance development in which the inherent metric
framework of music itself serves as the organizational structure for
the learning and performing process. He maintains that the rhythmic

organization of one's mental perception of music notation plays a major role in the developmental process. The learning approach emulates the prodigy or model learner whose perceptions generally guide both aural and physical aspects of music-making. The study includes a summary of Camp's approach as presented in his books, *Developing Piano Performance: A Teaching Philosophy* (1981) and *Teaching Piano: The Synthesis of Mind, Ear and Body* (1992).

Frantz, Mary L. *Richard Wilson: The Solo Piano Works, 1974–1986.* D.M.A. paper, Madison: University of Wisconsin, 1992, 155 p. UM 9218339. This document centers on Wilson's style as represented in three major works, *Eclogue* (1974), *Fixations* (1985), and *Intercalations* (1986). Each of these works is discussed separately and examined analytically in Chapters Two through Four. Issues that are addressed include pitch and rhythmic organization, large structural aspects, timbral and textural features, and pianistic issues.

Frejek, James Stephen. *A Method of Textural and Harmonic Analysis as Applied to Selected Piano Works of Debussy and Satie.* M.A. thesis, Long Beach: California State University, 1992, 217 p. In attempting to describe musical style, various theorists have written about melody, harmony, thematic development, meter, rhythm, form, etc., yet texture, an equally valid aspect of style, has received considerably less analytical attention. Harmony, in contrast, has been the topic of myriad writings; but because of the interrelationship of various aspects of texture and harmony, the two may be comfortably examined in parallel fashion.

The discussion of texture is limited to aspects of contrast and density. Likewise, two aspects of harmony and harmonic construction are considered: the examination and identification of vertical sonorities and the identification of constructive and organizational harmonic elements. The piano works of Debussy and Satie form a somewhat comparable terrain of these aspects of texture and harmony that may be examined while establishing the validity and workability of this method of parallel, bilevel textural and harmonic analysis.

Friedburg, Ruth C. *The Complete Pianist—Body, Mind, Syntheses.* Metuchen, N.J.: Scarecrow Press, 1993, 132 p. This is a no-nonsense, common observation book with plenty of helpful advice for the pianist. The "synthesis" portion was the most interesting to this author.

Topics discussed include the why and where of performance, preparation for performance, and performance. An extensive bibliography is included, but no index.

Friedman, Edward Arthur. *Texture and Ornament in the Music of Claude Debussy.* Ph.D. dissertation, Storrs: University of Connecticut, 1987, 213 p. UM 8800217. Motion is the central metaphor available for analysts' attempts to appreciate or account for musical activity. Yet, because the music of Claude Debussy is in so many ways puzzling to critics, a great deal of commentary neglects the question of his unique way of creating musical motion. The aim of this study is to show that Debussy did not reject motion in favor of color; rather, a new concept of musical motion generated (among other things) a new kind of color.

This study focuses on a group of selected songs and piano pieces published by Debussy over a period of about twenty-five years: "Passepied" (*Suite bergamasque*); "Clair de lune" (*Suite bergamasque*); "La flûte de Pan" (*Trois Chansons de Bilitis*); "Clair de lune" (*Fêtes galantes,* 1st collection); "Mandoline," "C'est l'extase" (*Ariettes Oubliées*); "Reflets dans l'eau" (*Images pour piano,* 1st set); "Feuilles mortes," "General Lavine—eccentric," and "La terrase des audiences du clair de lune" (all from *Preludes,* 2nd book); "Et la lune descend sur le temple qui fut" (*Images pour piano,* 2nd set); plus the first movement from the Sonata for Flute, Viola, and Harp.

Friedman, Richard Marc. *The Original Cadenzas in the Piano Concertos of Beethoven: An Analysis.* Ph.D. dissertation, Boston University, 1989, 315 p. UM 8820460. The study and analysis of all eight cadenzas written by Ludwig van Beethoven for the first four of his piano concertos reveals, as much as can be gleaned from this evidence, important information about Beethoven's approach to improvisation. This subject has long eluded investigation due to the paucity of musical and collateral evidence. The analyses of these cadenzas, seven of which are complete, reveal surprising information about the nature of the harmonic plan of the cadenzas and the choice of thematic material in each section of the cadenzas. They also uncover consistencies of pattern and compositional technique that clearly set these cadenzas apart from the late-eighteenth-century norms, best exemplified by those of Mozart.

Beethoven may have been prompted to commit these cadenzas to paper in 1809 by the fear of piracy, a fact he noted with increased attention, after his retirement from the concert stage in 1807. And by 1809 he had already begun study of Carl Philipp Emanuel Bach's *Versuch* and Daniel Gottlob Türk's *Clavierschule* in preparation for the anticipated education of the Archduke Rudolph. The keyboard fantasy, an important subject in the writings of both these theorists, had its own set of rules and compositional approaches. That Türk drew a connection between the fantasy and the cadenza as similar compositional forms, coupled with the amount of detailed description of the fantasy in Bach's treatise, may have served as an inspiration and perhaps guideline for Beethoven's composition of both the Fantasy, Op. 77, and the cadenzas in the same year.

Certain stylistic characteristics predominate in the cadenzas: the use of imitation at the outset; the greatest extent of fantasylike free modulation in the first of the three formal sections; the development of the subsidiary theme in the second section; and the strikingly careful avoidance of a strong dominant prolongation before the actual closing dominant of the cadenza. The cadenzas show an increasing predilection to grow in the direction of compositional, rather than extemporisational planning, a tendency that reaches its zenith in the written-in cadenzas in the Fifth Piano Concerto, the Violin Concerto, and the unfinished Sixth Piano Concerto.

Frieling, Randall. *A Guide to Transcription and Arrangements for Two Pianos.* D.A. dissertation, Muncie, Ind.: Ball State University, 1996. Transcriptions have recently become accepted by artist, critic, and listener. This dissertation is designed as a reference tool for the pianist and duopianist; 1378 entries are catalogued. Each entry contains some of the information from the following list: composer's name, birth and death dates, country, title of work, date arrangement written, publisher and publisher identification number, date of publication, arranger name, number of pages, length in minutes, library or source where found, origin of work, editor, comments, and level of difficulty.

The writer used a number of libraries for the research including the Library of Congress. In addition to the reading of scores of many of the entries, an original questionnaire was sent to 393 pianists who are listed as Master Teachers of College Faculty in the 1995 *Directory of Nationally Certified Teachers of Music.* The results are printed from the 219 replies.

Fritsch, Michael F. *Beethoven's Last Piano Sonatas as Fantasy Sonatas.*

D.M. paper, Evanston, Ill.: Northwestern University, 1987, 159 p. UM 8722555. The introduction to this study of Beethoven's late piano sonatas, "Developing an Underlying Conception that Explains 'Fantasy Sonata'," begins with a two-fold premise concerning the term *fantasy sonata*. The first part of this premise is that this term itself embodies a contradiction, since *fantasy* implies the following of one's whims, while *sonata* implies a stricter type of organization. The second part of the premise is that if a conception could be found that could rectify this apparent contradiction, a framework could be found within which "Fantasy Sonata," as applied to Beethoven's last sonatas, could be understood. It is suggested that the concept of personally autonomous expression, the idea of each sonata as a living being analogous to the person, conceived at once in the mind of its creator, satisfies the requirements of both sonata and fantasy, since the idea of personality involves both unity (experience within one personality) and diversity (varying perceptions by one personality).

Part Two of the Introduction, "Fantasy Expressions Resulting from 'Biological' and 'Psychological' Characteristics of Personally Autonomous Expression," illustrates by numerous examples from the sonatas the musical results of personally autonomous expression.

Part Three, "Deeper Expressions of Fantasy," sets forth the idea that the deepest expressions of fantasy in these works are those related to the illusion of the expression, musically, of absolute expression, that are not limited to the time frame of reference.

The ideas described above are supplied in a measure-by-measure analysis of all movements of Op. 101, and in the detailed analysis of several excerpts from the remaining sonatas (two from Op. 106, one from Op. 109, and one from Op. 110) that illustrate the shape these ideas take beyond Op. 101.

Frohlic, Martha. *Beethoven's "Appassionata" Sonata*. New York: Oxford University Press, 1992, 224 p. Includes a discussion of the final version, analysis of all the sketches and revisions for the third movement in the autograph, and complete transcriptions and facsimile reproductions of the sketches.

Furman, Pablo Eduardo. *An Analysis of Alberto Ginastera's "Piano Concerto No. 1" (1961)*. Ph.D. dissertation, Los Angeles: University of California, 1987, 108 p. UM 8723379. In the first part of the paper, the author presents a historical overview of Ginastera's three compositional periods, focusing on the influences operative in his *Piano Concerto No. 1,* such as traditional forms (i.e., variation and rondo forms), serial technique, and folklore. In the analytical component that follows, the author details the structural properties of the piece, its phraseology, unifying devices, and the pitch and thematic organization.

Galatas, Ruth Ann. *A Survey of Techniques in Imagery Training for the Treatment of Performance Anxiety.* D.M.A. paper, University of Miami, 1989, 75 p. UM 8922735. The present investigation surveys the literature on performance anxiety and imagery techniques (progressive relaxation, rational-emotive imagery, instructional desensitization, and cognitive retraining). The purpose of this study is to examine these techniques and determine possible effects on stage fright. Chapter One discusses the physical consequences of stage fright, and well-known performers give examples of their experiences with performance anxiety. Chapter Two defines "imagery" and provides a brief history on this product of imagination. Chapter Three describes a treatment program for relaxation through imagery training. Chapter Four discusses mental practicing, the use of positive images to reinforce that which has been practiced. In Chapter Five, systematic desensitization is explored in which the performer relearns his or her response to threatening stimuli through imagery training. Chapter Six discusses cognitive retraining, and the performer is instructed to analyze her thinking processes concerning the stage. The performer is encouraged to use these techniques to build a proper perception of the stage.

Galvan, Mary Grace. *Kinesthetic Imagery and Mental Practice: Teaching Strategies for the Piano Principal.* D.M.A. paper, University of Miami, 1992, 82 p. UM 9239657. This essay surveys the possible effectiveness of kinesthetic imagery and mental practice on the keyboard skills of the piano principal (an undergraduate music major not pursuing a degree in piano performance). Sports psychologists and movement artists (those trained in the study of theater movement) maintain that mental practice intensifies the correct kinesthetic image of a movement and increases the possibility of a successful physical execution. The memorization of pianistic movements is affected not only by kinesthetic images but also by visual images of the keyboard and the printed notes, as well as aural images of the resulting sounds. With mental practice, it is possible that the piano principal can learn to consciously translate printed notes into kinesthetic sensations (feelings in the hand) that produce spontaneous physical responses.

This essay offers an alternative learning method for the piano principal by applying mental practice strategies used by athletes, actors, and pianists.

Garcia, Susie Patricia. *Alexander Skryabin and Russian Symbolism: Plot and Symbols in the Late Piano Sonatas.* D.M.A. paper, Austin: University of Texas , 1993, 199 p. UM 9323309. This treatise focuses on both the neglected relationship between Scriabin's philosophy and his music, and on the relationship between his philosophy and that of the Russian poetic movement known as Symbolist. Through study of historical and biographical literature it can be shown that Scriabin was in the mainstream of the Russian art and culture of his time. His ideas were shaped by the commonly held beliefs of the Russian Symbolist school, particularly the branch known as Mystical Anarchism, whose stated goal was the universal transformation of humankind through Symbolist art.

Analysis of the late sonatas (nos. 6–10) shows that Scriabin imbued certain musical figures with mystical meanings which he indicated with verbal references placed within the body of each sonata. These expressive markings illuminate Scriabin's use of specific musical gestures in conjunction with certain verbal images, thus creating a body of symbols that remained consistent throughout the late sonatas.

Gates, Robert Edward. *The Influence of the Eighteenth-Century Piano on the Works of Joseph Haydn.* D.M. paper, Bloomington: Indiana University, 1982, 148 p. Reviews the historical evidence that relates Haydn to eighteenth-century keyboard instruments. Attempts to clarify which of his works were written for which instrument, and compares the action, tone, and damper mechanism of Viennese and English pianos. Traces the evolution of Haydn's keyboard style in terms of his notation of dynamic and expressive markings, use of new keyboard textures and registrar contrast, use of articulations, and the probable use of damper-lifting mechanisms.

Gilbert, Linda M. *The Practice Handbook: A Musician's Guide to Positive Results in the Practice Room.* Redondo Beach, Calif.: Damore Publications, 1993, 61 p.

Gillespie, John, and Anna Gillespie. *Notable Twentieth-Century Pianists: A Bio-Critical Sourcebook.* Westport, Conn.: Greenwood Press, 1995, 2 vols., 910 p. Extensive, documented evaluations of 100 notable twentieth-century pianists detailed through biographies, style analyses, representative discographies, selected performance reviews, and selected references.

Gitz, Raymond J. *A Study of Musical and Extra-Musical Imagery in Rachmaninoff's "Etudes-Tableaux," Opus 39.* D.M.A. paper, Baton Rouge: Louisiana State University, 1990, 88 p. UM 9123192. The nine *Etudes-Tableaux,* Op. 39 (1916–1917) for piano solo are the last important works written by Sergey Rachmaninoff (1873–1943) before his exile from Russia in 1917. The use of the word *Tableaux* in the title suggests an association with pictures, paintings, or scenes. Although the composer often wrote under the external influence of extra-musical sources, he rarely revealed them. This study examines the musical and extra-musical imagery that influenced Rachmaninoff, these elements being the *Dies irae* from the Roman Catholic Mass for the Dead, Russian chant, bell sonorities, and paintings by the Swiss artist Arnold Bocklin (1827–1901). In addition, Rachmaninoff's love of nature and his homeland is reflected throughout the study, and an explanation is given for the dark, somber sentiment that permeates many of the etudes.

Glenn Gould on Gould. Video cassette. Films for Humanities and Sciences, 24 minutes. ANE 5339. Gould's primary, all-encompassing goal was to give shape in the air to the sound in his head. The relationship between this overriding drive to communicate music and his audiences is the theme connecting this compilation of Glenn Gould film clips. Some date from his early years and others from near the end of his life; some show him thoughtful, others playful. Always, however, this carefully structured program retains its focus on the musical center of Gould as he alternately plays or explicates his voices, *allegro molto staccato,* itself a study in rhythmic variations.

Glenn Gould Plays Beethoven. Video cassette. Media for the Arts, Newport, RI 02840, 60 minutes. Gould plays (in his inimitable way) *The Emperor Concerto, Bagatelle,* Op. 126, No. 3, and the *Variations in F Major,* Op. 34.

Gloutier, David. *A Comparison of the Transcription Techniques of*

Godowsky and Liszt as Exemplified in Their Transcriptions of Three
Schubert "Lieder." D.M.A. paper, Denton: North Texas State University, 1987, 39 p. UM 8804309. This investigation seeks to compare
the transcription techniques of two pianist-composers, Godowsky and
Liszt, using three Schubert *lieder* as examples. The *lieder* are "Des
Wandern" from *Die Sahöne Müllerin,* "Gute Nacht" from *Winterreise,*
and "Liebesbotschaft" from *Schwanengesang.* They are compared
using four criteria: tonality, counterpoint, timbral effects, and harmony.
   Liszt, following a practice common in the nineteenth century, was
primarily concerned with bringing new music into the home of the
domestic pianist. The piano transcription was the most widely used
and successful medium for accomplishing this. Liszt also frequently
transcribed pieces of a particular composer in order to promulgate
them by featuring them in his recitals. The Schubert *lieder* fall into
this category. Liszt did not drastically alter the original in these compositions. Indeed, in the cases of "Liebesbotschaft" and "Des Wandern," very little alteration beyond the incorporation of the melody
into the piano accompaniment occurs.
   Godowsky, in contrast, viewed the transcription as a vehicle for composing a new piece. He intended to improve upon the original by
adding his own inspiration to it. Godowsky was particularly ingenious in adding counterpoint, often chromatic, to the original. Examples
of Godowsky's use of counterpoint can be found in "Des Wandern"
and "Gute Nacht." While Liszt strove to remain faithful to Schubert's
intentions, Godowsky exercised his ingenuity at will, being only loosely
concerned with the texture and atmosphere of the lieder. "Gute Nacht"
and "Liebesbotschaft" are two examples that show how far afield
Godowsky could stray from the original by the addition of chromatic
voicing and counterpoint. Godowsky's compositions can be viewed
as perhaps the final statement on the possibilities of piano writing in
the traditional sense. As such these works deserve to be investigated
and performed.

Gluckman, Isidore B. *A Comparative Study of Five Piano Works by*
   Bach, Beethoven, and Liszt. M.A. thesis, San Jose, Calif.: San Jose
   State University, 1995, 71 p. UM 1375689.
   This thesis covers the study of five piano works played by the writer
at a Master Recital: *Toccata in C minor, BWV 911,* by J. S. Bach;
Andante in F (Andante Favori), WoO 57, by Beethoven; and the three
Petrarch Sonnets, 47, 104, and 123, from *Années de Pèlerinage,* sec-

ond year, Italy, by Liszt. All originated during one of the three music periods, Baroque, Classic, and Romantic, and are most important to pianism as they spanned the entire great era of piano emergence and development.

The works are examined individually from a historical perspective, including pertinent associations with events, if any, of the respective composer's life, or possible influences such as poetry (e.g., Petrarch sonnets). They are then analyzed as to form, tonality, and style. The epilogue compares works and pertinent composer styles, showing differences and similarities.

Godoy, Monica. *Claudio Santoro: Overview of His Piano Works and Analysis of the Fourth Piano Sonata.* D.M.A. paper, Boston University, 1994, 104 p. UM 9408962. This document attempts to present the piano music of Claudio Santoro, a major twentieth-century Brazilian composer. In order to illustrate the composer's background, the first chapter addresses briefly the situation of Nationalist music from the beginning of the second decade of this century to the 1940s, when Claudio Santoro came into the Brazilian scene. A biography, focusing mostly in a personal account by the composer, serves to illustrate Santoro's family background, environment, education, and struggles to develop into a first-class musician.

The Fourth Sonata represents one of Santoro's most popular piano works. The analysis of this work focuses on clarifying how the structure may be organized and how the chromatic idiom supports Santoro's deceptive tonal goals.

Goertzen, Valerie Woodring. *The Piano Transcriptions of Johannes Brahms.* Ph.D. dissertation, Urbana-Champaign: University of Illinois, 1987. 407 p. UM 8803048. With the present-day emphasis on authenticity in music, there is a tendency to view nineteenth-century piano transcriptions as a necessary evil, a body of music not worthy of serious study from the era before recordings. Yet some of these pieces hold up to scrutiny even without reference to a model. The transcriptions of great composers may be of particular interest as demonstrations of their handling of the piano in isolation from the creation of musical material, as evidence of compositional process, or for the light they shed on matters having to do with biography. This dissertation examines Johannes Brahms's transcriptions of his own works and those of other composers—a total of forty items—as they relate to his biography and working methods and as illustrations of his transcribing techniques.

The discussion of Brahms's transcriptions of works of other composers focuses on arrangements of two chamber works of Schumann and three overtures of Joseph Joachim, which were completed early in his career, mainly for private use. Brahms began transcribing his own music to enhance offers of new works to publishers and to increase his income. But he was also concerned with the forms in which his music reached the public, and wished to contribute to the repertory of good four-hand pieces. He enjoyed playing his transcriptions with friends and used them to introduce new works to colleagues. The two-piano version of the B-flat Piano Concerto played a role in his refining of the work before publication. Brahms's concern that the transcription of his own music might injure his reputation as a serious artist led him to publish most of the arrangements anonymously.

Revisions in the manuscript sources show the care Brahms took in making his transcriptions faithful to their models and also pianistic. The examination of his techniques of transcribing is organized around four interrelated concerns: accommodation of voices of the texture, adaptation of melodic and rhythmic figuration, reinforcement of dynamics and of structural dramatic outlines, and adaptation of instrumental techniques and atmospheric effects.

Goldberg, Laurette. *The Well-Tempered Clavier of J. S. Bach: A Handbook for Keyboard Teachers and Performers*. Berkeley: Music Sources, 1996, 2 vols. Full of insightful information and written exclusively for piano and harpsichord teachers. Appropriate for the mature artist as well as teachers and students at every level.

Goldenzweig, Hugo. *Selected Piano Etudes of Frédéric Chopin: A Performance Guide*. Ph.D. dissertation, New York University, 1987, 290 p. UM 8803584. Schenker and phenomenological analysis of selected Piano Etudes of Frédéric Chopin uncovered a rich data base of information, including Schenker graphs and a descriptive phenomenological analysis in narrative form (with musical examples) for each work. It encompassed an analysis of musical form, texture, dynamics, and style. The methodological sources for the phenomenological analyses were based on the work of Thomas Clifton and Lawrence Ferrara. A performance guide follows, consisting of musical and interpretive "tips" based on the analyses. This in turn is followed by a technical explanation section that identifies the specific technical problems and offers solutions for them as well as guidance for study and practice. A videotape of the author's performance of the *27 Etudes* is included (Appendix B).

Goldstein, Johanna. *A Beethoven Enigma: Performance Practice and the Piano Sonata, Opus 111.* New York: Peter Lang, 1988. Based on the author's doctoral dissertation.

Göllerich, August. *The Piano Master Classes of Franz Liszt 1884–1886.* Ed. Wilhelm Jerger; trans., ed., enlarged by Richard Louis Zimdars. Bloomington: Indiana University Press, 1996, 209 p. These important diary notes of Göllerich provide a fascinating picture of the Liszt tradition. They show Liszt's approach to piano teaching by detailing the manner he taught the pieces played in the classes by various (now famous) pianists. Liszt's comments about his own works are highly interesting, especially when they differed from the printed score. One hundred fifty musical examples are included to clarify Liszt's remarks. Provides extraordinary insight into the little-known area of nineteenth-century performance practice.

Gonzalez, Ruben O. *Carlos Chavez's Concerto for Piano with Orchestra: A Spiritual Fusion of the Ancient and the Modern.* D.M.A. paper, University of Cincinnati, 1993, 61 p. UM 9329968. In this work two cultures are presented, the Aztec (Chapter One), and the Western (Mexico after the conquest, Chapter Two), to provide historical background to the diverse elements in Chavez's musical style. Chapter Three is an analysis of the concerto with conclusions drawn to show the influences of the two cultures.

Gordon, Stewart. *Etudes for Piano Teachers: Reflections on the Teacher's Art.* New York: Oxford University Press, 1995, 208 p. This collection of essays, many of which first appeared in the "New Davidites" series in *American Music Teacher,* examines the many challenges involved in piano teaching—not only the technical tasks of teaching students how to play the instrument, but also the more general challenges of how to inspire and shape students' learning and growth, personal identity, and how to offer career guidance. Divided into three parts— Fundamental Studies, Virtuoso Studies, and Transcendental Studies— the volume begins with the premise that teaching and performing should be given equal status. From there, the author addresses specific pedagogical considerations regarding pedaling, sight-reading, inner-hearing and counting techniques, practice procedures, memorizing, and improvising, as well as more philosophical questions such as how to adapt to the advent of technology and new music, and what to do about the diminishing market for Eurocentric classical music. Includes index.

————. *A History of Keyboard Literature*. New York: Schirmer Books, 1996, 528 p. Subtitled "Music for the Piano and Its Forerunners," this book is designed mainly as a text for piano literature courses. Beginning with literature for the clavichord, Gordon continues the discussion through the latter part of the twentieth century. Approached from a pianist's point of view, the author offers insights into structure, technical features, and frequently comments on how pianists regard the music in terms of frequency of performance and reputation. Also contains an extensive bibliography.

————. *Memorizing in Piano Performance*. Video cassette. Van Nuys, Calif.: Alfred Publishing Co., approximately 60 minutes. Very helpful for pianists who have trouble memorizing music or fear a memory loss in performance. Five memorization processes are outlined, followed by techniques that will aid in the correction of typical memorization problems. Suggestions for incorporating these ideas into the teaching process are also provided.

————. *Performance Practices in Late 20th Century Piano Music*. Video cassette. Van Nuys, Calif.: Alfred Publishing Co., 1995, 55 minutes. Gordon breaks through misconceptions about the musicality and performance appeal of contemporary music. He offers insights into how to interpret, teach, and perform the music—and enjoy the process. In three parts: I. Analysis and Performance, using pieces by Richard Faith and Halsey Stevens; II. Jazz Influence, featuring pieces by Leo Kraft and Sol Berkowitz; and III. Non-Tonal Music, exploring works by Bruce Wise and George Crumb.

Gorton, Judy Blanche Woods. *The Doctoral Programs in Piano at the University of Oklahoma as Viewed by the Graduates*. D.M.A. paper, Norman: University of Oklahoma, 1996. The purpose of this study is to evaluate the doctoral programs in piano at the University of Oklahoma based on the opinions and attitudes of the graduates between 1980 and 1995. Information for the study was gathered through a questionnaire sent to the forty-seven graduates of the programs. The results of the study were based on the response rate of 80.85 percent.

General information was obtained regarding age (age at graduation and current age), gender, race, degree, and date of completion. Participants were asked to provide information about their master's and bachelor's degrees, choice of doctoral degree programs, prestige and marketability of degree programs, sources of financial support, first position after doctorate, present employment, other employment, postdoctoral study, publishing and performance activity, professional affiliations, and duration of doctoral program.

The evaluation of course work and instruction was directed toward six different areas: music theory, music history, music education, applied piano study, research, and piano pedagogy. Questions regarding availability, appropriateness of courses, and usefulness in present employment were included. Also solicited was a description of the participants' morale and the factors affecting morale as they progressed through the doctoral course work, during preparation for general examinations, and during preparation of the dissertation or document. In-depth questions explored the general examinations experience and the dissertation or document process. Also addressed were the overall quality of the participant's doctoral degree program and the graduate music faculty.

Information was gathered from open-ended questions asking for strengths, weaknesses, and recommendations for improvement in seven areas regarding the doctoral programs in piano: advising; course requirements and course offerings; preliminary examinations; evaluation of instructors; physical facilities and equipment; general examinations; and the dissertation or document process. The following areas for further investigation were recommended: a comparative study of other doctoral programs in piano; an assessment of a five-to-ten-year span of all doctoral programs in music at the University of Oklahoma; a follow-up study of students who started doctorates in piano but did not finish; a comparative study with other universities; a study evaluating job performance of doctoral graduates in piano; and an evaluation of the programs by current doctoral students in piano.

Gould, Glenn. *Selected Letters.* Ed. and comp. John P. L. Roberts and Ghyslaine Guertin. New York: Oxford University Press, 1992, 260 p.

Over 200 letters covering a wide range of Gould's artistic activities. His detailed thoughts about piano repertoire are of special interest. Includes index.

Gracia, Ana Lucia Altino. *Brahms's Opus 34 and the 19th-Century Piano Quintet.* D.M.A. paper, Boston University, 1992, 223 p. UM 9225136. This study aims to present a comparative historical account of the nineteenth-century piano quintet. The centerpiece is an analysis of Brahms's F minor Piano Quintet Op. 34, together with a comparative account of the two versions of this work and a hypothetical reconstruction of the no longer extant string quintet which proceeded them. The reconstruction of the quintet was necessary for the sake of comparison with Schubert's C major String Quintet, which the author believes to have been the major influence on Brahms's Op. 34.

The development of the piano quintet throughout the nineteenth century, as shown through a discussion of the most representative works and the various influences that relate them, serves as one of the main goals of this study. Although Brahms's Op. 34 is the main focus of this work, the piano quintets of his predecessors, Prince Louis Ferdinand of Prussia and Schumann, as well as works of his followers, Antonín Dvořák, César Franck, and Max Reger, are extensively discussed.

Graff, Steven Lewis. *Chopin Performance Tradition and Its Relationship to Analysis.* D.M.A. paper, City University of New York, 1995, 123 p. UM 9431360. Have great Chopin interpreters of the past and present demonstrated in their performances an awareness of the same issues that analysts have written so much about? What types of analytical ideas seem directly related to performance, and what seem purely theoretical? In this study the author has taken his own analytical ideas and those of several analysts, determined what they suggest to pianism, compared them to various recordings, and arrived at conclusions regarding the relationship between the analysis and performance of a sampling of Chopin's music. Analyses are compared of the A Minor mazurka, Op. 59, No. 1, the A Major prelude, and the G Major prelude with recordings by Alfred Cortot, Moriz Rosenthal, Arthur Rubinstein, William Kapell, Jorge Bolet, and Emanuel Ax. As this study is designed primarily as a performance practice guide for the piano student, some of the pianistic devices are exposed that these Chopin interpreters have used to convey analytical concepts in their performances.

Graning, Gary Alan. *An Analysis for the Performance of the Piano Variations of Karol Szymanowski.* Ed.D. dissertation, New York: Columbia University Teachers College, 1989, 236 p. UM 8913113. The 1980s have shown an awakening of interest in the music of Karol Szymanowski. Scholars such as Jim Samson, Alistair Wightman, and Teresa Chylinaka, and also the publication in 1982 of the *Complete Works of Szymanowski,* have focused attention on the composer who was perhaps the most important Polish composer of the first half of the twentieth century. The music of Szymanowski's "early period," including the Variations for Piano, Op. 3 and Op. 10, have received less attention than the later periods. The Variations provide a unique outlook from which to view Szymanowski: the music typifies the early works, presages the later works, and reveals the composer's creativity at its most basic level—how he achieves unity amid diversity.

This study is intended to acquaint performers and teachers with Szymanowski's treatment of the theme and its subsequent variations in his piano Variations, Op. 3 and Op. 10. An analysis of the harmonic and melodic patterns, phrase structure, texture, tempo, key and dynamic plans of each variation, and how each variation relates to the surrounding variations has been followed by an analysis of performance and interpretative problems. In addition, consideration of Szymanowski's position in the musical history of Europe and Poland, pertinent biographical details, and an analysis of three piano works from the "early, middle, and late periods" place the composer and his music in perspective.

The examination of the Variations shows not only the development of pianistic and compositional techniques from the works which preceded them, but also shows a greater musical maturity in the later set of Variations, the *Variations on a Polish Folksong,* Op. 10, which are generally considered outstanding examples of the late romantic character variation. While not well known in this country, the Variations are frequently performed in Europe and are as characteristic of Szymanowski as his later music, and as worthy to be heard.

Granville-Price, Paulina Delp. *An Approach for a Keyboard History/Literature Minicourse for Performing Adolescent Students in Summer Keyboard Music Programs.* Ph.D. dissertation, Tallahassee: Florida State University, 1987, 365 p. UM 8802827. The purpose of this study is to develop a comprehensive musicianship approach for a keyboard history and literature minicourse for performing adolescent students in summer keyboard music programs.

Reasons justifying the study were found in reported literature which noted an imbalance between the teaching of performance skills and comprehensive musicianship; summer camp literature, which illustrated this imbalance; and a lack of sufficient research into the above concerns directed specifically to the summer music program.

Since there did not appear to be a minicourse that specifically addressed the aforementioned needs in summer music programs, this study sought to develop an approach for such a course. A five-step procedure was used. Step one was the identification of the problem, based on the purpose and need for the study. Step two was the critical review of related literature for collection of data in light of the above-identified problem. Step three was the presentation of a rationale stated as twelve principles of comprehensive musicianship developed from the review of related literature, and the application of this rationale to development of an instructional goal, course objectives, content components, instructional objectives, overall instructional strategy, and lesson strategies for a minicourse approach. Step four was an examination by a panel of five outstanding music educators and performers of the minicourse's consistency with comprehensive musicianship rationale, and an analysis of the panelists' responses. Step five was a statement of conclusions and recommendations for further study.

According to the panelists' responses, the researcher's approach for a minicourse was effective in addressing a persisting need to find additional ways to instruct adolescent keyboardists in comprehensive musicianship. Recommendations for further study include continuing revisions and testing of the course in an appropriate setting, and constructing similar courses for other musical groups.

Gray, Steven Earl. *Tempo Indication in the Piano Music of Béla Bartók: Notation and Performance.* D.M.A. paper, Stanford, Calif.: Stanford University, 1990, 67 p. UM 9024307. Bartók recorded his own works for piano beginning in 1912 and continuing through January 1945. The Bartók Record Archive collection of those recorded performances provides a valuable resource for the modern performer in the interpretation of Bartók's tempo indications. His performances indicates that tempi were significant to Bartók's musical expression and that the relative change from one tempo to the next was an important part of the compositional concept. While many studies investigate Bartók's use of pitch and the connection to folk melodies, there is little or no mention of tempo. This study investigates Bartók's notation and his performance of those works within which a tempo change is notated above the staff. The pieces included are as follows: *Ten Easy Pieces, Two Rumanian Dances, Sonatina, Rumanian Folk Dances, Suite, Improvisations, Nine Little Piano Pieces,* and *Mikrokosmos.*

The study examines the recording media used to record Bartók's performances, as well as his writings on the subject of musical style and on the use of tempo words. Bartók's notation is analyzed according to his use of tempo words, metronome markings, total time indications, recurrence of tempo words, modification of a primary tempo, and types of tempo changes (e.g., slow-fast, fast-slow-fast, fast-faster). The recorded performances are analyzed according to the percentage of variation from the notation, the nature of that deviation, and its context within the form. Appendixes list the notated and recorded tempi, the percentage change from notation to performance, the chronology of recording, the original recording information, and the metronome numbers associated with tempo words.

Conclusions drawn from this study indicate that in Bartók's general performance style, music that is directly related to a folk tradition is most likely to vary from the notated tempo, while the movements that show the least deviation are those which are shorter and simpler in tempo design. Also, music of a narrative character, which Bartók termed "parlando-rubato," requires the notation to be interpreted through the rhythmic inflections of speech, whereas music related to bodily motion (dancing or marching) requires a stricter regulation of the pulse, which Bartók termed "tempo giusto."

Graziano, Vivian. *A Descriptive Analysis of Various Relationships Between Home Environment and Success in Piano Study.* Ed.D. dissertation, New York: Columbia University Teachers College, 1991, 237 p. UM 9210534. A serious concern music educators have is keeping students participating and succeeding in music programs. Since piano is chosen by many students and involves family settings, it is valuable for music educators to understand relationships between home environment and musical participation and success of piano students. The purpose is to explore these relationships and determine what home environmental factors influence those variables.

Research methodology was theoretically based on exploration and discovery, and includes qualitative analyses of twelve in-depth interviews with parents of children who were succeeding at piano lessons. The primary data were obtained by recommendation from twenty piano teachers from Dutchess, Orange, Ulster, and Sullivan counties of New York State. The parents interviewed include a wide range of occupations and backgrounds and have children of varied ages and time spent on studying piano.

The interviews revealed that parental values, such as concern for education, having goals and expectations, gaining basic musical skills, maintaining regular practice, developing discipline, commitment, responsibility, and perseverance have positive influences on children's participation and success. These values were manifested in parents' desires to expose children to activities fostering personal growth; choose piano teachers based on certain criteria; develop responsibility through scheduling and supervision of practice; foster commitment to an activity once started; and encourage perseverance through flexibility and adapting to children's changing needs.

Green, Barry. *The Inner Game of Music.* New York: Doubleday, 1986. Barry Green, a professional cellist, has written this book with Tim Galwey, author of *The Inner Game of Tennis,* which popularized the concept of two "selves" (Self #1 and Self #2) that interact in ways that may either enhance or diminish skilled performance. The book is organized into a series of chapters that deal with various facets of preparation and performance, and benefits from Green's background as a musician.

————, and Phyllis Lehrer. *The Inner Game of Music, Solo Workbook and Cassette: Piano.* Chicago: G.I.A. Publications, 1995, 172 p. Thirty-seven clear exercises help the pianist develop the main ideas of the 1986 book: awareness, will, and trust. Questions follow activity sections. The cassette contains Lehrer's beautiful playing.

Grindea, Carola. *Piano Technique.* Video cassette available from the author at 28 Emperor's Gate, London SW7 4HS, England, 56 minutes. This video focuses on the kind of piano technique that will help prevent and cure physical problems and injuries and help reduce anxiety and stress. A booklet comes with it discussing in more detail the areas described in the video. The "Grindea Technique" is based on natural movements of the body. Also available from the same address is a 34-minute video on *Focal Dystonia,* which is basically incoordination and loss of control of certain movements.

Groves, Susan Elizabeth. *Bach Pianists: A Performance History.* D.M.A.

paper, Austin: University of Texas, DMA paper, 1992, 116 p. UM 9239199. The history of pianists who play Bach begins primarily in the nineteenth century, particularly in the realm of virtuoso piano transcriptions. It was not, however, until well into the current century that both pianists and their public developed any real knowledge about the full range of Bach's keyboard literature in its original form. This study reviews a cross-section of the currently available Bach piano recordings from the 1930s to the present, with an emphasis on those pianists who have recorded large segments of the literature, such as the *Well-Tempered Clavier,* the *Goldberg Variations,* and the various suites.

Spanning approximately the last forty years, three pianists have stood out as representatives of their respective generations. While they all share a technical mastery of Bach's rigorous demands, they also display radically different but equally valid approaches toward bringing this music to life, ranging from the scholarly but lively style of the American pianist, Rosalyn Tureck, to the brilliantly eccentric Canadian Glenn Gould, and finally to the polished eclectic approach of the most recent Bach specialist, the young Hungarian Andras Schiff.

Grueninger, Diana Page. *An Analysis of the Nine Preludes for Piano by Ruth Crawford Seeger.* D.A. paper, Greeley: University of Northern Colorado, 1990, 244 p. UM 9107355. The purpose of the study is to analyze in detail and according to the basic parameters of music the *Nine Preludes for Piano* by Ruth Crawford Seeger. The parameters examined are melody, rhythm, meter, texture, range, harmony, dynamics, and developmental techniques. The analysis identifies specific compositional techniques and traits of Crawford's style as evidenced in these works.

In Crawford's piano preludes, melodic material is frequently based on motivic cells of two or three notes which are repeated in sequence or in slightly modified versions. The forms are ternary (ABA) in half the preludes, and through-composed in the remaining half of the preludes. Dynamics and range are used to enhance the building of form. In earlier preludes, harmonic structures are mostly tertian, though very dissonant; in the later preludes, more sevenths, seconds and tritones are found. Rhythm and meter are straightforward in some preludes and more ambiguous and fluid in other preludes, though more instances of complexity and ambiguity are to be found than are straightforward meters and prominent rhythms. In addition to the detailed analysis, considerable weight has been given to biographical data and to the influence of events and people on the development of Crawford's style. Suggestions for the performance of the preludes have also been included in the study.

By means of a computer program, set-theory analysis has been applied to the vertical structures in the preludes in order to identify their harmonic organization. The charts generated by the computer program reveal, in the vocabulary of set-theory, a high degree of relationships of various kinds between the vertical structures, both within a single prelude and among all the preludes. These set-theory charts, along with the musical scores, are included in the appendix. A list of sets used in the preludes is also included in the appendix.

Guerry, Jack. *Silvio Scionti: Remembering a Master Pianist and Teacher.* Denton: University of North Texas Press, 1991, 220 p. Guerry, a former Scionti student, has collected many stories about this colorful and zestful master teacher-pianist. Organized in three parts: The Early Years, The Years in Texas, and The Years of "Retirement." Contains information about how Scionti taught and his wonderful way of working with students. Scionti is a name to remember in the history of teaching piano in twentieth-century America, and we are grateful for Guerry's documentation.

Guhl, Louise. *Odyssey of a Small Town Piano Teacher.* San Diego: Kjos Music Co., 1994, 40 p. The author offers helpful advice on practicing, psychology, and sight-reading. Also contains a valuable appendix on supplementary reading list for first-year students, an unusual catalog of emotions, plus a list of seventy pieces that Guhl kept in performance shape until she was eighty. Comments about two of her former teachers, Guy Maier and Bernhard Weiser, are most interesting.

Guy, Suzanne W. *If . . . You Would Add to the Beauty in the World.* Published by the author, 718 Botetourt Gardens, Norfolk, VA 23507, 44 p. Some thoughts on practicing and performing. Arranged by thought bytes, one per page; it is full of wisdom and tradition.

Haimberger, Nora Elizabeth. *The Piano Sonatas of Carl Maria von Weber.* Thesis, Seattle: University of Washington, 1964.

Halbeck, Patricia Gisela. *The Development of a Computer Database to Select Piano Repertoire from the Romantic Era for Intermediate Students.* D.M.A. paper, Norman: University of Oklahoma, 1992, 189

p. UM 9311009. This document develops a computer data base that aids teachers in the selection of piano repertoire from the Romantic era for intermediate level students. Repertoire by Burgmüller, Grieg, Gurlitt, Heller, Karganov, Kirchner, Mendelssohn, Schumann, and Tchaikovsky are included in the data base. Repertoire entries created for 100 pieces include the following information: title, composer, key, time signature, level of difficulty, mood, prominent rhythm pattern or note value, length, tempo, selected editions, and performance skills. Performance skills focus on technical and musical patterns such as scales, chords, double notes, articulation, textures, pedalling, ornaments, and dynamics. The user can access pieces by a single element of information such as key, tempo, or by combinations of elements such as mood, tempo, and specific performance skills.

Hammill, Jennifer Lee. *The Development of Compositional Style in the Piano Music of Federico Mompou.* Thesis, Seattle: University of Washington, 1991.

Hancock, Robin James. *Rachmaninoff's "Six Moments Musicaux," Op. 16, and the Tradition of the Nineteenth-Century Miniature.* D.M.A. thesis, Boston University, 1992, 128 p. Sergey Rachmaninoff's piano cycle *Six Moments Musicaux* (Op. 16, published in 1896) is an enigma among his works for piano solo. The six pieces of Op. 16 have traditionally been seen as a step to his compositional maturity. Completely overlooked, however, is the retrospective nature of this cycle. With these pieces Rachmaninoff effectively reinterpreted models of specific works by Schubert, Chopin, and Wagner. Indeed, the title pays homage to the only other set of six piano pieces to carry the same designation, Schubert's *Moments musicals* (Op. 94, 1828). Structural, harmonic, and strategic references in Rachmaninoff's pieces suggest a link to two pieces in the Schubert set: Rachmaninoff's Op. 16, No. 1, corresponds to Schubert's Op. 94, No. 1, while Rachmaninoff's Op. 16, No. 2, corresponds to Schubert's Op. 94, No. 4. The virtuoso writing and etude texture of the fourth and sixth pieces in the Rachmaninoff set, and especially the focus on the left hand in the fourth piece, are reminiscent of two of Chopin's etudes, the Revolutionary etude (Op. 10, No. 12) with its predominant left-hand part, and the Ocean etude (Op. 25, No. 12). An interesting tie to Wagner is found in Rachmaninoff's third piece, a song without words which corresponds in many particulars to "Im Treibhaus" from the Wesendonck Lieder.
Comparing the pieces in Rachmaninoff's cycle to specific models from

Schubert, Chopin, and Wagner reveals both similarities and differences. More important, this examination suggests that Rachmaninoff's highly individual style emerged, in part, out of his confrontation with works of the past, a confrontation that allowed him to clear mental working space for the masterpiece to come.

Hankla, Jesse R. *Mozart's Four-Hand Piano Sonatas with a Theoretical and Performance Analysis of K. 358 in B Flat Major and K. 497 in F Major.* D.M.A. paper, Norman: University of Oklahoma, 1986, 156 p. UM 8629028. The purpose of the study is twofold. First, a brief overview of each of the one-piano, four-hand sonatas by Mozart is presented through a series of formal-structural abstracts. The written literature addressing the subject of Mozart's life and works, with emphasis upon the literature discussing the four-hand sonatas, is reviewed. A number of recordings of the sonatas are surveyed. Additionally, several editions of these works are examined. (For the purposes of the present study, the childhood Sonata in C Major, K. 19d, was not considered.)

In the second phase of the study, a theoretical and performance analysis of the Sonata in B Flat Major, K. 358 (186c) and the Sonata in F Major, K. 497 is presented. The thrust of the analysis of these two sonatas is to present a number of musical examples in which analytical considerations assist in making performance decisions.

Among the findings gleaned from the study is that each of the sonatas exhibited expected high-level formal-tonal schemes. Also, each of the four middle movements was cast in the key of the subdominant, an expected compositional procedure in the works of Mozart. The most interesting findings were observed in the F Major Sonata. This is likely a result of the fact that the F Major Sonata is a later and much more mature work than the B Flat Major Sonata. One of the most fascinating findings of this study was the observation of the role of phrase rhythm. While phrase rhythm was found to be significant in both sonatas, its greatest impact was noted in the F Major Sonata.

With regard to recommendations for further study, there is a need for an intensive study of the two sonatas that were not considered in detail in this study, the D Major Sonata, K. 381 (123a) and the C Major sonata, K. 521.

Hansen, Mark R. *The Pedagogical Methods of Enrique Granados and Frank Marshall: An Illumination of Relevance to Performance Prac-*

tice and Interpretation in Granados' "Escenas Romanticas." D.M.A.
paper, Denton: University of North Texas, 1988, 70 p. UM 8908915.
Enrique Granados, Frank Marshall, and Alicia de Larrocha are the
chief exponents of a school of piano playing characterized by special
attention to details of pedaling, voicing, and refined piano sonority.
Granados and Marshall dedicated the major part of their efforts in
the field to the pedagogy of these principles. Their work led to the
establishment of the Granados Academy in Barcelona, a keyboard
conservatory which operates today under the name of the Frank Marshall Academy. Both Granados and Marshall have left published method books detailing their pedagogy of pedaling and tone production.
Granados's book, *Método Teórico Práctico para el Uso de los Pedales
del Piano* (Theoretical and Practical Method for the Use of the Piano
Pedals) is presently out of print but is available in a photostatic version from the publisher. Marshall's works, *Estudio Práctico sobre los
Pedales del Piano* (Practical Study of the Piano Pedals) and *La Sono-
ridad del Piano* (Piano Sonority) continue to be used at the Marshall
Academy and are available from Spanish publishing houses. This study
brings information contained in these three method books to the fore-
front and demonstrates its relevance to the performance of the music
of Granados, specifically the *Escenas Románticas*. Alicia de Larrocha,
Marshall's best-known pupil, currently holds the directorship of the
Marshall Academy and, as such, is perhaps the best living authority
on this entire line of pianistic and pedagogical thought. An interview
conducted with Madame de Larrocha in April 1983 adds detail and
provides valuable perspective about the present use and relevance of
these materials and concepts.

Harris, Conwell Ray, Jr. *Unifying Techniques in the Anniversaries of
Leonard Bernstein.* D.M.A. paper, Baton Rouge: Louisiana State University, 1993, 101 p. UM 9419892. Although most of Bernstein's compositions are large-scale works, he also composed a number of miniatures for solo piano entitled "Anniversaries." There are four sets: *Seven
Anniversaries* (1944), *Four Anniversaries* (1945), *Five Anniversaries*
(1964), and *Thirteen Anniversaries* (1989). This monograph illustrates
that within the highly compact structure of these brief pieces, a variety of unifying techniques has been used. The analysis of all the anniversaries shows how Bernstein unified the pieces by manipulation of
motives and themes through inversion, augmentation, and transposition, in addition to ostinati and phrase repetition and extension.

Harris, John M. *A History of Music for Harpsichord or Piano and Orchestra.* Lanham, Md.: Scarecrow Press, 1997, 473 p. This reference work has much to recommend it: 1. basic information on an enormous number of concertos; 2. biographic information related to many of the composers; 3. unique organization by period and country. It pulls together much information about this genre; thus it is a timesaver for the reader. For instance, in Part IV, After Brahms to the Present (ca. 1897–1992), the United States section, there are approximately 1,110 composers of concertos discussed and/or listed. There are hundreds of such entries in the rest of the book.

Hatch, David Glen. *An Examination of the Piano Teachings Skills of Master Teacher, Joanne Baker.* D.M.A. paper, Kansas City, Mo.: University of Missouri, 1987, 151 p. UM 8725694. The purpose of this dissertation is to study the various teaching skills of Joanne Baker in an effort to better define qualities of master teaching. This study describes her early life prior to her appointment as professor of music in Missouri, her life following her appointment to the present day, her philosophy and thoughts on piano performance and pedagogy, the reflections and evaluations of her influence as a pedagogue by present and former students, and her influence and reputation as described by professional colleagues.

In order to facilitate the preparation of this study, research and acquisition of material was completed through forty hours of personal interviews with Joanne Baker; investigation of various primary documents including sample reviews, articles, and programs; questionnaires requesting information about pedagogical and personal influences of Baker on present and former students including results of their professional endeavors; personal interviews with eight former students; and questionnaires requesting commentary and reflective impressions of colleagues drawn from a local, regional, national, and international representation. Findings from this research indicate that Baker, who has devoted a lifetime of service to the progression of the pianistic art, is indeed a Master Teacher.

Hatch, Sarah J. *The Governance Style of Il Allison, Sr., As Evidenced in Documentation of the Development of the National Guild of Piano Teachers, 1929–1963.* Ph.D. dissertation, Denton: University of North Texas, 1991, 147 p. UM 9201523. The purpose of this study is to examine the governance style of Il Allison, Sr., as evidenced in documentation of the development of the National Guild of Piano Teachers (NGPT). Chapter One includes a discussion of literature on leaders and leadership style. Chapter Two contains a historical background of Allison, focusing on his role in the development of the NGPT, 1896 to 1979. Chapters Two, Four, and Five provide in-depth studies of Allison's governance style, including recruitment of new members; the NGPT Yearbook; the selection of judges; the addition of new projects; issues involving Guild standards and certification; and the need for a Guild forum. Chapter Six is a summary with conclusions, discussion, and recommendations for further study.

Haupt, Helen Doria. *Form in the Pianoforte Sonatas of Franz Schubert.* M.M. thesis, Urbana-Champaign: University of Illinois, 1941, 47 p. Chapters: Introduction, Expositions, Development, Recapitulation, Conclusion, Tables, Examples, and Bibliography.

Haydon, Geoffrey Jennings. *A Study of the Exchange of Influences Between the Music of Early Twentieth-Century Parisian Composers and Ragtime, Blues, and Early Jazz.* D.M.A. paper, Austin: University of Texas, 1992, 181 p. UM 9239200. In studying the music of early-twentieth-century Parisian composers and certain early American jazz musicians, a relationship emerges revealing a mutual exchange of ideas. Composers such as Claude Debussy, Maurice Ravel, Erik Satie, Darius Milhaud and Igor Stravinsky were compelled to incorporate elements derived from American popular music into some of their compositions. In similar fashion, American jazz musicians such as Bix Beiderbecke and George Gershwin were intrigued by the impressionistic compositions of these French composers. Gershwin and Beiderbecke were among the first jazz musicians to successfully utilize many impressionistic devices in their improvisations and compositions.

Ragtime, American minstrelsy, and the cakewalk are considered to be strong influences in Debussy's *Minstrels, "General Lavine"—eccentric, Golliwog's Cakewalk,* and *Le petit Nègre.* Milhaud visited Harlem in the early 1920s, where he heard authentic versions of American jazz and blues. His *La Création du monde* reveals these American influences in his choice of instruments, use of blues material, and in sections reminiscent of the early New Orleans style of jazz. Ravel took an active interest in jazz in the 1920s. The "Blues" movement from the Sonata for Violin and Piano and the two piano concerti of Ravel effectively incorporate blues components, and on occasion are reminiscent of certain compositions of George Gershwin.

Haydon, Sona. *Piano Technique: Is There One Way?* Video cassette. Van Nuys, Calif.: Alfred Publishing Co., 1995, 40 minutes. After a serious injury to her right hand, Haydon conducted detailed research in therapeutic techniques to help her regain strength and mobility. In this video Haydon combines ideas from her own recovery treatment with technique by master teachers. She discusses and demonstrates posture, hand position, drills, isometrics, stretching, scales, arpeggios, and much more.

Hayner, Phillip Avery, II. *The Role of the Piano Etude in the Compositions of Karol Szymanowski.* D.M.A. paper, University of Cincinnati, 1982. Karol Szymanowski's four Etudes for Piano, Op. 4, represent a synthesis of the style of Frédéric Chopin and Alexander Scriabin and are excellent examples of the late Romantic character piece. His twelve Etudes, Op. 33, represent a synthesis of Claude Debussy, Scriabin, and Max Reger. Each set of etudes served as a proving ground for exploring new devices and sonorities, which were then incorporated into a larger, more complex genre—the sonata.

Heartling-Lint, Ann Elisa. *A Graded Annotated Bibliography of Selected Solo Piano Works of Alexandre Gretchaninoff.* Ph.D. dissertation, Columbus: Ohio State University, 1988, 516 p. UM 8812257. The purpose of this study is to survey systematically and classify Gretchaninoff's published piano works; provide a rationale for the use of his piano works as an educational tool; discuss problems and concerns related to teaching and performing Gretchaninoff's music; present a historical background on Gretchaninoff as educator, performer, and composer; examine the form and compositional devices used in Gretchaninoff's solo piano works; and recommend republication of commendable piano works that are currently out of print.

The study includes information related to Gretchaninoff's life and music compositions. Also discussed are the compositional devices, forms, and characteristics appearing in the piano solo works listed in the study, including recommendations for application of the selected repertoire as ideal teaching pieces. The appendixes contain lists of research tools, music examples cited in the study, and a catalog of the composer's solo piano works.

Hendricks, Renee Christine. *An Examination of the Teaching Methods of Seven Nineteenth-Century Piano Pedagogues.* M.A. thesis, Washington, D.C.: American University, 1988, 67 p. UM 1334061. This thesis examines the teaching methods of seven nineteenth-century piano pedagogues, Johann Nepomuk Hummel, Carl Czerny, Frédéric Chopin, Franz Liszt, Theodor Kullak, Ludwig Deppe, and Theodor Leschetizky, in an effort to trace the development of piano instruction in the nineteenth century from its beginning as a secondary job or hobby of performer-composers to a full-time and sophisticated occupation. It is an observation of the growth in each musician's role as teacher as well as the approach to teaching piano as it developed in the nineteenth century. A single chapter is devoted to the teaching methods of each instructor and includes the major ideas, philosophies and techniques employed and imparted by that teacher. An appendix is included containing a list of pedagogical compositions and writing by each instructor.

Henning, Dennis John. *Charles-Valentin Alkan: An Introduction with Special Reference to the Etudes Op. 35 and Op. 39.* M.Phil. thesis, Oxford, U.K.: University of Oxford, 1975, 117 p. UM 1332854. The author attempts to identify the position of Charles-Valentin Alkan within the nineteenth-century virtuoso piano repertoire as both a performer and composer through a detailed analysis of his studies in the twenty-four major and minor keys and by a survey of contemporary accounts of his performances and criticisms of his compositions. The analysis is prefaced by a chapter that examines musical life in Paris during the first half of the nineteenth century and then traces Alkan's activities as recorded in contemporary French music journals. From the two collections, Op. 35 and Op. 39, a comprehensive survey of Alkan's conception of piano playing is drawn—from purely didactic studies to grand virtuoso epics. The analyses are followed by a final chapter that deals with the chief characteristics of Alkan's style, and in which these studies are then cross-referenced with Alkan's other published works.

Hensel, Fanny Mendelssohn. *Letters of Fanny Hensel to Felix Mendels-*

sohn. New York: Pendragon Press, 1987, 687 p. The collected letters of Fanny, Felix's sister, edited and translated with introductory essays and notes by Marcia J. Citron.

Hepp, Christopher Marshall. *Piano Performance as a Heuristic Process with Appendix: Implications of the Heuristic Process for Piano Instruction.* D.M.A. paper, Boulder: University of Colorado, 1986, 159 p. UM 8618952. This dissertation addresses the relationship between two distinct topics: piano performance and heuristic. By piano performance, the author means public concert performance and the preparatory stages leading to it. The stages include the learning, memorization, and interpretation of the repertoire to be performed. The concert artist is that individual whose livelihood is accomplished through piano performance. The heuristic process denotes a method of solving problems that utilizes heuristic. Heuristic is used to solve complex problems; the author shows piano performance to be a complex problem and, thus, an appropriate area for the use of heuristic. By examining the heuristic process inherent in piano performance, the author is describing the heuristic used by concert pianists.

In order to define and identify heuristic, the author investigates the field of computer science where the use of heuristic is more common and systematic. The heuristic computer program designed by Allen Newell and Herbert Simon and called the General Problem Solver, or GPS, is of particular interest because of its resemblance to human problem-solving in mathematics. The GPS program together with the contributions of George Polya constitute a model that the author uses to identify and describe the general and specific heuristics used by concert pianists at the artistic level of performance.

The occurrence of a heuristic process of problem-solving provides a new understanding of the development of piano technique. The field of Constructivist psychology, specifically the work of Jean Piaget, supports the relationship between problem-solving and the development of motor skill. This relationship is applied to the heuristic process of problem-solving exhibited by concert pianists; the author asserts that the superior technical achievements of concert pianists are a result of their use of heuristic.

The author contends that the heuristic process exhibited by pianists at the artistic level of performance imparts a clearer understanding of music-making at the piano. This understanding has implications for piano instruction. Piano teachers can improve the level of piano performance in students by improving their problem-solving abilities. Improvement in problem-solving abilities takes place through the use of heuristic.

Herbert, Constance Giesey. *Lynn Freeman Olson: Technical and Pedagogical Elements of His Music for Piano.* D.M.A. paper, Kansas City, Mo.: University of Missouri, 1992, 397 p. UM 9239638. Lynn Freeman Olson (1938–1987), born in Minneapolis, was a prolific American composer whose catalogue of compositions includes over 1,250 works for piano. In addition, he composed music for children's educational radio and television, for dance, and for religious education records and books. Many articles in leading music journals are also to his credit. The first part of the dissertation details the background of Olson's life and musical career, documenting his place in the profession. A discussion of his musical philosophy is included, extensively referencing many of Olson's published articles, interviews, letters and videotapes. His system of grading piano works is included, as well as a discussion of his concept of piano technique and his approach to teaching the instrument.

Hernandez, Alberto Hector. *Puerto Rican Piano Music of the Nineteenth Century.* Ed.D. dissertation, New York: Columbia University Teachers College, 1990, 152 p. UM 9033830. Although a considerable amount of Puerto Rican piano music of the nineteenth century has been identified by musicologists since 1915, a large number of the scores remain inaccessible to teachers and students. An absence of literature on this subject is due mainly to the lack of organization of bibliographical sources and because the music itself has not been published during this century.

Research procedures were divided into three phases: preliminary study of the available literature, on-site visits to selected libraries and music collections in the United States, Puerto Rico, and Europe, and the classification and the selection of compositions. As a result of the investigation, sixty-four piano pieces by thirteen composers were compiled and properly identified, some of them unknown and omitted in previous musicological studies. The selected piano scores included are now available for the first time in many years, some of them since 1881 or 1893. Six biographical essays are followed by a brief analysis of the pieces and a section on pedagogical points.

The musical, historical, and bibliographical information of sources contained in the study will establish a solid base for further study and research. Piano pedagogues and musicians will definitely expand their piano and musical repertory.

Hess, Carol. *Enrique Granados—A Bio-Bibliography.* Westport, Conn.: Greenwood Press, 1991, 192 p. Includes Biography, Bibliography, Works and Performances, Discography, Appendix 1: Listing of Original Works by Scoring, Appendix 2: Chronology of Important Events during Granados' Lifetime, and Index.

Hess, Debra Lynn. *The Pedagogical Works of Johann Christian Gottlieb Graupner.* Ph.D. dissertation, Gainesville: University of Florida, 1992, 154 p. UM 9331148. Johann Christian Gottlieb Graupner (1767–1836) was a highly regarded musician and influential champion for the development of music in Boston during the first quarter of the nineteenth century. Among his publications, Graupner included six books for instruction in playing the piano, flute, and clarinet. Five of these works are extant.

The purposes of this study are to present a comprehensive analysis of these pedagogical works to determine the type of musical instruction available during this period of American history; to consider these works within the historical context of postrevolution America, a society in its infancy in terms of its development and support of the arts; and to supplement the currently available musicological research on Gottlieb Graupner and his contributions to music instruction and curriculum in Boston during the first three decades of the nineteenth century.

Hester, Richard. *Introduction to the Fortepiano in 20 Questions, More or Less.* (Rte. 143, Box 41, Coeymans Hollow, N.Y. 12046): R. Hester Pianos, 1987, 33 p. Neither scholarly nor comprehensive, but answers basic questions frequently asked about this instrument. New edition in progress.

Highfill, Nadine Antoinette. *Incomplete Notation: Melodic and Textural Additions to Selected Piano Concertos of W. A. Mozart.* M.A. thesis, Fullerton: California State University, 1995, 90 p. UM 1361905. Many of Mozart's piano concertos written for his own performance contain passages in the piano parts that appear fragmentary. This incomplete notation can be attributed to the great haste in which they were written. The modern performer must decide not only if these passages need to be completed but, if so, how to complete them. This study attempts to assist the performer in preparing a convincing and historically authentic performance by offering possible solutions for completing these passages.

Chapter One provides an introduction to the problem and explains the procedures for this study. Chapter Two presents important sources and a historical background. Chapter Three examines the appropriateness of adding embellishments. Chapter Four explores the issue of completing sketched passages. Chapter Five provides the summary and conclusions. This study concludes that the addition of ornaments and figurations is appropriate for passages that may be arguably incomplete.

Higson, Jamos. *Amateur at the Keyboard: A Practice and Study Guide for Nonprofessional Pianists.* Jefferson, N.C.: McFarland & Co., Inc., 1991, 208 p. A manual for amateur pianists interested in rekindling their piano studies. Included is information on selecting an instrument, music, practice techniques, and resources.

Hildebrandt, Dieter. *Pianoforte—A Social History of the Piano.* Trans. Harriet Goodman, with introduction by Anthony Burgess. New York: George Braziller, 1988, 207 p. The piano, according to the author, is the secret hero of the nineteenth century, and forms the connecting link between the colorful stories, legends, and anecdotes Hildebrandt weaves into this witty and captivating account of the memorable social and artistic currents of the time. The memorable pianists are included as well as the great duels at the piano (Bach versus Marchand, Scarlatti versus Handel, Mozart versus Clementi), the technical improvements to the instrument, the piano as part of the storm of romanticism that overtook Paris in the 1830s, and the dawning era of the concert tour and the power of the music critic. It includes many quotations from diaries and letters, and an index.

Himes, Douglas D. *W. A. Mozart's Sonatas for Solo Clavier: Recent Developments in Chronology, Transmission, and Biographic Context.* Ph.D. dissertation, University of Pittsburgh, 1988, 271 p. W 8816998. Mozart's sonatas for solo clavier are among the earliest significant works in piano literature, yet they have received comparatively little scholarly attention. They comprise eighteen completed sonatas, four others presumably completed but long since lost, and seven fragments of sonata movements. Since the mid-nineteenth century, with the appearance of Köchel's first catalog and the Jahn biography, there have been unresolved questions about the chronology of the sonatas and the reasons for their composition. Erroneous conclusions have been perpetuated from one generation of scholars to the next. Mistakes in the identification of sonatas cited in the Mozart family correspondence have added to the confusion. This study proposes a new chronology for the solo clavier sonatas, based on handwriting analyses of Wolfgang Plath and paper studies of Alan Tyson, with refinements suggested by a close reading of the Mozart correspondence and other historical documents. It also proposes a historical context for each of the sonatas and suggests revised identifications for sonatas cited in the correspondence.

Hinson, Maurice. *Performance Practices in Baroque Keyboard Music.* Video cassette. Van Nuys, Calif.: Alfred Publishing Co., 1997, two cassettes, 120 minutes (in two parts). Cassette I includes an introduction to the Baroque period, characteristics of the Baroque period (architecture, painting, music, Doctrine of Affections, opera, programmatic keyboard music), dance, figured bass, emphasis of contrast, keyboard instruments, touch, rhythmic values, articulation, dynamics, ornamentation, notation, and repertoire. Hinson performs and discusses fourteen pieces.

Cassette II, The Baroque Dance, includes a discussion of the historical background of the dance and keyboard music and the most popular court dances of the period. Each dance is broken down into component steps so the viewer can learn them; then Hinson accompanies the dancers (from the Dance Department of the University of Kansas) so the viewer can practice what he or she has learned. A discussion of the basic steps is followed by the introduction of the individual dances including the minuet, allemande, courante, sarabande, bourrée, gavotte, polonaise, gigue, and the rigaudon. These musical dances (found in so many keyboard suites of the period) take on a new life when the dance steps are understood.

————. *Performance Practices in Classical Piano Music.* Video cassette. Van Nuys, Calif.: Alfred Publishing Co., 60 minutes. In Part One, Hinson defines "performance practice" and discusses the musical characteristics of the classical period and the strong dance influence at work during this time frame. In Part Two, a dancer gracefully demonstrates the gigue and minuet. Various dances are then discussed and performed. Frequently misinterpreted Italian terms are redefined, providing clues to performing the music with more accuracy. Finger pedaling is demonstrated, along with other performance conventions that were rarely indicated in the composer's manuscript. Part Three is devoted to exploring the repertoire. Repertoire covered in whole or part includes Beethoven, Country Dances, WoO 14/1 and 7, Bagatelle, Op. 33/3, Sonata in G Major, Op. 2/1; Clementi, Sonatina in G Major, Op. 36/5 (6th edition); Haydn, Sonata in B Minor, Hob. XVI:32, Sonata in E-flat Major, Hob. XVI:49; Mozart, Fantasy in D Minor, K. 397, Sonata in F Major, K. 280, Sonata in F Major, K. 332; and Schubert, Hungarian Melody, D. 817.

――――. *Performance Practices in Early 20th-Century Piano Music*. Video cassette. Van Nuys, Calif.: Alfred Publishing Co., 68 minutes. In Part One (Ragtime Influences), Hinson discusses the influence of ragtime on contemporary composers such as Debussy, Satie, Ravel and Milhaud. Part Two (Nationalistic Music) focuses on the importance of folk song in various national schools and their unique types of piano music. In Part Three (New Tonal Directions), Hinson looks at the development of serialism (twelve-tone writing), Hindemith's "Gebrauchmusik," and other new developments during the period of 1890–1914. Repertoire covered in whole or part includes Bartók, Bagatelle, Op. 6/4, Bear Dance; Joplin, Ragtime Dance; Arthur Farwell, Approach of the ThunderGod; Percy Grainger, The Sussex Mummers Christmas Carol; Schoenberg, Short Piano Piece, Op. 19/2; Edward MacDowell, From a Wandering Iceberg, Op. 55/2; Samuel Coleridge-Taylor, Deep River, Op. 59/10; Enrique Granados, Dance of the Rose; and Hindemith, Foxtrot and Let's Build A Town.

――――. *Performance Practices in Impressionistic Piano Music*. Video cassette. Van Nuys, Calif.: Alfred Publishing Co., 66 minutes. In Part One (Early Influences), Hinson discusses how impressionistic painters, symbolist poets, and composers such as Chopin, Liszt, and Grieg set the stage for Debussy and other composers of the day to begin exploring new compositional techniques. Part Two (Performance Techniques) focuses on exercises for controlling pianissimo dynamic markings commonly found in impressionistic piano music, as well as applicable pedaling techniques. In Part Three (Musical Characteristics),

Hinson discusses specific musical characteristics that impressionist composers incorporated into their music, such as ancient plainsong, the whole tone scale, the pentatonic scale, and more. Part Four (Exploring the Repertoire) concludes with detailed discussions and performance of a number of Debussy pieces. Repertoire covered in whole or part includes Debussy, Doctor Gradus ad Parnassum, The Snow Is Dancing, Dancers of Delphi, Footprints in the Snow, The Girl with the Flaxen Hair, The Sunken Cathedral, Pour le Piano, Prelude and Toccata, Reverie, Clair de lune; and Ravel, Sonatine.

————. *Performance Practices in Romantic Piano Music.* Video cassette. Van Nuys, Calif.: Alfred Publishing Co., 60 minutes. In Part One (Literary Influences), Hinson examines how nineteenth-century composers were inspired by poetry and literature, explored the extreme ranges of their emotions, and were moved by nature, folklore, magic, and anything medieval or Romanesque. Part Two (Musical Characteristics) begins with a discussion on how Romantic-period composers created new compositional forms to help express their musical ideas. In Part Three (Exploring the Repertoire), Hinson summarizes his lecture by performing additional repertoire from the period. Repertoire covered in whole or part includes Brahms, Intermezzo in E-flat Major, Op. 117/1; Chopin, Mazurka in F Minor, Op. 68/4, Waltz in A-flat Major, Op. 69/1, Valse Melancolique, KK Anh. 1a/7; Liszt, Eglogue, S. 160, Consolation III in D-flat Major, G. 172/3; Mendelssohn, Venetian Boat Song, Op. 30/6; and Schumann, Warum?, Op. 12/3.

————. *The Pianist's Guide to Transcriptions, Arrangements, and Paraphrases.* Bloomington: Indiana University Press, 1990, 159 p. Includes more than 2,000 transcriptions that can stand on their own as musical entities, are well suited to the piano, and are in good taste. Includes transcriptions, arrangements, and paraphrases for solo piano, duet, and two pianos, as well as outstanding transcriptions for one hand. In an alphabetical listing of composers, pieces are described under the name of the original composer, and cross-references appear under the name of the transcriber. The only book of its kind that provides a convenient reference tool for an important aspect of piano literature.

————, comp. and intro. *The Vienna Urtext Guide to Piano Literature.* Valley Forge, Pa.: European American Music Corp., 1995, 240 p. Written by the editors of the Vienna Urtext Edition. This is a collection of the front notes from the various piano editions of this publisher that range from J. S. Bach to Paul Hindemith. These notes include in-depth discussions of sources, critical notes, historical background, and suggestions for interpretation. Most of the writers of these notes are outstanding performers and scholars in their fields. The compilation of these commentaries makes this an important book for teachers and pianists. Includes an index of composers plus an index of authors and editors of the Prefaces and Notes on Interpretation.

Holland, Samuel S. *Teaching toward Tomorrow.* Van Nuys, Calif.: Alfred Publishing Co., 1996, 112 p. This book is a music teacher's primer for using electronic keyboards, computers, and MIDI in the studio. The author provides valuable insight into the evolution of keyboard instruments, electronic media, and the revolution that computers have caused in the performance and teaching of music. It contains clear, concise, and easy-to-apply explanations of terms and cutting-edge technology.

————. *The Contributions of Louise Wadley Bianchi to Piano Pedagogy.* D.M.A. paper, Norman: University of Oklahoma, 1996. The purpose of this study is to document and analyze Louise Wadley Bianchi's contributions to music education and piano pedagogy. A pragmatic and at times visionary music educator, Bianchi contributed to the development of piano pedagogy and preparatory departments in American universities, to the elementary piano method series, and to the literature on piano pedagogy. As piano pedagogy enters its fourth decade as a field of degree-oriented academic endeavor, its historical base is still in need of fundamental roots. This study contributes to one aspect of this need.

Basic historical and ethnographic research techniques were employed to establish Bianchi's role in the development of pedagogy and preparatory programs in higher education. These included reviews of primary and secondary literature, interviews with individuals who worked closely with Bianchi, and questionnaires that were sent to all former students who had received a degree in piano pedagogy under Bianchi.

The study is divided into eight chapters. Chapter One provides an introduction, including purpose, need, and procedures for the study, survey of related literature, and limitations. Chapter Two provides a synopsis of Bianchi's life and career as it leads to an understanding of the historical and philosophical bases of her contributions to piano pedagogy. Chapter Three documents the history of Bianchi's piano pedagogy programs at Southern Methodist University in Dallas, Texas, and Chapter Four examines the Piano Preparatory Department at Southern Methodist University. Administrators, faculty and staff members, and former students were queried. Documents in university archives, music department archives, and other locations were consulted in the attempt to present a historical portrait of this benchmark program in piano pedagogy from its inception in the early 1960s to Bianchi's retirement in 1986.

Chapter Five examines Bianchi's articles, her monograph on piano pedagogy that has been a major occupation since her retirement from Southern Methodist University, and her workshops and lectures. Chapter Six evaluates the *Music Pathways* series and Bianchi's contributions to it. The working relationship and contributions of the co-authors Olson, Blickenstaff, and Bianchi are explored. Chapter Seven provides a snapshot of Bianchi as viewed by her former students. Chapter Eight summarizes Bianchi's contributions to piano pedagogy and makes recommendations for further research. Appendixes include letters, questionnaires, and interview guides for Bianchi and her colleagues; a complete catalog of Bianchi's publications; a catalog of master's theses prepared under Bianchi's direction; and a list of workshops and lectures presented by Bianchi.

Hollander, Jeffrey Mark. *Shaping the Interpretation, Interpreting the Shape: A Comparative Performance Study of Selected Works of Frédéric Chopin.* Ph.D. dissertation, Berkeley: University of California, 1993, 449 p. UM 9430537. Can we gain fundamental information about musical works from comparison and analysis of performances of those works? This dissertation is an empirical exercise in comparative performance criticism; the materials for this study are numerous recorded performances of four works by Frédéric Chopin made throughout this century. The many possible interpretations represented by these recordings—an important critical resource—suggest a flexible conception of the musical work; the performer stands as an important reader of the text. Recordings of the Berceuse, Op. 57, and the C-sharp Minor Waltz, Op. 64, No. 2, illustrate distinct patterns of interpretative change. Also discussed is the E-flat Nocturne, Op. 9, No. 2 and the A-flat Ballade, Op. 47.

Holzaepfel, John. *David Tudor and the Performance of American Experimental Music, 1950–1959.* Ph.D. dissertation, City University of

New York, 1994, 420 p. UM 9417470. The first two chapters discuss Tudor's early training and the radically new musical orientation he underwent at the end of 1950 through a fortuitous encounter with the aesthetics of Antonin Artaud. The remaining four chapters concentrate on Tudor's realizations of selected works by the principal American experimental composers of the 1950s: Morton Feldman's *Intersections 2, 3*; Earle Brown's *Twenty-five Pages* and *Four Systems*; Christian Wolff's *Duo for Pianists I and II*; and John Cage's "Solo for Piano" from the *Concert* for Piano and Orchestra.

Hominick, Ian Glenn. *Sigismond Thalberg (1812–1871), Forgotten Piano Virtuoso: His Career and Musical Contributions.* D.M.A. paper, Columbus: Ohio State University, 1991, 138 p. UM 9130450. The author has attempted to bring together existing data to form the first comprehensive survey of Thalberg and his career achievements. The primary purpose is to provide information on Thalberg's career as a pianist-composer and to show the significant influence he had on his contemporaries and on future generations of composers and pianists. This work traces Thalberg's career throughout Europe and North and South America, including the infamous "duel" with Franz Liszt. It provides an abundance of firsthand accounts of Thalberg's performances and a glimpse at his character.

Hong, Barbara Blanchard. *The Five Piano Concertos of Selim Palmgren: A Finnish Nationalist Meets the Challenge of the Twentieth Century.* Ph.D. dissertation, Bloomington: Indiana University, 1992, 405 p. UM 9231555. The piano concertos of the Finnish composer Selim Palmgren (1878–1951) show in microcosm Finland's nationalistic struggle, its fluctuating interest in participating in Central European trends and ideas during the first half of the twentieth century, and Palmgren's own stylistic changes. With each concerto, he adapted to a new set of national and international influences. His five piano concertos form a group of large-scale works extending over his whole career, dating from 1904 to 1941, illustrating the changes in style and techniques.

Each of the concertos shows a search for new structural solutions. While one-movement forms, thematic transformations, and interrelationships preoccupied Palmgren in the first two concertos, the next three focused on other aspects: programmatic variations in the Third; three linked movements in the Fourth, including a telescoped sonata form and a cyclic finale; and creation of a Neoclassical style with traditional forms in the Fifth.

Hong, Yat-Lam. *Three Essays on Chopin's "Etudes," Opp. 10 and 25.* D.M.A. paper, University of Cincinnati, 1991, 84 p. UM 9200447. The first essay is an attempt to trace the origins of the concert etude by examining the development of the piano, the rising popularity of the instrument among amateur musicians, the method books, the technical exercise, and its eventual merging with the character piece to become the concert etude. Clementi's *Gradus ad Parnassum* is also examined in some detail.

The second essay is a study of nine current editions of the Chopin *Etudes,* edited by Liszt, Debussy, Cortot, Esteban, Mikuli, Friedheim, Badura-Skoda, Paderewski, and Zimmermann. Features of particular interest in each version are discussed in detail.

The last essay examines the cyclic nature of Chopin's twenty-four *Etudes,* Opp. 10 and 25, by investigating the numerous ways in which these pieces are connected to each other: by key relationships, cadences, end-to-beginning tie-ins, attacca designation, etc. The total number of such connections between the *Etudes* in their published order is also compared with that of the *Etudes* in their chronological order to provide statistical evidence that, while the organizational scheme here is not as tightly structured as that of his *Preludes,* Chopin's decision to publish the *Etudes* in their present order is far from random.

Horan, Leta Gwin. *A Performer's Guide to Emma Lou Diemer's "Seven Etudes for Piano."* D.M.A. paper, Louisville: Southern Baptist Theological Seminary, 1987, 95 p. UM 8800192. The purpose of the dissertation is to provide a guide for performers and teachers to be used in the preparation and performance of *Seven Etudes for Piano* by Emma Lou Diemer. A short biographical sketch of the composer is presented in Chapter Two, and Chapter Three is devoted to a discussion of the etudes. Each etude is examined separately through a discussion focusing on performance implications such as tempo, pedaling, and phrasing as dictated by its musical and technical content. Stylistic considerations, which include tonal language, form, and texture, are discussed as they relate to performance and interpretation.

Horn, Daniel Paul. *Change and Continuity in the Music of George Rochberg: A Study in Aesthetics and Style as Exemplified by Selected Piano Solo and Chamber Compositions.* D.M.A. paper, New York: The Juilliard School, 1987, 168 p. Chapters include Introduction; Career and Contemplations; The Early Works; Serialism and the Quest for Musical Expression (1952–1963); Collage and the Search for the

Past (1965–1969); Multi-Gesturalism and the Reclamation of the Past (1971–1979); Reintegration (Music since 1980); and Common Threads and Tentative Conclusions: Towards an Understanding of Rochberg's Style, with an Examination of Critical Assessments and Some Speculation about the Composer's Relation to Posterity.

Horne, Aaron. *Keyboard Music of Black Composers: A Bibliography.* New York: Greenwood Press, 1992, 331 p.

Hornick, Andrew M. *Ensemble and Solo Works of Ignaz Pleyel Originally Composed for Keyboard: A Style-analytic Review.* Ph.D. dissertation, New York University, 1987, 360 p. UM 88001543. In the latter part of the eighteenth century, a gradual change occurred in the dissemination and performance of chamber music, which historically had taken place within aristocratic circles. The growing middle class and the emerging popularity of amateur music-making caused an increasing demand for playable, witty compositions that frequently centered around the pianoforte. Ignaz Pleyel was a principal factor in both the composition and the publication of *Hausmusik* for keyboard and accompanying instruments. Between 1783 and 1803 Pleyel wrote forty-nine trios (accompanied sonatas) for keyboard, violin or wind, and cello, fifteen duos (accompanied sonatas) for keyboard and violin or wind, and a plethora of generally shorter pieces for solo keyboard. Pleyel was not only a prolific composer but also an important music publisher in the early nineteenth century. These publishing associations, combined with the naturally vivacious nature of the music itself, aided the dissemination of Pleyel's piano music throughout Europe. Between 1787 and 1792, the central period of the keyboard works, Pleyel was the most published composer on the Continent. This fact affirms the need for an intensive analytic review of Pleyel's music, as it illuminates the critical palette of the amateur musician of the time. From the resulting comprehensive observations, a number of cogent conclusions about the musical style of Pleyel can be suggested. In his youth, Pleyel was a student of Joseph Haydn, and this association is evident in the extensive use of rhythmic activation in the accompanied sonatas. Although little stylistic development appears during Pleyel's twenty-year period of composition, certain elements unify early and late keyboard trios, with the final set showing a number of truly unique musical traits.

Hoskins, Janina W. *Ignacy Jan Paderewski, 1860–1941: A Biographical*

Sketch and a Selective List of Reading Materials. Washington: Library of Congress, 1984, 32 p. A biographical sketch and a selective flat of reading materials. Available from the Library of Congress, European Division, Washington, DC 20540. Includes Works by Paderewski, Works about Paderewski, Key to Symbols, and List of Works in Chronological Order.

Hostetter, Elizabeth Ann. *Jeanne Behrend: Pioneer Performer of American Music, Pianist, Teacher, Musicologist, and Composer.* D.M.A. paper, Tempe: Arizona State University, 1990, 282 p. UM 9101885. Jeanne Behrend (1911–1988) made significant contributions to American music. As a student of Josef Hofmann and Rosario Scalero at Curtis Institute of Music, she was in the first graduating class in 1934, receiving the only diploma given in both piano and composition. Her pioneering efforts began with three recitals of American music in 1939. Behrend composed primarily songs and piano works and also wrote for string quartet, women's chorus, and orchestra. Due to difficulty in getting her works published and performed, she gave up composition and concentrated on the performance of American music. Her 1940 recordings of American piano music were a first of their kind. In 1945 she was the first woman sent by the United States Department of State on a goodwill concert tour of Brazil. At The Juilliard School of Music, Behrend taught one of the earliest courses in American music. Her expertise as a performer and musicologist led to recordings of works by Griffes and Gottschalk and editions of early American choral music, solo piano works of Gottschalk, the travel diary of Gottschalk, and unknown songs of Stephen Foster. She specialized in composers of America's past and often played works by Ives and Farwell. Throughout her life she was a champion for lesser-known composers, particularly John Edmunds and Tibor Serly. In the 1960s Behrend returned to teaching and discovered a special interest in the beginning adult piano student. To consider one area singularly is to do a great injustice to her. Only when her total accomplishments are viewed collectively can her work be fully measured. Behrend can well be considered a model for today's performer to realize the interdependence of performer, composer, and musicologist.

The writer gathered most of the research from Behrend's personal files during two trips to Philadelphia, where she met with Behrend. The files contain much correspondence with American musicians, paticularly Samuel Barber and Josef Hofmann. While primarily a bi-

ography, the research paper includes a complete catalog of her compositions.

Houser, Virginia McNair. *Instructional Units to Develop Listening Skills
in Pre-College Pianists Based on Lower Intermediate Repertoire.*
D.M.A. paper, Norman: University of Oklahoma, 1991, 319 p. UM
9210499. The purpose of this study is to create a series of instructional units designed to teach listening skills to junior high and high
school pianists based on lower intermediate piano teaching repertoire.
These units serve as listening guides to direct students toward important aural features of the work under consideration and help develop
skills in making critical judgments, forming opinions, and expressing
a personal aesthetic experience. These units were designed for both
private and group lessons in which students studied this specific literature. They would also be applicable to group classes of non-key-
board music majors studying this repertoire on the collegiate level.

This project was limited to eight pieces with two chosen from each
stylistic period—Baroque, Classical, Romantic, and Contemporary.
The works were chosen from the collection *Favorite Classics,* Solo
Book I, selected and edited by E. L. Lancaster and Kenon D. Renfrow
and published by Alfred Publishing Co. This collection was chosen
because it includes well-known repertoire from all four musical periods. Selections are on a lower intermediate level and are familiar to
most piano teachers.

How to Choose a Piano Teacher. Video cassette. Kansas City, Mo.: SH
Productions, 1995, 40 minutes. This video answers all of the basic
questions to this perennial question. Experts Christopher Hepp and
Virginia Houser cover thoroughly such areas as: When should my child
start lessons? What about private versus group lessons? How much
do lessons cost? What about electronic pianos and computers? Which
schools offer scholarships for students? Includes what you need to
know the right questions to ask prospective teachers, learn the various methods and latest trends in piano teaching, and gain tips on pur-
chasing a new or used piano. Parents of all prospective piano students
should see this video.

Hsu, Madeleine. *Olivier Messiaen, The Musical Mediator. His Major
Influences: Liszt, Debussy and Bartók.* Cranbury, N.J.: Associated
University Presses, 1996. This book analyzes selected piano works of

Messiaen, provides a guide for the interpretation and performance of the works, and gives pedagogical instruction for each composition under six major headings: rhythm, phrasing/slurring, dynamics, touch/tone production, pedaling, and technique. It also offers background on Messiaen's philosophy of music, particularly the religious, literary, visual, and musical experiences that affected his compositions.

Hudson, Richard. *Stolen Time*. New York: Oxford University Press, 1995, 480 p. Traces the complex history of tempo rubato, melodic, and structural. Suggests new ways of approaching rubato in composers such as Chopin, Liszt, and Stravinsky.

Hughes, Walden Dale. *Liszt's Solo Piano Transcriptions of Orchestral Literature*. D.A. paper, Greeley: University of Northern Colorado, 1992, 212 p. UM 9231154. Although many important musicians such as Karl Tausig, Hans von Bülow, and Ferruccio Busoni contributed significant examples of piano arrangements to the body of transcription literature, Franz Liszt overshadows all other transcribers of the century. His efforts in this area constitute an even larger endeavor than his original works. The major considerations contemplated in this study include how Liszt solved the problems encountered in transcribing multifarious orchestral scores to the piano, whether his solutions were successful, and whether his transcriptional techniques were modified over time. Comparisons regarding Liszt's transcriptional techniques drawn between his arrangement of Berlioz's Symphonie Fantastique, representing an early effort, and his transcription of the Beethoven Ninth Symphony, representing a late undertaking thirty-five years later, have revealed consistency of approach, and no significant deviation in either intent or technique.

Hukill, Cynthia Louise. *A Stylistic Analysis of Selected Piano Works of Leroy Robertson (1896–1971)*. D.M.A. paper, Kansas City, Mo.: University of Missouri, 1988, 228 p. UM 8814606. Leroy Robertson was born in Fountain Green, Utah, December 21, 1896, of Mormon parents. Despite a childhood of financial hardship and limited opportunities for exposure to music, he became one of the preeminent American composers of the 1930s and 1940s, studying with such noted teachers as George W. Chadwick, Ernest Bloch, Hugo Leichtentritt, Ernst Toch, and Arnold Schoenberg.

Robertson's most productive years were those immediately following his European study, 1933–1946, during which he also produced some of his finest piano compositions. This study, which was made from a performer's perspective, is a stylistic analysis of six compositions from this period: the Quintet in A minor for Piano and String Quartet, the Three Concert Etudes for Pianoforte in B-flat Major, G minor, and E-flat Major, the *Rhapsody for Piano and Orchestra,* and the *Novelette for Piano.* Such elements as formal structure, melodic material, harmonic, contrapuntal, and rhythmic aspects, technical demands, and pedaling are addressed with the intent of helping a pianist to prepare for a performance.

Humber, Ingrid. *An Analysis with Interpretive Suggestions of Seven Keyboard Works of Alessandro Scarlatti.* Ed.D. dissertation, New York: Columbia University Teachers College, 1986, 276 p. UM 8620368. Alessandro Scarlatti's musical fame and historical significance are so deeply rooted in his vocal and orchestral compositions that the keyboard toccatas and sonatas have been neglected. A careful study of a representative portion of fifty-four keyboard compositions composed by Scarlatti confirms their significance as performance works.

The purpose of this dissertation is to offer a structural analysis with interpretative suggestions of seven keyboard compositions including two sonatas and five toccatas. Since the Milan sonatas were unsigned, it was necessary to offer scholarly authentication that these two sonatas were indeed composed by Scarlatti. In addition, five signed Scarlatti toccatas located in the Yale University Manuscript were compared for structural discrepancies to another five toccatas found in the Milan Manuscript.

Another purpose of this dissertation is to edit the seven compositions and include a discussion of the unnecessary emendations found in the earlier editions of these works. The editions involved the reconstruction of measures, the realization of harmonies, and the proper placement of ornaments.

This study examined the Milan and Yale University Manuscripts including twenty toccatas, one dance and fugue, and three other fugues in order to determine their basic structural characteristics. In the Milan Manuscript, it was necessary to eliminate non-Scarlatti compositions. The Milan Manuscript was found to contain seven Scarlatti keyboard compositions. Two other Milan sonatas were signed "Del Signore Sassone," meaning "of the Saxon," and indicated that these sonatas were composed by G. F. Handel or Johann Adolf Hasse who resided in Italy in the early eighteenth century. Three other unsigned Milan sonatas were determined not to be by Scarlatti because of the mature nature of their galant style. One toccata in the manuscript was of doubtful origin because of the delayed resolution of chords and intervallic expansion. A sonata in A major followed by a gigue was also eliminated as a Scarlatti composition because of its peculiar galant style.

This analysis of seven keyboard compositions of Alessandro Scarlatti revealed technically demanding works with a wide range of harmonic and melodic complexity. Generally, the sonatas, which utilized a I–IV–V harmonic structure, were not as complex harmonically or melodically as the toccatas. The results of this study can be used by music instructors who wish to include the harpsichord compositions of Alessandro Scarlatti in the standard concert repertoire.

Hunter, Colleen Marie. *A Study of Repertoire Performed in Degree Recitals by Piano Performance Majors at Selected United States Schools of Music.* D.M.A. paper, Kansas City, Mo.: University of Missouri, 1993, 261 p. UM 9318550. The analysis of 332 recital programs resulted in a tabulation of 1,864 compositions, representing 123 composers, 62 of whom were listed one time. Works performed two or more times, as well as those played only one time, were specified for each academic year and placed into one of seven style periods. Repertoire from the twentieth century was listed for each academic year.

Huot, Joanne Marie. *The Piano Music of Federico Mompou (1893–).* Thesis, Seattle: University of Washington, 1965.

Husarik, Stephen, ed. *American Keyboard Artists.* 2nd ed., Chicago Biographical Center, 1992, 488 p. Contains biographical listings of approximately 2,000 keyboard professionals, i.e., concert artists, cathedral and church organists, orchestra members, chamber musicians, entertainers, award winners, authors, administrators, educators, and those who set the standards and initiate trends in American music.

Hutton, Judy Foreman. *The Teaching and Artistic Legacy of French-born Pianist Daniel Ericourt.* D.M.A. paper, Greensboro: University of North Carolina, 1993, 248 p. UM 9419163. The principal purpose of this study is to investigate the professional career of French-born pianist Daniel Ericourt (b. 1903) and, more specifically, to explore Ericourt's contributions as artist-in-residence at the University of North Carolina at Greensboro from 1963 to 1976. Secondary objectives include compiling biographical data in order to establish Ericourt's educational and professional background, identifying important teachers and associates, and disclosing events, philosophies, and achievements which influenced his artistic development and led to his career as pianist and pedagogue.

Hyde, Carol Shannon. *A Case Study of an Artist-In-Residence: Ruth Slenczynska, Concert Pianist.* Ed.D. dissertation, Urbana-Champaign: University of Illinois, 1988, 432 p. UM 8908714. The purpose of this case study is to document and describe the process of transition in Ruth Slenczynska's musical career from concert pianist to artist-in-residence and the factors that kept her in the position for twenty-three years. Data for the study was collected from interviews with Slenczynska, administrators and colleagues at Southern Illinois University at Edwardsville, published and unpublished documents including Slenczynska's childhood scrapbook, letters, press releases, and a Slenczynska performance videotape.

Slenczynska's formative lifestyle and early years as a widely acclaimed child prodigy are traced and attention is given to the conditions existing during her career as a concert pianist in the decade prior to her acceptance of an artist-in-residence position. In addition, the incentives that drew her toward a career as artist-in-residence are investigated. The career change from concert pianist to artist-in-residence brought about numerous changes in Slenczynska's professional and personal life, detailed in the study. Her role as a faculty member was also researched.

Analysis of data revealed that as an artist-in-residence, Slenczynska made a great number of adjustments regarding her public performances. From necessity, she became her own manager, lowering the number of concert engagements in order to also fulfill her teaching responsibilities. As an educator, new opportunities arose for Slenczynska to write articles on piano pedagogy and conduct workshops which she scheduled frequently. Research findings showed that numerous changes also occurred in Slenczynska's personal life. She moved from a large city to a small town in a rural area; she met and eventually married a professor from the same university at which she taught. Slenczynska also gained a sense of financial security stemming from her steady income as an artist-in-residence. Finally, the university offered and succeeded in maintaining a nonrestrictive attitude toward Slenczynska's employment, never confining or stifling her appetite to perform.

Igrec, Srebrenka. *Béla Bartók's Edition of Mozart's Piano Sonatas.* D.M.A. paper, Baton Rouge: Louisiana State University, 1993, 141 p. UM 9419898. This study examines Bartók's editorial work, providing evidence about his playing and teaching of Mozart. The first chapter, an introduction, briefly discusses Bartók's editorial activities, establishes his sources for the Mozart edition, and discusses his editorial style and the order of sonatas as they appear in his edition. The next two chapters examine Bartók's articulation and dynamics. In Chapters Four and Five Bartók's expression markings, tempo modifications, and pedaling are discussed. His metronome markings, fingerings, ornament realizations, and formal analyses are investigated in Chapter Six.

Indenbaum, Dorothy. *Mary Howe: Composer, Pianist and Music Activist.* Ph.D. dissertation, New York University, 1993, 445 p. UM 9317667. Mary Howe's career is presented in three categories: as a solo pianist and as a partner in a two-piano team, in which she gained competence and confidence in public performance; as a composer, including her methods of work, collegial relationships, and promotional activities; and her contributions to the wider musical community, both as an advocate of American music and as an organizer and founder of institutions in Washington, D.C., particularly the National Symphony Orchestra.

Issacs, Nicholas Stephen. *The Keyboard Cadenza.* D.M.A. paper, Stanford University, 1986, 82 p. UM 8619850. This paper considers the origin, theory, aesthetics, and some surviving written examples of the keyboard cadenza from the mid-eighteenth to the nineteenth centuries. A summary of the eighteenth-century view is given, as represented by Quantz, Bach, Türk, and Kollman, followed by a discussion of examples by Haydn, Mozart (original cadenzas), Clementi, Müller, and Hoffman (cadenzas for others' concertos), with special attention given to common principles of structure and compositional procedures, as well as to stylistic authenticity. After discussing nineteenth-century musical trends, the paper considers the role of Fantasy in music, its effect on the cadenza and musical structure in general, and its relationship to eighteenth-century musical theory and practice. Distinction is made between the innovative approach of Beethoven, Chopin, Mendelssohn, and Liszt and the relatively conservative styles of Schumann, Brahms, Tchaikovsky, and Grieg, in cadenzas and compositional style in general. Three cadenzas by the author are included, written for the first movement of Mozart's *Piano Concerto in C major,* K. 503 and for the first two movements of Beethoven's *Piano Concerto in B-flat major,* Op. 19, that attempt stylistic authenticity according to the principles of style and structure defined by Quantz and his successors. Illustrations include harmonic reductions of numerous cadenzas discussed, and reproduction in the appendix of Clementi's set of cadenzas written in the style of several of his contemporaries (1803).

Iverson, Jane Marie Leland. *Piano Music of Agathe Backer Grondahl.* D.M.A. paper, Greeley: University of Northern Colorado, 1993, 142 p. UM 9323111. This source provides an in-depth examination of twenty pieces based on Norwegian folk songs, folk dances, and folk stories. The examination includes analyses of these pieces with regard to compositional style and pedagogical value. Musical examples and recommendations for pedagogical use and performance are included in the analysis. The analysis culminates in an audio recording of these piano works performed by this writer.

Jacobson, Daniel Christopher. *Franz Schubert: Expanding the Realm of Harmonic and Formal Thought, c. 1810–1828.* Ph.D. dissertation, Santa Barbara: University of California, 1986, 2 vols., 715 p. UM 8703654. Despite the existence of over 350 articles and books about Franz Schubert (1797–1828) and his music, a definitive study of his compositional development has not yet been provided. Researchers have been quick to praise Schubert's melodic and interpretative gifts; however, they have failed to recognize fully the significance of functional harmonic distance as his primary means of development and expression. Since the Romantic period was heralded by a gradual expansion of the limits of functional tonality and an increased reliance on non-standard formal procedures, a study of these aspects would seem to be one of the more reliable methods for tracing gradual changes in Schubert's musical thought.

This dissertation attempts to shed new light on Schubert's harmonic and formal procedures by proposing and applying a systematic approach to the analysis and evaluation of eighty selected works from five chronologically representative musical genres: mass, symphony, chamber music, solo piano literature, and song. In all, over 40,000 measures of music are analyzed in this study, and the evaluation of this information reveals four distinct style-periods in Schubert's output: Period 1 = c. 1810–18, Period 2 = c. 1819–23, Period 3 = c. 1824–26, and Period 4 = c. 1826–28. In each of these four periods, Schubert consistently employed a unique set of tonal procedures, regardless of genre; thus, such harmonic evidence can help to establish relative dates of composition for many of his works. In order to demonstrate the validity of this approach, its methods are applied to the dating of two problematic works, the "Great" C Major Symphony (D. 944) and the Piano Trio No. 1 in B-flat (D. 898). After careful consideration of the statistics, this study provides substantial evidence that the "Great" C Major Symphony was almost certainly written in 1825–26, and that the Piano Trio No. 1 was probably conceived during the latter half of 1827.

Jacobson, Jeanine N. *A Catalogue of Movement-Based Instructional Activities for Beginning Piano Students Correlated to* The Music Tree *Series by Frances Clark and Louise Goss.* D.M.A. paper, Norman: University of Oklahoma, 1989. The purpose of this study is to create a catalog of elementary movement-based activities for piano teachers to use in the private piano lesson with average-age elementary piano students. The resulting catalog provides a comprehensive introduction to and mastery of all musical parameters through movement. The movement-based activities have been adapted to correlate with *The Music Tree,* a four-book beginning piano series by Frances Clark and Louise Goss.

Because music is an aural experience, every music educator hopes that the student will develop listening skills. These skills foster musical sensitivity, aid in the learning of one's chosen performance instrument, and provide a lifelong joyful experience with music. Aural development is not achieved through a natural developmental process but must be taught, just as reading and technique are taught. Educators believe that learning is more efficient if the learning mode is experiential rather than simply an intellectual process. Research indicates that large body movement is essential for learning and development in general. Movement-based instruction is used by music educators because it is experiential and because it involves a relationship between the aural and the kinesthetic.

The catalog includes 302 series of activities for the four books, presents a movement activity series for two to four pieces in each unit of study, and also provides up to five more series of activities per unit for the preparation and reinforcement of other musical parameters, following a systematic sequencing for a gradual development of musical sensitivity and response. Approximately twenty-seven preliminary activities are also presented. Because it is so important that the musical cues elicit an appropriate response on the part of the student, ninety music examples of suggested improvisations are included within the body of the document. It is recommended that future studies apply the Dalcroze principles of eurythmics, improvisation, and solfège to *The Music Tree* series and other beginning piano series. Further, future studies should attempt to develop a catalog of movement-based activities that could be adapted for use with any beginning piano series.

James, Michael Joseph. *The Evolution of Pedagogical Thought in American Piano Teaching of the Twentieth Century.* D.M.A. paper, Columbia: University of South Carolina, 1995, 97 p. UM 9430900. This study presents five patinas of thought that have evolved out of the development of piano pedagogy in America during the twentieth century. These paths of thought focus on the following topics: the inseparability of technique from conception and musical interpretation; the incorporation and coordination of the whole body in piano performance; the use of rhythmic control as a means of achieving musical organization and continuity; the necessity of mental concentration, aural awareness and self-evaluation in piano study and performance; and the humanistic facet of piano instruction.

Janis, Byron. *In the Steps of Chopin: A Portrait by Byron Janis.* Video cassette. Films for the Humanities and Sciences, 58 minutes. Janis takes us through the stations of Chopin's life, demonstrating the pianistic techniques Chopin taught his pupils, examining differences between manuscript and published versions of some pieces, and showing both his own technical virtuosity and exceptional affinity with Chopin in performances of a broad range of Chopin pieces.

Jiorle-Nagy, Linda A. *A Study of Phrase Structures and Unifying Devices in George Crumb's "Makrokosmos I and II."* D.M.A. paper, Boston University, 1993, 317 p. UM 9319017. This document presents a detailed analysis of the first two books of the *Makrokosmos* with special emphasis on the forms and phrase structures used by the composer. Structural unity is examined in terms of the motivic connections within the individual movements and also within the *Makrokosmos* as a whole. Unconventional methods of phrase construction are discussed along with the specific methods Crumb chooses to define his forms and phrase lengths. Likewise, specific propulsional forces and their effect upon the overall emotional curve of the pieces are studied.

Johnson, Mary Teel. *A Parent's Guide to Piano Lessons.* Montery, Calif.: Funchess Jones Publishing, 1987, 112 p. Distributed by Somma Publishing, P.O. Box 762, Seaside, CA 93955. An excellent book (twenty-one chapters) for helping the public appreciate the qualified piano teacher and to seek proper instruction for their children.

Johnson, Wayne David. *A Study of the Piano Works of Alan Hovhaness.* D.M.A. paper, University of Cincinnati, 1986, 194 p. UM 8708125. Alan Hovhaness has written nearly a hundred works for piano. Although they remain little known, these compositions represent a significant contribution to twentieth-century keyboard literature. The purpose of this study, therefore, is to examine them within a biographical, historical, and stylistic context.

The study commences with a brief biography of Hovhaness in relation to his keyboard works, also exploring the impact of travel outside the West on his style, and including a discussion of the religious and philosophical influences which have formed a basis for his worldview and his eclectic compositional approach.

Hovhaness's evocative titles provide strong clues to his musical language and a stimulus for musical imagery. Because of his use of so many non-Western terms, the purpose of Chapter Two is to provide specific explanations and translations of problematic titles and foreign terms. The discussion of stylistic features in Chapter Three begins with his practice of imitating non-Western instruments at the keyboard. The characteristics of such instruments as the *kanoon,* the *oud,* and the *jhaltarang* are discussed, with illustrations of how these Near Eastern and Indian instruments were utilized as models. This is followed by a brief analysis of his use of counterpoint, an examination of his use of exotic modes and scales, and a brief study of his harmonic practices. Rhythmic features, including cycles, free rhythms, and chance procedures are examined next, and the chapter concludes with an overview of both traditional and non-Western structural concepts employed in the piano works.

Chapter Four provides information which would be of specific interest to a performer, including a discussion of Hovhaness's techniques of using various implements "inside" the piano, as well as interpretive suggestions for selected works. The study concludes with an appendix containing a catalog of published and unpublished piano works (including solo, four-hand, and concertos) through 1986.

Jones, Charles Howard. *The "Wiener Pianoforte-Schule" of Friedrich Starke: A Translation and Commentary.* D.M.A. paper, Austin: University of Texas, 1990, 542 p. UM 9031765. To date, there has been no English translation of the *Wiener Pianoforte-Schule* (Viennese Pianoforte School), a pedagogical treatise published by Friedrich Starke (1774–1835) in 1819, 1820, and 1821. Starke was a performing musician, respected pedagogue, and composer in Vienna who was most noted for being the teacher entrusted by Beethoven with the musical instruction of his nephew Carl. Recent writers, most notably Robert Winter in his article "Second Thoughts on the Performance of Beethoven's Trills," (*Musical Quarterly* LXIII, Fall 1977), William S. Newman in his 1988 book *Beethoven on Beethoven,* and Sandra P. Rosenblum in her 1988 book *Performance Practices in Classic Piano Music,* have cited Starke's treatise in support of points they make about early-nineteenth-century performance practice. For these reasons, the author deemed it useful to make this work accessible to English-speaking readers.

The English translation of this work is preceded by an introductory chapter that contains biographical information about Starke, a comparison of this treatise with similar works published during the late eighteenth and early nineteenth centuries, a catalog of repertoire selections by Starke and other composers contained in this work, and an evaluation of the significance of the Starke treatise. The entire three-volume treatise has been translated. All examples, tables, and repertoire selections are included.

Jones, Leslie. *The Solo Piano Music of Vivian Fine.* D.M.A. paper, University of Cincinnati, 1994, 299 p. UM 9502565. Vivian Fine's approach to composition and the evolution of her style are traced through a comprehensive survey of her fifteen solo piano works. Encompassing a period of nearly seventy years (1925–1994), the essence of Fine's composing—her hallmark characteristics of linear writing and harmony defined by dissonance—has remained relatively unchanged. This survey examines her work from the earliest, *Four Polyphonic Pieces* (1931–1932), written in an extremely harsh, dissonant style, through *Toccatas and Arias* (1987), a culmination of all the qualities of balance and symmetry that are displayed in Fine's writing—contrasting consonance and dissonance, counterpoint and homophony, subject and retrograde, and unrelenting drive and lyrical beauty.

Joyner, David Lee. *Southern Ragtime and its Transition to Published Blues.* Ph.D. dissertation, Memphis, Tenn.: Memphis State University, 1986, 211 p. UM 8627178. The purpose of this study is to trace the development of published ragtime in the South, its composers and publishers through historical investigation, and musicological analysis of the sheet music. This study also investigates the transition in the South from ragtime music to formalized published blues songs by citing early blues influences in Southern rags and ragtime retentions in mature published blues compositions. This study begins with an evaluation of Southern ragtime and published blues scholarship to date and attempts to define and identify "ragtime" and "blues." The inadequacies of existing scholarship on southern rags and published blues are pointed out as well as possible needs for the future.

The development of Southern ragtime is discussed, including the important role of the Jesse French Piano Company of Nashville. The history of ragtime in various southern cities is given, including its composers and publishers. The geographical areas considered in this study reach from Nashville to Georgia to Texas. Previously unknown biographical information and rag pieces are introduced and discussed, especially on such figures as H. A. French, Geraldine Dobyos, and Elma Ney McClure. Also discussed are formalized published blues songs, first made famous by W. C. Handy with the publication of his "Memphis Blues" in 1912. Other blues composers, especially those in Memphis around the years of Handy, are discussed and their blues styles compared with Handy's. The rags and blues surveyed in this study are analyzed for their regional distinction, general musical quality, and the individuality of their composers.

Kalil, Timothy Michael. *The Role of the Great Migration of African Americans to Chicago in the Development of Traditional Black Gospel Piano by Thomas A. Dorsey, circa 1930.* Ph.D. dissertation, Kent,

Ohio: Kent State University, 1993, 204 p. UM 9419241. This dissertation seeks to show how Thomas A. Dorsey, Chicago in the 1920s, and traditional Black gospel piano are inextricably linked via the Great Migration. In short, traditional Black gospel piano could not have happened at any other time or place. Furthermore, traditional Black gospel piano joins ragtime, blues, and jazz piano as one of Black America's most important musical contributions.

Kallberg, Jeffrey. *Chopin at the Boundaries: Sex, History, and Musical Genre.* Cambridge: Harvard University Press, 1996, 301 p. Essays on various aspects of Chopin, written over a number of years, have led the author to the ideas offered here. A "new" Chopin is revealed, according to Kallberg. Charles Rosen says this is "the most stimulating book of Chopin criticism I have ever read." Contains illustrations, music examples, and index.

———. *The Chopin Sources: Variants and Versions in Later Manuscripts and Printed Editions.* Ph.D. dissertation, University of Chicago, 1982, 399 p. Explores the musical issues revealed by Chopin's revisions, the cultural and economic milieu from which they emerged, and the nature of the sources in which they occurred. Restricts the musical discussion to Chopin's later works (1842–1847) and considers only revisions after the sketch stage. Assesses music publishing in the nineteenth century and Chopin's relations with his publishers, and describes the nature of his manuscripts. Examines compositional problems in selected manuscripts and printed editions, treating both text-critical and musical issues.

Kaminsky, Peter Michael. *Aspects of Harmony, Rhythm and Form in Schumann's "Papillons," "Carnival," and "Davidsbündlertänze."* Ph.D. dissertation, Rochester, N.Y.: University of Rochester, Eastman School of Music, 1990, 2 vols., 324 p. UM 9012232. This study focuses on structural principles in three of Schumann's piano cycles, *Papillons, Carnival,* and *Davidsbündlertänze.* The three works share the untransposed repetition of motives and progressions across movements ("cross reference") as an important structural element. The strategic placement of cross references and the tonal context in which they occur imply structural levels analogous to the role of motivic parallelisms within individual movements. By tracing the process of cross reference, this study shows a progressively more sophisticated

approach to large-scale structure in the cycles, from the tenuous organization of *Papillons* to the highly complex scheme of *Davidsbündlertänze*.

An understanding of cross reference necessitates examining more
general aspects of Schumann's rhythmic and harmonic style. His rhythmic practice is characterized by symmetrical phrase organization and
the frequent use of hemiola, metrical displacement, and other conflicts
with the notated meter. The analysis takes recent work in contemporary rhythmic theory on metrical dissonance and hypermeter as a point
of departure in examining the interaction of rhythm, tonal progression, and form. Discussion of Schumann's harmonic practice begins
with characteristic local progressions and leads to progressively larger
analytical contexts. For *Papillons* and *Carnival* the harmonic language
is primarily diatonic, and it frequently involves the tonicization of the
relative mode, sometimes at relatively deep structural levels. In turn,
relative mode tonicization often provides the basis for the grouping
of adjacent movements, a comparatively local but important factor in
large-scale structure.

Davidsbündlertänze stands apart from the two earlier cycles in the
sophistication of its tonal and rhythmic achievement and in the depth
of its expressive content. Chromatic as well as diatonic cross references articulate a highly complex and multilayered formal organization. In addition, rhythm becomes a structural determinant through
the use of metrical means to emphasize repeated progressions across
movements.

Kang, Mahn-Hee. *Robert Schumann's Piano Concerto in A Minor, op.
54: A Systematic Analysis of the Sources.* Ph.D. dissertation, Columbus: Ohio State University, 1992, 201 p. UM 9307795. Because of
the notational difficulties of the autograph, the first edition contains
many errors and inconsistencies. The first full-score edition, published
posthumously in 1862, stems from the 1846 edition, but the anony-
mous editor tried to correct the errors and regularize the notation.
His work was flawed by his lack of access to the autograph manuscript. The edition in Robert Schumann's Werke, perhaps the work of
an assistant rather than Clara Schumann herself, virtually reproduces
the readings of the 1862 edition. Only in a pedagogical edition published in 1887 did Clara—who had performed the solo piano part at
the premiere—offer personal ideas on performance. A new critical
edition is clearly needed; recent scholarly editions rely uncritically on
readings stemming from the 1862 edition.

Kang, Yunjoo. *The Chopin Prelude, Opus 28: An Eclectic Analysis with Performance Guide.* D.A paper, New York University, 1994, 243 p. UM 9502425. The focus of this study is the analysis of four selected preludes by Chopin in order to uncover compositional techniques and to support a performance guide. Criteria used for selection include inherent problems of compositional idiosyncrasy, performance practice and technique, and aesthetic comments. The works selected are No. 15 in D-flat Major, No. 16 in B-flat minor, No. 17 in A-flat Major, and No. 22 in G minor. A historical survey of the development of the piano prelude is presented. In addition, the extant literature concerning the performance practice of Chopin's piano music is reviewed.

Kaplan, Iris. *The Experience of Pianists Who Have Studied the Alexander Technique: Six Case Studies.* Ph.D. dissertation, New York University, 1994, 224 p. UM 9422998. The experiences of six pianists who have studied the Alexander Technique, and how they incorporated it into their piano playing, are explored, described, and compared. Open-ended in-depth interviews were conducted, recorded, and transcribed. The first and second levels of analysis were organized around the participants' individual experiences and perceptions. The data were then coded and organized into categories that seemed meaningful for the participants: Impetus for Study, Musical Education, the Alexander Technique Process, the Application of the Alexander Technique to Piano Playing, Results of Alexander Technique Study, and Disciplines that Complement the Alexander Technique. The themes that emerged from each category are presented and comprise the third level of analysis.

Karpati, Janos. *Bartók's Chamber Music.* Trans. Fred Macnicol and Maria Steiner. Stuyvesant, N.Y.: Pendragon Press, 1994, 412 p. Includes bibliographical references and index.

Kashner, Sam, and Nancy Schoenberger. *A Talent for Genius: The Life and Times of Oscar Levant.* New York: Random House, 1994, 512 p. This is a reliable account of Levant's life and career. Of special interest is the account of Levant's relationship with the Gershwin family and the description of music in New York and Hollywood.

Keith, Nancy Alton. *A Comparative Analysis of the Fugue in the Twentieth-Century American Piano Sonata.* M.M. thesis, University of Cincinnati, 1987, 228 p. UM 1331171. A comparative, parametric analysis of three fugues within the twentieth-century American piano sonata, found in Samuel Barber's *Piano Sonata* Op. 26 (1949), Elliott Carter's *Piano Sonata* (1946), and Paul Hindemith's *Third Piano Sonata* (1936). The objective of the thesis is twofold: to compare and contrast the composer's handling of the fugue procedure, and to examine each composer's fugue technique as it relates to and reflects his overall style.

Each fugue is examined individually. A sectional overview summarizes the parametric activity within each portion of the fugue. Then, a detailed thematic analysis deals with the fugue's progressive motivic development. Following this analysis are individual discussions on the compositional parameters of rhythm and meter, dynamics and register, harmony, and tonality. Finally, a summary reviews the most significant stylistic aspects of each fugue.

Kelly, Pamela Preston. *The "Ponteios" of Camargo Guarnieri.* D.M.A. paper, College Park: University of Maryland, 1993, 195 p. UM 9407725. The fifty *Ponteios* for piano solo are the perfect embodiment of Guarnieri's versatility as a composer and of the folk and popular influences in his music. They range from intermediate to virtuosic in difficulty, reflecting different moods, textures, and harmonic treatments. Because of the contrast within the five volumes of *Ponteios,* they make effective recital pieces when grouped in performance. They are an unexplored treasure for pianists of all nationalities. This Performance-Tape Project, comprised of a written document and a tape recording of all the *Ponteios,* will hopefully make these pieces better known.

Kemmerling, Sarah Ellen Moore. *Selected Piano Compositions Written Since 1960 for the Intermediate Piano Student.* D.M.A. paper, Austin: University of Texas, 1980, 131 p.

Kidd, Leonice T. *They All Sat Down.* Florence, Ky.: Willis Music Co., 1994, 152 p. Charming vignettes of some of the great piano personalities. Contains entertaining, little-known facts that show the performers to be human like the rest of us. The list of pianists runs from Johann Christian Bach to Emma Lou Diemer. Aimed at teenage readers.

Kiel, Claudia Margaret. *The Piano Etudes of Prokofiev and Stravinsky: An Interpretive Analysis for Performers.* D.M.A. paper, University of Miami, 1989, 153 p. UM 9003124. The four Prokofiev etudes, written in 1909, mark the beginning of this composer's mature style. Their energetic motion provides for the study of broken chords and octaves, ostinato patterns, polyrhythms, finger independence, and voicing of contrapuntal texture. The four Stravinsky etudes, from 1908, show very little resemblance to the mature Stravinsky style. The influence of Scriabin is seen in their chromatic harmony and extensive use of polyrhythms. Broken and blocked octaves and chords, voicing, and finger independence, along with polyrhythms, are the technical difficulties within the set.

This study provides a structural and interpretative analysis of these two rarely performed sets of etudes. Structural analysis includes that of form, melody, thematic relationships, motivic material, textures, harmony, rhythms, and meters. Interpretative analysis involves phrasing, tempi, dynamics, climaxes, moods, voicing, tonal quality, and pedaling. Biographical information pertinent to the etudes' composition is also included.

Kim, Hae-Jeong. *The Keyboard Suites of Matthew Locke and Henry Purcell.* M.M. thesis, Denton: University of North Texas, 1989, 88 p. UM 1338036. This work largely concerns the roles of Matthew Locke and Henry Purcell in the history of English keyboard music as reflected in their keyboard suites. Both, as composers of the Restoration period, integrated the French style with the more traditional English techniques—especially, in the case of Purcell, the virginalist heritage—in their keyboard music. Through a detailed examination of their suites, the author reveals differences in their individual styles and sets forth unique characteristics of each composer. Both composers used the then traditional almain-corant-saraband pattern as the basis of the suite, to which they added a variety of English country dances. At the same time they modified the traditional dances with a variety of French and Italian idioms, thereby making distinctive individual contributions to the genre.

Kim, Kyungsook Lee. *Traditional Music and Contemporary Piano Music of Korea.* D.M.A. paper, Chicago: American Conservatory of Music, 1991, 96 p. UM 9130025. Korean Music can be divided into three basic categories: aristocratic music, folk music, and religious music. Each of these types of music has its own musical character and style from which contemporary Korean composers draw modern inspiration. A brief history of Western music in Korea highlights the significant events leading up to the introduction of the techniques of Western musical composition into Korean music. Analysis of selected contemporary piano compositions by five noted composers, Suk-Hi Kang, Jung-Gil Kim, Byung-Dong Paik, Young-Jo Lee, and Young-Ja Lee, points out the specific Western musical techniques which these modern Korean composers have incorporated into their work.

Kim, Young Sook. *The Artist-Teacher as College Music Educator.* Ed.D. dissertation, New York: Columbia University Teachers College, 1993, 234 p. UM 9400575. This work addresses two current topics in college-level music education: the philosophical questions of an artist-teacher, and analysis of musical works. The first topic deals with the emotional and psychological questions faced by those who have majored in music performance in college without any preparation for becoming a teacher, and who nevertheless do teach after graduation, but with a sense of frustration. The second topic deals with the belief that an in-depth analysis of a music piece gives an artist-teacher insight into the world of the creator of the music and thus enables him or her to have a creative approach in the performance and teaching of the music. For this purpose, five piano pieces by Bach, Beethoven, Chopin, Liszt, and Yun are analyzed, each in separate chapters.

Kindall, Susan Carol. *The Twenty-Four Preludes for Solo Piano by Richard Cumming: A Pedagogical and Performance Analysis.* D.M.A. paper, Norman: University of Oklahoma, 1994. The purpose of this document is to provide a pedagogical and performance analysis of Richard Cumming's *Twenty-Four Preludes for Solo Piano* that will promote interest, interpretative understanding, and continued performance of these pieces. The preludes form Cumming's most extensive work written for the piano. They are of high artistic value and deserve a place in the standard repertoire. This document includes an introductory chapter, followed by three chapters which include a summary with recommendations for further study.

Chapter One consists of an introduction that provides an overview of the awards, commissions, and acclaim Cumming has received for his works. It also contains the purpose of the study, related literature, need for the study, limitations, and design and procedure. Chapter Two provides background valuable for understanding Cumming's compositional style. A brief biography explores topics pertinent to his development as a musician: ancestry and birth, formative years, high school years, piano teachers, college years and composition teachers, the Aspen Summer Music Institute, the Music Academy of the West, European solo concert tour, and other performances as solo concert pianist. Cumming's work as composer for theater and his positions with Trinity Repertory of Providence, Rhode Island, as Director of Educational Services and co-author and literary manager are also explored. Cumming's position as college instructor, his current pursuits as composer and teacher, and his performances as composer complete the biography. The remainder of the chapter consists of an overview of Cumming's works for solo voice, chorus and opera, orchestra and chamber ensemble, solo piano, theater, film, television, and radio. The chapter concludes with a brief look at stylistic traits inherent in Cumming's music.

Chapter Three provides an extensive examination of Cumming's twenty-four preludes. It begins with an introductory section which highlights the compositional climate in which the preludes were conceived by discussing compositional forerunners and stylistic influences, the world premiere in New York City, subsequent performances, and the critical acclaim the work has received. The pedagogical and performance analysis consists of three steps for each prelude: a brief formal analysis, identifying structural selections and tonal areas of each piece; interpretive comments; and questions to help prepare each piece for performance. Musical examples are incorporated within the text.

Chapter Four includes a summary and a list of recommendations for further study. The summary consists of a biographical sketch, with a look at influences, stylistic traits, and concluding comments concerning the preludes. Following the bibliography, seven appendixes provide lists of interview questions, discographies of Cumming as both pianist and composer, a catalog of works by Cumming, two unpublished alternate versions of *Prelude No. 9 in E Major,* photographs, selected concert programs, and the composer's analysis of *Prelude No. 5 in D Major.*

Kinderman, William. *Beethoven's Diabelli Variations.* New York: Oxford University Press, 1987, 244 p. Greatly enhances our understanding of this great set of variations. Based on the author's doctoral dissertation.

King, Robert A., Jr. *A Study of Tomas Svoboda's* Nine Etudes in Fugue Style for Piano, Op. 44. D.M.A. paper, Eugene: University of Oregon, 1993, 188 p. UM 9402026. The study is in five parts: an introduction, which includes a description of the etudes, the goals of the study, and the methods used; an interview with Tomas Svoboda, including a brief biography, biographical questions, and general and specific questions regarding the etudes; analysis of the etudes; pianistic challenges and recommendations; and conclusions. The interview with Svoboda, along with published biographical information and sources on piano technique, provides support for the study.

Kirby, F. E. *Music for Piano: A Short History.* Foreword by Maurice Hinson. Portland, Oreg.: Amadeus Press, 1995, 466 p. Includes bibliographical references and index. This is a completely rewritten and updated version of the author's *A Short History of Keyboard Music.* This new version focuses only on piano music. The section on twentieth-century piano music is especially interesting. Contains perceptive insights and superb documentation. An excellent text for piano literature courses.

Kirk, Kenneth Patrick. *The Golden Ratio in Chopin's* Preludes, Opus 28. Ph.D. dissertation, University of Cincinnati, 1987, 145 p. UM 8712729. Each of the 24 Preludes, Op. 28, of Frédéric Chopin (1810–1849) exhibits a "turning point" (TP) after which the motion of the music is better characterized as toward the end rather than away from the beginning. A model is proposed for the TP. Statistical analysis demonstrates that the proportional placements of the twenty-four TPs cluster around the golden ratio ($p=.618$). The golden ratio is widespread in nature and has been claimed to have artistic significance. The clustering of the TPs and other approximately golden sectioning of the preludes are shown to be important to the form and aesthetic of the preludes.

Kitchens, Melinda Leunette. *Free Polyphonic Texture in Selected Early Piano Works of Robert Schumann.* D.M.A. paper, Tuscaloosa: University of Alabama, 1993, 59 p. UM 9403310. The purpose of this document is to identify free polyphonic texture in selected piano works of Robert Schumann; to determine the extent to which Schumann was influenced by the polyphony of the past; to articulate contrapuntal elements employed by Schumann in his solo piano music and other musical genres; and, finally, to emphasize polyphonic texture as a significant aspect of the composer's style. The project includes a survey, a comparison, an analysis of the texture of Schumann's music, and additional biographical material on the composer's life and works. This project also includes a comparison of Schumann's compositional style with the compositional styles of his contemporaries.

Klein, Andreas. *The Chopin "Etudes": An Indispensable Pedagogical Tool for Developing Piano Technique.* D.M.A. paper, Houston: Rice University, 1989, 88 p. UM 9012816. Today's pianists perform with a high degree of technical efficiency and versatility demanded by the recording industry and expected by audiences worldwide. The piano student with aspiration toward a major performing career needs to develop such a standard of skill in order to find recognition in the competitive musical scene. It is the obligation of every pedagogue to introduce specific pieces to the student at the appropriate time to give him or her a calculated technical challenge. Even though exercises are usually a prominent part of the systematic training, most students dislike practicing them because they are mechanical and worthless toward building a performance repertoire. In addition, too much emphasis on technical studies will lead the student to think that skill is the most important goal of practicing. Therefore, the teacher has to find pieces which stimulate technical progress and feature musical beauty at the same time.

The twenty-seven Etudes by Chopin represent a collection of pieces which contain many technical and musical tasks. Compared to other etudes written in the early nineteenth century (e.g., by Czerny, Moscheles, Hiller, and Thalberg), they have earned superiority through their many pianistic and musical innovations. Because the Chopin Etudes were written over many years, they feature many similarities to other works by the composer, which facilitates their performance. In addition, the thorough study of these etudes will give the pianist the necessary skill to deal with many other technical problems in late classical and romantic pieces. The Chopin Etudes are not suitable for the beginner. However, when the student has acquired proficiency with arpeggios, trills, and scales in the Baroque and Classical repertoire, the Chopin Etudes will not only serve to expand the technical ability, but can be added to the performance repertoire as well.

Kline, Donna Staley. *Olga Samaroff Stokowski: An American Virtuoso on the World Stage.* College Station: Texas A & M University Press, 1996, 288 p. Kline looks at Samaroff, one of America's greatest piano teachers, from many angles: her family background and musical training, her recordings, her newspaper career, her great teaching success, the Schubert Memorial competition, the Layman's Music Courses, lecturing, and the media. Many former students were interviewed, and Stokowski is revealed through the eyes of these students. A fine documentation of this remarkable visionary.

Knafo, Claudio. *Tradition and Innovation: Balances Within the Piano Sonatas of Alberto Ginastera.* D.M.A. paper, Boston University, 1994, 115 p. UM 9424870. The three piano sonatas of Alberto Ginastera represent the composer's early and late periods; therefore, they offer insight into his compositional process. The popularity of Sonata No. 1 paralyzed Ginastera to the extent that he did not write the Sonata No. 2 until thirty years later. The three works reveal Ginastera's ability in creating synthesis of traditional techniques with the musical language of his native Argentina. Strong rhythms, folklike thematic material, and the influence of nature are incorporated into a strong architectural design.

Koch, Karen Kuhfuss. *A Rationale and Materials for Introducing Music History to Intermediate Piano Students.* M.M. thesis, St. Louis: Webster University, 1986, 38 p. UM 1329136. Piano students between the ages of eight and fourteen need music history information as a framework for assimilating musical and cultural information. Educational rationale, curriculum, and materials inspired by the ideas of Maria Montessori promote acquisition of a skeletal framework of important information at these ages. Parameters of this basic framework include dates and a few defining characteristics and personages of importance to keyboard music during four historical periods (Baroque, Classical, Romantic, and Twentieth Century). By beginning with an overview of the whole time period, students have a schema with which to classify and learn details. Four types of learning materials are included. These materials include a room-size time line, matching games, student notebook materials, and cassettes of intermediate piano literature organized by historical period.

Koehler, William Alan. *The Late Independent Keyboard Rondos of Carl Philipp Emanuel Bach.* D.M.A. paper, Austin: University of Texas, 1986, 102 p. UM 8700318. The treatise views a small but important group of Carl Philipp Emanuel Bach's keyboard works, the late rondos, against the background of the historical development of the rondo form in theory and practice. Chapter One investigates the evolution of the rondo concept from 1702 to 1802 through excerpts from treatises and dictionaries of the period. Chapter Two is a survey of selected keyboard rondos written in France, Italy, and Germany between c. 1650 and 1790. Chapter Three discusses Bach's keyboard rondos and includes analyses that view the works empirically rather than force them arbitrarily into pre-existing formal conceptions. Specific problems of performance practice are addressed in Chapter Four, and concluding comments evaluate the rondos' strengths and weaknesses.

Koh, Boyoung Yum. *Ravel's "Le Tombeau de Couperin": A Study of the Work and its Historical Significance.* D.M.A. paper, University of Miami, 1986, 88 p. UM 8706499. A study of the related literature has shown that French composers traditionally wrote pieces in tribute to their predecessors or colleagues. Ravel followed this tradition by writing *Le Tombeau de Couperin* in the form and style of the Baroque and Classical periods. Also, this work relates to early-twentieth-century Neoclassicism. Therefore, *Le Tombeau de Couperin* is a synthesis of the French tombeau tradition and Neoclassicism. This paper discusses the historical significance of the work and Ravel's pianistic style by analyzing the formal, harmonic, and melodic aspects of *Le Tombeau de Couperin*. This study surveys the works which are in the French tombeau tradition or are related to twentieth-century Neoclassicism. Performance problems with *Le Tombeau de Couperin* are discussed in conjunction with Ravel's pianistic and technical aspects. A comparison with the orchestral transcription of *Le Tombeau de Couperin* reveals Ravel's conception of orchestral tone colors and their application to this work.

Komlós, Katalin. *Eighteenth-Century Pianos and Their Music: Germany, Austria, and England, 1760–1800.* New York: Oxford University Press, 1995, 256 p. Includes bibliographical references and index. Concentrates on the keyboard writing of the last third of the eighteenth century, as inspired by the fundamentally different constructions of the German/Viennese and the English pianoforte. Also provides a description of late-eighteenth-century performing styles.

———. *Fortepianos and Their Music: Germany, Austria, and England,*

1760–1800. Oxford: Clarendon Press, 1995, 147 p. This short book is important as it covers the history, music, and performance practices of the instrument. The interrelationships of composers, instruments, and performers of the first forty years of the fortepiano are carefully discussed. It is an excellent guide to use with the London Pianoforte series (edited by N. Temperley). A fine bibliography adds to the usefulness of this excellent resource.

————. *The Viennese Keyboard Trio in the 1780s: Studies in Texture and Instrumentation.* Ph.D. dissertation. Ithaca: Cornell University, 1986, 2 vols., 501 p. UM 8607338. This study deals with questions of texture, instrumentation, and form in the keyboard trios published in Vienna between 1780 and 1790. This repertoire comprises seventy known works by eight composers: Clementi, Joseph Haydn, Hoffmeister, Kozeluch, W. A. Mozart, Pleyel, Sterkel, and Vanhal. In style and technique, the trios by Clementi, Hoffmeister, Kozeluch, Pleyel, Sterkel, and Vanhal range from modest works for amateurs to pretentious and virtuosic works apparently intended for performance by professionals. The more familiar works of Haydn and Mozart take on a new aspect when understood in the context of the hitherto unknown works of their contemporaries.

The analytical procedures examine the functional relationships of the three instruments in the ensemble, in terms both of their textural variety and the relations of these textures to musical form. In general, the keyboard instrument is most prominent; the roles of the strings vary widely. In nearly all the works, the intended keyboard instrument seems to have been the fortepiano, not the harpsichord. The violin tends to remain subordinate, but not infrequently it functions as an equal partner of the keyboard, and occasionally it even becomes the soloist of the whole ensemble.

The common notion that, before Beethoven, only Mozart's trios include independent cello parts is incorrect. About one-half of the repertoire exhibits primarily continuolike cello parts which double the keyboard left hand; this includes Haydn, whose cello writing, however, is rhythmically and registrally independent, and is an essential component of the sound of the ensemble. The other half, however, including Mozart, features partially or wholly independent lines in the cello. Unlike Mozart and Haydn, the other composers vary the weight and function of the cello considerably, even within a single opus. Pleyel and Sterkel write completely independent, even concertante cello parts. Thus, the texture of the Viennese keyboard trio in the 1780s, as a whole, represents a fairly advanced stage in the development of the genre during the Classical period. A thematic catalog of the trios in the repertoire by the composers other than Haydn and Mozart appears as an appendix. Volume II contains a complete work by each of these six composers.

Kong, Joanne Lan-Funn. *A Comparison of the Technical and Interpretive Qualities of the Piano and Harpsichord, Accompanied by Performance Editions of the Chromatic Fantasy and Fugue (BWV 903) by Johann Sebastian Bach.* D.M.A. paper, Eugene: University of Oregon, 1986, 152 p. UM 8629566. The purpose of this study, as outlined in the introduction, is to provide keyboardists with a thorough understanding of the technical and interpretative aspects of harpsichord and piano performance. This information is particularly useful for pianists, as a significant portion of their repertoire includes works of Johann Sebastian Bach which were originally conceived for the harpsichord. It is the premise of this paper that, despite their differences, the unique musical qualities of both the piano and harpsichord can be knowledgeably applied to produce stylistically convincing performances of Baroque keyboard music.

   The comparison of piano and harpsichord playing begins with an examination of the instruments' physical characteristics, included in Chapter One, Physical Properties of the Harpsichord, and Chapter Two, Physical Properties of the Piano. These chapters compare the actions, construction, and acoustical properties of the two instruments. Chapter Three, Technique, consists of a detailed discussion of the keyboardist's playing mechanism and of the ways in which a basic keyboard technique can be effectively adapted to the contrasting physical properties of the piano and harpsichord. Discussions about the interpretative aspects of harpsichord and piano performance are included in Chapter Four, Rhythm and Phrasing, Chapter Five, Tone Quality and Dynamics, Chapter Six, Articulation, and Chapter Seven, Fingering. Descriptions of the specific musical resources of each instrument, illustrated with numerous musical examples, are provided. A brief survey of historical and current trends in the performance of Bach's works is given in Chapter Eight, Performance of J. S. Bach's Music on the Harpsichord and Piano.

Koosin, Timothy Victor. *The Solo Piano Works of Toru Takemitsu: A Linear/Set-Theoretic Analysis.* Ph.D. dissertation, University of Cincinnati, 1989, 316 p. UM 8917941. Prior to Japan's recovery from the Second World War, Japanese composers were polarized into two opposing groups, one which rejected indigenous Japanese modes of musical expression to emulate Western models, and a "nationalistic school," which attempted to graft traditional Oriental elements on to Western forms. By the 1950s, however, traditional distinctions between Japanese and Western music began to be obscured as Japanese composers mastered an international musical vocabulary and achieved a new sense of artistic confidence. Toru Takemitsu (b. 1930) is the foremost representative of this new era in Japanese musical composition. This analysis focuses on Takemitsu's complete published works for solo piano, a significant and little-studied body of music which spans thirty years of the composer's creative output.

The first chapter provides historical perspective, tracing developments in modern Japanese music from the influx of Western influence during the Meiii Restoration to the activities of Takemitsu and his contemporaries during the past three decades. The second chapter explores how elements of traditional Japanese art and philosophy have been shaped by Japanese conceptions of time. Examples from the piano works are cited to describe how Takemitsu employs modern Western musical materials to construct a characteristically Japanese temporal image.

In the analyses which follow, musical surface features are related to global forces of linear and vertical pitch organization. Structural graphs are used to represent large-scale linear connections projected through contextual emphasis on focal pitch-classes. The study traces Takemitsu's developments of an additive process by which linear and vertical structures are built up from octatonic-referential cells. In Takemitsu's most recent solo piano pieces, *Les yeux clos* (1979) and *Rain Tree Sketch* (1982), local and global pitch relations are generated through an interpenetration of references to octatonic and whole-tone collections. In these works, Takemitsu creates continuity and variety through octatonic and whole-tone references without conforming to the tonal limitations of either collection, creating a subtle and original pitch structure which is free and yet true to a contextually defined internal logic.

Kopelson, Kevin. *Beethoven's Kiss: Pianism, Perversion, and the Mastery of Desire.* Stanford, Calif.: Stanford University Press, 1996, 198

p. The publisher says of this book: " . . . problems posed by the key players —erotic anxieties of musical amateurs, sexual myths concerning child prodigies, prurient interests in leading virtuosos. Castrating figurations of 'maiden' piano teachers . . . the piano resonates with intimations of both homosexuality and mortality."

Kottick, Edward L., and George Lucktenberg. *Early Keyboard Instruments in European Museums.* Bloomington: Indiana University Press, 1997, 276 p. The reader is directed to unusual holdings of sixteen countries, thirty-five cities, and forty-seven museums. More than 100 photographs show the varied styles of construction. Contributions of important makers such as Broadwood, Dulcken, Graf, Kirkman, the Silbermanns, Stein, Walter, and others make this volume unique. Also includes a glossary of technical terms and an index of makers.

Kowalchyk, Gayle. *A Descriptive Profile of Piano Pedagogy Instructors at American Colleges and Universities.* Ed.D. dissertation, New York: Columbia University Teachers College, 1989, 135 p. UM 8913117. Although piano pedagogy is firmly established in the college and university curriculum, research in this area has focused on the curriculum itself and not on the person who is teaching piano pedagogy courses. The purpose of the study is to develop a descriptive profile of piano pedagogy instructors at American colleges and universities. The profile includes personal information, educational background, teaching experience, and current teaching responsibilities. Based upon data from those currently teaching in the field, recommendations for the training of future piano pedagogy instructors are offered. Comparisons are made between those who teach at institutions offering degrees in piano pedagogy and those who teach at institutions not offering degrees in piano pedagogy.

The data was collected through a questionnaire sent to the 558 piano pedagogy instructors at American colleges and universities listed in the 1986–1988 *College Music Society Directory.* The results were based on data from 279 questionnaires. The results show that the typical piano pedagogy instructor is female and between the ages of 46 and 55. She has a master's degree in piano performance and holds a full-time appointment at the level of associate professor. She has 24.5 years of piano-teaching experience and has taught piano pedagogy for 10.6 years. Piano pedagogy is 24 percent or less of her collegiate teaching load.

Recommendations include that the profession address the training of future piano pedagogy instructors and that research be conducted in the following areas: the changing keyboard technology and its impact on piano teaching and piano pedagogy, the actual course content of piano pedagogy courses, and the design and implementation of a course specifically concerned with how to teach piano pedagogy.

Kramer, Dean Fredric. *The Old School and the New School: A Comparative Study in the Art of Interpreting Piano Music.* D.M.A. paper, Austin: University of Texas, 1992, 320 p. UM 9239201. This treatise discusses various changes in the interpretation of piano music during the past hundred years and studies the lives and the recorded interpretations of five outstanding pianists in order to discover large patterns in the evolution of the art of interpretation. The pianists chosen for the study are Sergey Rachmaninoff (1873–1943), Artur Schnabel (1882–1951), Arthur Rubinstein (1887–1982), Alfred Brendel (b. 1931), and Vladimir Ashkenazy (b. 1937). The first part of the treatise presents brief biographies of the pianists under discussion. The biographical information given is very condensed and selective, focusing primarily on the development of each pianist as an interpreter.

Kraus, Richard. *Pianos and Politics in China: Middle-Class Ambitions and the Struggle over Western Culture.* New York: Oxford University Press, 1989, 288 p. Presents the story of China's urban middle class and its music through biographies of four Chinese musicians whose careers embody the contradictions of China's response to Western culture. Kraus explores the lives of composer Xian Xinghai and virtuoso pianists Fou Ts'ong, Yin Chengzong, and Liu Shikun to illustrate China's place at the furthest edge of an expanding international order. The piano provides an apt metaphor for Western cultural influence in China.

Kreaky, Jeffrey. *A Reading Guide to the Chopin Preludes.* Westport, Conn.: Greenwood Press, 1994, 130 p. This helpful interpretative concordance is a combination of analysis, musings, and opinion. Includes bibliographical references.

Kuo, Tsong-Kai. *Chiang Wen-Yeh: The Style of His Selected Piano Works and a Study of Music Modernization in Japan and China.* D.M.A. paper, Columbus: Ohio State University, 1987, 202 p. UM 8726582.

Chiang Wen-Yeh, a Taiwanese pioneer in the early development of modern Chinese music, was born in 1910 and studied in Japan in 1923. In 1938, he moved to Beijing, where he died in 1983. He was one of the most productive and active composers, whose compositions won several national and international competitions in Japan during the 1930s and 1940s. His early works were strongly influenced by Bartók, Prokofiev, his teacher Tcherepnin, and Debussy; his later works demonstrated Chinese nationalism. His music exhibited originality and creativity in the assimilation of musical styles between East and West.

The historical context of the Japanese and Chinese music environment that led to the formation of Chiang Wen-Yeh's musical style is investigated. Also discussed are the musical conflicts between East and West and how Chiang solved the problems in his compositional style.

Kvarnstrom, Jonas Erik. *A Structural Analysis of George Enescu's* Piano Sonata in D Major, *Op. 24, No. 3.* D.Mus. paper, Vancouver: University of British Columbia, 1992, 60 p. UM NN 75394. Enescu, a contemporary of Bartók and Kodály, found himself caught in the current of nationalism that asserted itself in Europe during the first decades of the twentieth century. Seeking a personal, expressive idiom in which he could fuse the musical elements of both Western tradition and his native Romanian folk heritage, Enescu experimented with diverse compositional trends and styles.

The focus of this paper is to examine to what extent these compositional techniques are incorporated into Enescu's work and to direct attention to those elements, i.e., both structural and non-structural, that were most distinctive of his musical style. Owing to its concentration of key stylistic elements and its stature as perhaps the most accomplished piano composition in Enescu's output, the *Sonata for Piano in D Major,* Op. 24, No. 3 (1934) serves as the model for this analytical study.

Lai, Li-Chin. *"Variations on a Theme by Robert Schumann," Op. 20 by Clara Schumann: An Analytical and Interpretative Study.* D.M.A. paper, Philadelphia : Temple University, 1992, 123 p. UM 9302128. Clara Schumann is recognized as one of the foremost female composers of her time, yet analytical studies of her music are lacking. This monograph, therefore, focuses on one of her finest compositions, *Varia-*

tions on a Theme by Robert Schumann, Op. 20, for piano (1853, published in 1854). The work is conservative in its approach to variation form, but it may be admired for its clarity of texture, lyricism, tonal color, and elegance of style.

The study provides performance practice recommendations, especially as they relate to the analytical discussion. Performance suggestions are also based upon Clara Schumann's own teaching methods and pianistic style.

Landon, Robbins H. C. *The Mozart Companion.* New York: Schirmer Books, 1990, 452 p. This compendium touches on nearly every facet of Mozart's personal and professional life: the influence of his father, his emotional attachment to his wife, musical patronage in Vienna, his virtuosity on the keyboard and the violin, and his personal attitudes toward death. It includes a chronological survey of his music, a glossary, and an index.

Lane, David H. *A Book for Music Teachers.* Bryn Mawr, Pa.: Theodore Presser, 1987, 80 p. This book will reinspire flagging spirits and also hone the skills and sensibilities of those whose enthusiasm has never dulled. More oriented toward the public school music teacher, it discusses many points applicable to the private teacher.

Lang, Bertha F. *Practice Does Not Make Perfect—Only Correct Practice Does.* Wakefield, N.H.: Hollowbrook Pub., 1992.

Laor, Lia. *Piano Pedagogy (1800–1850): History and Methodology.* Ph.D. dissertation, Tel-Aviv University, 1989, 263 p. A consideration of the evolution of piano pedagogy, 1800–1850, and a discussion of various pedagogical methods, analyzing the educational options they provide for teacher and student. The ideas of Rousseau, Kant, Hegel, and Jean Paul (Johann Paul Friedrich Richter) on education and the way in which they were applied by leading educators of the time, such as Johann Heinrich Pestalozzi and Claude-Adrien Helvétius, are discussed. Since modern piano pedagogy is founded largely on nineteenth-century methods, this study should have implications for current practice. Summary in Hebrew.

Laredo, Ruth. *The Ruth Laredo Becoming A Musician Book.* Valley Forge, Pa.: European American Music Corporation, 1992, 72 p. A guide for the aspiring pianist. Laredo describes how to warm up and how to practice, talks about her teachers, and gives lessons on Chopin's Etudes.

Larsen, Janeen Jess. *Teaching Basic Jazz Piano Skills to Classically Trained Adult Pianists: A Mastery Learning Approach.* Ph.D. dissertation, Gainesville: University of Florida, 1986, 261 p. UM 8704186. This is a descriptive study of the sequential process used by this investigator for the development of a short course in basic jazz piano skills. The problem of this study is whether systematic, linear procedures could be used in the development, design, and evaluation of a course involving creative subject matter. The development of the course was based upon a three-stage model suggested by Markle, the design of the course was based upon the mastery learning theory of Carroll and Bloom, and the evaluation of the course was based upon the formative-summative evaluation theory of Scriven. The course was intended for group instruction of classically trained adult pianists. The process of course development was undertaken over a two-year time span and consisted of a sequence of prototypical workshops in jazz piano. Each workshop was evaluated and revised in order to produce the final methodology for teaching the course.

Summative evaluation data were collected during the final stage of course development (a five-week, fifteen-hour workshop in basic jazz piano skills). The data indicated that most students achieved success at improvisation in a jazz context and were able to acquire skills in using seventh chords. All students attained a mastery score on an exam which tested cognitive knowledge of the jazz idiom. Participation in a carefully structured, developmental sequence of activities provided in a group situation had a positive effect on all students' attitudes toward their improvisational ability.

This study provides detailed lesson plans and evaluation materials for a sequence of activities that will enable classically trained adult pianists to acquire a selected set of basic jazz piano skills in a short amount of time. The viability of linear systems of course development and design is also demonstrated, and new information about the applicability of mastery learning theory to the field of music education is provided. This study will serve as a useful model for music educators interested in developing their own curriculum materials, and it will provide valuable information for teachers and students of jazz piano.

Lasarenko, Kim Andrei. *A Style Change in Rachmaninoff's Piano Music as Seen in the "Second Piano Sonata in B-Flat Minor, Opus 36" (1913* *and 1931 Versions).* D.M.A. paper, Columbus: Ohio State University, 1988, 101 p. UM 8813376. Rachmaninoff's piano music underwent a style change during the middle period of his career. The document shows this style change by means of a comparative examination of the *Second Sonata in B-flat minor* in the original (1913) and the revised editions (1931). A brief biography is included that chronicles the major events in Rachmaninoff's life and discusses the type of training that Rachmaninoff received as a child.

A discussion of the formal structure of both versions is presented along with a schematic analysis. The change of style is revealed through a comparative examination of both structure and revisions of texture. Included in the comparative discussion of textures is an examination of the problems of performance found in both versions of the sonata, and some possible solutions to these problems are offered.

The conclusion of the document recapitulates the differences of structure and texture found in the comparative examination of the sonata. A discussion concerning the advantages and disadvantages of performing either version is also presented. As a result, a third version, a personal performance version consisting of a combination of the 1913 and 1931 editions, is presented.

Layton, Robert, ed. *A Companion to the Piano Concerto.* London: Christopher Helm, Ltd., 1988, 369 p. This book offers a survey of the growth and development of the concerto form from its origins in the seventeenth century to the present day. Written by a team of internationally renowned scholars and critics under the editorship of Robert Layton, the analyses are original and penetrating. It includes concerti for all media, but the piano concerto receives the most emphasis.

Leach, Francis Orin. *The Dances for Solo Piano of Paul Creston: A Pedagogical and Performance Overview.* D.M.A. paper, Norman: University of Oklahoma, 1994, 149 p. UM 950179. The purpose of this document is to provide a pedagogical and performance overview of four solo piano works by Paul Creston: *Five Dances for Piano,* Op. 1 (1950), *Five Little Dances for the Piano,* Op. 24 (1946), *Prelude and Dance,* Op. 29, No. 1 (1942), and *Prelude and Dance,* Op. 29, No. 2 (1942). This study is intended to serve as a reference work for teachers and students of contemporary piano literature.

A pedagogical and performance overview of the chosen works includes three steps: a brief formal overview identifying structural sections and tonal areas of each piece, a study and practice guide that includes the identification of technical pianistic problems and specific practice directions, and performance questions for the student to help prepare each piece for performance.

LeClair, Lynn Bridget. *An Historical and Comparative Study of the Influences of Edvard Grieg and Robert Schumann on the Piano Studies of Edward MacDowell.* M.M. thesis, University of Cincinnati, 1994, 74 p. UM 1375048. The music of Edward MacDowell was heavily influenced by several composers, but evidence of the greatest influence can be found in the piano music of Edvard Grieg and Robert Schumann. Historical and nonmusical influences also exist, such as the shared admiration and correspondence between Grieg and MacDowell. The short piano works of Grieg, Schumann, and MacDowell serve as an informative body of material in which to prove the influence in question. The following parameters are addressed: programmatic titles, formal structure, textural similarities, harmonic idiosyncrasies, and rhythmic tendencies. In conclusion, the attitudes of these composers concerning various topics, as well as parallels in their practical life, are explored to further clarify similarities.

Lee, Chen-Tien. *Mussorgsky's "Pictures at an Exhibition": An Analytical and Performance Study.* D.M.A. paper, Columbus: Ohio State University, 1993, 123 p. UM 9325438. The document is organized into four chapters. Chapter One introduces Mussorgsky's personal background and his achievements in composition, and Hartmann's personal background and his significance as an architect, painter, and stage designer. Chapter Two contains the compositional backgrounds of "Pictures at an Exhibition," including the original piano version of Mussorgsky and the orchestrated version by Ravel.

Chapter Three discusses sections from the suite, including the literary references of the "Pictures" and analyzes the music in terms of structural, melodic, harmonic, and rhythmic characteristics. Chapter Four discusses some of the technical problems encountered with the suite by the author during preparation for public performance.

Lee, Esther Yee-Wah. *A Formal and Stylistic Study of the Chopin Etudes.* Thesis, Seattle: University of Washington, 1965.

Lee, Eun Young. *Fugues for Piano in the Early Nineteenth Century.*

D.M.A. paper, Austin: University of Texas, 1994, 214 p. UM 9428432. This treatise concentrates on the piano fugue written during the earlier part of the nineteenth century. In the first chapter, there is a discussion of the general historical background. Chapter Two is devoted to ten individual composers, containing the biographical information relating to each composer's fugal composition, a general discussion of his or her fugal writing, a list of his or her fugal compositions for piano, and analyses of representative works. The concluding chapter deals with the general aspects of fugal writing in the early nineteenth century. The appendix includes a comprehensive list of fugues written for the piano from approximately 1790 to 1860.

Lee, Myung-Sook. *The Solo Piano Music of George Perle: A Performance Guide.* Ph.D. dissertation, New York University, 1991, 340 p. UM 9134757. This dissertation offers biographical information about George Perle and presents a brief overview of ten of the composer's published piano works. A lengthy and detailed discussion is devoted to the analysis of piano works from each of the composer's stylistic phases. The works analyzed are *Pantomime, Interlude, and Fugue* (1937), *Toccata* (1969), and *Ballade* (1982). The analysis of each piece is divided according to categories of form, sound, harmony, melody, and rhythm. An extensive performance guide is presented for each piece.

Lee, Sun Kyung. *Bartók's Unfolding Performance History: A Comparative and Critical Review.* D.M.A. paper, Boston University, 1994, 177 p. UM 9415028. Béla Bartók (1881–1945) left several recordings of his own piano music from 1912 to 1945. This document examines differences between Bartók's scores and his recordings, classifies the changes, and shows how they affect compositional structure. The changes include incidental, "ossia" type, and "informality," which is defined as a notational convention that can be altered as needed by a performer depending on the written context. This document also provides a detailed analysis of two pieces by comparing interpretations by Bartók and other pianists.

Lee, Tze Fung Alfred. *Tonal Perspectives in the Selected Piano Preludes of Shostakovich (Op. 34: Nos. 1, 3, 6, 14, and 24): An Analytical Study.* M.A. thesis, Denton: University of North Texas, 1994, 59 p. UM 1358736. This study is an investigation of tonal structures in selected preludes of Shostakovich's Op. 34. Explanations and analytic perspectives provide support of tonality-oriented interpretation for the compositions which often appear to be "atonal." Chapter One is divided into historical perspectives of the prelude as form and a summary of Shostakovich's life and work. Chapter Two contains a historical background of the development of Shostakovich's compositional styles, emphasizing his early style of piano composition, and the impact of his "Lady Macbeth," the Crisis, and its influence on later works. Chapter Three deals with the problems of and analytical approaches in the study of the selected preludes.

Le Guerrier, Claire. *The Physical Aspects of Piano Playing.* New York: Vantage Press, 1987, 93 p. Chapters: Finger Exercises, The Fingers, From Thumb to Fingerings, The Hand, The Joints, Digital Pressure, Posture at the Piano, Conclusion, and Bibliography. This book is based mainly on C. P. E. Bach's *Essay on the True Art of Playing Keyboard Instruments.*

Lehrer, Charles-David. *The Nineteenth Century Parisian Concerto.* Ph.D. dissertation, Los Angeles: University of California, 1990, 634 p. UM 9028386. During the early years of the nineteenth century, composers throughout Europe gradually began to alter the accepted Classical style structure of the concerto. No group of musicians was more vigorous in bringing about change in that medium than the dynasty of composers initiated by Pierre Rode and Antoine-Joseph Reicha in Paris. This family, with its roots in the great establishments of the Paris Opera and Conservatoire, eventually produced such artists as Franz Liszt, Henryk Wieniawski, Gabriel Fauré, and Camille Saint-Saëns.

In order to understand the compositional procedures of this great Parisian family, the author analyzed ninety of their concertos. Autograph manuscripts, nineteenth-century orchestral parts, and twentieth-century editions, primarily from the holdings of the Bibliothèque Nationale in Paris and the New York Public Library, were utilized for this purpose. The result has been the discovery that the Parisians used six additional approaches for the composition concertos beyond their unique version of the three-movement Classical Style.

The initial chapter acquaints the reader with terminology and models for each of seven Parisian concerto styles. These are designated as Classical Style Types I and II, Scena Style, French Romantic Style Types I and II, and German Romantic Style Types I and II. The next five chapters present the ninety concertos within the context of nineteenth-century French history, stretching from the Napoleonic Era to the early years of the Third Republic. Each of these chapters begins with an overview of a specific period and a summation of the various concerto styles which were in use in Paris at the time. The works of individual composers are then discussed in detail.

Leikin, Anatoly. *The Dissolution of Sonata Structure in Romantic Piano Music (1820–1850)*. Ph.D. dissertation, Los Angeles: University of California, 1986, 295 p. UM 8621101. The piano music composed during the first half of the nineteenth century retains its perennial popularity, both in the concert hall and at home. Paradoxically, such popularity has not translated into corresponding scholarly attention. Romantic forms, and particularly sonata form, head the list of neglected —or even disparaged—issues. Traditionally, Romantic sonata form has been viewed as the Achilles heel of Romantic music. However, the particularities (or, as some might say, the peculiarities) of nineteenth-century forms fit into an orderly evolutionary process that bespeaks a self-conscious, purposeful effort on the part of the composers.

This investigation focuses on the piano music of three central figures in the early Romantic movement: Franz Schubert, Robert Schumann, and Frédéric Chopin (when appropriate, music of other composers and genres is included). Their treatment of sonata form reveals an intentional blending of sonata elements and their functions, as well as of the entire recapitulatory and developmental traits. For example, a sonata form could merge with variation, etc. This dissolution of sonata structure grew both out of the nineteenth-century reaction against an excessive formal predictability and out of the Romantic obsession with ambiguity.

Four methodological approaches inform this study. The first is a semiotic approach to music, viewing it as an act of communication. This goes a long way toward clarifying the so-called problem of normative standards in music, including that of the sonata pattern. Second, principles of general system theory help to illuminate sonata structure as a complex organism whose elements are interrelated through their functional characteristics, while the whole system interacts with its environment. Third, the manner in which the analyses of specific musical works are conducted is indebted to a modern Russian school of music theory, especially to what is known as "integral analysis." Finally, in spite of the apparent abstractness of the first two approaches, each and every analysis here is aimed squarely at the practical needs of the listener, the performer, and the teacher.

Lemons, Christopher Hoyt. *The Keyboard Concertos of Georg Mathias Monn.* Ph.D. dissertation, Evanston, Ill.: Northwestern University, 1991, 924 p. UM 9129022. Although G. M. Monn's groundbreaking work with the symphony has long been acknowledged, his eleven keyboard concertos have attracted little attention and are commonly thought to be conservative works. Unlike Monn's symphonies, no modern editions of his keyboard concertos have appeared to correct such an impression. After describing the sources and their authenticity, this study presents substantial excerpts from every movement of each concerto together with an analysis of the form, harmony, and thematic structure of each movement.

Letnanova, Elena. *Piano Interpretation of the Seventeenth, Eighteenth and Nineteenth Centuries.* Jefferson, N.C.: McFarland & Co., 1991, 208 p. Focuses on how to interpret music of another century. The author has compiled a detailed analysis of such keyboard "methods" as existed in Europe in the seventeenth, eighteenth, and nineteenth centuries. Theoretical works of C. P. E. Bach, Türk, J. S. Bach, Mozart, Chopin, Liszt, Kullak, and Lussy are discussed, with English translation.

Leung, Jackson Yi-Shun. *A Selective Study of Sonata-Fantasies in the First Half of the Nineteenth Century.* D.M.A. paper, University of Cincinnati, 1990, 150 p. UM 9108731. By the mid-1770s the Viennese Classical Sonata had evolved into a more or less standardized structure. This multimovement form became the most expansive, well-proportioned, closely knit, and expressive musical structure for the keyboard. The development of the eighteenth-century fantasy can be traced in the works of J. S. Bach, C. P. E. Bach, and Mozart. Several aspects prevail in these fantasies, including improvisatory passages, scales and arpeggios, virtuosic and declamatory passage-work, sectional structure, recitative-like sections, and rich and daring modulations.

Up to the end of the eighteenth century, the sonata and the fantasy had been kept apart except for the introductory fantasy. The two musical structures clearly contrast with each other—the Classical sonata had a well-defined structural basis, with a fairly rigid key scheme, whereas the fantasy from the same period provided composers with the opportunity to express their flights of fancy without a certain formal design or a strict harmonic structure.

The most explicit association of the two forms came when Beethoven wrote his Sonatas, Op. 27, Nos. 1 and 2, both of which bear the description "Sonata quasi una fantasia." Beethoven's idea of equating the two strikingly contrasted formal structures and the fusion of their principal characteristics was taken up by other composers in the first half of the nineteenth century.

Of the five works discussed in this thesis, three (the two Beethoven sonatas and the Liszt "Dante Sonata") were published with the inscription "Sonata quasi una fantasia" or "fantasia quasi una sonata." The other two (Mendelssohn, Op. 28 and Schumann, Op. 17) were originally conceived as sonatas and later published as fantasias. The combination of these two forms indicates the current trend of infusing fantasy elements into other genres such as the sonata, string quartet, symphony, opera, and oratorio. The change of title from sonata to fantasy also signifies the originality, free imagination, experimentation, and symbolism of these works. These works also exemplify the slow, gradual transformation of stylistic traits that took place at the beginning of the nineteenth century.

Lewis, Leonne Jan. *Robert Schumann's Symphonic Etudes, opus 13*. M.A. thesis, Long Beach: California State University, 1986, 64 p. UM 1328928. Robert Schumann's most creative period of piano composition extended from 1834 through 1844. During the years 1834 to 1837, *Symphonic Etudes*, Op. 13 was composed. The purpose of this project is to investigate the historical and stylistic aspects of *Symphonic Etudes*. An introduction presents a historical perspective of Schumann and his contemporaries. Investigation of sources, historical background, and analyses of the variation form and musical style of *Symphonic Etudes* follow in subsequent chapters. A facsimile of an 1835 manuscript of *Symphonic Etudes* appears in Appendix A.

Lewis, Ronald Edwin. *The Solo Piano Music of Frederic Rzewski*. D.M.A. paper, Norman: University of Oklahoma, 1992, 148 p. UM 9311015. Frederic Rzewski has only four published works for solo piano. Rzewski's piano compositions represent a cross-section of contemporary avant-garde music. His major works for solo piano were written beginning in the mid-1970s. He has written seven works for solo piano since his last published work in 1979.

The purpose of this document is to provide an introduction to the solo piano works of Rzewski. The number of works, as well as the complexities found in each, prohibit an in-depth study of each composition in a document such as this. Instead, the author addresses the most important features of each work, and in doing so, develops a synthesis of Rzewski's style as it pertains to his solo piano music.

Lewis, Thomas P., ed. *A Source Guide to the Music of Percy Grainger.* White Plains, N.Y.: Pro/Am Resource Guide, 1991, 356 p. Includes sections on Biographical/Artistic Vignettes, Catalog of Works, Locations of Scores, Program Notes, Discographies, and Books and Articles. Of special interest is the section on program notes which include some of Grainger's performance directions and suggestions for vocal and instrumental treatment.

Lichtenwanger, William. *The Music of Henry Cowell: A Descriptive Catalogue.* I.S.A.M. monograph, New York: Brooklyn College, 1986. A definitive catalog of the music of a highly original and prolific composer. For almost 1,000 works this catalog supplies date and circumstances of composition, instrumentation, text sources, details of first performance, locations and description of manuscripts, and publication information.

Lin, Wen-Ching. *The Scriabin Sound and Style: An Analysis of Twelve Etudes, Opus 8.* D.M.A. paper, University of Miami, 1994, 121 p. UM 9432879. This dissertation contains an analysis of Scriabin's musical style; a discussion on the influence of Chopin's music on Scriabin's compositions, especially his early works; and a comparison of Scriabin's Op. 8 to Chopin's Op. 10 and Op. 25. For example, Scriabin followed a precedent set by Chopin for using triple metric units, to which Scriabin confined himself exclusively. Scriabin developed techniques such as hand stretching and pedaling for performing his works, which require considerable stamina, especially for a pianist who has small hands. In Scriabin's composition for piano in his later period, the influence of Chopin's music was not prevalent. In rhythm, melody, harmony, and form, Scriabin's sound and style became his own.

Lindeman, Stephen D. *Structural Novelty in the Early Romantic Piano Concerto.* Stuyvesant, N.Y.: Pendragon Press, 1998, 500 p. Focuses on the experimental treatment of this genre by J. B. Cramer, C. M. von Weber, Felix Mendelssohn, V. Alkan, Clara Wieck, Robert Schumann, and Franz Liszt. Includes measure-by-measure timeline analyses of the first movements of over 100 concertos (including those of Mozart, Cramer, Beethoven, Hummel, and others) and offers a detailed examination of a critical time in the development of the form.

Lipke, William Alan. *Liszt's "Dante Fantasia": An Historical and Musical Study.* D.M.A. paper, University of Cincinnati, 1990, 137 p. UM 9108574. This study examines the historical, literary, and philosophical context of Franz Liszt's *Après une lecture de Dante, Fantasia quasi sonata* (Dante Fantasia). The study begins by tracing the literary, religious, and musical influences on Liszt from 1811 to 1839. His interest in the works of François-Auguste-René de Chateaubriand and Victor Hugo is discussed with reference to nineteenth-century medievalism, and his belief in the humanitarian role of the artist is linked to his associations with the Saint-Simonist movement and Félicité-Robert de Lamennais.

Liszt's desire to give musical expression to Dante Alighieri's *Divina commedia* is shown to be a reflection of his own artistic ideal, and parallels are drawn between the philosophy of the medieval poem and his own philosophy. The notion of the interrelationship of the arts is set forth as an important aspect of Liszt's thought and is illustrated in an examination of the other works in the *Années de pèlerinage*. The introduction of poetry into the music of the piano is shown to be central to his concept of musical expression at the time and to lead eventually to the actual portrayal of specific poems through symphonic music.

The original and progressive aspects of the work's form, harmony, melody, and pianistic devices are discussed, particularly the dichotomous nature of sonata-fantasy form, the employment of forward-looking techniques of tonal structure and coherence, and the use of thematic metamorphosis. An investigation is made into the history of the work including a review of its premiere and the significance of its evolving title. Evidence is given documenting the association of the work with the *Divina commedia* from its inception to its publication, and the programmatic implications of that association are explored.

Lister-Sink, Barbara. *Freeing the Caged Bird.* Video cassette. P.O. Box 10912, Winston-Salem, NC 27108, 130 minutes. This video provides help in developing a well-coordinated, injury-preventative piano technique. Areas covered include exploration of piano and body mechanisms; a step-by-step training program; potentially harmful technical habits; slow-motion analysis of movement; and a systematic approach to virtuoso technique—how not to accumulate tension. Superb presentation.

Liszt: A Self-Portrait in His Own Words. Comp. David Whitwell. Northridge, Calif.: Winds, 1986, 241 p. Liszt's thoughts on a variety of subjects, drawn from many years and a variety of sources. Part One: Liszt: A Self-Portrait; Part Two: Liszt's View of the World of Music; Part Three: Liszt's Reflections on His Own Music.

Little, Meredith, and Natalie Jenne. *Dance and the Music of J. S. Bach.* Bloomington: Indiana University Press, 1991, 249 p. Bach wrote a great deal of stylized dance music and music based on dance rhythms. Part One describes the French Court dance practice in the cities and towns where Bach lived. Part Two presents the dance forms used by Bach, annotating all of his named dances. Appendix I lists all of Bach's named dances with the BWV number for each piece, date of composition, the larger work in which it appears, the instrumentation, and the meter. Appendix II gives the same data for pieces clearly recognizable as dance types but not named as such. A stimulating look at the rhythmic lifeblood of Bach's incredible repertoire of dance-based music.

Lively, Judy Sharon. *Extra-Musical Associations in Selected Pieces from "Années de Pèlerinage—Troisième Année," by Franz Liszt.* D.M.A. paper, Denton: University of North Texas, 1990, 123 p. UM 9105038. Volumes One and Two of *Années de Pèlerinage* contain travel impressions. The pieces in Volume Three serve as a means of expressing a religious pilgrimage. The religious meaning is implied by the titles and by letters Liszt wrote concerning specific pieces. For the pieces to have programmatic significance, the music must support the verbal clues. This dissertation maintains that selected pieces in *Années de Pèlerinage III* are programmatic and that Liszt provided musical clues that have not been discovered or, if noticed, have not been analyzed in detail. The dissertation also explores similarities between selected pieces of *Années de Pèlerinage III* and other programmatic or texted works by Liszt sharing the same subject. The findings reinforce the premise that Liszt deliberately intended to express certain extra-musical ideas within the music itself.

The paper briefly analyzes the musical reasons for labeling *Années de Pèlerinage III* a cycle. Different sources call these pieces cyclic, citing the shared common religious theme as the reason. This dissertation discusses musical reasons that reinforce the idea of a cycle.

Chapter Two discusses Liszt's views on program music. Chapter Three identifies common themes in Liszt's programmatic works and discusses the symbolic significance of thematic transformation. Chapter Four suggests an approach to analyzing program music. Chapter Five discusses Liszt's musical narrative and his use of common rhetorical devices. Chapter Six analyzes extra-musical associations in selected pieces from the *Années de Pèlerinage—Troisième Année*. Five pieces have been selected for analysis: "Angelus!," "Aux Cyprès de la Villa d'Este" I and II, "Marche funèbre," and "Sursum corda."

Lloyd-Watts, Valery, and Carole L. Bigler, with the assistance of Willard A. Palmer. *Ornamentation: A Question and Answer Manual.* Van Nuys, Calif.: Alfred Publishing Co., 1995, 64 p. This volume presents a clear, concise approach for realizing ornaments in all eras of music. It is an easy-to-understand manual and a succinct and thorough guide for every musician.

Lo, Stephen Yuet-Din. *A Reading Course for Suzuki Piano Students.* Ph.D. dissertation, Lubbock: Texas Tech University, 1993, 214 p. UM 9416618. This dissertation attempts to design a well-balanced reading course for Suzuki students who have completed Volume I of the Suzuki Piano School. The reading course is in three parts: Rhythmic Drills, Keyboard Orientation Exercises, and Reading Exercises. The general purpose of this course is to introduce reading to the students using familiar musical materials, and gradually to add new materials that will prepare them to learn the pieces in Volume II.

Loft, Abram. *Ensemble! A Rehearsal Guide to Thirty Great Works of Chamber Music.* Portland, Oreg.: Amadeus Press, 1992, 365 p. Contains study and rehearsal guides to thirty well-known chamber works, mainly quartets. Includes Haydn's piano trio Hob XV: 25 in G. Mainly oriented toward strings.

Logan, Christine Janice. *Some Aspects of Australian Piano Music Since 1945.* D.M.A. paper, University of Cincinnati, 1988, 159 p. UM 882330. A study of Australian piano music from 1945 to 1985, presenting a historical survey of the repertoire and an analysis of the pitch structure of four selected works. The analyses test the precept that in eliminating any atonal music, the "integer model of pitch" is a valuable concept. Details of pieces suitable for recital purposes are listed in an appendix.

Long, William C. *An American Romantic-Realist Abroad: Templeton*

Strong and His Music. Metuchen, N.J.: Scarecrow Press, 1994. Includes bibliographical references and index.

Lopes, Richard Clarence. *The Piano Concertos of Carl Maria von Weber: Precursors of the Romantic Piano Concerto.* D.M.A. paper, Columbus: Ohio State University, 1989, 223 p. UM 9011109. Carl Maria von Weber is a recognized figure in the history of German Romantic opera. However, as a composer for the piano, he has received little attention from performers and scholars. His two piano concertos, *Concerto No. 1, in C Major* and *Concerto No. 2, in E Flat Major,* and his one-movement work for piano and orchestra, the *Konzertstück,* are rarely performed by modern pianists and orchestras. Yet, in his day, Weber was a respected virtuoso performer, a writer of music criticism, and an innovator as an orchestral conductor. Weber's operas have received a measure of the attention they deserve. As an instrumental composer, Weber's works have fared less well. Although there are a few studies that deal with the four piano sonatas, there is very little written about the piano concertos. These works form an important part of Weber's compositional output and give a clear picture of his style. The aim of this document is to study all three concerted works for piano and orchestra in order to bring attention to important melody and rhythm, and to demonstrate their importance as precursors of the Romantic piano concerto. This document draws attention to elements of Weber's formal approach and virtuoso piano style which can be seen in the concertos of Mendelssohn, Schumann, Chopin, and Liszt. Weber developed many of the techniques employed by these composers at a time when Beethoven was still active. Weber's experiments with form and programmatic compositions had a direct influence on the development of the one-movement Romantic concerto and the symphonic poem.

A further aim of this document is to bring attention to the intrinsic artistic value of these concertos, and to stimulate performers to program these works more frequently, thereby enriching their own repertoires and broadening the musical horizons of the audiences for whom they perform.

Lopez, Jose Raul. *Alkan's "Symphonie," Op. 39: An Analysis and Pedagogical Aspects.* D.M.A. paper, University of Miami, 1993, 135 p. UM 9412921. This essay is a study of Alkan's *Symphonie* for solo piano, a composite of four etudes (nos. 4–7) from his *Douze Etudes* *dans les tons mineurs,* Op. 39. This cycle, along with the *Douze Études dans les tons majours,* Op. 35, traverses all major and minor keys, and represents Alkan's contributions to the genre, worthy of inclusion with Chopin's and Liszt's etudes among the nineteenth-century's formidable musical-technical pianistic legacy. The introduction establishes the need for a detailed study of the *Symphonie,* and the four subsequent chapters present a detailed analysis (harmonic and structural), combined with an exploration of pedagogical aspects.

Lorenz, Ricardo, comp. and ed. *Scores and Recordings at the Indiana University Latin American Music Center.* With Luis R. Hernández and Gerardo Dirié. Bloomington: Indiana University Press, 1995, 478 p. This book is loaded with information to help the pianist looking for repertoire from Latin American composers. It includes biographical information on over 950 composers, plus many piano works and recordings when available. The book is a treasure for all pianists looking for repertoire from this part of the world. The material may be borrowed on interlibrary loan.

Lozier, Frederick Joseph. *Idiomatic, Notational, and Stylistic Elements in the Piano Works of David Del Tredici.* D.M.A. paper, Athens: University of Georgia, 1993, 111 p. UM 9329805. Pulitzer Prize–winning composer David Del Tredici, most noted for his orchestral works, has published three compositions for solo piano and one for piano four hands: *Soliloquy* (1958), *Fantasy Pieces* (1959–1960), *Virtuoso Alice* (1984), and *Scherzo* (1960). They represent his early and recent compositional styles. This study focuses on attributes associated with idiomatic piano writing found in Del Tredici's piano music, pianistic logic inherent in the notation of his piano works, and other considerations that define his compositional style.

Lu, Emily. *The Piano Concerto of Samuel Barber.* D.M.A. paper, Madison: University of Wisconsin, 1986, 117 p. UM 8702318. The *Piano Concerto* of Samuel Barber is the composer's last major work for the piano. It is the writer's belief that a stylistic analysis of this work can provide interesting and valuable insights into Barber's pianistic style as a whole. To this end, several stylistic traits common in much of the composer's works have been selected for detailed explorations. The concerto is used as a springboard throughout the dissertation, fortified by numerous references to the solo piano works as well.

The main chapters discuss form, principal motives, the usage of counterpoint, ostinato, and rhythm, as well as the traits, lyricism, and drama, with relationship to the piano writing and orchestration in the concerto.

As a result of his thorough training in counterpoint and form, Barber's concerto abounds with lively and interesting contrapuntal writing, while the first movement is a creative interpretation of the traditional sonata form. In place of the opening orchestral ritornello, Barber has substituted a piano introduction containing all the motives from which the movement derives.

The ostinato device plays an important and varied role in the *Piano Concerto*. The wide spectrum ranges from the interesting "coloring" ostinato of the first movement and the accompaniment of the Canzone, to the intensity of the driving Rondo ostinato as well as the calmer ostinatos from the playful episodes.

Barber's rhythms tend to be varied and active, while avoiding the obvious. Rhythmic displacement and written-out accelerando occur frequently in the first movement. The third movement of the concerto oscillates between the (3+2) and (2+3) groupings of the 5/8 meter to accommodate the melodic material involved.

Lyricism and drama are two of the most outstanding qualities in the *Piano Concerto*. The composer draws the utmost lyric-dramatic effects from the music through idiomatic piano writing as well as expert and imaginative orchestration.

Luther, Sigrid. *The Anniversaries for Solo Piano by Leonard Bernstein.* D.M.A. paper, Baton Rouge: Louisiana State University, 1986, 133 p. UM 8625343. Leonard Bernstein wrote three sets of dedicatory piano miniatures: *Seven Anniversaries* (1943), *Four Anniversaries* (1948), and *Five Anniversaries* (1949–1951). Each piece is in honor of a close friend, relative, or family member of a friend of the composer. The titles bear the names of the respective dedicatees (for example, "For Aaron Copland"); the titles in all but the first set also include the date of birth. The purpose of this monograph is to provide background information about each dedicatee and to analyze each tribute in terms of significant musical features, with brief reference to pedagogical considerations. It has been found that the anniversaries are well-integrated motivically, yet they come across with seemingly spontaneous turns of melody and rhythm. Harmony is refreshingly elusive but not devoid of tonal orientation. Jazz elements and generally moderate technical demands add to the appeal of the anniversaries as teaching pieces. Several have been incorporated into orchestral works, gaining in the process additional musical and extra-musical associations. Two unpublished anniversaries (1965) are briefly discussed in the appendix to this monograph.

Lyman, Janet Palmberg. *Administrative Aspects of Intern Teaching in Piano Pedagogy Courses.* Ph.D. dissertation, Norman: University of Oklahoma, 1991, 167 p. UM 9128671. The purpose of the study is to gather information concerning administrative aspects of intern teaching in piano pedagogy course. Based upon the data collected, several conclusions have been drawn. At most institutions, more than one setting was used for intern teaching. At many institutions, the level of funding accorded to intern teaching arrangements could be increased. The piano pedagogy teacher was often the victim of work overload and under-compensation, while intern supervisors, in general, were under-compensated. Among respondents reporting compensation for supervisors, a majority were satisfied with the mode of compensation. When load credit was the mode of supervisor compensation, it was most often given as an amount that remained the same regardless of the number of interns supervised. The number of institutions with interns teaching independently use their own pupils (47.0 percent), laboratory programs (38.8 percent), preparatory departments (32.7 percent), and independent piano studios (16.4 percent). The percentage with piano studios was small due to lack of funding for these arrangements and dissatisfaction with the amount of load credit given to intern supervisors in independent piano studios. Recommendations for the administration of intern teaching conclude the study.

Macahilig, Suzanne. *A Method for the Interpretation of Beethoven's Middle Period Piano Sonatas.* Ph.D. dissertation, New York University, 1992, 465 p. UM 9306870. The extant literature in musical analysis provides approaches with inherent strengths and weaknesses. The assumption of this study is that no existing system of analysis has been developed specifically for the performance of Beethoven piano sonatas. This study investigates Beethoven piano sonatas from the Middle Period (1803–1814) for the development of an analytical tool that is tailored to those works and that will also incorporate a guide for their performance.

The steps in this research study are an overview examination of the Classic Era and the Beethoven piano sonatas, selection of piano sonatas from Beethoven's Middle Period, a review of traditional methods of analysis and how performance needs are met, the syntheses of a method of analysis, the analyses of the "selected" sonatas which include a guide for their performance, and an assessment of the strengths and weaknesses inherent in the method of analysis synthesized and its implementation.

MacDonald, Claudia Sue. *Robert Schumann's F-Major Piano Concerto of 1831 as Reconstructed from His First Sketchbook: A History of Its Composition and Study of Its Musical Background.* Ph.D. dissertation, University of Chicago, 1986. Music for a piano concerto in F major is found scattered through the pages of Robert Schumann's first sketchbook. That the solo parts of this concerto's first movement were complete is shown, first, by entries in Schumann's diary, and second, by his own table in the first sketchbook labeling sections and subdivisions of the movement in full detail, and giving measure numbers for each. Examination of the sketchbook permits reconstruction of the concerto movement in the form in which Schumann must have performed it in August 1831, when he played the entire movement for his friends. This reconstruction is one of two main subjects of the thesis.

The other main subject is to show that the form and effects of Schumann's movement are modeled on the concertos of his contemporaries, notably those of Johann Nepomuk Hummel and Henri Herz. In his sketchbook, Schumann gives direct evidence of using Herz's A Major Concerto, Op. 34 as a model. No such direct evidence exists connecting the Schumann work with Hummel's as a model, but the demonstrable fact of his own movement and the first movement of Hummel's A minor Concerto, Op. 85, a movement which was part of his repertoire by 1828, strongly suggests this must be the case. Hummel's concerto was particularly important in shaping the solo exposition which Schumann brought from Heidelberg to Leipzig in the fall of 1830. Thereafter, the sketches related to his work during December 1830 and May and August 1831 reveal that Schumann increasingly adopted the Romantic style of writing in Herz's concerto, as opposed to the Classical style of his former model, Hummel.

As a background for these two main subjects, the first chapter of the thesis addresses the question of Schumann's purpose in writing the concerto and the circumstances that made him drop the project, the decisive one being the laming of his finger in October 1831. At this time, only the solo part of the first movement was completed. The final version, as it is found in Schumann's first sketchbook, is given in an appendix.

MacMillan, Duncan. *The Piano Music of Michael Hennagin: An Introductory Examination.* D.M.A. paper, Norman: University of Oklahoma, 1987, 269 p. UM 8808076. This document provides an introduction to the piano music of American composer Michael Hennagin (b. 1936). No research has been done on Hennagin or his piano works in particular, even though he has received critical acclaim for trio compositional efforts in a variety of genres. A substantial portion of Hennagin's compositional output is published and nationally recognized, particularly in the choral idiom. His published piano solos include only the *Sonata (No. 1)* and the *Children's Suite.* He has written in addition *Three Inventions,* a *Sonata for Two Pianos,* and three other sonatas for solo piano. To date, two of the sonatas remain unpremiered.

The initial chapter of the study provides a biography of Hennigan and deals with such topics as early influences, important teachers, places of study, major compositions and circumstances surrounding them, professional and academic appointments, and important personal relationships and their significance to Hennagin's development as a composer. Ensuing chapters are devoted to a survey of specific piano compositions. Biographical and theoretical aspects of the music are discussed. Biographical details include programmatic content, sources of inspiration, and statistics regarding premieres and subsequent performances. The theoretical elements considered include form, harmonic vocabulary, intervallic/motivic content, rhythmic treatment, and relationships between works (related or borrowed ideas). Pianistic idioms and general stylistic features are also considered. The concluding chapter summarizes stylistic characteristics of Hennagin's piano writing as a whole.

Source materials include books, interviews with the composer and pianists who have played his works, published scores and manuscripts, reviews, and tapes of performances from private collections. Appendixes include miniature scores of the unpublished compositions for piano and a complete catalog of works, courtesy of the composer.

Magrath, Jane. *The Pianist's Guide to Standard Teaching and Performance Literature.* Van Nuys, Calif.: Alfred Publishing Co., 1995, 569 p. Provides information on solo piano teaching literature graded from Levels 1 to 10. Mainly for the piano teacher but also valuable for the piano student. Covers the easier literature from Baroque to present.

Manno, Mark Anthony. *An Investigation into the Nature of Musical Expression and Its Application in Elementary Piano Teaching.* D.M.A. paper, Austin: University of Texas, 1993, 507 p. UM 9323311. Twenty-five expressive characteristics pertaining to piano performance were identified from the existing literature. A questionnaire distributed to piano and piano pedagogy experts was used to validate the list of characteristics and to identify those characteristics which are both essential to an expressive piano performance and suitable for teaching to elementary level piano students. In order to provide the reader with practical suggestions on how other elementary level literature might be taught, eight pieces from elementary level piano music by Dmitri Kabalevsky were analyzed and discussed in terms of expressive factors found in the music.

Manshardt, Thomas. *Aspects of Cortot.* Northumberland, England: Appian Publications and Recordings, 1994, 150 p. Manshardt studied with Alfred Cortot from 1957 to 1962. Much of the book is devoted to a clearly presented series of exercises aimed at developing emotional freedom. Much discussion focuses on the use of the wrist.

Manwarren, Matthew Clark. *The Influence of Liszt's Sonata in B Minor on Julius Reubke: A Study of Reubke's Sonata in B-Flat Minor for Piano and the Sonata on the Ninety-fourth Psalm for Organ.* D.M.A. paper, University of Cincinnati, 1994, 108 p. UM 9424554. Friedrich Julius Reubke (1834–1858) is relatively unknown today as a nineteenth-century composer and performer primarily because of his short life. His most important contribution as a composer consists of his two sonatas, the *Sonata in B-flat Minor* for piano and his *Sonata on the Ninety-fourth Psalm* for organ, both of which were composed in 1857. The primary influence of these two works was Liszt's *Sonata in B Minor* (1853). Chapter One discusses Reubke's early study with Hermann Bonicke, Adolf Bernhard Marx, and Theodore Kullak, as well as his study with Liszt. Chapter Three summarizes some of the trends and characteristics of the sonata as a genre in the mid-nineteenth century and how these are reflected in Reubke's sonatas.

Maple, Douglas Alvin. *D'Anglebert's Autograph Manuscript, Paris, B.N.*

Res. 89 - : An Examination of Compositional, Editorial, and Notational Processes in 17th-century French Harpsichord Music. Ph.D. dissertation, University of Chicago, 1988. Although Res. 89 is smaller and less comprehensive than some of the better-known French harpsichord manuscripts like those of Bauyn or Parville, the nature of its contents and the fact that it is a rare autograph actually make it more valuable for certain purposes than the other larger sources. In addition to several of d'Anglebert's pieces that appear nowhere else, it contains a number of his pieces in pre-publication versions. Examination of these pieces that exist in both manuscript and printed versions reveals that d'Anglebert made numerous detailed changes as he prepared them for publication. These affected meter and barring, rhythmic notation, slurs and beams, texture, and especially ornamentation. The discussion argues that most of these were merely improvements in notation, and that d'Anglebert was one of the first to concern himself with presenting detailed and literal renditions of his music to the public.

D'Anglebert also included pieces by other harpsichordists in his manuscript, principally Chambonnières. Comparison of d'Anglebert's readings of these pieces with those published a few years earlier by Chambonnières reveals numerous small but significant differences. Since these variant readings are unique to 89 and show many similarities to d'Anglebert's own style, it is fairly certain that he intentionally "recomposed" these borrowed pieces. The apparent contradiction between d'Anglebert's free treatment of music by other composers with his efforts to notate his own pieces in a very explicit fashion leads to a discussion of the whole question of authenticity of musical text in the seventeenth-century repertoire.

D'Anglebert's manuscript also contains numerous transcriptions of lute pieces and excerpts from stage works by Lully. The presence of these lute transcriptions might be seen as further evidence of the connection between the lute and harpsichord styles. However, even though there are some signs of lute influence in d'Anglebert's music, the discussion shows that these are relatively limited. His true purpose in making these transcriptions, as well as his arrangements of the Lully pieces, was simply to take well-known pieces from other media and to rework them so that they would be in his own idiomatic keyboard style.

Margolis, Victor. *The Plate Spinner: Playing with Time.* Cupertino, Calif.: Marik Publishing, 1995, 330 p. Margolis is a former psychologist who now travels throughout the country putting out the message of this book: "expressing ourselves, particularly through the arts, might be our most important self-obligation." The author is convinced that the principles used in learning a musical instrument can also be applied to life. This book about making music makes the practice of the piano irresistible, provides a strategy (platespinning) for maintaining a large repertoire, and shows how principles of music practice can affect one's life. Full of refreshing and innovative ideas and loaded with wit and humor.

Markoff, Mortimer. *The Art of Playing the Piano: Conversations with Mortimer Markoff.* Palo Alto: London Road Books, 1993.

Marks, Brian Roberts. *Sources of Stylistic Diversity in the Early Piano Sets of Sergei Prokofiev.* D.M.A. paper, Austin: University of Texas, 1994, 265 p. UM 9428433. The early works of Sergey Prokofiev are remarkable for their diversity of compositional techniques. This is particularly true of the sets of piano pieces composed through the end of the First World War, a span of time encompassing nine opuses: *Four Etudes,* Op. 2, *Four Pieces,* Op. 3, *Four Pieces,* Op. 4, *Ten Pieces,* Op. 12, *Sarcasms,* Op. 17, *Visions Fugitives,* Op. 22, *Tales of the Old Grandmother,* Op. 31, and *Four Pieces,* Op. 32. The treatise is organized into three chapters. Chapter One focuses on historical background: cultural life in turn-of-the-century Russia, Prokofiev's interaction with the artistic trends of his time, and the reception of his music by the musical establishment and the general public. Chapter Two presents an overview of the nine works to be examined, their circumstances of composition, stylistic makeup, and general analytical remarks. Chapter Three provides detailed analyses of those works which most clearly illustrate the various techniques employed by Prokofiev, and relates their use to his stylistic development.

Marsh, Ozan. *The Pianist's Spectrum.* With Anna Norvelle. Wolfeboro, N.H.: Longwood Academic, 1987, 125 p. Marsh was a distinguished concert pianist and outstanding piano teacher. Here, he draws on his years of teaching experience to present a consistent philosophy of how piano should be taught and how it should be learned. He places strong emphasis on technical training and discusses the "tricks of the trade." An important book for piano teachers and advanced students.

Marshall, Robert L., ed. *Eighteenth-Century Keyboard Music.* New York: Schirmer Books, 1994, 443 p. A collection of essays by various well-qualified authors on the keyboard music of J. S. Bach through the early works of Beethoven. Includes bibliographical references and Index.

Marston, Nicholas. *Beethoven's Piano Sonata in E, Op. 109.* New York: Clarendon Press, 1995, 230 p. Includes bibliographical references. Provides a thorough study of this sonata's sources and an analytical approach to the structure of the work. Includes early sketches and parts of the autograph score.

————. *Schumann, Fantasie, Op. 17.* Cambridge, England, and New York: Cambridge University Press, 1992, 130 p., illustrated. Includes bibliographical references and index. A thorough discussion, musical, theoretical, and historical, of this great masterpiece. A Cambridge Music Handbook.

Martin, Mauricy. *Sonata Brève: A Synthesis of the Piano Works of Oscar Lorenzo Fernandez.* D.M.A. paper, Boston University, 1993, 97 p. UM 9330151. This document focuses on the *Sonata Brève,* Lorenzo Fernandez's last work for piano solo, written in 1947. This sonata is not only the composer's largest composition for the instrument, but it also represents a synthesis of his piano output. In addition to a detailed analytical study of the *Sonata Brève,* this project gives an account of the composer's life with a list of his complete works and also includes a chapter giving an overview of the stylistic development and characteristics of his piano works, especially with regard to nationalism.

Martin, Terry Nathan. *Frédéric Chopin and Romantic Nationalism: An Examination of His Correspondence.* Ph.D. dissertation, St. Louis: Washington University, 1990, 164 p. UM 9103104. This dissertation explores Chopin's relationship to nineteenth-century Romantic Nationalism through pertinent information found in his complete correspondence. In order to dispel misconceptions and exaggerations about Chopin's nationalist sensibilities, this work approaches the matter from a more objective vantage than what has been done to date. Chopin and his nationalist genres are presented in light of recent scholarship on nationalism and music.

The work extracts all of Chopin's known comments about nationalism, patriotism, and current events of his day and offers commentary on these utterances. In addition, there are chapters on Polish history

and political events during Chopin's years in Poland, important Polish
contributions to Romantic nationalist philosophy, Chopin's relationship and conflicts with Polish nationalists, and Chopin's use of Polish
folk music forms. Rather than being stereotyped as a "nationalist,"
Chopin is presented as an example of the quintessential Romantic
composer who, like his contemporaries, chose occasionally to include
national characteristics in his compositions.

Martinez, Maria Dolores. *Psychophysical Aspects of the Interchange
Between Piano and Harpsichord: A Study of Experiences and Opinions of Current Performers and Educators.* Ph.D. dissertation, Lubbock: Texas Tech University, 1990. UM 9104760. This investigation
arose from focusing on specific technique problems which initially sur-
faced in the author's playing when interchanging piano and harpsichord performance with relative frequency.

Chapter One of this dissertation contains introductory material, giving the purpose and scope of this study, and a description of the methodology used in collecting survey data. Chapter Two treats the subject of the intrinsic differences between harpsichord and piano playing,
citing specific technical problems which may occur in the transfer from
one instrument to the other. Chapter Three deals with the learning
and performance of skills as a motor-programming process, including
the dynamics of practicing, the creation of habits, and an analysis of
motor learning concepts from the sport sciences. Chapter Four is the
conclusion, and gives the author's suggestions for future research. Two
appendixes accompany the study, the second being of special interest
as it contains the results of the survey, with comments of pedagogues
from throughout the United States.

Martyn, Barrie. *Rachmaninoff: Composer, Pianist, Conductor.* Aldershot,
Hants, England: Scholar Press, 1990, 584 p. Distributed by Ashgate
Publishing, Old Post Road, Brookfield, VT 05036–9704. This is the
most important book to appear on Rachmaninoff since 1956. The
subject's life and works are discussed in detail. Rachmaninoff's piano
music gets a well-balanced going-over and is placed in perspective to
his other works.

————. *Nicholas Medtner: His Life and Music.* Aldershot, Hants, England: Scholar Press, 1995, 288 p. Distributed by Ashgate Publishing.
Medtner's music is carefully analyzed and its German Romantic influ-

ence is discussed. Martyn's understanding of Medtner's piano music is especially perceptive.

Matheson, Lynn Marie. *The Genesis of Beethoven's Piano Sonata in A flat, Op. 110.* M.A. thesis, Victoria, B.C.: University of Victoria, 1993. 135 p. UM 84329. Although Beethoven's Piano Sonata in A flat, Op. 110, is one of his outstanding compositions, it has not been exhaustively discussed in the literature. In particular, aspects of the genesis of the work are in need of clarification. One body of sketch materials has remained unknown to previous scholars and is examined here in detail for the first time. Study of the sources in question—Paris Manuscripts 51, 51/3 and 80—makes possible a reevaluation of Beethoven's compositional process.

The thesis assesses the work of other scholars who have written about the sonata, placing emphasis on studies of the primary sources. Various manuscripts are examined in detail and their relation to one another clarified. Important as well is the examination of the structure and chronology of the source materials—including the autograph scores. Both the physical structure and musical content of the source materials require close attention. Robert Winter's source study in *The Beethoven Sketchbooks* (Oxford, 1985) is reconsidered here against the evidence of the original manuscripts.

The largest part of this thesis concerns the genesis of the sonata as documented in manuscripts held in Berlin and Bonn, as well as Paris. Various stages of the compositional evolution are traced in the sources, with special attention given to the complex final movement of the work, for which many layers of revision are preserved in the manuscripts. Certain sketches for this movement are surprisingly different from the final version and can therefore offer a new basis for analytical insight into the finished work.

Maxwell, Grant L. *Music for Three or More Pianists: An Historical Survey and Catalogue.* D.Mus. dissertation, Edmonton: University of Alberta, 1992, 327 p. Also published by Scarecrow Press, Metuchen, N.J., 1993, 467 p. A fascinating, albeit generally unknown area in the literature for keyboard ensemble is the evolution of a remarkably large repertoire—original and transcribed—for three or more pianists at one or more keyboards with or without other acoustic and electronic instruments or singers.

The history of keyboard music for three or more players was initiated c. 1730 by J. S. Bach, who transcribed two concertos for three harpsichords and one for four. As well as duet and two-fortepiano works, Mozart pioneered original team piano repertoire. The "Lodron" Concerto, K. 242, was scored for three fortepianos and orchestra. Original compositions for three or more pianists continued to be written—with Czerny, Kalkbrenner, Moscheles, Smetana, Glazunov and Rachmaninoff—for particular pianists and occasions.

By the early twentieth century, a mass of transcriptions and arrangements had accumulated. These works were an effective way for most pianists to familiarize themselves with the rarely heard orchestral literature. Before the invention of the radio and phonograph, it was once a standard practice for publishers to issue orchestral and chamber music repertoire for four, six, eight or more hands at one or more pianos.

McAlexander, Dan R. *Works for Piano by William Bolcom: A Study in the Development of Musical Postmodernism.* D.M.A. paper, University of Cincinnati, 1994, 107 p. UM 9502525. Attempting to understand the development of musical postmodernism by better understanding the evolution of Bolcom's style, this study explores his work for solo piano as a microcosm of both. The early works, which were composed in a rationalist style, and the subsequent rags, which resulted from his rebellion against academicism, are examined for evidence of tendencies which influence such mature recent works as the *Twelve New Etudes,* winner of the 1988 Pulitzer Prize for music.

McBee, Karen Lee. *Nena Plant Wideman: Her Life and Work with Student Concerti Performances, 1949–1983.* D.M.A. paper, Kansas City, Mo.: University of Missouri, 1993, 208 p. UM 9418465. Nena Plant Wideman was a piano teacher whose involvement in the Shreveport, Louisiana, musical culture from 1940–1983 included the founding of the Shreveport Symphony Society and the initiation of a piano concerto contest.

Major areas concerning Wideman are presented in individual chapters. Chapter One provides an introduction to the document. Chapter Two presents biographical information on Wideman including her childhood, early music training, education, marriage, teaching positions, activities, and honors. The third chapter details the history of the Wideman Piano Competition and records Wideman's activities in the formation and early years of the Shreveport Symphony Society. The workings and financial aspects of the Wideman benefit concert series—an annual twenty-five year event—appear in Chapter Four. Chapter Five summarizes the document's information.

McCabe, John. *Haydn Piano Sonatas.* London: BBC Publications, 1986, 91 p. A discussion of all the piano sonatas and the most important other solo keyboard works. McCabe has recorded all of the sonatas, and his comments from the performer's point of view are most enlightening and helpful.

McCain, Claudia Jean Forney. *Current Piano Teaching Practices in Music Store Education Programs.* Ed.D. dissertation, Urbana-Champaign: University of Illinois, 1993, 196 p. UM 9411713. The purpose of this study is to investigate current practices in piano teaching in music store education programs as related to teacher qualifications, instructional materials, business policies, and the stated rationale for selected programs. These practices were compared with college and university piano pedagogy instructors' opinions on realistic minimum standards for piano teaching in music store education programs.

McCalla, Shan Eileen. *The Piano Works of Dane Rudhyar: An Overview and Stylistic Study.* D.M.A. paper, Tempe: Arizona State University, 1988, 182 p. UM 8815627. Dane Rudhyar was a twentieth-century French-American who contributed to the fields of astrology, oriental philosophy, and modern music. The purpose of this study is to provide detailed information on the life, musical philosophies, and piano works of Rudhyar. His music can best be appreciated if one is familiar with his philosophies because for Rudhyar the two fields are interrelated. He composed some thirty works for the keyboard over the course of his life, nearly all of which feature his compositional technique of "orchestral pianism." This study provides a complete overview of Rudhyar's piano works and focuses on a stylistic analysis of pieces from his early and late periods of composition. *Grandes* and *Epic Poem* were chosen from these respective periods because they are among his best-known piano pieces. The study reveals that the works are stylistically similar, although the latter is greater in length and complexity.

McClain, Barbara Lois. *Some Influences on the Early Pianoforte Works of Frédéric Chopin.* M.M. thesis, Urbana-Champaign: University of Illinois, 1956, 69 p. John Field and Johann N. Hummel are singled out for their strong influence on Chopin. Chapters: Dissonance and Chromaticism, Oramentation, Parallel Melodic Movement, Wide Figurations and Leaps, and Summary.

McClendon-Rose, Helen Jean. *The Piano Sonatas of Louise Talma: A Stylistic Analysis.* D.M.A. paper, Hattiesburg: University of Southern Mississippi, 1993, 99 p. UM 9239408. The chief purpose of this study is to furnish an analysis of each of the piano sonatas by Louise Talma with regard to melody, harmony, tonality, rhythm, form, and texture. Observations pertaining to style characteristics and compositional techniques are included, as well as comments on technical and musical difficulties for the performer. A short biography of Louise Talma, a complete listing of her works, and a discography are also included.

McGillen, Geoffrey Eugene. *The Teaching and Artistic Legacy of Olga Samaroff Stokowski.* D.A. dissertation, Muncie, Ind.: Ball State University, 1988, 505 p. UM 8914095. The purpose of this research is to investigate the life and piano teaching of Olga Samaroff in order to determine her contribution to American music. The sub-problems were to survey the important influences upon her life; examine her association with wealthy patrons, concert managers, and conductors; scrutinize her personal relationship with Leopold Stokowski; define and discuss her piano teaching method; assess her application of it with a cross-section of students; and reveal the problems that her method encountered.

Olga Samaroff (1882–1948), christened Lucie Mary Olga Agnes Hickenlooper, first studied piano with her grandmother, Lucie Loening Grunewald. Grunewald emphasized the importance of recreating accurately the composer's text. Much of Samaroff's teaching method evolved from her early training with Grunewald. Samaroff was the first American woman to win a scholarship at the Paris Conservatoire and entered it in 1896. Studies in Berlin (1898–1900) followed with Ernst Jedlickza and Ernest Hutcheson. In Paris and Berlin, Samaroff personally experienced a slavish attitude toward musical tradition, and later eschewed such adherence to any single school or style.

Her first marriage (1900) to a Russian named Boris Loutzky subsequently caused her to settle in St. Petersburg (now Leningrad). After leaving Loutzky in 1904, Samaroff returned to the United States and began her concert career. The vicissitudes of her career presented her with firsthand experience. Samaroff withdrew several times from the concert stage, retiring officially in 1926 due to an arm injury. In the meantime, she married and later divorced conductor Leopold Stokowski, whose rehearsal technique she cited as an important influence on her teaching. She began teaching at the newly established Juilliard Graduate School in 1924. She also taught at the Philadelphia Conservatory (1924–1948).

Samaroff's two-part approach of artistic independence and human development contrasted with the artist-coach method of other prominent teachers of the day. Her students were surveyed about the efficacy of her teaching. In addition, Samaroff's own files and personal correspondence, hitherto unavailable, are included as evidence in support of the author's findings.

McGowan, James John. *Harmonic Organization in Aaron Copland's Piano Quartet.* M.M. thesis, Denton: University of North Texas, 1995, 84 p. UM 1375491. This thesis presents an analysis of Copland's first major serial work, the *Quartet for Piano and Strings* (1950), using pitch-class set theory and tonal analytical techniques. The first chapter introduces Copland's *Piano Quartet* in its historical context and considers major influences on his compositional development. The second chapter takes up a pitch-class set approach to the work, emphasizing the role played by the eleven-tone row in determining salient pitch-class sets. Chapter Three reexamines many of these same passages from the viewpoint of tonal referentiality, considering how Copland was able to evoke tonal gestures within a structural context governed by pitch-class-set relationships. The fourth chapter reflects on the dialectic that is played out in this work between pitch-class sets and tonal elements, and considers the strengths and weaknesses of various analytical approaches to the work.

McKinney, David Conley. *The Influence of Parisian Popular Entertainment on the Piano Works of Erik Satie and Francis Poulenc.* D.M.A. paper, Greensboro: University of North Carolina, 1994, 109 p. UM 9502709. These two prolific and inventive composers incorporated a wide range of popular styles into their writing, from Parisian cafe-concert, music-hall, and cabaret songs, to the popular chanson and music for the circus. Both composers frequented popular establishments throughout their lives and introduced characteristic aesthetic principles such as diversity, parody, banality, and nostalgia into their piano writing—features all founded in Parisian popular entertainment.

McMullen, Edwin Lyle. *The Keyboard Technique of Domenico Scarlatti.* Thesis, Seattle: University of Washington, 1942.

McRay, Elizabeth Norman. *The Impact of the New Pianofortes on Classical Keyboard Style: Mozart, Beethoven and Schubert.* West Midlands, England: Lynwood Music (Books Division), 1987, 114 p. A study of performance practices in the piano music of Mozart, Beethoven, and Schubert. Chapter One focuses on Mozart's "Je suis Lindor" variations; Chapter Two, Beethoven's response to the development of the new pianofortes, as seen through his Bagatelles; Chapter Three: the influence of Viennese dance music on Schubert's music for the pianoforte. Excellent for discussion of the pianos used by these three composers.

Mecker, Rachel Elizabeth. *Text, Melody Line, and Sentogram: Emotion in Selected Piano Works of Claude Debussy.* M.M. thesis, Tucson: University of Arizona, 1994, 162 p. UM 1358523. This study examines a technique of applying sentic analysis (established by Manfred Clynes) to selected piano works by Claude Debussy: *La fille aux cheveux de lin* and *Des pas sur la neige.* Sentograms for anger, grief, hate, joy, and love were visually compared to line graphs of the melodies and melody inversions to discover similar shapes within the line graph, further referred to as musical sentograms.
  Analysis results were based on the relationship between melodic direction and sentogram structure and the degree to which musical support was provided for those musical sentograms through phrase structure, dynamic intensity, and texture change. Very few musical sentograms were found to have support within the phrase structure or correspondence between melodic direction, dynamic intensity, and texture intensity. The results question the application technique and the validity of sentic analysis as a useful method of musical analysis for these and other works.

Mei Ling Tye, Nancy. *Selected Intermediate-Level Solo Piano Music of Robert Starer: A Pedagogical and Performance Analysis.* D.M.A. paper, Norman: University of Oklahoma, 1995. The purpose of this document is to provide a pedagogical and performance analysis of the intermediate solo piano music of Robert Starer published between 1980 and 1995: *At Home Alone* (1994), *Four Seasonal Pieces* (1985), and *MOUNTAINCALLS* (1994). It is intended to serve as an informative guide for teachers who want to add more accessible contemporary music to their students' repertoires.

The first chapter provides an introduction that discusses both the importance of Starer as a twentieth-century composer and the piano works for young students. The second chapter presents a biographical sketch of Starer, followed by a brief overview of his piano works and a section on the general style characteristics of his music. Three succeeding chapters contain the pedagogical and performance analyses of the selected works respectively: *At Home Alone, Four Seasonal Pieces,* and *MOUNTAINCALLS.* A brief, introductory background is provided for each work. The following analytical procedures are applied to each individual piece: 1) a structural analysis, briefly identifying main sections, tonal areas, and twentieth-century compositional techniques; and 2) practice and performance suggestions, identifying pianistic and technical elements for practice, teaching, and performance.

The study concludes with a summary, conclusions, and recommendations. Appendix A lists Starer's published and unpublished piano music; Appendix B includes a discography of the solo piano music; and Appendix C includes written correspondence from Starer to the author.

Mellers, Wilfrid. *Percy Grainger.* New York: Oxford University Press, 1992, 176 p. A detailed, analytical look at the music and an insightful assessment of Grainger's hard-to-classify contribution.

Merned, Orhan. *Seventeenth-Century English Keyboard Music: Benjamin Cosyn.* New York: Garland Publishing Co., 1993, 2 vols. Outstanding dissertations in music from British universities.

Meza, Esequiel, Jr. *External Influences on Rachmaninov's Early Piano Works as Exemplified in the "Morceaux de Salon," Opus 10 and "Moments Musicaux," Opus 16.* D.M.A. paper, Tucson: University of Arizona, 1993, 79 p. UM 9328606. This study examines the development of these two compositions and provides information regarding important experimental processes related to Rachmaninoff's own musical materials. Op. 10 was written shortly after his graduation from the Moscow Conservatory. Like many of his early works, it was written under the constraints and structural models of his conservatory training. The Op. 16 collection, however, shows evidence of extended compositional experimentation and freedom from the previous constraints.

Millican, Brady. *The London Piano Trios of Joseph Haydn: A Performer's Survey of Neglected Masterpieces.* D.M.A. paper, Boston University, 1992, 326 p. UM 9223510. This survey seeks to offer performers a sound analytical and interpretational examination of a third great series of Haydn masterpieces dating from his years in England, his piano trios. It is hoped that these efforts will increase awareness of these works as worthy companions of the symphonies and string quartets written at this time.

The study begins with an exploration of the identity and disposition of Haydn's trio ensemble. A primary goal of this chapter concerns exploration of the numerous links between the trio ensemble c. 1795 and the contemporary orchestra. If performers grasp Haydn's allusions in these works to the larger ensemble, and join them to his invocation of traits appearing in the ethnic music of both Great Britain and Central Europe, they will be able to better appreciate the individual contributions to the music, even when they are not articulating melodic material.

The study thoroughly examines Haydn's imaginative use of sonata form, and links the trios to the virtuoso world of the concerto. The topic of appropriate embellishment by performers receives major consideration, as do currently available editions and recordings of this repertoire. A detailed examination of the Trio, H. 29, provides the focal point of the dissertation, bringing together all of these strands.

Milliman, Ann L. *A Survey of Graduate Piano Pedagogy Core Course Offerings.* Ph.D. dissertation, Norman: University of Oklahoma, 1992, 316 p. UM 9223057. The purpose of this study is to identify the content of the graduate piano pedagogy core course(s) at selected colleges and universities. Data for the study were gathered through a questionnaire sent to the 128 institutions offering graduate-level courses in piano pedagogy as listed in the 1991 Directory of Piano Pedagogy Offerings in American Colleges and Universities, compiled by the National Conference on Piano Pedagogy Committee on Administration/Piano Pedagogy Liaison. The results of the study were based on a 65.6 percent response rate.

Information was obtained regarding enrollment of the institution, the number of graduate piano performance majors and graduate piano pedagogy students, the number of graduate piano pedagogy faculty, and type of graduate degrees offered with an emphasis or major in piano pedagogy. Institutions offering a graduate piano pedagogy core course(s) were asked to provide information regarding the core course structure, core course enrollment, core course requirements, and specific topics addressed in the core course(s). Additional areas of investigation included circumstances in which undergraduate students were allowed to enroll in the graduate piano pedagogy core course(s), circumstances in which graduate students could be exempted from the core course(s), requirement differences for master's and doctoral students, ways for incoming graduate students to meet deficiencies in specific areas of pedagogy, and alterations made in the core course content to compensate for a student's previous pedagogy study.

The study investigated specific core course content, including the topics addressed in the course and the type of teaching and observation experiences encountered by the pedagogy students. Respondents were asked to indicate whether specific topics were included, as well as to describe the amount of emphasis placed on each topic. Information was gathered concerning the amount of observation of teaching required in the core course(s), the type of educational settings available for student teaching and observation of teaching, and the specific level and classification of students taught or observed by the pedagogy student.

Mills, Charlotte Rae. *Grazyna Bacewicz: A Stylistic Analysis and Evaluation of Selected Keyboard Works.* Greeley: University of Northern Colorado, 1986, 139 p. UM 8621966. The following five selected keyboard works of Grazyna Bacewicz (1909–1969) represent her unique compositional style during her most important years, 1933–1965, and, as such, are worthy of evaluation as teaching and performing repertoire: *Suita Dziecieca na forte pian* (1933), *Piano Sonata II* (1953), *Etiuda Nr. II and VII z cyklu Ten Etiud* (1957), and *Maly Tryptyk forte pian* (1965).

The first chapter traces Bacewicz's life and professional activities as a composer, virtuoso violinist, and teacher. Her compositions, numbering over two hundred, are imposing in quantity and diversity. This prolific list includes her keyboard compositions which form an impressive stylistic inheritance in the realm of piano literature.

The stylistic analysis and pedagogical evaluation are the focus of Chapters Two and Three, respectively. The analysis of these five works reveals rhythmic structures consisting of both motorlike rhythms and fluid, relaxed rhythmic patterns; a melodic line which transforms from a simple lyrical line in the early works to a total dissolution of the melodic line in her last work; a harmonic vocabulary that relies heavily on chromaticism; formal structures which include mainly ternary forms (with the exception of several movements from the Suita and Sonata II), and which delineate Bacewicz's varied textural designs; and certain technical and musical characteristics—expanded intervals and chords requiring a wide hand span, total tonal control, articulate pedaling, agility, and speed—all of which clearly identify the music as her own.

These technical and musical considerations make Bacewicz's keyboard works appealing to the pedagogue, performer, and student. Her keyboard compositions represent an integral link in the lineage of Polish keyboard literature and are deserving of recognition and study as performance and teaching literature.

Mitchell, David William. *A Comparison of Embellishments in Performances of BeBop with those in the Music of Chopin.* M.M. thesis, Tucson: University of Arizona, 1992, 149 p. Significant similarities can be found in the origins of the music of the bebop style of jazz of the 1940s and 1950s and the music of Chopin. Chopin's music, like that of the beboppers, has an improvisatory quality. And many of the beboppers' complex embellishment figures have significant corollaries in the music of Chopin.

In comparing bebop embellishments with those in the music of Chopin, the author has selected Charlie Parker, Dizzy Gillespie, and Clifford Brown as exponents of the bebop style. This study finds similarities between Chopin's use of embellishments and that of Parker, Gillespie, and Brown which include the use of delayed passing motion, the use of consecutive embellishing tones, the use of figures which converge on a note from both sides, and the frequent use of changing tone figures of all types.

Mizrahi, Joan Berman. *The American Image of Women as Musicians and Pianists, 1850–1900.* D.M.A. paper, College Park: University of Maryland, 1989, 404 p. UM 8924275. Piano playing has traditionally been perceived as a feminine avocation, yet more men than women have become concert pianists. This dissertation explores the link between women and the piano in late-nineteenth-century America. Many

authors have observed varying and seemingly contradictory ideas about
the nature of women in the literature and art of the nineteenth century. Thus, women might be portrayed by some as angelic and responsible for preserving morality and transmitting culture, and by others
as dangerous and sinister. During the same period, ideas about music
were also varied and contradictory. Some authors spoke of music as a
link with the divine, while others reviled it as frivolous and "effemi-
nate." This dissertation examines the interrelatedness of nineteenth-
century ideas about music with concurrent perceptions of female pianists and musicians.

The material for this study is drawn from general and specialized
(musical) periodical literature and from works of fiction. The selected
periodicals are *The Saturday Evening Post* in 1850 and 1900, *The
Message Bird* (a music journal) in 1850, and *The Etude* (a music journal devoted primarily to the piano) in 1900. Fiction studied includes
Kate Chopin's *The Awakening*, Harold Frederic's *The Damnation of
Theron Ware*, and Henry James's *The Portrait of a Lady*.

References to female musicians and pianists in the above sources are
analyzed, and five common images of women as musicians and pianists are discovered and illustrated. For the music journals, female
authors and advertisers are noted, and articles about women are count-
ed and categorized according to the images discovered. Female musicians and pianists are found to have been frequently idealized as
comforters and inspirers of men. Women were praised for sacrificing
concert careers to care for homes and families, but they were encouraged to teach children and to work together in clubs to further the art
of music. Stereotyped images of female musicians and pianists affected
women's lives in the nineteenth century and still influence us today.

Mohr, Franz. *My Life with the Great Pianists*. With Edith Schaeffer.
Grand Rapids, Mich.: Baker Book House, 1992, 192 p. Mohr was
head technician at the Steinway factory in New York, and he shares
his stories of tuning for some of the world's greatest pianists.

Momany, Sharon Miller. *Form and Genre in Selected Keyboard Works
from Rossini's "Pêches de Vieillesse."* D.M.A. paper, Memphis, Tenn.:
Memphis State University, 1990, 137 p. UM 9025509. The purpose
of the dissertation is to present a study of *Album pour les enfants
adolescents, Album pour les enfants dégourdis, Album de chaumière,
Album de château,* and "Quatre hors d'oeuvres" from *Quatre mendi-*

ants et quatre hors d'oeuvres. The aspects considered are genres, forms, and sub-topics of form such as recurring ideas, introductory portions, cadenzas, and codas.

Rossini compositions may be grouped into three genres: character piece, prelude, and dance. There is no clear dividing line between a Rossini character piece and a prelude, with the exception of prelude-and-fugue combinations. The dances, on the other hand, are usually cast in the same formal structure and even feature literal repetition of sections.

Of the dozen forms found in "Pêches," there are four forms that occur most frequently. ABA or unicellular movements usually occur as the first movement of a two-movement scheme. ABACA may be regarded as the Rossini dance-form, and character pieces with this structure are usually dance-type compositions. One of the outstanding traits found in the keyboard works is the use of a recurring idea. The recurring idea appears in the introduction. It may reappear to link sections, reappear in the coda, or be present in another movement of the composition. Most of the compositions feature an introductory section. The Rossini introduction is one of three basic types: single line or octaves in the cello register of the keyboard, four-part harmony in the center of the keyboard, or a combination of the octaves and the four-part texture.

All of the movements feature codas. The codas may be divided into two main groups, slow and fast. Slow tempo codas feature augmentation or ritard; fast tempo codas are more unusual. These Rossini codas are called "momentum" codas. Rossini achieves momentum in several ways: through acceleration, through compression, or through repetition. Rossini favors constant reiteration of the tonic chord at the conclusion of a piece.

Morris, Gregory W. *Copland's "Single Vision" and the "Piano Sonata."* D.M.A. paper, Denton: University of North Texas, 1990, 53 p. UM 9105042. Difficulties are encountered in any discussion of Copland's style, for his works cover the spectrum from harsh, dissonant works to folk music. To avoid the task of defining a style which encompasses this array of vastly different pieces, a sharp distinction is frequently made between the abstract and popular works. However, Copland repeatedly objected to such categorization, claiming that he composed from a single vision. A careful examination of his total output proves the validity of his claim. Many common characteristics are found throughout works from all categories and time periods. These traits include a basic economy of materials, emphasis on thirds, consistent method of development, use of declamation, jazz-influenced rhythms, cyclicism, and a slow/fast/slow sequence of movements, as well as within single movements.

This document uses the *Piano Sonata* as a model of Copland's style, for it exemplifies these characteristics more clearly than any other major piece for piano. By making numerous comparisons with other works, Copland's single vision is revealed.

Morrow, Craig Martin. *Franz Liszt's Life and Music: A Dramatic Monodrama Piano Recital.* Ph.D. dissertation, New York University, 1993, 209 p. UM 9411197. The purpose of this study is to incorporate a historical investigation of Franz Liszt's life and music as a basis for the creation of a dramatic monodrama piano recital in order to develop a model capable of providing an alternative to the traditional piano recital. The investigation is divided into four chapters. The first provides an introduction. The second chapter presents a biography of Liszt. The third chapter introduces the monodrama piano recital, Franz Liszt: The Passions of a Virtuoso, and the final chapter investigates the theatrical form used in the third chapter.

Moss, Earle. *More Than Teaching.* Toronto: Gordon V. Thompson Music, 1989, 97 p. This is a manual of piano pedagogy in which the author details his ideas regarding piano teaching, playing and interpretation, and some of his "secrets" or views on piano teaching today. Shows teachers and pianists ways to improve performance and instruction.

Mozart on Tour. Video cassette. 7 vols. Philips NTSC VHS 440–070–243. This series follows Mozart through his life and travels. Concert halls, royal residences, and houses related to Mozart's life are part of this fascinating tour. Andre Previn narrates, and fine performances of fourteen concertos are included. Some of the pianists include Ashkenazy, Frager, Lupu, Previn, Kocsis, Ranki, and Uchida. A memorable experience.

Munger, Shirley Annette. *Gigue Types in Keyboard Music from John Bull to J. S. Bach.* Thesis, Seattle: University of Washington, 1950.

Nauhaus, Gerd, ed. and trans. *The Marriage Diaries of Robert and Clara*

Schumann. Preface by Peter Ostwald. Boston: Northeastern University Press, 1993, 256 p. These carefully edited diaries, kept for the first four years of the Schumanns' marriage from 1840 to 1844, illuminate the intimate relationship of this famous couple. They reveal many candid views of the Schumanns' contemporaries.

Nelita True at Eastman. Video cassette. Kansas City, Mo.: SH Productions. No. 101: Portrait of a Pianist Teacher, 60 minutes. Provides the foundation of True's approach to performance and teaching. Contains a thirty-minute lecture on important aspects of pedagogy, a short lesson with a junior high school student on Bach's Prelude to the A Minor English Suite, No. 2, plus two performances of Beethoven's Op. 2, No. 3, first movement, and Chopin's D-flat Nocturne.

———. Video cassette. No. 102: The Studio Lesson, 30 minutes. Takes you inside True's studio for a private lesson on Schumann's Papillons, Op. 2.

———. Video cassette. No. 103: Technique Through Listening, 45 minutes. A lecture on the basic techniques of piano playing.

———. Video cassette. No. 104: Principles of Style for the Young Pianist, 35 minutes. Uses special effects that enable you to follow the measure-by-measure analysis of Mozart's Sonata in G Major, K. 283 (first movement) and Brahms's Rhapsody in G Minor, Op. 79, No. 2.

Nelson, Mary Janean. *A Comparison of Unilateral, Coordinated, and Aural Model Practice Procedures in Learning Piano Music.* D.M.A. paper, Austin: University of Texas, 1993, 151 p. UM 9413635. The purpose of this investigation is to compare the effectiveness of unilateral (one-hand) versus coordinated (both hands) practice procedures on learning piano music. The effectiveness of an aural model during unilateral practice also is investigated. The present study compared the roles of unilateral and coordinated practice trials in terms of learning efficiency, performance accuracy, and musical expression.

Neumann, Frederick. *Essays in Performance Practice.* Ann Arbor: UMI Research Press, 1982, 321 p. Includes sixteen essays on music and subjects from Quantz to Mozart. Extensive endnotes and a thorough index add to the usefulness of the book.

————. *New Essays on Performance Practice.* Ann Arbor: UMI Research Press, 1989, 275 p. Following his successful first volume (listed above), the author offers a companion work which extends his consideration of issues in this controversial and evolving area of musical scholarship. Among the eighteen essays in this collection, spanning performance issues in music from Vivaldi and Bach to Mozart and Haydn, five are published here for the first time. Contains six essays on ornamentation that should be read by all applied music teachers. Both witty and provocative (in both volumes), Neumann substantiates his arguments with extensive documentation and musical illustration. Both volumes provide student, teacher, and scholar with a strong foundation not only in the principles behind the controversies in musical performance, but in the different sides of those controversies.

Nicholas, Jeremy. *Godowsky: The Pianist's Pianist.* P.O. Box 1, Wark, Hexham, Northumberland, NE 48 3 EW, England: Appian Publications and Recordings. Contains a bibliography as well as a list of Godowsky's compositions and recordings. Appian also has available four of Godowsky's recordings of his own works.

Norris, Geoffrey. *Rachmaninoff.* New York: Schirmer Books, 1994, 208 p. Includes recent findings and the author's research at Ivanovka, Rachmaninoff's estate in Russia.

Norris, Jeremy. *The Russian Piano Concerto.* Bloomington: Indiana University Press, 1994, vol. 1, 232 p. This first volume explores an important yet little-studied period (the nineteenth century) in the history of a glorious and popular genre.

Novak, John Kevin. *A Synthesis of Style in the Piano Music of Leoš Janáček.* Thesis, Austin: University of Texas, 1987, 97 p.

Nyquist, Janet Eloise Brown. *The Solo Piano Works of Aaron Copland.* Thesis, Austin: University of Texas, 1963, 172 p.

Oki, Diana Kyoko. *Performance Problems in Béla Bartók's Suite Opus 14 and "Out of Doors."* M.M. thesis, Long Beach: California State University, 1993, 58 p. UM 1354524. The purpose of this report is to discuss the performance problems found in two of Béla Bartók's piano works: *Suite,* Op. 14 (1916) and *Out of Doors* (1926). These problems include the accurate interpretation of Bartók's score markings; terminology for fingerings, tempi, phrasing, articulation, and dynamics; the correct understanding and articulation of rhythms, texture, and character of the pieces; as well as any unique technical and musical difficulties encountered in the performance of these works. In addition, a discussion of Bartók's recording are used to illustrate specific performance problems found in *Suite*, Op. 14.

Ong, David. *The Association of Right Hand Characteristics and Practice Habits with the Prevalence of Overuse Injury Among Piano Students.* M.C. paper, Edmonton: University of Alberta, 1992, 133 p. UM MM 77051. This study examines some of the factors associated with overuse injury among piano students. One of the intentions of this study was to investigate the prevalence of overuse injury among piano students in the Edmonton, Alberta, area.

Piano student volunteers were recruited from post-secondary institutions in the Edmonton area. The subjects' right-hand characteristics were measured, and the students were interviewed to determine their practice characteristics. Fifty-four subjects were analyzed, and an overuse injury rate of 53.7 percent was determined.

The results did not show any association between right-hand characteristics and overuse injury, except for male hand stretch, which was a factor that might protect against overuse injury. The habit of practicing through pain was significantly higher for the overuse group of piano students.

Orvis, Joan. *The Smaller Piano Works of Johannes Brahms.* Thesis, Seattle: University of Washington, 1954.

Oshima-Ryan, Yumiko. *American Eclecticism: Solo Piano Works of Louise Talma.* D.M.A. paper, University of Cincinnati, 1993, 125 p. UM 9329970. The first chapter of the thesis contains a biographical sketch, dealing principally with Talma's musical education and early career. The second chapter discusses the influence of Nadia Boulanger and Igor Stravinsky on young American composers in the 1930s and 1940s. The discussion of Talma's solo piano works is found in the third and fourth chapters. The analysis of form, melody, harmony, texture, and rhythm are discussed in connection with the early works, *Alleluia in Form of Toccata, Piano Sonata No. 1,* and the late works, *Six Etudes, Piano Sonata No. 2, Passacaglia and Fugue,* and *Tex-*

tures. The final chapter analyzes several aspects of performing Talma's solo piano works, such as Talma's own musical markings, along with the technical difficulties and problems.

Ostwald, Peter F. *Glenn Gould: The Ecstasy and Tragedy of Genius.* New York: W. W. Norton, 1997, 386 p. Psychiatrist-musician Ostwald details aspects of Gould's personality disorders—information drawn from the files of 15 doctors. It is a fascinating story about the private and professional life of this musical genius. A chapter on Gould's teacher Alberto Guerrero will be of great interest to pianists.

Ott, Bernard. *Lisztian Keyboard Energy.* Lewiston, N.Y.: Mellen Press, 1992, 261 p. Gives an account of the composer's playing, emphasizing not only Liszt's own playing, but its enormous influence on pianism in general. Ott analyzes very carefully what made Liszt such a great pianist. Much of it had to do with the way Liszt used active retropulsive energy. Contains some technical physiological jargon.

Ott, Margaret Saunders. *Countdown to Performance.* Video cassette. Spokane, Wash.: Teacher's Pet Productions, 60 minutes. Ott gives directions for six days of positive practicing that will help the student "gear down" the excitement before a performance and help him or her play their very best.

————. *Getting Your Act Together.* Video cassette. Spokane, Wash.: Washington State Music Teachers Association, 2903 East 25th, No. 328, Spokane, WA 99223, 1996, 23 minutes. How to prepare for performance events, for pianists from five to seventy-five years old, and beginners through concert artists. Discusses the two most critical times in learning a piece—the first and last weeks—as well as what to do for seven days before the performance. Superb practical advice.

————. *If the Beat Goes On.* Video cassette. Spokane, Wash.: Teacher's Pet Productions, 60 minutes. Ott teaches you how to validate the pulse in music and how to make music engage the audience. Learn the relation of gesture to rhythm, and how to reproduce the sound of other instruments on the piano.

————. *Master Lessons on Favorite Piano Pieces.* Spokane, Wash.: Teacher's Pet Productions, 60 minutes. Master lessons by a great teacher on "Für Elise" by Beethoven, a Chopin Prelude from Op. 28, and "Clair de Lune" by Debussy.

———. *Speaking from Experience*. P.O. Box 267, Deer Park, WA 99006: Ott/Patterson, 1997, 29 p. The author's experiences from a lifetime of teaching and performing, some practical, some philosophical, but all of unique interest from this great lady.

Outland, Joyanne Jones. *Emma Lou Diemer: Solo and Chamber Works for Piano Through 1986*. D.A. paper, Muncie, Ind.: Ball State University, 1986, UM 8703642. Chapter One: Emma Lou Diemer, currently Professor of Composition at the University of California at Santa Barbara, is an rexcellent representative of the mainstream of twentieth-century American music. In 1959, she was awarded a Ford Foundation Grant and assigned to the secondary schools of Arlington, Virginia. During this time, her simpler works for bands and choirs resulted in requests from publishers and commissions from many sources. The choral works have become her largest category of compositions. However, she has also written some twenty-six chamber and solo works for piano.

Chapter Two: Her earliest works reflected her stated models, Rachmaninoff, Debussy, and Gershwin, in their programmatic titles, energetic rhythms, and full keyboard sound. She frequently used chord structures in thirds, within an atonal harmonic framework.

Chapter Three: At Yale, she fell under the Neoclassic influence of Hindemith. Characteristics used included tighter forms, fugues and imitative textures, motivic melodic construction, strong metric rhythm with ametric and syncopated patterns, ostinatos, and a harmonic language of tonics, modal key schemes, and intervals.

Chapter Four: With the solo piano works, she melded the Neoclassic structured language with her earlier romantic style. Ideas once again flowed directly from improvisations, while she also wrote her first large twelve-tone work.

Chapter Five: In the 1970s, she combined the sonorities of the electronic world with intrinsically pianistic techniques, including the new sounds of the avant-garde. Rhythm returned as pulsing beats, contrasted with free and aleatoric sections. Neoclassic motivic development generated dramatic forms.

Chapter Six: Diemer integrates many techniques, new and old, into a highly successful and personal style, one which places ultimate value on expression and communication. Retaining a strong tie to the past, she is a cautious explorer, rarely breaking new ground, but eventually encompassing even the most advanced trends into wonderfully effective works.

Page, Tim. *William Kapell: A Documentary Life History of the American Pianist.* College Park: University of Maryland, International Piano Archives, 1992. The vast majority of the material is drawn from the Kapell Collection at the International Piano Archives at Maryland. Includes index.

Palmieri, Paul, ed. *Encyclopedia of Keyboard Instruments.* Vol. I, *The Piano.* New York: Garland Publishing, 1994, 521 p. The first volume of an encyclopedia devoted solely to keyboard instruments, this work features approximately 600 articles, arranged alphabetically. Entries deal with artisans, composers, events, companies, instrument construction, culture and history, instrument popularity in various countries, research discoveries, and current and future trends. The emphasis is on developments that had wide influence and on the historical evolution of each instrument, but the *Encyclopedia* also examines specialized topics ranging from Viennese actions to aliquot scaling.

Signed articles by contributing experts range from fifty to 7,000 words, providing basic information for ready reference. Comprehensive in scope, the volume traces the evolution of the major versions of the piano to the present day, including fortepiano, player piano, electronic piano, and synthesizer. Special attention is given to historical instruments, reconstruction, contemporary manufacturers and builders, and current favorites. Selected bibliographies with each entry cite the best sources for further research. Illustrations, charts, lists, full indexes, and internal cross-references enhance the coverage.

Panetta, Vincent Joseph, Jr. *Hans Leo Hassler and the Keyboard Toccata: Antecedents, Sources, Style.* Ph.D. dissertation, Cambridge: Harvard University, 1991, 402 p. UM 9132014. This dissertation examines the keyboard toccata as cultivated by Hans Leo Hassler and several important contemporaries.

Parakilas, James. *Ballads Without Words: Chopin and the Tradition of the Instrumental Ballade.* Portland, Oreg.: Amadeus Press, 1992, 358 p. Discusses ballades by Chopin, Liszt, Brahms, Grieg, and Fauré, plus orchestral ballades and concerto ballades by D'Indy, Franck, Dukas, Delius, Tchaikovsky, Janáček, Frank Martin, and others. Includes a detailed analysis of the Chopin Op. 23 ballade, a bibliography, notes, discography, and index.

Park, Myeongsuk. *An Analysis of Isang Yun's Piano Works: A Meeting of Eastern and Western Traditions.* D.M.A. paper, Tempe: Arizona State University, 1990, 146 p. UM 9025791. Isang Yun is a representative Korean composer who has contributed to the fields of Oriental and modern music. Through his seventy-two years, Yun has lived in Korea, Japan, and Germany. The purpose of this study is to provide insight into his musical ideas, as evidenced by the piano works. Through an analysis of two works, *5 Stücke für Klavier* (1958) and *Interludium A* (1982), the researcher finds that Yun used twelve-tone techniques in the first work; in the second, however, he more fully developed his own musical ideas and style, which are related to Oriental philosophy and traditional music.

Park, Younghae Noh. *Four-Hand Piano Sonatas of the Nineteenth Century.* Ph.D. dissertation, Austin: University of Texas, 1985, 2 vols., 444 p. UM 8609623. This study deals with an unduly neglected and yet historically interesting genre of nineteenth-century piano music, the four-hand sonata. It is based on selected but highly representative examples. This study is presented in two volumes, the first of which contains the text, while the second holds the musical examples and a thematic index of the works discussed. Chapter Two provides a brief discussion of Mozart's contribution to the genre as historical background for the nineteenth-century four-hand sonatas. Chapters Three through Five are chronological surveys of four-hand sonatas from the three historical periods—the turn of the century, the first half, and the second half—and assess their individual contributions to the genre. These chapters proceed by composer in the approximate chronological order of the appearance of the works. In some cases, however, it was not possible to establish either a firm date of composition or date of publication. Among the questions explored here are the different types which the sonatas represent, the approaches to the form of outer and inner movements, and to what extent they reflect general or specific trends. Chapter Six is an abstract summary of formal and stylistic features, and of indigenous four-hand writings discussed in the preceding chapters. It also examines how the various composers dealt with the specific possibilities given by the presence of two players at one keyboard, and to what degree they followed traditional procedures or explored new modes of four-hand writing and established trends which others would follow in the course of the century.

Parker, Mary Elizabeth. *Bartók's "Mikrokosmos": A Survey of Pedagogical and Compositional Techniques.* D.M.A. paper, Austin: University of Texas, 1987, 153 p. UM 8902419. The importance of Béla Bartók's *Mikrokosmos,* a graded set of one hundred fifty-three pieces for piano, lies in its comprehensive and systematic organization of both keyboard and compositional techniques. Written between 1926 and 1939, the *Mikrokosmos* was described by Bartók as "a little world of music." The collection offers a microcosmic view of the style and content of his musical language, displaying the influence of all of the aspects of Bartók's multifaceted career as a composer, pianist, piano teacher, and ethnomusicologist.

This study draws together both pedagogical and theoretical analyses of the pieces, which have frequently been examined from only one of these two perspectives. Chapters One and Two provide introductory and historical information. Chapters Three through Five summarize the pedagogical content of each volume of the *Mikrokosmos,* using specific musical examples to illustrate Bartók's approach to building technical facility at the keyboard and basic musical skills. The collection provides an excellent source of solo repertoire, ensemble pieces, and sight-reading material in a twentieth-century tonal idiom that is suitable for pianists of all levels.

Chapters Six through Eleven examine pitch organization in *Mikrokosmos* and include theoretical analyses of pieces from all six volumes. Each chapter focuses on a different type of pitch organization based on distinct kinds of intervallic combinations in the melodic and harmonic structures of the pieces. Pantatonic and modal formations reflect the pervasive influence of authentic folk music sources on Bartók's musical language. His use of polymodality led Bartók toward what he called "a new modal chromaticism," which has primarily a melodic function. Bartók also developed special techniques of abstract pitch organization, including the use of simple (uni-intervallic and compound) interval cycles. The full evolution of Bartók's style joins the concept of inversional symmetry with that of interval cycles. Traditional concepts of modal centers often are juxtaposed and interact with tonal centers based on an axis of symmetry. Bartók's didactic aim of providing progressive levels of pianistic difficulty in the *Mikrokosmos* is paralleled by the increasing complexity of pitch organization. In light of its manifold value for students of piano, music theory, and composition, as well as for historians and ethnomusicologists, the *Mikrokosmos* will undoubtedly endure as a major twentieth-century pedagogical resource.

Paul, Robert Christian. *Improvisation in Twentieth-Century Solo Piano Repertoire, as Represented in Alvin Curran's First Piano Piece (1967) and Pieces Selected from "Squares" (1978) and Four North American Ballads (1978–1979), by Frederic Rzewski.* D.M.A. paper, University of Miami, 1993, 159 p. UM 9412922. The purpose of the study is twofold: first, to discuss in detail the problems encountered in preparing and performing the improvisational elements in the selected works; and second, to abstract a general insight into the problem of improvisation across a broad stylistic spectrum.

Paulson, Georgia H. *The Piano Music of Franz Schubert.* Thesis, Seattle: University of Washington, 1964.

Peace, John. *The Complete Pianist.* Liverpool, England: Castillon Press, 1993. Serious study of this book will lead to increased command of the piano. A holistic approach for all levels.

Pearsall, Thomas Armstrong. *The Advanced Solo Piano Music of Benjamin Britten: An Analysis for Teaching and Performance.* D.M.A. paper, Norman: University of Oklahoma, 1996. The purpose of this document is to provide an analysis for teaching and performance of the advanced solo piano music of Benjamin Britten. Four of the six published works for solo piano fall into this category and are examined. These include *Three Character Pieces* (1930), *Twelve Variations* (1931), *Holiday Diary,* Op. 5 (1934), and *Night-Piece* (1963). The study is intended to serve as a reference for teachers and performers interested in gaining familiarity with these works.

The first chapter provides an introduction that examines Britten's significance as a composer. Additional pertinent background on the composer is provided in the second chapter, including a biographical sketch, overview of the piano works, discussion of his philosophy, and examination of musical style and influences. Chapters Three through Six contain analyses for teaching and performance of the selected works: *Three Character Pieces, Twelve Variations, Holiday Diary,* Op. 5, and *Night-Piece.* An introduction and structural analysis is provided for each work, along with suggestions for practice and performance. Tonal areas and sectional divisions are illustrated in the structural analysis. Included in the suggestions for practice and performance are recommendations for tempo, pedaling, fingerings, and other pertinent musical and pianistic considerations. The study concludes with a summary, conclusions, and recommendations. An appendix lists the piano music of Britten.

Pelley, James Frederic. *A Transcription for Cello and Piano of Six Baryton Trios by Joseph Haydn, with a History of the Baryton.* Ph.D. dissertation, Eugene: University of Oregon, 1986, 217 p. UM 8705885. Joseph Haydn wrote 126 trios for baryton, viola and cello, but they are rarely performed today because the baryton has been virtually obsolete for 150 years. Since the baryton shares many characteristics with the cello, and since there is a scarcity of cello repertoire from the Classic era, a transcription of these works for cello with piano accompaniment would serve both a pedagogical purpose for cellists and cello teachers, and a musical purpose for acquainting the public with a large segment of Haydn's creative output which is generally unknown.
Six of Haydn's trios for baryton, viola, and cello have been selected and transcribed for cello and piano. The trios selected are numbers 86, 98, 104, 109, 113, and 117. They were selected to present a variety of musical forms, keys, technical challenges for the cellist, and suitable adaptability from the original. In addition to the score, a cello part has been prepared with suitable bowings and fingerings indicated. A short history of the baryton is given, elucidating its use in seventeenth-, eighteenth-, and nineteenth-century music, and the role of Haydn's baryton trios in that history is discussed.

Peppercorn, Lisa M. *Villa-Lobos: The Music—An Analysis of His Style.* Trans. Stefan de Haan. White Plains, N.Y.: Pro/Am Music Resources, 1992, 136 p. The author shows how the Brazilian composer's unique style developed from simplistic beginnings through acquaintance with European traditions into the mature style that is known around the world. Peppercorn analyzes the principal works by category, beginning with the piano music, and graduating to the orchestral works by way of the music for violin and cello, voice, chamber music, and music for solo instruments with orchestra. Packed with valuable information.

Perlemuter, Vlado, and Helene Jourdan-Morhange. *Ravel According to Ravel.* Ed. Harold Taylor. Trans. Francis Turner. White Plains, N.Y.: Pro/Am Resources, 1988, 92 p. Perlemuter studied with Ravel all of Ravel's solo piano works. The composer would carefully explain why he had written the music in a particular way and how it should be interpreted. This book is based on those sessions and on subsequent radio interviews and discussions. It is a fascinating companion to Ravel's piano music.

Perlman, Seth Harte. *Tonal Organization in the Twenty-Four Preludes and Fugues of Dmitri Shostakovich, Rodion Shchedrin, and Niels Viggo Bentzon.* D.M.A. paper, Baltimore: Peabody Conservatory of Music, 1988, 153 p. UM 8827008. Tonal organization in the twenty-four preludes and fugues of Dmitri Shostakovich, Rodion Shchedrin, and Niels Viggo Bentzon illustrates the conflict between traditional fugal textures and modern harmonic practices. After brief biographical summaries of these three composers are presented, the fugue of Bach's *Well-Tempered Clavier* is examined briefly as a useful model for comparative analysis with modern fugal collections of similar scope.

Passing consecutively from Shostakovich to Shchedrin to Bentzon, the chromatic, harmonic language increases in complexity, thereby negating the controls of the major-minor system. Concomitantly, the ability to present fugal entries within a coherent tonal structure and the quantity of procedures based on traditional fugal characteristics diminish.

Shostakovich employs a procedurally formulaic paradigm for his fugal expositions. Horizontal key movements are shown to be significant in providing directionality toward the tonic key area within each fugue. Whereas the design of the Shostakovich fugue can be partially explained by the major-minor system, those of Shchedrin and Bentzon often cannot. Both have a chromatic, harmonic language that makes key progressions obscure. Nevertheless, Shchedrin is shown to rely heavily on a procedural framework derived from the traditional fugue. Traditional precedents are least evident in the figures of Bentzon, however. His diverse, often enigmatic designs demonstrate the ability of the modern fugue to metamorphose into another musical form, such as an ostinato form, or simply to be a way of developing a polyphonic texture.

The tonal-organizational elements that connect the preludes to their fugues are then briefly discussed, followed by a concluding summary and bibliography.

Peskanov, Alexander. *In Search of Sound.* P.O. Box 7506, Kingsport, TN 37664: Classical Video Concepts, Inc. Three videos that cover the course of technical requirements used in special music schools and conservatories in Russia. 1. Beginner: Levels I & II; 2. Advanced: Levels III–V; 3. Virtuoso: Levels VI–VII. Peskanov demonstrates the technical requirements and performs various compositions.

Petree, Katherine Frances. *Performance Practices in the Piano Music of Arnold Schoenberg.* D.M.A. paper, Lawrence: University of Kansas, 1986, 134 p. UM 8619871. In this study, the piano music of Arnold Schoenberg is considered from the performer's point of view. The subjects of tempo, metronome markings, German character indications, dynamics, articulation, phrasing, and pedaling are discussed; musical examples drawn from the piano music are given to illustrate the text. The primary sources for the paper are Schoenberg's written performing prefaces to the piano music, his letters, and the essays concerning performance in *Style and Idea.* This material has been supplemented by the writings of Schoenberg's colleagues and contemporaries, namely Rudolph Kolisch, Erwin Stein, Ernst Krenek, Ferruccio Busoni, Edward Steuermann, and Egon Wellesz. The preface includes information on Schoenberg's attitudes toward performers and his philosophy of the performer's role in the process of musical re-creation. Some important additional aspects of interpreting Schoenberg's music are briefly considered in the final chapter.

Petteys, M. Leslie. *Julie Rive-King, American Pianist.* D.M.A. paper, Kansas City, Mo.: University of Missouri, 1987, 448 p. UM 8800639. Julie Rive-King (1854–1937), an American pianist, was considered one of the foremost piano virtuosi during the last quarter of the nineteenth century. Despite the fact that European and American women were encouraged to study and perform music only as amateurs, Rive-King pursued a professional career which proved to be more successful than those of most American male pianists of her era. Between 1874 and 1900, Rive-King performed with all of the prominent conductors and orchestras and made numerous concert tours throughout the United States and Canada.

This study discusses Rive-King's family and education, the influence exerted on her career by her husband and manager, and her life as a professional concert artist and teacher. Also included is an analysis of her method of practice and memorization, her choice of repertoire, and her pianistic abilities based on a study of her performance reviews. Finally, Rive-King's professional career is documented concerning the growth of her reputation, musicians with whom she worked, business relationships and agreements, and the hardships encountered by and demands made of traveling musicians in America during the late nineteenth century. Appendixes have also been compiled which include annotated lists of Rive-King's compositions, concert appearances, repertoire, and piano rolls.

In a field that was dominated by the male European virtuoso, Rive-King's career served as a role model for other women and American performers. Her willingness to travel throughout the country afforded her great opportunity to assist in America's musical education. Through her concerts, Rive-King helped to establish higher performance standards, and to introduce to her audiences a wide variety of piano repertoire by European and American composers.

Pfeiffer, Theodor. *The Piano Master Classes of Hans von Bülow.* Trans. and ed. Richard L. Zimdars. Bloomington: Indiana University Press, 1993, 196 p. Accounts of Bülow's master classes by Pfeiffer and Jose Vianna da Motta. These in-depth accounts preserve for today's pianists vital elements of the Liszt tradition, and the book contains valuable finger exercises that Bülow recommended to his students.

Pflanz, Barbara Claire. *Beethoven's Pianos and Piano Sonatas: A Study of the Piano as an Instrument in the Time of Ludwig van Beethoven and its Relation to Problems of Performance in the 32 Sonatas.* Thesis, Seattle: University of Washington, 1961.

Phelps, Consoella Ward. *The Keyboard Works of Johann Kasper Ferdinand Fischer (ca. 1665–1746).* Thesis, Seattle: University of Washington, 1973.

Phemister, William. *American Piano Concertos: A Bibliography.* Detroit, Mich.: Information Coordinators, 1985, 323 p. The listings range from Abrams to Zimbalist. Includes composer dates, a description of many of the works, publisher or where manuscript can be located, performance time, orchestration, composition date, first performance, and recordings (when appropriate). The most complete work on the subject.

Piano. Video cassette. Princeton, N.J.: Films for the Humanities and the Sciences, 28 minutes. ABS 2707. Concentrates on the piano, the most frequently featured solo instrument. Includes extracts from Tchaikovsky's *First Piano Concerto,* Brahms's *Variations on a Theme of Haydn,* and Schumann's *Piano Concerto in A Minor.* Hosted by Dudley Moore, Sir Georg Solti, conductor, with the Schleswig-Holstein Music Festival Orchestra.

Picton, Howard J. *The Life and Works of Joseph Anton Steffan (1726–1797): With Special Reference to His Keyboard Concertos.* New York: Garland Pub., 1989.

Pollens, Stewart. *The Early Pianoforte.* Cambridge, England: Cambridge University Press, 1994, 284 p. This is the first comprehensive historical and technological study of the pianoforte based on primary source material. It begins with the earliest fifteenth- and sixteenth-century manuscript sources, and then focuses on the "invention" of the piano by Bartolomeo Christofori in Florence in 1700, the early exportation of Florentine pianofortes, and the building of copies in Portugal, Spain, and Germany. The text is illustrated with many photographs, measurements, line drawings, and tables. Includes bibliographical references and index.

Potter, Susan Marie. *The Piano Method in Mid-Nineteenth Century America: A Study of Method Writers and Their Works Published in the United States.* D.M.A. paper, Philadelphia: Temple University, 1994, 275 p. UM 9434725. The purpose of this study is to examine the role of the piano pedagogue in mid-nineteenth-century America by investigating the careers and methods of thirty-three piano method writers whose works were published in the United States between 1820 and 1870. Additionally, a list was compiled to show the printing history of more than 100 methods known to have been published in the United States during that fifty-year span.

Prado, Sharon S. *The Decadent Aesthetic in France, 1880–1914: Musical Manifestations in the Works of Debussy and His Contemporaries.* Ph.D. dissertation, University of Cincinnati, 1992, 374 p. UM 9232316.

The decadent aesthetic in France influenced musical modernism in the development of a musical style analogous to stylistic innovations in decadent French poetry and literature during the 1880s. Musical manifestations of decadent style appear in selected works of Claude Debussy and Erik Satie, both closely associated with literary figures and the milieu of the Chat Noir, where the new aesthetic known as decadence was cultivated.

This dissertation provides paradigmatic analytical models of musical decadence in Debussy's *Proses lyriques* and the piano piece "Masques," as well as in Satie's *Prélude de la porte héroïque de ciel* and *Ogives*. Debussy's and Satie's interest in new models of expression and new means of manipulating musical elements parallels similar concerns of their literary contemporaries, which this thesis rightly calls decadence.

Prater, Pamela Jo. *A Comparison of the Techniques of Piano Playing Advocated by Selected Twentieth-Century Pedagogues.* D.M.A. paper, Austin: University of Texas, 1990, 139 p. UM 9105501. An analysis of the techniques of Theodor Leschetisky (1830–1915), Tobias Matthay (1858–1945), Rudolf Maria Breithaupt (1873–1945), Otto Ortmann (1889–1979), and Arnold Schultz (1903–1972).

Price, Dcon Nielsen. *Accompanying Skills for Pianists.* Culver City, Calif.: Culver Crest Publications, 1991, 152 p. The most practical book on the subject. Includes biographical references and index.

Prieur, Thierry Guy Patrice. *A Critical Analysis of the Premises Underlying North American Introductory Piano Methodologies.* M.A. thesis, Montreal: Concordia University, 1994, 137 p. UM 97597. This thesis critically examines the introductory stages of piano instruction as they are presented in contemporary North American piano methods. Proceeding from an interdisciplinary perspective—with references drawn from relevant sources in the pedagogical, psychological, and educational literatures—it focuses on the current practice of reducing information to prescriptive formulas, while confining student-teacher interaction to unilateral verbally and visually transmitted instruction. The underlying assumption here is that the more complex aural, tactile, choreographic, and aesthetic experiences will naturally follow.

This assumption not only oversimplifies the initial stage of an extremely complex and demanding skill, but communicates a vision of the relationship of pianist, piano, and score that can be as counterpro-

ductive as it is naive. In developing its critical argument, the thesis treats
the members of this relationship in terms of their interaction, rather
than as mutually exclusive entities. The value of prescriptive methodologies is thrown into question when considered in the light of its neglect of the long-term realities of music as a discipline. While they
may, in some cases, produce apparently quick results, they have neither the philosophical acumen nor the methodological tools to set the
pace for higher order musical performance. Indeed, a faithful adherence to the principles embodied in these prescriptions is more likely
to plant the seeds of performing "blocks" that could seriously compro-
mise the artistic development of the aspiring pianist. As an alternative,
suggestions are offered for the development of a methodology that
cues more directly into the student's native musical potential by establishing links between his or her existing knowledge and intuitive resources.

Pruett, Jeffrey Mark. *J. S. Bach's Chaconne in D Minor: An Examination of Three Arrangements for Piano Solo (Ernst von Pauer, Arthur
Briskier, Karl Hermann Pillney).* D.M.A. paper, Baton Rouge: Louisiana State University, 1991, 89 p. UM 9200085. The chaconne from
the *Second Partita for Solo Violin* by Johann Sebastian Bach is one of
the most often arranged compositions in the history of music. From
the years 1879 and 1893, respectively, came the most famous arrangements—those by Johannes Brahms and Ferruccio Busoni (both for
solo piano).

   This monograph consists of an examination of three versions of Bach's
Chaconne in D Minor—those by Ernst von Pauer (1867), Arthur
Briskier (1954), and Karl Hermann Pillney (1968). In addition, a brief
comparison of piano accompaniments written for the chaconne by
Felix Mendelssohn and Robert Schumann (1847 and 1853, respectively) comprises the remainder of the study. The author chose to examine Pauer's Chaconne because of its display of virtuoso keyboard technique, a quality that removes it dramatically from the original source.
Briskier's and Pillney's arrangements are examined in light of their similar compositional geneses—both are works dating from the twentieth century and subsequently reflect a more conservative view of the
interpretation of Bach's original work.

Puckett, Mark A. *Twelve Bagatelles by George Rochberg: Background,
Structure, and Performance.* D.M.A. paper, Lawrence: University of

Kansas, 1986, 51 p. UM 8619872. The *Twelve Bagatelles* (1952) for piano mark the beginning of George Rochberg's period of serial composition. The purpose of the lecture-recital is to provide insights and approaches to aid in their performance.

Part One includes biographical information on the composer, a discussion of the bagatelles in relation to his total output, and a survey of works that might have been an influence on the bagatelles. The overall structure of the work and other compositional aspects are also examined. Part Two explores the musical "gesture" of each bagatelle.

Each piece is examined in detail and such aspects as mood, tempo, structure, texture, articulation, and dynamics are considered. Because of the straightforward style and small traditional structures, the fact that the bagatelles are serial should matter little in the performer's approach. On the whole, they are quite accessible and have similarities to character pieces of earlier eras.

Two of the basic problems in the interpretation of sets of character pieces are to establish an overall cohesiveness while maintaining the individuality of each movement. The problem of cohesiveness in the bagatelles is approached by structural and compositional analysis. The pieces are drawn together by characteristic sonorities and motives, similarities of formal structure, and by the fact that only four of the possible forty-eight forms of the twelve-tone set are used.

The problem of maintaining the individuality of each movement within the set of pieces is approached by close observation of the score. Descriptive titles such as *Tempo di marcia* (no. 4), *Quasi parlando* (no. 5), and *Intenso, con un sentimento di destino* (no. 9) indicate strong individual characterizations for each piece. The serial aspect is not considered important by the composer, nor should it be a concern to the performer. The author suggests that programmatic images be used by the performer to aid in imagination and to enhance the changing moods of the pieces. This approach aids in realizing the sounds and nuances inherent in the work.

Purrone, Kevin C. *"Danses Concertantes" by Igor Stravinsky: An Arrangement for Two Pianos, Four Hands.* Ph.D. dissertation, Lubbock: Texas Tech University, 1994, 151 p. UM 9506786. Stravinsky's *Danses Concertantes* is a five-movement work for chamber orchestra. It was commissioned by Werner Janssen of Los Angeles for his own orchestra, and was conducted by the composer at its premier on February 8, 1942, in Los Angeles.

In addition to the two-piano arrangement of *Danses Concertantes* (conceived as a performing edition), this study includes a review of those general principles used to create the arrangement as well as detailed notes on each measure of the arrangement. The subject of these notes concerns the incorporation and distribution of the instrumental parts into the two-piano texture, and the criteria that were used to decide upon these incorporations and distributions.

Rabin, Rhoda. *At the Beginning: Teaching Piano to the Very Young Child.* New York: Schirmer Books, 1996, 304 p. Rabin leads readers on a step-by-step journey through the elements of teaching piano to the very young child (ages three through seven). Three appendixes supplement the text with musical games and exercises that have been created or adapted by Rabin to help children absorb information.

Rachmaninoff Piano Concerto No. 2. Video cassette. Princeton, N.J.: Films for the Humanities and Sciences, 60 minutes. ABS 4115. Barry Douglas, pianist, with Michael Tilson Thomas conducting the London Symphony Orchestra. Includes rehearsal sequences, discussions between soloist and presenter (Dudley Moore) that explore the technical and creative demands of the work, and a full performance of the concerto.

Randall, Mayumi Ogura. *The History of Piano Improvisation in Western Concert Music.* D.M.A. paper, University of Cincinnati, 1993, 97 p. U.M. 94244584. The purpose of this study is twofold. The main purpose is to present the type of piano improvisation practiced during the eighteenth and nineteenth centuries and to discuss the art's gradual decline during the twentieth century. The second purpose is to clarify the definition of improvisation and to give examples of how the art was taught in the past. Many times, improvisatory skill was considered a special talent that a few privileged musicians possessed. Talent is undoubtedly very important, but many pedagogues in the past agreed that through systematic study and diligence, any musically inclined student could acquire improvisation skill of a sufficient and fluent quality.

Rangel-Ribeiro, Victor, and Robert Markel. *Chamber Music: An International Guide to Works and Their Instrumentation.* New York: Facts on File, 1993, 271 p. Lists more than 8,000 pieces written between the sixteenth century and the present that are scored for three to twenty musicians. Part Three is a master quick-reference index.

Rastall, Roberta Luckey. *Using the Orff-Schulwerk Process in Pre-Piano Lessons for Early Elementary-Aged Children.* M.A. thesis, Fullerton: California State University, 1989, 101 p. UM 1336966. Whereas the current method series available on the market are quite adequate for teaching elementary school children to play the piano, they do not provide as sufficient a beginning for preschool children who lack musical experiences. This gap can be filled by Orff-Schulwerk (currently used in elementary school classrooms) if the Orff techniques are applied to the teaching of individual preschool and early elementary–aged children.

Before learning to read music can be accomplished, the child needs experience with a wide variety of musical activities. A set of lesson plans was developed showing how the process of the Orff-Schulwerk can be integrated into pre-piano lessons. A study was also done to demonstrate ways to integrate these musical experiences with the four surveyed teaching books. The techniques of the Orff-Schulwerk can provide both pre-piano musical experience and musical experiences found to be lacking in older students.

Ray, Brenda C. *Franz Liszt's Settings of Three Petrarch Sonnets.* D.M.A. paper, Baton Rouge: Louisiana State University, 1986, 169 p. UM 8710586. Franz Liszt's transcriptions of his own works and the works of others represent a significant segment of his keyboard compositions. These transcriptions (and his numerous revisions of them) provide opportunities for studying the development of his compositional styles. For example, the four versions of three Petrarch sonnets reveal the manner in which he used his own basic musical material in two different areas of performance (vocal and keyboard), and they illuminate the path he took that led to his late style.

The purpose of this study is to examine Liszt's four versions of sonnets (the 1838–1839 tenor songs, the 1846 keyboard transcriptions, the 1858 keyboard revisions, and the 1861 baritone songs) from a historical and stylistic standpoint, examining in particular the characteristics that indicate a change in style which, in turn, pointed to his late works of 1869–1886.

Of the four sets, the 1858 piano transcriptions are particularly effective examples of their genre—the nineteenth-century character piece for piano. In them, Liszt's skillful and tasteful transference of extra-musical ideas to the keyboard can easily be grasped and appreciated. They have eclipsed the more virtuoso 1846 transcriptions to such a degree that the latter are rarely performed. The "operatic" 1838–1839 songs, with their expansive accompaniments, display characteristics that have prompted criticisms of Liszt's early songwriting technique. Just as the 1858 piano revisions represent a refinement and sophistication in style, the 1861 song rewrites reveal a certain control and restraint. Characteristics are found in them that predict the changes in Liszt's style that were to occur during the last seventeen years of his life.

Redford, John Robert. *The Application of Spanish Folk Music in the Piano Suite "Iberia" by Isaac Albeniz.* D.M.A. paper, Tucson: University of Arizona, 1995, 70 p. UM 9426340. Albéniz has made full use of the wealth of Spanish folk music in his compositional style, and the movements of Iberia represent a synthesis of the characteristic elements of Spanish folk music. These elements may be considered according to the following three main categories: the rhythms of Spanish dance, especially those belonging to the body of Andalusian folk music known as flamenco; the characteristics of Spanish folk song; and the guitar idiom. This study identifies and examines the numerous aspects of folk music employed in Iberia, and in several instances compares Albéniz's stylizations with quotations of authentic folk music.

Reed, Carl Hadley. *The Keyboard Works of Johann Kuhnau.* Thesis, Seattle: University of Washington, 1956.

Reich, Howard. *Van Cliburn: A Biography.* Nashville: Thomas Nelson Publishers, 1993, 428 p. Numerous myths surround the pianist Van Cliburn who, in 1958, won the first Tchaikovsky International Piano Competition in Moscow. At the time, relations between the U.S. and the USSR were so tense that the jury needed Khrushchev's permission to award the prize to an American. The twenty-three-year-old Texan went on to become a major concert and recording artist during the next two decades. Then Cliburn suddenly stopped and it was not until 1987, when he charmed the Gorbachevs at a White House concert, that he performed in public again.

Part of the story is told in the words of fellow musicians, critics, friends, and Cliburn himself. Reich disputes the claim advanced by some that Cliburn's talent was overrated, his repertoire limited, and his artistry not taken seriously by the musical establishment. He does a thorough job of showing that the long period of silence was due to burnout rather than failure. Van Cliburn emerges as a likable and modest musician, dedicated to helping others, and devoted to his mother, who was his first teacher. Includes bibliographical references and discography.

Reighard, Geoffrey Mark. *A Theoretical and Performance Analysis of the Eighteen Transcriptions from George Gershwin's "Songbook."* D.M.A. paper, University of Oklahoma, 1993, 261 p. UM 94090260. The purpose of this study is a theoretical and performance analysis of all eighteen songs of the *Songbook*. The premise for a thorough theoretical researching of the work is to help pianists understand the music, thus enhancing performance. The study also focuses on the art of improvisation, which has a direct correlation to the song transcriptions.

Reimler, Walter. *A Gershwin Companion: A Critical Inventory and Discography, 1916–1984.* Ann Arbor: Popular Culture, 1991, 488 p. Part One contains information about 318 Gershwin pieces that have been published, but publishers are not included. Part Two contains information (for 1913–1946) about unpublished works by Gershwin. Part Three includes three indexes of recording artists, of compositions, and general index.

Renfrow, Renon Dean. *The Development and Evaluation of Objectives for Educating Graduate Piano Pedagogy Students to Use Computer and Keyboard Technology.* Ph.D. dissertation, Norman: University of Oklahoma, 1991, 210 p. UM 9135052. The purpose of this study is fourfold: to develop objectives for educating graduate piano pedagogy students to use computer and keyboard technology; to determine the status of computer and keyboard technology education within the graduate piano pedagogy offerings of selected colleges and universities; to identify and interview the experts in piano pedagogy and keyboard technology as it relates to piano pedagogy; and to evaluate the objectives and make recommendations on implementing them into graduate piano interviews.

Renwick, William Jonathan Michael. *Voice-Leading Patterns in the Fu-*

gal Expositions of J. S. Bach's Well-Tempered Clavier. Ph.D. dissertation, City University of New York, 1987, 375 p. UM 8713790. Although Heinrich Schenker's theory of tonal music goes very far toward uniting the traditionally independent domains of counterpoint and harmony, it does not deal directly or deeply with the connective role which imitative texture often plays in this synthesis. The obligations inherent in a canonic or fugal texture may limit composition choices, but they also provide an underpinning of control and direction to voice leading. This dissertation demonstrates the structural role of imitation in tonal music by comparative analysis of a selected body of imitative music: the fugues of J. S. Bach's *Well-Tempered Clavier.*

Rezits, Joseph. *Beloved Tyranna: The Legend and Legacy of Isabelle Vengerova.* Bloomington, Ind: David Daniel Music Publications, 1995, 226 p. Describes Vengerova, who was one of the most important piano teachers of the twentieth century. Focuses on her superlative musicianship combined with her ability to impart this rare quality to others. This book also reveals how we as musicians can apply her principles to our own playing and teaching.

Rhee, Meehyun. *A Background and an Analysis of Mozart's Piano Concerto No. 24 in C Minor, K.491: Aids Towards Performance.* D.M.A. paper, Columbus: Ohio State University, 1992, 114 p. UM 9218947. Based upon her experience in performing the work, the writer explores the elements of classical concerto form and style defined by the concerto. Chapter One discusses the background of the concerto, including a historical summary of Mozart's life and structure of the concerto.

  Chapter Two provides information regarding literature and sources for the concerto, including a description of research methods and music. Chapter Three presents a general analysis of each movement, including thematic characteristics, key relationship, structure, technical problems, and interpretation. Chapter Four lists the writer's summary and conclusions, including recommendations for further study and performance.

Rhein, Robert. *Johann Peter Milchmeyer's "Die Wahre Art das Pianoforte zu Spielen": An Annotated Translation.* D.M.A. paper, Lincoln: University of Nebraska, 1993, 275 p. UM 9322813. J. P. Milchmeyer's *Die wahre Art das Pianoforte zu spielen* (The True Art of Playing the

Pianoforte) was a keyboard instruction manual published in Dresden, Germany, in 1797. It was addressed to a middle-class audience either of students attempting to learn without an instructor, or of teachers who lacked training and experience. The present dissertation is a translation of the first (and only) edition, "as clear and readable as possible, while reproducing the book in a form as much like the original as practical" (from the translator's preface).

There are six chapters: The Position of the Body, the Arm, the Hand, and the Fingers (including advice on styles of articulation and on rhythm); On Fingering (the longest chapter); On Ornamentation (with many written-out examples); On Musical Expression (terminology); On Knowledge and Modification of the Pianoforte (evaluating pianos and employing the various special-effects pedals); and Several General Remarks.

Riggs, Robert Daniel. *Articulation in Mozart's and Beethoven's Sonatas for Piano and Violin: Source-Critical and Analytic Studies.* Ph.D. dissertation, Harvard University, 1987, 461 p. UM 8800842. In 1954 a musicological competition focused investigations into Mozart's possible use of different signs to indicate nuances of staccato. The majority verdict (with a few dissenting votes) ruled that Mozart did intend such distinctions, and that two signs, the dot and the stroke, should be used in critical editions. This policy was adopted for the *Neue Mozart Ausgabe.* The same problem has also plagued the editorial evaluations of Beethoven's notation, and it has produced conflicting expert opinions.

This dissertation attempts to solve the "staccato problem" by placing it in a broader context. The tandem study of both composers widens the perspective and thus avoids possible misconceptions created by irrelevant personal idiosyncrasies of notation. Also, the significance of articulation (including but not limited to staccato) is considered in relation to their general compositional and performance styles.

The first of the three sections is an analysis of the supportive function played by articulation in achieving clarity of structure and in the creation of contrast—two of the most important features of classical style. In section two, which narrows to concentrate on the staccato problem, the author makes the controversial assertion that neither Mozart nor Beethoven indicated nuances of staccato by employing different signs. This conclusion is based on evidence from the autograph and printed sources, the eighteenth- and nineteenth-century instruction books, and biographical clues. Section three is an examination of the performer's obligation to make decisions regarding the interpretation of articulation. These must be guided, not by the appearance of the autograph notation, but by an understanding of contemporary views concerning musical expression and character.

Rivera-Gusman, Felix. *A Rhythmic Riddle: A Guide to the Performance of Rhythms in the Piano Danzas of Juan Morel Campos.* D.M.A. paper, University of Miami, 1993, 74 p. UM 9412923. After a historical account regarding the confusion that surrounds their performance, the seventy-nine danzas in the original edition of Olimpio Otero are rhythmically analyzed. Guidelines for the proper performance of Morel Campos's danzas are furnished, allowing any pianist, not only regional ones, to arrive at a correct and musical performance of the danzas.

Robbins, Mary Lauren. *Mozart's Cadenzas for the First Movements of His Piano Concertos: The Influence of Harmonic Symmetry on Their Function and Structure.* D.M.A. paper, Austin: University of Texas, 1992, 117 p. UM 9309315. The symmetrical tonic-dominant-tonic harmonic relationship that characterizes Mozart's sonata-type works is also exhibited in his first movement cadenzas for the piano concertos. This dissertation discusses harmonic symmetry on two structural levels in relation to a Mozart first movement cadenza: the cadenza contributes to the overall tonal symmetry of the movement in which it occurs, and a type of harmonic symmetry is exhibited in the cadenza itself as well. This symmetry in the cadenzas is shown by analyses based largely on emphasized occurrences of the tonic harmony or its chord tones.

Robert, Walter. *From Bach to Brahms: A Musician's Journey through Keyboard Literature.* Bloomington, Ind.: Brown Composition Systems, 1993, 147 p. Robert's brilliant mind and wit are evident on every page of this book, which is primarily Robert's lecture notes from his years of teaching piano literature. He describes religious, cultural, political, and technological conditions that influenced the creation and reception of keyboard music from 1700 to 1900. Robert hopes the reader will play the music under dicussion for, as he says, "words without songs" are meaningless. "Playing, even with only one finger, is more profitable than taking tonal baths in the record library" (from the introduction). Most of the book is easy to read and follow, while parts (Bach's World and Music, Beethoven—Lessons from Sociology) will require more than one reading if they are to be thoroughly understood.

Roberts, Jean Elizabeth. *Alec Wilder (1907–1980) as Composer of Piano Music: A Study of Stylistic and Structural Aspects of Five Piano Works.* D.M.A. paper, Austin: University of Texas, 1988, 113 p. UM 8901432. Wilder was an American composer, primarily self-taught, whose life and works are gaining increased recognition since his death. He began writing popular songs in the 1920s, but by the 1950s had turned his attention to more serious forms, mostly instrumental. This treatise examines five of his largest piano works: the *Sonata-Fantasy* and *Piano Suites Numbers One, Two, Three*, and *Four. Piano Suite Number Three* has been published by Margun Music. The other pieces are still in manuscript but can be obtained from the publisher, Margun Music.

The Introduction explores the personal history of Alec Wilder, much of which is based on his book *Letters I Never Mailed*, published by Little, Brown and Company. This profile describes Wilder as a very shy and modest person who composed not for posterity or financial gain, but for the purpose of communicating specifically with close friends. In Chapters Two through Seven, the *Sonata-Fantasy* and *Piano Suites Numbers One, Two, Three*, and *Four* are examined for melody, rhythm, harmony, and form. Special attention is given to the areas of counterpoint, melodic transformation, chromaticism, and the use of blue notes. In each chapter there is a discussion of stylistic elements such as the unpredictable and unique style of his melodic writing, use of syncopation, added-note chords, and the adaptation of these elements into traditional forms. By discussing the various aspects of Wilder's composition and examining the dichotomy of influences and characteristics in his music, the author attempts to clarify the unusual position Wilder occupies in the world of composition.

Roberts, Paul. *Images: The Piano Music of Claude Debussy.* Portland, Oreg.: Amadeus Press, 1996, 396 p. Pianist Roberts probes the sources of Debussy's artistic inspiration, relating the "impressionist" titles to the artistry and literary ferment of the time. With clarity and insight, Roberts touches on all the principal technical problems facing a performer of Debussy's piano music. Richly illustrated. Also available is a CD, *Debussy: Piano Music*, the first of a series of recordings of the complete piano works, performed by Paul Roberts. The CD is available separately.

Roberts, Peter Deane. *Modernism in Russian Piano Music: Skriabin, Prokofiev, and Their Russian Contemporaries.* Bloomington: Indiana University Press, 1993, vol. I, 175 p., vol. II, 236 p. Volume I contains text and excellent analyses. Volume II contains more than 300 musical examples, many from scores that are difficult to attain. Includes bibliographical references and index.

Roberts Bell, Carol Ann. *A Performance Analysis of Selected Dances from the "Hungarian Dances" of Johannes Brahms and the "Slavonic Dances" of Antonín Dvořák for One-Piano, Four-Hands.* D.M.A. paper, Norman: University of Oklahoma, 1990, 274 p. UM 9110007. The purpose of this project is to provide a performance analysis of *Hungarian Dances* Nos. 6 and 11 by Johannes Brahms and *Slavonic Dances* Op. 46, No. 7 and Op. 72, No. 1 by Antonín Dvořák. An overview of each collection precedes the analyses. Few documents have dealt with more than one or two dances from either collection, and none has analyzed these specific dances for performance.

The analyses of the dances are approached from an ethnic viewpoint with a broad historical perspective preceding the analyses. The background explores the development of the duet up to the nineteenth century as well as the rise of nationalism in the nineteenth century. Prior to each overview, further background is given that discusses the countries and people associated with each collection. Within this discussion, the musical characteristics of each folk group are defined. Acknowledging popular as well as folk elements in the dances, this document also addresses the absorption of these features into the personal styles of Brahms and Dvořák.

Each analysis begins with a general description of basic musical elements as well as any discoveries as to the dance's origin. A detailed phrase-by-phrase analysis proceeds with special attention to stylistic traits and performance problems. The outcome is a clearer understanding of compositional features. From this vantage each analysis should enhance a more stylistic performance of the duets.

Robertson, Kaestner D. *Arm-Weight and Weight-Transference Technique: Its Systematic Use as a Technical and Artistic Vehicle in Piano Playing.* D.M.A. paper, Boston University, 1991, 118 p. UM 9122870.

This dissertation reexamines weight-transference technique and takes the position that this technique is not just one of several equally effective piano-playing techniques, but the only one.

Robinson, Schuyler Watrous. *B-A-C-H Motive in German Keyboard Compositions from the Time of J. S. Bach to the Present.* Thesis, Urbana-Champaign: University of Illinois, 1972, 136 p.

Rodman, Ronald Wayne. *Thematic and Tonal Processes in the Development-Reprise Forms of Claude Debussy, 1880–1905.* Ph.D. dissertation, Bloomington: Indiana University, 1992, 351 p. UM 9235302. Claude Debussy is considered an innovator in musical composition in the early twentieth century, especially in his manipulation of extended tertian harmonies, nontraditional scales, and unorthodox thematic construction to create unique formal structures. While Debussy's forms are often cited as iconoclastic for this time and as prototypes of much subsequent twentieth-century composition, this dissertation surveys to what extent Debussy was influenced by the archetype of sonata design in four of his early compositions: the *Symphonie en si mineur* (1880), the first movement of the *Quatuor* (1892), the prelude to the suite *Pour le piano* (1902), and *L'Isle joyeuse* (1905).

An analytic method is devised, following d'Indy's ideas of tonal motion and prolongation, to trace the linear deployment of themes and tonal areas in each of the four pieces. Themes are recognized as adhering to one of five functions of sonata form: exposition, recapitulation (recurrence), introduction, transition, and development. Results of the analyses reveal that Debussy retained the ternary conception of sonata design, but interpolated into the linear course of the design juxtaposed and stratified thematic and tonal segments. Thematically, themes often recurred at unexpected locations, creating small-scale arch designs.

Roe, Stephen. *Keyboard Music of J. C. Bach: Source Problems and Stylistic Development in the Solo and Ensemble Works.* New York: Garland Publishing Co., 1989, 490 p.

Rogers, Barbara Jean. *The Works for Piano Solo and Piano with Other Instruments of Mary Carr Moore (1873–1957).* D.M.A. paper, University of Cincinnati, 1992, 376 p. UM 9313822. Two chapters discuss the life and musical career of Mary Carr Moore. An active performer and teacher, Moore participated in musical organizations and worked for the advancement and appreciation of American music. She composed throughout her life.

The remaining chapters examine Moore's music for piano solo, chamber music including piano, and piano concerto. Her style evolved over time; three stylistic periods are discernible in her work. At first (1898–1922) she gained skill in handling established rules. Gradually (1923–1934) she responded to new influences, particularly those associated with Impressionism. Her mature works (1935–1950) show Moore integrating new materials and old.

Rolder, Michael Thomas. *A History of the Concerto.* Portland, Oreg.: Amadeus Press, 1994, 480 p. Includes bibliographical references and index. This lucid guide to the concerto consists of four parts corresponding to the major periods of music—Baroque, Classical, Romantic, and Twentieth-Century. The compositions of each composer are discussed in detail.

Rosenblum, Sandra P. *Performance Practices in Classic Piano Music: Their Principles and Applications.* Bloomington: Indiana University Press, 1988, 544 p. Assists the performer on the fortepiano and pianoforte to arrive at musical, expressive, and historically informed performance. The author examines the principles of performing the music of Haydn, Mozart, Beethoven, and their contemporaries as revealed in a variety of historical sources. The finest book on the subject.

Rosfeld, Marilyn Dalgliesh. *The Development of a Series of Instructional Units for Teaching Improvisational Principles to Pianists.* D.M.A. paper, Norman: University of Oklahoma, 1989. Improvisation is essentially the formulation of musical constructs in a musician's mind and the simultaneous performance of those tonal images. While improvisation has been a significant factor in Western music of the past, its role in art music has declined since the mid-1800s. It still thrives in folk, popular, and church music and has attracted some interest in academia in recent years. The need for instructional materials designed to aid students in acquiring improvisational skills prompted the present study.

The purpose of this study is to develop a series of instructional units for teaching improvisational principles to pianists. Each unit is based on selected theoretical principles. The study identifies procedures that composers and improvisers have successfully used and creates a means of focusing experimentation by the student in systematic productive learning using these procedures. This material has several potential uses: 1) it may serve as a textbook for a college course in keyboard improvisation; 2) it may be used as the textbook for the keyboard section of the freshmen-sophomore theory sequence; 3) it may be a supplementary text in private or class piano for the study of improvisation; 4) it may be a self-paced instructional tool for those wishing to develop improvisational skills; and 5) it may help composers and arrangers in improvising progressions at the keyboard that will culminate in the written score.

The format of each unit is divided into six sections: description of the theoretical concept, preparatory practice steps involving the concept, application of the concept to the "Ode to Joy" theme from Beethoven's Ninth Symphony, examples for examination from piano literature that illustrate the concept, melodies with chord symbols for harmonization by the student, and suggested titles of other melodies for further harmonic improvisation.

The theoretical concepts developed in the sixteen units are far from exhaustive. Similar studies in several areas are suggested: contrapuntal improvisation; accompaniment patterns and texture variation; stylistic features of additional idioms such as jazz, rag, gospel, and rock; and church music. It is hoped that these instructional units will provide a medium to help raise the level of improvisation within educational institutions from stepchild status to full legitimacy.

Rowland, David. *A History of Pianoforte Pedalling*. Cambridge, England: Cambridge University Press, 1993. Pedaling technique was a major feature of nineteenth-century piano performance and, coupled with new developments in piano structure, inspired many composers to write innovative works for the literature. Rowland examines this topic through the technique and music of composer-pianists such as Beethoven, Liszt, and Chopin and follows the transition from harpsichord and clavichord to piano. Includes bibliographical references and index.

Rownd, Gary R. *Musical "Tombeaux" and "Hommages" for Piano Solo*. D.M.A. paper, Lexington: University of Kentucky, 1990, 200 p. A consideration of "tombeaux" and "homages" for piano solo from 1709 to the present, organized into eleven categories: celebration, character portrait, explanatory note given, in memory of, imitations, piece for . . . , "soggetto cavato," style portrait, tombeau intent, homage intent, and piece in a commemorative set. An appendix of over 300 titles provides publication information and details of each tribute.

Roys, Katie Clare. *A Stylistic Analysis of the Pianoforte Sonatas of Franz Schubert.* Thesis, Seattle: University of Washington, 1950.

Rubinstein. *See Arthur Rubinstein*

Ruckman, Robert Craig. *The Etudes of Alexander Scriabin: A Performance Perspective.* D.M.A. paper, University of Cincinnati, 1987, 237 p. UM 8712719. In spite of a renaissance of Scriabin's music during the past two decades, much of his music continues to be ignored or underrated. The etudes, twenty-six studies of a consistently high quality, are a case in point. Scriabin's etudes are of interest not only for their pianistic qualities, but also because they illustrate, by virtue of their placement in his complete works, his compositional development, which went from simple diatonic harmony to ultrachromaticism and atonality. This development, which is seen less dramatically and more continuously in the ten sonatas and especially in the ninety preludes, is highlighted in a study of the etudes, which appear as landmarks along the way in his stylistic development.

The purpose of this study is to illustrate, through an examination of the etudes, performance problems the pianist will encounter in Scriabin. Many, if not most, of the idiosyncracies involved in playing Scriabin remain throughout his three stylistic periods. The study presents the etudes of each period, relates their general characteristics, and elucidates by way of musical examples. Each etude is discussed. This study is not a measure-by-measure analysis or a problem-solving commentary. The pianist who approaches the Scriabin etudes must, as a prerequisite, have well-developed technique and exhibit sensitive musicianship, both of which presuppose abilities in fingering, pedaling, phrase-shaping, and obtaining clear balance. Rather, this study seeks to point out situations that are intrinsic to Scriabin's style, and which present musical and technical challenges. It is the author's belief that all musical problems have technical solutions. This kind of presentation will be of particular value to the pianist who is embarking on the performance of Scriabin's music, particularly the etudes.

Ryan, Sylvia Watkins. *The Solo Piano Music of Gian-Carlo Menotti: A*

Pedagogical and Performance Analysis. D.M.A. paper, Norman: University of Oklahoma, 1993, 204 p. UM 9320224. The purpose of this document is to provide a pedagogical and performance analysis of Gian-Carlo Menotti's published solo piano works: *Poemetti* (1937), *Ricercare and Toccata on a Theme from "The Old Maid and the Thief"* (1953), and the piano version of *Amahl and the Night Visitors* (1951). This study is intended to serve as a reference work for teachers of contemporary piano literature.

Sachs, Harvey. *Rubinstein: A Life.* New York: Grove Press, 1995, 525 p. This carefully researched book straightens out many of the facts from Arthur Rubinstein's books *My Young Years* (1973) and *My Many Years* (1980). Sachs lists some of Rubinstein's best recordings, and Donald Manildi's discography (thirty-three pages) is thoroughly welcomed. Also includes fifty highly interesting photographs.

Sadoff, Ronald Hayden. *The Solo Piano Music of Charles Ives: A Performance Guide.* Ph.D. dissertation, New York University, 1986, 470 p. UM 8614345. The study begins with a biographical chapter that uncovers significant information that pertains to Ives's eclectic compositional style. This includes a discussion of Ives's literary work: "Essays before a Sonata." Its close relationship with the *Piano Sonata No. 2* ("Concord Mass., 1840–1860") is highlighted. An overview of the complete published solo piano works is also included.

The logic of Jan La Rue's (1970) approach to style analysis is presented next. This serves as a formalistic method for analyzing all of the published solo piano works. Traditional musical elements are discussed in the first part of each analysis: sound, harmony, rhythm, and melody. A scale model of each work and movement appears in the form of a time line. This gives one an overall sense of structural proportion and motivic unity.

Lawrence Ferrara's phenomenological method is examined in depth in the opening of the fourth chapter. The *Concord Sonata* was chosen through a selection process because of its overwhelming quantitative presence (in relation to his other piano works). Moreover, it is highly representative to his overall solo piano corpus. Ferrara's method was then utilized to present a detailed analysis of this work. In the fifth chapter, the knowledge gained from the data accumulated is integrated in the construction of a performance guide to the *Concord Sonata*. Conclusions are presented that synthesize biographical, formalistic, phenomenological, and practical perspectives.

Saffle, Michael Benton. *Liszt in Germany, 1840–1845.* Stuyvesant, N.Y.: Pendragon Press, 1994. The Franz Liszt studies series; No. 2. Includes bibliographical references and index. Traces Liszt's reception by German critics, and the "German" compositions Liszt completed for voice, male chorus, and piano during these tours.

Saldarriaga-Ruiz, Juanita Susana. *The Fifty "Ponteios" for Piano of Camargo Guarnieri.* D.M.A. paper, Chicago: American Conservatory of Music, 1991, 176 p. UM 9130026. The fifty Ponteios were written over a period of twenty-eight years, from 1931 to 1959. This document includes a discussion of style, influence of jazz music, impact of folk music, influence of Alexander Scriabin, and pianistic style.

Salmon, John Cameron. *The Piano Sonatas of Carl Loewe (1796–1869).* D.M.A. paper, Austin: University of Texas, 1988, 452 p. UM 8909776. While Carl Loewe was perhaps best known in his day as a composer and performer of his own ballads, he also wrote a sizable amount of instrumental music—two symphonies, three piano concerti, several string quartets, and five piano sonatas—most of which has never been examined thoroughly. Until now, for example, there have been only a few brief studies of Loewe's piano sonatas, notably by Leopold Hirschberg (1919), Paul Egert (1934), Hans Engel (1934), and William S. Newman (1969).

By looking at Loewe's five diverse piano sonatas (composed 1819–1847) in a thoroughgoing fashion, it becomes possible to place them in some kind of historical and stylistic context as well as to evaluate them in terms consistent with modern sensibilities. Perhaps more significantly, taken together, the sonatas constitute an encapsulation for mid-nineteenth-century trends, such as the musical unification of several movements or the use of a specific, sometimes elaborate, program.

Several subthemes emerge in this study that have ramifications outside the scope of the ostensibly narrow topic. One is the abiding influence of Beethoven, and to a lesser extent Weber, on sonata composers of the early nineteenth century. Another is the manifestation of "pastoral style" and "gypsy style" (as seen in Loewe's Frühling and Zigeuner sonatas), both healthily blossoming traditions in the nineteenth century. Still another subtheme concerns the identification of German critical taste from 1833–1852, the years within which Loewe's sonatas were reviewed. From critiques by Schumann (*Neue Zeitschrift für Musik*), Rellstab (*Iris im Gebiete der Tonkunst*), Fink (*Allgemeine musikalische Zeitung*), Referstein (*Cecilia*), and others, one gains insight into what was considered new and what was considered normal.

Loewe's sonatas straddle Romantic and Classical styles. Thus, while some formal ideas, such as basing several movements on one motif as in Op. 41, look forward, they tend to reflect the earlier pianism of Cramer or Weber rather than the more instrumentally exploitative approach of Chopin or Liszt. Still, Loewe's Op. 16—with the curious slow-movement Romance for tenor and soprano—is a satisfying and original contribution to Romantic piano literature.

———. *The Piano Sonatas of Carl Loewe*. New York: Peter Lang, 1997, 247 p. Loewe's training and musical background are discussed following a close look and analysis of his five piano sonatas. Loewe (1796–1869) straddled the Classical and Romantic eras. Also includes an index of Loewe's works. An interesting body of compositions. Based on the author's doctoral dissertation.

Salmon, Paul. *Notes From the Green Room: Coping With Stress and Anxiety in Musical Performance*. New York: Lexington Books/ Macmillan Publishers, 1992, 231 p. Written primarily for students, teachers, and clinicians who wish to look into therapeutic techniques for dealing with performance stress based on cognitive-behavioral therapy. A central thesis of the book is that performance stress can be effectively managed through a process of self-assessment and the cultivation of a wide range of coping skills.

Salvador, Miguel. *The Piano Suite "Goyescas" by Enrique Granados: An Analytical Study*. D.M.A. paper, University of Miami, 1988. 153 p. UM 8820805. This study presents a multifaceted analysis of the piano suite *Goyescas* by Enrique Granados. The aim of the research has been to obtain a more objective insight into the distinctive language of the music.

Factual data and critical commentaries on *Goyescas* are presented in the Introduction, followed by an outline of the purpose and need for the study. A brief review of the extent and nature of the available literature devoted to *Goyescas* is also included. Background information on the *Goyescas,* including a historical account of the Goyesque period and Granados's source of inspiration, is presented in the first chapter.

Stylistic features found in *Goyescas* are illustrated by way of musical examples and discussion in Chapter Two. The presentation is organized around the areas of harmony, melody, rhythm, and meter,
and the simulation of specific sound idioms on the piano. Chapter
Three examines the formal structure of the suite. The analytical discussion is preceded by general background information on each piece
and a brief survey of the art works which inspired the music. A formal, thematic, and tonal diagram is provided for each movement as
an aid to the reader. Granados's transformation of the piano suite into the opera *Goyescas* is presented in Chapter Four. The piano writing is traced in the vocal score in order to establish the relationship
between the two. A synopsis of the operatic plot is also included.

The Conclusion consists of a summary and suggestions for further
study. Art works by Francisco Goya related to the *Goyescas* comprise
the appendix to the essay. An extensive bibliography, a selected discography, and an index to musical examples are also included.

Samson, Jim. *The Cambridge Companion to Chopin.* New York: Cambridge University Press, 1992, 289 p., 8 illustrations, 120 music examples, paperback. This book is designed to provide the enquiring
music lover with helpful insights into a musical style that recognizes
no contradictions between the accessible and the sophisticated, between the popular and the significant. Twelve carefully structured chapters by leading Chopin scholars make up three parts. Part One discusses the sources of Chopin's style in the music of his predecessors
and the social history of the period. Part Two profiles the mature
music, and Part Three considers the afterlife of his music—its reception, its criticism, and its compositional influence on the works of
subsequent composers.

———. *Chopin: The Four Ballades.* New York: Cambridge University
Press, 1992, 104 p. A survey of manuscript sources and later editions
points out some of the many inconsistencies that continue to vex critics and performers. The discussion of the nature and musical content
of the works includes so many different viewpoints that the reader is
left somewhat confused. The introductory chapter is the finest.

———. *The Music of Chopin.* New York: Oxford University Press, 1994,
264 p., paperback. First published in hardback by Routledge in 1985.
This book is a critical study of Chopin's music and of the creative proc-

ess. Provides a detailed analysis of the style and structure of the music in the light of recent Chopin scholarship on the one hand and recent analytical methods on the other.

Samulski-Parekh, Mary V. *A Comprehensive Study of the Piano Suite "Goyescas" by Enrique Granados.* D.M.A. paper, Kansas City, Mo.: University of Missouri, 1988, 243 p. UM 8814609. This study of the piano suite *Goyescas* begins with a sketch of Enrique Granados's life and continues with an in-depth review of the major influences on Granados's music and life, including Romanticism, Spanish folk music, and Francisco Goya. Discussions and musical examples illustrate how Schumann, Chopin, and Liszt affected Granados's early piano works and the suite *Goyescas.* Also, specific instances of the various traits of Spanish folk music found in the *Goyescas* are presented after considering the significant influence of Felipe Pedrell on Granados and his colleagues. Granados's fascination with Goya is placed in a political and historical context, which shows that Granados was not alone in his admiration for the great painter. This is followed by a thorough study of the structure of each movement of the *Goyescas* and a consideration of the possible thematic unity of the suite. A brief summary of the opera *Goyescas* concludes the body of this paper.

Sanchez, Theresa Cosette Bush. *A Study of the Twenty-Four Preludes for Solo Piano (1968) by Richard Cumming.* D.M.A. paper, Hattiesburg: University of Southern Mississippi, 1992, 112 p. UM 9321738. This study opens with a biography of the composer Richard Cumming, contains a discussion of his musical training, and details his career as a piano soloist, professional accompanist, and composer of music for piano, theater, chamber groups, and singers. The main portion of the study provides a stylistic and harmonic analysis of each of the twenty-four preludes of Cumming with sixty-one musical examples, as well as background information on their composition. A summary chapter discusses Cumming's compositional techniques in the preludes, with regard to melody, harmony, rhythm, texture, form, and technical difficulty.

Sauerbrei, Patricia Margaret. *The Keyboard Concertos of Georg Christoph Wagenseil (1715–1777).* Ph.D. dissertation, University of Toronto, 1983. Wagenseil made a significant contribution toward the transformation of the keyboard concerto from Baroque to Classical style, a contribution underestimated to the present time owing to an in-adequate study of the sources.

A full sonata-form exposition, development, and recapitulation are consistent features of Wagenseil's first-movement concerto form. An initial Tutti presents the orchestral first subject, transitional material, and closing subject. The accompanying ensemble then takes on a sec-ondary role to the soloist, who, after restating the opening theme, in-troduces a distinctive keyboard subject which becomes the vehicle for elaboration throughout the movement. The recapitulation, often initi-ated by the soloist, includes a recall of all significant material. Slow movements range in scope from full-fledged concerto form to a brief binary form with perfunctory ritornellos. Binary structure is used in many slow and final movements, especially those modeled on the key-board sonata or divertimento. Although binary repeat marks persist in some of the concerto-form movements in later works, they do not obscure the three-part sonata-form plan.

The nature of Wagenseil's thematic writing provides a determinant of compositional maturity. Disjunct, small-jointed thematic units of the 1750s and early 1760s gave way to a more expansive melodic style in later works. Wagenseil experimented with thematic extension and elaboration, and often effectively rearranged small modular units in subsequent statements.

Wagenseil wrote skillfully for the orchestra, especially when wind instruments were added to the usual trio of two violins and bass. Al-though many concertos are of small dimensions, the writing for strings usually suggests an orchestral rather than soloistic performance. As a harpsichord virtuoso, Wagenseil knew how to show his instrument to greatest advantage, and the few extant examples of cadenzas and fer-matas, as well as discussions of his style and influence in contempo-rary writings, give further evidence of the nature of his keyboard style and the widespread esteem in which he was held. Through his numer-ous concertos, Wagenseil helped to promote the keyboard to its fa-vored position as a solo instrument for the emerging Classical concerto.

Saver, Benjamin. *The Most Wanted Piano Teachers in the USA*. Pasade-na, Calif.: Xin Hua Ma Publishing, 1994, 3 vols. Comprehensive ref-erence program offers much expertise, knowledge, experience, and invaluable insights about piano teaching, studying, and performing. Saver visited forty-eight of the most sought-after piano teachers in the United States, interviewed them, and recorded their coaching sessions.

Scanlan, Mary Kathryn. *The Development of Guidelines to Assess the Relative Difficulty of Intermediate Level Romantic Piano Repertoire.* Ed.D. dissertation, Urbana-Champaign: University of Illinois, 1988, 151 p. UM 8908826. This study develops guidelines to assess the relative difficulty of intermediate level Romantic piano repertoire. A preliminary group of 256 pieces was compiled from standard piano repertoire listings. Using criteria which were derived from related literature and consultation with piano pedagogy specialists, a sample of thirty pieces representative of Romantic genre and composers was chosen for analysis. This sample was divided into three groups of ten pieces. Each group was representative of one of the three levels of difficulty within early, intermediate, and advanced.

The sample was analyzed using a framework consisting of nine categories: figuration, harmony, melody, rhythm, formal structure/phrasing, articulation/touches, dynamics, pedal, and ornamentation. These categories were derived from two resource areas: books and articles dealing specifically with the intermediate level, and books and articles dealing with piano pedagogy at all levels. The resulting analyses were summarized for each level. Comparisons within levels were made and guidelines for each level were formulated. These guidelines described typical contents and expectations within each of the nine analytical categories.

A checklist consisting of the nine categories was formulated. Using the guidelines for each level, the investigator and a panel of three piano pedagogy specialists independently evaluated six randomly selected Romantic piano compositions. There was significant agreement between the investigator and panel members as to the level of difficulty of the compositions. Results indicated that the guidelines and checklist were suitable evaluation tools in determining the degree of difficulty of intermediate Romantic piano repertoire.

Schermerhorn, Marta. *An Historical and Analytical Study of Beethoven's Fortepiano Sonata in A Major, Opus 101.* M.A. thesis, San Jose, Calif.: San Jose State University, 1991, 165 p. UM 1345819. This study examines historical and analytical aspects of Beethoven's *Fortepiano Sonata in A Major,* Op. 101, from the perspective of historically informed performance practices. The first part focuses on the biographical context of the sonata beginning with Beethoven's life and works from 1814 to 1816. The discussion of the chronological place and significance of Op. 101 illustrates Beethoven's emergence into his late period. The simultaneous developments of the fortepiano and Beethoven's late style are presented. Differences between the fortepiano and the modern piano are addressed. A detailed discussion of tempo indications and metronome markings for Op. 101 illustrates the importance Beethoven placed on selecting his intended tempos.

The second part of the study contains a formal analysis of the sonata with particular emphasis on the fantasy-sonata style. Beethoven's lyricism and interest in counterpoint are discussed as key expressive characteristics of his late style. The study concludes with a philosophical exploration regarding a hermeneutic interpretation of Op. 101.

Schniederman, Barbara. *Confident Music Performance: The Art of Preparing.* St. Louis: Magnamusic-Baton, 1991, 142 p. Excellent suggestions and superb outline of ways to make the preparation procedure more secure.

Schonberg, Harold C. *Horowitz: His Life and Music.* New York: Simon & Schuster, 1992, 427 p. This brilliantly written book reads like a detective story. It explores some of the darker sides of Horowitz: his bouts with depression and insecurity, his obsession with critics who disliked his high Romantic style, and his troubled relationship with his daughter Sonia. Schonberg gives us a full and rounded portrait of Horowitz's life and music. Includes sixteen pages of photos, a discography, and indexes.

Schubert, Kathleen Louise. *Willard A. Palmer's Contribution to Piano Pedagogy.* Ph.D. dissertation, Norman: University of Oklahoma, 1992, 332 p. UM 9305962. This study documents and analyzes Willard Palmer's contributions to music education. The study is divided into six chapters. Chapter One serves as an introduction. Chapter Two is a biographical study of Palmer's childhood and education, his family life, his early career as an accordionist and teacher, and his work as a musicologist, lecturer, choral director, and clinician.

Chapter Three documents the evolution of the American beginning piano method from 1950, with emphases on the middle-C, multiple-key, and intervallic reading approaches. Chapter Four evaluates Palmer's piano methods and supplementary materials using criteria established by significant piano pedagogues. A description of the pedagogical principles behind Palmer's keyboard editing procedures and policies, through his contributions to Alfred's Masterwork Series, comprises

Chapter Five. The final chapter summarizes Palmer's contributions to music education and recommends further research.

Schulenberg, David. *The Keyboard Music of J. S. Bach.* New York: Schirmer Books, 1992, 475 p. This unique reference provides a comprehensive survey of all of Bach's keyboard music, integrating recent discoveries and ongoing debates with analytical and interpretative problems and recommendations.

Schults-Berndt, Elfie Diana. *Friedrich Heinrich Himmel's Grande Sonate Pour Deux Pianoforte: A Performance Edition.* Ph.D. dissertation, East Lansing: Michigan State University, 1986, 2 vols., 152 p. UM 8707187. Friedrich Heinrich Himmel (1765–1814), in addition to being an outstanding pianist, was one of the premier composers of his day. He was especially noted for his dramatic works, including opera seria in the neo-Neapolitan style, Singspiel, and Liederspiel; secular and sacred cantatas; oratorios; and lieder. Surprisingly, he composed very few works for the piano, but notable among these is the *Grande Sonate pour Deux Pianoforte* (1801).

Both Himmel and his *Grande Sonate* are largely forgotten today. This fact appears particularly lamentable in view of the need of performance literature for the two-piano medium from the Classic era. The *Grande Sonate* is a substantial work belonging to that period in the development of the medium which followed the duo works of Mozart and Muzio Clementi, and which led to the era of the "Grand Duo" that blossomed in the 1820s. Influences of the keyboard music of Jan Ladislau Dussek and Mozart are evident in Himmel's work, and it shares stylistic similarities with the keyboard music of Felix Mendelssohn.

Examination of Himmel's *Grande Sonate* reveals a three-movement work employing sonata allegro for the first movement, ternary form for the second, and rondo for the third. Elements which enhance the unique qualities of the work include extensive use of variation and contrapuntal techniques within sections; sharp contrasts of harmony, texture, color, and rhythm within sections; integration between sections through motivic recurrence and development; and an overall cyclic form.

Scialli, Carmen. *A Study of Ferruccio Busoni's Transcriptions of Six Organ Chorale Preludes by Johannes Brahms.* D.M.A. paper, Baton

Rouge: Louisiana State University, 1992, 76 p. UM 9316997. Refer-
ring to Busoni's writings on transcribing as found in the appendixes to
his edition of Bach's *Well-Tempered Clavier,* this monograph examines Busoni's transcriptions of six organ chorale preludes by Brahms,
focusing on 1) the adaptation of a work written for two manuals and
pedals to the single keyboard of the piano, considering organ pedals,
doubling, and dynamics; and 2) the pianistic treatment of organ reg-
istration, concerning texture, voicing, and use of piano pedals.

Scionti, Silvio, ed. Jack Guerry. *Essays on Artistic Piano Playing.* Denton,
Tex.: University of North Texas Press, 1998. Jack Guerry has compiled and edited this superb collection of essays written throughout
Scionti's life. It is a delight to have these "words of wisdom" from this
great piano teacher collected in one volume. The book is divided into
three parts: I. Basic Points in Fine Piano Playing (18 chapters); II. The
Art of Pedaling (13 chapters); and III. Other Essays, including a chapter on two-piano playing, as well as the maestro's famous recipe for
spaghetti sauce!

Seitzer, Janet E. *The Solo Piano Works of Jack Beeson.* D.M.A. paper,
Baltimore: Peabody Institute of the Johns Hopkins University, Peabody
Conservatory of Music, 1986, 182 p. UM 8617869. Jack Beeson,
noted primarily for his operas and other vocal compositions, has also
written music for the solo piano. This dissertation provides analyses
of the complete piano works, to date comprised of five sonatas and a
suite entitled *Sketches in Black and White.*

First, Beeson's life and career are chronicled briefly, including many
of his own observations on the people and events that influenced his
music, especially in the early years. Of particular interest are his comments concerning composers who influenced the works described here.

The main part of the dissertation is devoted to analyzing the piano
works. Because Beeson's music is best described as Neoclassical, analyses are structured to isolate and discuss traditional style components:
form, melody, harmony, texture, and rhythm. The goal of the analysis
is to show how these components are used to give the music its distinctive sound. Compositions are divided into two categories: Early
Works (1942–1944), the first two sonatas and the first movement of
the third sonata (all presently withdrawn from publication), and Later
Works (1951–1958), the revised second and fifth sonatas, and *Sketches.*
The analysis illustrates how Beeson's compositional approach changed,

particularly in the areas of treatment of developmental forms, thematic character, and textural aspects.

Finally, the main components of Beeson's style are summarized. Melody, the most significant feature of his piano works, is united with predominantly multivoiced textures, careful plotting of climactic points, and absence of nonrelated material. Combined, these components give Beeson's music its unique sound: lyrical, craftsmanlike, and unpretentious.

Selesner, Eugene. *A Study of the Solo Piano Music of Maurice Ravel.* M.M. thesis, Urbana-Champaign: University of Illinois, 1952, 104 p. Chapters: The Piano Works of Ravel's First Period, The Piano Works of Ravel's Second Period, Conclusion, Summary, and Bibliography.

Sellek-Harrison, Maria B. *A Pedagogical and Analytical Study of "Granada" ("Serenata"), "Seville" ("Sevillanas"), "Asturias" ("Leyenda") and "Castilla" ("Sequidillas") from the "Suite Española," Opus 47 by Isaac Albeniz.* D.M.A. paper, University of Miami, 1992, 183 p. UM 9314534. The first chapter is an outline of the purpose of the doctoral essay and includes a summary of the extent and nature of the literature presently available on Albéniz. The second chapter is a biography of Albéniz. The third chapter describes the contents of the *Suite Española,* Op. 47, including a diagram giving the individual titles of pieces, their key, date and dedication of each composition, and date of first edition.

The first part, "Analysis," of Chapters IV to VII discusses the form and stylistic features of the individual works, illustrated by musical examples, a form diagram, and general background information. The second part, "Pedagogical and Performance Considerations," discusses various physical and technical difficulties and problems of musicianship, and provides by way of examples the author's exercises, specific fingering, and interpretative solutions.

Shank, Carl Dean. *The Piano Technology Course as a Key to Better Artist-Technician Communication.* D.M.A. paper, Austin: University of Texas, 1988, 172 p. UM 8901433. This treatise deals with the problems caused largely by the lack of understanding, on the part of pianists, of the technical-physical and acoustical nature of their instrument. A solution to the problem is offered through a structured course in piano technology involving historic as well as modern perspectives. The first chapter provides an overview of the present-day situation. It cites the inability of many of today's pianists to communicate with the existing technicians.

Chapter Two looks at the present piano marketplace and the problems that the pianist faces because of poorly maintained performance instruments. Due to lack of environmental and maintenance control in many homes and concert halls, the pianist often confronts an instrument that may even dictate serious musical compromises.

Chapter Three sets forth the basic definitions of the piano technology skill areas: tuning, mechanical regulation, restoration, and tone regulation. Additionally, some important guidelines are given for selecting a high-quality restoration facility.

Because of a lack of technical knowledge possessed by pianists in this country, Chapter Four addresses the problem by outlining a one-semester piano technology course specifically designed for the piano major. In addition to giving the student an introduction to all the basic areas of technology, this type of course is structured in such a manner to supply the students with a synopsis of the historical background of keyboard instruments. There will be a "hands-on" practicum provided as well.

Chapter Five argues in favor of a two-semester course in piano technology, over the one-semester course presently offered at a few institutions, by proposing and discussing an expanded practicum. It thoroughly compares the suggested course proposal with other courses currently offered at major universities. Because of the shortage of qualified piano technicians, Chapter Five concludes with an epilogue which illustrates how the two-semester course could be expanded into a music degree program in piano technology. Currently offered at only one school in the nation, Michigan State University, this approach to training piano technicians truly elevates the field from a mere trade to a highly skilled profession.

Sheadel, Michael John. *Schumann's "Waldezenen": From Analysis to Performance.* D.M.A. paper, Philadelphia: Temple University, 1993, 159 p. UM 9332843. Although this study provides historical background and a documentation of the sources, the principal focus is a critical analysis of the cycle. The question underlying the analysis at every point is, "What is the effect?" Individual compositional elements such as harmony, texture, and form are examined, but are isolated for discussion only as a means to illuminate their relationship to the overall character.

What does this imply for performance? Viewpoints presented include the results of experimentation at the keyboard and evaluation of recorded performances. Interpretative markings such as dynamics, articulations, and tempo indications are taken into account. Through this approach it is demonstrated that a synergy between conscious analysis and intuitive responses is not only possible but in fact desirable for performers and scholars alike.

Sheets, Randall Keith. *The Piano Sonatas of Carl Czerny.* D.M.A. paper, College Park: University of Maryland, 1987, 179 p. UM 8725608. A student of Beethoven and the teacher of Liszt, the Viennese composer Carl Czerny (1791–1857) is generally recognized as one of the greatest piano pedagogues in the first half of the nineteenth century. Modern research has also revealed Czerny's invaluable contributions as a reliable source of information on the performance practices of Beethoven, as well as of the early Romantics in general. In spite of this interest, Czerny's works as a serious composer, in particular the piano sonatas, have remained almost completely unexplored. The little-known series of eleven sonatas shows Czerny to have been a composer of considerable stature. Largely written between 1820 and 1827, they foreshadowed in style and emotional content the works of the later Romantics. The first sonata, Op. 7, was highly praised by Liszt, who performed the work throughout Europe. Since the piano sonatas of Czerny are not available in modern editions, this study is based on original nineteenth-century editions which are in the holdings of the Library of Congress, the British National Library, the Catholic University of America, and the University of Michigan at Ann Arbor. After presenting a biographical sketch of the composer, this study addresses the position of the sonatas in Czerny's total output, problems of publication dates, Czerny's own comments on the sonatas, and contemporaneous reviews. It then surveys the important structural and stylistic traits evidenced in these works. Concluding chapters present analytical descriptions of each of the eleven sonatas, as well as a summary and assessment of these works.

Sherman, Robert, and Alexander Sherman. *Nadia Reisenberg: A Musician's Scrapbook.* College Park: University of Maryland, International

Piano Archives, 1986, 192 p. This book, by Reisenberg's sons, affectionately recalls some of the high points, both professional and personal, of a warm, vibrant life in music. Chapter titles are Early Years, A New Life in America, The 1930s, The 1940s: New Friendships, New Horizons, The 1950s and 60s, Master Teacher, The Israel Connection, Three Sisters, and The Last Years. This book gives the reader revealing glimpses of almost three-quarters of a century of the musical life of Reisenberg, both in the United States and abroad.

Shieh, Shiow-Lih Lillian. *A Pianist's Reference Guide to Beethoven's Piano Sonatas.* D.M.A. paper, Greensboro: University of North Carolina, 1992, 136 p. UM 9302647. Beethoven's thirty-two piano sonatas are such cornerstones of piano literature that no serious pianist fails to include at least a few of them in his or her repertoire. The purpose of this document is to compile an annotated bibliography of Beethoven's thirty-two piano sonatas to serve as a reference guide for pianists. Three types of sources are listed: books, dissertations, and journal articles. The author has elected to limit the document to literature in English published in the second half of the twentieth century.

The bibliography contains over 400 citations and is divided into two sections: studies of all sonatas and studies of selected sonatas. Three indexes are included: author, opus number, and general.

Shilo, Nilly Epstein. *Rendition, Form and Temporal Modification in Robert Schumann's "Kreisleriana," Op. 16.* D.M.A. paper, Boston University, 1993, 269 p. UM 9322310. Written in 1838, the *Kreisleriana,* Op. 16 is a product of Robert Schumann's maturity as a keyboard composer, a maturity reflected in the complex piano writing, variety of material, and depth of expression. A piano cycle of eight pieces, it poses intricate problems for the performer. The main part of the paper presents detailed analyses of the eight pieces, with particular emphasis on performance-related issues that evolve from the different textures, including an assessment of the two authentic versions of the work, namely, the original of 1838 and the revised editions of 1850.

Shinn, Ronald Rulon. *The Mirror Inversion Piano Practice Method and the Mirror Music of Vincent Persichetti.* D.M.A. paper, Tuscaloosa: University of Alabama, 1990, 123 p. UM 9105968. The noted American composer Vincent Persichetti created a number of piano works which employ strict mirror inversion: *Reflective Keyboard Studies,* Op. 138 (1981), *Little Mirror Book,* Op. 139 (1983), *Mirror Etudes,* Op. 143 (1980), and *Twelfth Piano Sonata,* Op. 145 (1982). Since these works use such a restrictive compositional technique, an examination of the etudes and the sonata through performance, research, and analytic study is undertaken to reveal motivations for their composition. Dominating Persichetti's rationale was his belief in the value of this approach as an effective piano practice system.

A study of the mirror inversion piano practice approach has shown that a number of other important pianists, composers, and pedagogues have strongly advocated the use of this method in learning new repertoire; mastering difficult passage work; developing hand equality; advancing keyboard comfort, balance, topographical accuracy, and touch control; and heightening acceptance of twentieth-century sounds. Important musicians employing this approach through composition or written testimony include Bartók, Kochevitsky, Fink, Duckworth, Ziahn, Ganz, and Bacon.

Because mirror inversion is not widely understood, Chapter One is devoted to a discussion of inversion in its wider compositional sense, examination of mirror compositions written during the last several centuries, and study of pieces for piano which use exact mirror inversion. Compositional implications of mirror writing are discussed, and a section is devoted to the formation of a clear visualization of mirror keyboard work. Since the mirror practice approach is not as widely advocated as some methods, and since it may be perceived as a radically new and unorthodox approach, it was important to acquire objective data related to some of the assertions regarding mirror practice. Consequently, an experimental pilot study was conducted, using an electronic piano and a number of computer programs to assess MIDI information, and examining the effects of three piano practice approaches—left hand alone, hands together in parallel motion, and hands together in mirror imaging—on the development of touch control. Descriptive examination of the data shows evidence of the efficacy of this practice approach.

Shockley, Rebecca Payne. *Mapping Music: For Faster Learning and Secure Memory.* Madison, Wis.: A-R Editions, 1997. An excellent strategy for learning and memorizing music more efficiently. The unique ingredient is diagramming the main features of a piece and using this diagram as a "map" for learning the music. It can be used at any stage of learning.

Sicsic, Henri-Paul. *Structural, Dramatic and Stylistic Relationships in Prokofiev's Sonatas No. 7 and No. 8.* D.M.A. paper, Houston: Rice University, 1993, 124 p. UM 9408666. Chapter One explores the historical context of the War Sonatas and an overview of Prokofiev's piano works, focusing on the nine Piano Sonatas. In Chapter Two, the structural relationships, motivic material, and stylistic differences of Sonata No. 7 and Sonata No. 8 are summarized. The introductory theme of the seventh sonata, its "Grundgestalt," contains all of the other themes in essence. Chapter Three examines how the drama of the sonatas influences their structure and the use of their motives. The seventh sonata is subjected to formal, tonal, and motivic analysis. Chapter Four continues the process with a full analysis of all three movements of Sonata No. 8. In conclusion, these ideas are brought together in an overview of performance practice in the seventh and eighth sonatas.

Siebenaler, Dennis James. *Analysis of Teacher-Student Interactions in the Piano Lessons of Children and Adults.* D.M.A. paper, Austin: University of Texas, 1992, 201 p. UM 9239203. The purpose of this investigation is to identify and describe the characteristics of effective teaching in the piano studio. Thirteen piano teachers were videotaped with one adult student and one child student during three consecutive lessons each. An eight- to twelve-minute segment containing work on a piece in progress was excerpted from each of the seventy-eight lessons.

With regard to younger students' attitudes toward the lessons observed and toward piano in general, the frequency of teacher questions was inversely related to students' self-assessment and expressed enjoyment. Talking about music during the lesson was directly related to positive attitudes expressed by adult students. Overall, adult lessons and child lessons were differentiated by few variables: teachers devoted more lesson time to talking in lessons with adults, and adult students initiated questions more frequently than did children. Teachers posed questions to child students more frequently than they questioned adult students and devoted more of the overall lesson time to questions in lessons with children.

Siek, Stephen C. *Musical Taste in Post-Revolutionary America as Seen Through Carr's Musical Journal for the Piano Forte.* Ph.D. dissertation, University of Cincinnati, 1991, 349 p. UM 9205478. This study examines the work of the Carr family, musicians and publishers who emigrated to America from their native England in the early 1790s and established businesses in Philadelphia, Baltimore, and New York. For nearly a decade after their arrival, Joseph Carr and his son Benjamin published vast quantities of music, which established them as the unquestioned leaders of their field. Carr's *Musical Journal for the Piano Forte,* which appeared in five volumes from 1800 to 1804, was at the time the largest collection of secular music yet issued in America. By examining this work, the author seeks to answer questions concerning the community of immigrant musicians active in this period and their relationship to American musical taste. Because foreign-born musicians faced little competition in the major American cities at the time, and in fact even dominated the music publishing field, to what extent were they able to shape the musical tastes of their era? With respect to the music they published, were they essentially leaders or followers?

Although significant research already exists concerning many of the individuals discussed here, little has been done to relate their practices to their European background. For this reason, this investigation begins with an examination of the conditions in England which gave rise to an "immigrant school." A brief overview is also provided of both colonial and post-Revolutionary American musical culture. The Carrs' pre-immigration activities are examined in detail, as are the circumstances which may have led to their emigration.

An overview of American music publications in the 1790s is presented, and the Carrs' earlier publications through this period are also surveyed. It is the author's contention that an understanding of the American stage at this time is essential to grasp the significance of the "Musical Journal"; therefore, the nature of theater in both Philadelphia and New York has been extensively discussed. The contents of the "Musical Journal" have been examined in as much detail as possible. The study concludes by examining the Carrs' patrons with respect to their wider roles in American society and the extent to which the Carrs may have been able to influence their patrons' musical tastes.

Siepmann, Jeremy. *Chopin: The Reluctant Romantic.* Boston: Northeastern University Press, 1995, 288 p. Frédéric Chopin (1810–1849) retains his status as a major composer nearly a century and a half after his death. A spectacular prodigy in Poland, a dazzling virtuoso lionized by Parisian society, and the lover of George Sand, Chopin was in many ways archetypical of the Romantic imagination. This biography makes clear that the familiar image of Chopin masked a man largely out of sympathy with the very age he came to personify. The author draws extensively on the diaries and correspondence of the composer and his intimate friends, which included Liszt, Mendelssohn, and Delacroix, as well as on contemporary accounts, thus providing a revealing portrait of Chopin set against a backdrop of the turbulent times in which he lived.

Penetrating discussions of Chopin's music are woven through the text. Siepmann reviews the extraordinary transformation achieved by the composer in such genres as the polonaise, mazurka, and waltz. There is a selective discography which features discussion of the various approaches to Chopin's music chosen by the nineteen pianists listed. A second appendix on interpretation features interviews with a number of performers. There is also an appendix providing a full chronology, and another listing the principal people involved.

Signor, John Frederick. *A Study of the Bowed Piano String Techniques Utilized by Stephen Scott in "Minerva's Web" and "The Tears of Niobe."* D.M.A. paper, University of Miami, 1992, 89 p. UM 9239666. *Minerva's Web* (1985) and *The Tears of Niobe* (1986), by Stephen Scott, are scored for one grand piano to be bowed and plucked by an ensemble of ten musicians. The primary focus of the research has been to examine the bowed piano technique utilized by Scott to achieve highly original timbres from the strings of the piano.

Chapter Three examines technical difficulties, which include an explanation of the various bowing techniques used by Scott. Interpretative problems such as difficulties in phrasing, dynamics, and subtleties in articulation are discussed in a chapter devoted to performance aspects. Attention is also given to unique ensemble problems arising from ten musicians performing on one piano.

Silbiger, Alexander, ed. *Keyboard Music Before 1700: Studies in Musical Repertoire and Genres.* New York: Schirmer Books, 1995, 384 pp. Covering music for the organ as well as the harpsichord and clavichord, this volume surveys the rich diversity of the central keyboard repertoire prior to Bach, from the late fourteenth to the early eighteenth centuries. This is the finest book on the subject since Willi Apel's *The History of Keyboard Music* (1972).

Simms, Beverley Singleton. *The Solo Piano Works of John Corigliano: "Etude Fantasy" (1976) and "Fantasia on an Ostinato" (1985).* D.M.A. thesis, Denton: University of North Texas, 1990, 102 p. John Corigliano (b. 1938) is a contemporary American composer who has in the last twenty years established himself as one whose versatility and accessibility are appreciated by a wide range of audiences. He has labeled himself an eclectic composer who unashamedly borrows from other musical styles and periods in an effort to create works that appeal to a variety of listeners. He has been mentioned along with George Rochberg, George Crumb, and Jacob Druckman as an advocate of the post-modern movement in contemporary American music, a trend that has been crucial to the development of contemporary concert music. The purpose of this study is to examine the two solo piano works of Corigliano in terms of style, structure, and musical influences.

The *Etude Fantasy* (1976) is a set of five etudes, performed without pause. The etudes are unified through an elaborate use of thematic transformation in which a row-like idea generates most of the material. The keyboard writing is varied and dramatic, with similarities to Debussy, Bartók, Prokofiev, and Copland.

Fantasia on an Ostinato (1985), commissioned for the Van Cliburn International Piano Competition, is an atmospheric tone poem that transforms the theme from Beethoven's *Symphony No. 7* (second movement). The rhythmic and harmonic structures of this theme are retained through much of Corigliano's work. Full quotations and fragments of the symphony are combined with newly composed material influenced by Beethoven's theme. Influence of minimalist techniques associated with Terry Riley, Steve Reich, and Philip Glass is apparent throughout the work; rhythmic phasing, repetitive patterns, and musical stasis are used extensively in the second section.

A comparison of the *Etude Fantasy* and *Fantasia on an Ostinato* confirms the eclectic nature of Corigliano's style. In both works, the composer borrows freely from a variety of musical traditions, combining and modifying traditional and avant-garde techniques. It is this intelligent combination of elements, along with expert craftsmanship, that has become Corigliano's trademark and has earned him an important place in contemporary American music.

Simon, Robert. *Percy Grainger: The Pictorial Biography.* White Plains, N.Y.: Pro/Am Resources, 1987, 146 p., 297 photos. Grainger's life in pictures, one of the world's most photographed musicians. Also includes photographs of Busoni, Grieg, Delius, Vaughan Williams, Stravinsky, Duke Ellington, and Henry Cowell, among others.

Sisman, Elaine R. *Haydn and the Classical Variation.* Cambridge: Harvard University Press, 1993, 304 p. In this first full-scale examination of the theme-and-variations form in the Classical era, Sisman demonstrates persuasively that it was Haydn's prophetic innovations—placing the variation in every position of a multimovement cycle, broadening its array of theme types, and transforming its larger shape—that truly created the Classical variation. She elucidates the concept and technique of variation, traces Haydn's development and use of the form in symphonies, chamber music, and keyboard works, and then shows how Mozart and Beethoven in their individual ways built on his contributions.

Sitton, Michael Randy. *The "Album Des Six" and Pianism in the Works of Les Six, 1917–1925.* D.M.A. paper, Urbana-Champaign: University of Illinois, 1991, 125 p. UM 9124490. This inquiry examines the role of the piano in the work of the composers known as "Les Six" at the time of their collaboration, here defined as 1917–1925. Central to the study is the *Album des Six* (1920), a collection of piano music to which each contributed one piece, and one of few musical documents attesting to their association. It is shown that the album preceded and influenced the 1920 article by Henri Collet usually credited with establishing them as a group. Each of the album's pieces is analyzed, and other piano works written during the period in question are surveyed.

Skroch, Diana. *A Descriptive and Interpretive Study of Class Piano Instruction in Four-Year Colleges and Universities Accredited by the National Association of Schools of Music with a Profile of the Class Piano Instructor.* Ph.D. dissertation, Norman: University of Oklahoma, 1991, 317 p. UM 921502. The purpose of the study is to collect and interpret descriptive data on the current status of class piano instruction in four-year degree-granting institutions of higher education which are accredited by the National Association of Schools of Music (NASM). More specifically, the research sought information in three areas: The study elicited information about the nature and scope of instruction, including a comparison of program goals with NASM standards. The study provided a profile of the class piano instructor, including the nature of the pedagogical preparation for class piano teaching. The study afforded an organized source of updated information about materials, instruments, and equipment in use, focusing on the incorporation of new technology into the classroom. The research was conducted by means of a survey sent to class piano instructors at accredited institutions listed in the 1988–1990 College Music Society Directory. The results are based on 383 responses.

Smallman, Basil. *The Piano Quartet and Quintet: Style, Structure, and Scoring.* New York: Oxford University Press, 1994, 208 p. Surveys the development of the piano quartet and quintet from their beginnings in the mid-eighteenth century to the present day. Includes bibliographical references.

————. *The Piano Trio: Its History, Technique, and Repertoire.* New York: Oxford University Press, 1990, 240 p. Avoids mere listing and usefully sorts things out. Well researched.

Smith, Edwin L. *An Analyzation and Comparison of the Chopin Mazurkas.* B.M. thesis, Urbana-Champaign: University of Illinois, 1965, 52 p. Seven chapters, including introduction, table of reference (opus, key, form), introduction of schematic diagrams, schematic diagrams for all mazurkas, tabulations of specific structural details, detailed descriptions of representative mazurkas, and conclusion.

Smith, Janet Bass. *The Golden Proportion in the Published Solo Piano Music of Vincent Persichetti.* D.M.A. paper, Kansas City, Mo.: University of Missouri, 1987, 165 p. UM 8725702. Golden proportion is found in the most ancient structures and artifacts in all cultures, as well as in the human body and in nature. Recent studies have suggested its occurrence in literature, music, psychological relationships, stock market predictions, motivational pacing, and advertising effectiveness. Other studies have related it to human evolution in the prenatal imprinting of the heartbeat and face.

Vincent Persichetti's published solo piano music (thirty-one works) was analyzed for golden proportions in large structural relationships. This writer calculated the ratio of a structural event to the total length of the movement; only ratios falling within a 3 percent range of either the positive or negative section were said to be significant. This range was determined by increasing or decreasing .6180 or .3820 by those values. Golden proportions exist in 71 percent of the sections or movements.

Sokasits, Jonathan F. *The Keyboard Style of Sergei Rachmaninoff as Seen Through His Transcriptions for Piano Solo.* D.M.A. paper, Madison: University of Wisconsin, 1993, 151 p. UM 9318643. Although several critical studies exist of Rachmaninoff's free compositions for piano, his piano transcriptions generally receive only slighting references in relation to his entire output. This is surprising given the enduring fascination that transcriptions as an art form held for Rachmaninoff as both concert pianist and composer. The piano transcription is, in fact, the only form to which Rachmaninoff regularly returned during the final third of his life. During this period of self-imposed exile from his homeland, Rachmaninoff often expressed great difficulty in finding time and energy to compose. With the transcriptions, however, he seemed able to overcome these difficulties and create lasting works of art.

Somfai, Laszlo. *The Keyboard Sonatas of Joseph Haydn: Instruments and Performance Practice, Genres, and Styles.* Translated from Hungarian by the author in collaboration with Charlotte Greenspan. Chicago: University of Chicago Press, 1994, 416 p. This book has had an enormous influence on how Haydn, Mozart, and Beethoven are performed in Hungary. This translation should be read by all who are interested in this great repertoire. Includes bibliographical references and indexes.

Sossner, Doris Kert. *Revisiting Artur Schnabel: Artur Schnabel as Performer, Teacher, Editor, Composer, with Special Focus on "Seven Pieces for Piano Solo," 1947.* Ph.D. dissertation, San Diego: University of California, 1986, 210 p. UM 8706266. The primary focus of this dissertation is to shed light on the compositions of Artur Schnabel. The first chapter describes Schnabel's successful career as a concert pianist and the changes he made in program building. His almost complete recordings of the piano music of Beethoven have made a strong impact on future generations. The second chapter examines Schnabel's method of teaching musical form rather than piano technique. Interaction with his pupils is discussed as well as his unique contribution to musical editing, the use of Roman numerals to define phrasing.

Part Two delves into Schnabel's little-known career as composer with a general survey of his works and a detailed analysis of his last composition for piano, *Seven Pieces for Piano Solo* (1947). Schnabel's style is essentially contrapuntal in nature with much use of chromaticism. His harmonic language is atonal with frequent bichordality. Formal organization and phrasing are considered. Melodies are usually generated from cells of the opening motive which are repeated with variation. Schnabel's idiom is freely rhapsodic and lyrical in character. Only a relatively small proportion of his musical output was written for piano. The appendix points out the relationship between Schnabel and Ernst Krenek, translating pertinent letters from Schnabel to Krenek.

Speer, Donald Ray. *An Analysis of Sequential Patterns of Instruction in Piano Lessons.* Ph.D. dissertation, Baton Rouge: Louisiana State University, 1991, 127 p. UM 9207531. The purpose of this study is to investigate verbal behaviors of independent piano teachers in the setting of the private piano lesson. Twenty-five piano teachers from south east Louisiana participated in the study. Teachers recorded the individual lessons of two students on audiotape. Verbatim transcripts were developed from a total of forty-seven recorded lessons. Transcripts were coded, identifying verbal behaviors with regard to components of sequential patterns established by Yarbrough and Price (1981, 1989). Verbal behaviors were analyzed for time spent in the categories of teacher presentation, student participation, and teacher reinforcement. Frequencies were obtained for the number of complete/correct, complete/incorrect, and incomplete teaching patterns observed.

Results demonstrated significant differences due to student age in the areas of overall presentation of musical information, teacher talk, and coaching by the teacher, as well as student participation. Results also indicated that students perceived as "average" by their teachers received significantly more directive comments than students perceived as "better."

Stark, Lucien. *A Guide to the Solo Songs of Johannes Brahms.* Bloomington: Indiana University Press, 1995, 396 p. The author analyzes in detail more than 200 solo songs of Brahms and gives a translation of the texts. Stark, an outstanding pianist, has performed all of these songs and has lived with them for many years. His love for this literature will make you want to know more of this rich and varied repertoire.

Starr, S. Frederick. *Bamboula! A Life of Gottschalk, American Composer.* New York: Oxford University Press, 1994, 560 p. Based on extensive research, this is a major biography and it should help to reestablish Gottschalk's place in American musical history. Includes bibliographical references and index.

Staves, Heather Jean Coltman. *Variation Sets for Solo Piano of the Early Nineteenth Century.* D.M.A. paper, Austin: University of Texas, 1990, 277 p. UM 9031770. The many variation sets for solo piano written by pianist composers of the early nineteenth century are largely unknown to the majority of modern performers and audiences. This study will focus on selected variation works by six composers from that era: Johann Ladislav Dussek, Carl Maria von Weber, Johann Nepomuk Hummel, Ferdinand Ries, Frederic Kalkbrenner, and Ignaz Moscheles. Although their works are seldom heard today, these men were widely acclaimed during their lifetimes for their pianistic and compositional talents. A study of these works demonstrates the great variety of compositional styles and technical developments taking place even within this somewhat rigid and restricted genre. A deeper knowledge of this repertoire could enhance the musical understanding and literacy of performers and audiences.

Chapter One presents a survey of historical and social conditions of the era. Chapter Two is an overview of the variation form and structure of the period. In addition, the influence that the variation works of both Mozart and Beethoven had on each of the six composers is discussed. The remaining six chapters focus on the biographies and careers of the individual composers. Emphasis is placed on each composer's general treatment of the genre, and selected variation sets are analyzed.

Steen-Nøkleberg, Einar. *Onstage with Grieg.* Bloomington: Indiana University Press, 1997, 413 p. Each of Grieg's piano works is discussed, and a chapter treats the *Piano Concerto in A minor.* The author, an outstanding interpreter of Grieg, provides valuable advice for pianists at all levels of development. The finest work on the subject in any language.

Steeves, Cynthia Dawn. *The Origin of Gospel Piano: People, Events, and Circumstances that Contributed to the Development of the Style; and Documentation of Graduate Piano Recitals.* D.M.A. paper, Seattle: University of Washington, 1987, 136 p. UM 8802341. In most American Evangelical churches, the piano is used in such a way as to have equal or even greater importance and prominence than the organ. The use of the piano in this way began around the turn of the twentieth century. A unique style of playing the piano, indigenous to the Evangelical church, was developed that remains for the most part today.

This study is an examination of the events that brought about the development of this new style: the new gospel songs, the development of which culminated during the last part of the nineteenth century, that created a need for a more percussive accompanying instrument than the organ; the ready availability and popularity of the piano; and the worldwide revival meetings that provided a means of dissimilating the style in such a way that millions of people heard it.

Particular attention is paid to three individuals who contributed to the development of the style: Ira D. Sankey, who, although he was not a pianist himself, popularized a new song literature that was rhythmically and melodically more conducive to the piano than the organ; Charles M. Alexander, the flamboyant song leader who first employed a pianist to accompany gospel songs for revival meetings; and Robert Harkness, the first pianist to play in gospel style as well as the author of a gospel piano method.

Stephenson, Trevor John. *Heavy and Light Execution: The Correspondence Between Touch and Expression in Keyboard Music of the Classical Era.* D.M.A. paper, Ithaca: Cornell University, 1991, 129 p. UM 9131422. While the interpretation of specific articulatory markings has received a good deal of attention in recent performance-practice research, the subject of heavy and light execution has been relatively neglected. In this essay, after establishing the fundamental biases of middle- and late-eighteenth-century articulation through a brief overview of normal touch practices, the author examines the principles of heavy and light execution—using as a point of departure Daniel Gottlob Türk's thorough chapter on this topic from his Klavierschule of 1789—and then demonstrates how these principles apply to various examples of Classical keyboard works. A concluding chapter discusses how the nature of the Classical style manifested itself through lighter forms of execution.

Sterk, Valerie Stegink. *Robert Schumann as Sonata Critic and Composer: The Sonata from Beethoven to 1844, as Reviewed by Schumann in the "Neue Zeitschrift Fuer Musik."* Ph.D. dissertation, Stanford, Calif.: Stanford University, 1992, 684 p., 2 vols. UM 9302318. From 1834 to 1844, Robert Schumann was a principal writer and editor for the *Neue Zeitschrift für Musik.* Of his several hundred reviews on compositions of the 1830s and early 1840s, a majority were on recent piano music. These reviews offer a potential wealth of insight into the context and ideas behind his own piano compositions, many of which were composed precisely during this decade. The methodology within the dissertation is a critical examination of Schumann's reviews of sonatas, with simultaneous study and consultation of the sonatas under discussion.

Steward, Janet Gail. *The Encore Piece for Piano from 1920 to 1990: Historical Overview and Programming Patterns.* D.A. paper, Muncie, Ind.: Ball State University, 1991, 150 p. UM 9213811. The encore piece for piano is viewed both as a historical study and an investigation of current programming trends. Data from the *New York Times* music reviews and questionnaires completed by distinguished American pianists provided information that was compiled and charted. A study of the years 1920 through 1990 showed a discernible move away from extended encore segments, with a shift toward a single encore offering.

Stewart, Nancy Louise. *The Solo Piano Music of Marion Bauer.* Ph.D. dissertation, University of Cincinnati, 1990, 268 p. UM 9108622. Marion Bauer (1887–1955) was a significant figure in early-twentieth-century American music. One of the first Americans to study with Nadia Boulanger, she served in leadership positions in the American Composers Alliance, the American Music Guild, and the League of Composers, often as the only woman. She wrote numerous articles and several books, including *Music through the Ages,* a popular music history text, and *Twentieth Century Music: How It Developed, How to Listen to It,* a widely praised discussion of new styles and techniques. Bauer taught at New York University and Juilliard, spoke regularly at the Contemporary Trends Series of the Chautauqua Institute, and conducted seminars and classes at other prestigious schools. Her expertise on new trends in music made her a sought-after lecturer and respected critic. She was an outspoken advocate for American music and American composers, and wrote often on the subject.

Composition was an integral part of Bauer's career, and she left an impressive body of music, including works for piano, chamber ensemble, orchestra, chorus, and solo voice. Although her works were well received and often performed during her lifetime, they have fallen into obscurity in recent years. This study represents the first in-depth examination of a portion of her music. Bauer's piano works date from every decade of her career, spanning a period of more than fifty years, and the forty-two pieces provide an ideal opportunity to examine her development as a composer. Her music combines a concern for tradition, formal control, and expressiveness with a fascination with modern trends and developments. Most of the piano pieces are short, often grouped into sets of three to six, and thematically united by their descriptive titles. More than half are set in some kind of ternary form. The music reveals a steady progression from early diatonicism, through highly chromatic post-Impressionism, to late experiments with twelve-tone serialism. Thick chords and multilayered textures characteristic of many early works frequently give way in later years to a spare, linear style. Often technically demanding, many of the works exhibit vigorous, continuous rhythmic patterns as well as extremes of range and dynamics.

Stowell, Robin, ed. *Performing Beethoven*. New York: Cambridge University Press, 1994, 300 p. The eleven essays in this volume explore different aspects of the performance of instrumental works by Beethoven. Each essay discusses performance issues from Beethoven's time to the present, whether the aim is to realize a performance in a historically appropriate manner, to elucidate the interpretation of Beethoven's music by conductors and performers, to clarify transcriptions by editors, or to reconstruct the experience of the listener in various different periods.

Strahle, Graham. *Early Music Dictionary: Musical Terms from British Sources, 1500–1740*. New York: Cambridge University Press, 1995, 469 p. Definitions of musical terms are listed in chronological order for each term so that changes of meaning can be traced. Includes all aspects of music. Bibliography.

Sturgis-Everett, Barbara Ann. *The First Movements of Beethoven's "Piano Sonata in E Major, Op. 14, No. 1" and His "String Quartet in F Major, Op. 14, No. 1": A Critical Comparison.* D.M.A. paper, University of Cincinnati, 1986, 92 p. UM 8627612. This study explores the first movements of Beethoven's two versions of his Op. 14, No. 1: the *Piano Sonata in E Major* (1799) and the *String Quartet in F Major* (1802). Chapter One focuses on the motivic, formal, and tonal structure of the piano sonata with attention to voice-leading, keys, phrasing, dynamics, and articulation. Chapter Two examines the very different string quartet, showing where the changes occur, how they contribute to the quartet, and what significance these revisions have in light of the earlier sonata. Concluding remarks demonstrate that the recomposition is one of structural clarification rather than of practical necessity.

Sulton, Randall Steve. *Aspects of the New Romanticism in William Albright's "Five Chromatic Dances."* D.M.A. paper, Austin: University of Texas, 1992, 122 p. UM 9309316. William Albright's *Five Chromatic Dances for Piano* (1976) reflects a trend in much of the music since 1970 that critics and historians have called the New Romanticism. This treatise examines Albright's *Chromatic Dances* from an analytical and historical perspective, drawing particular attention to those aspects of the music that are neoromantic in nature.

In such works as Albright's *Five Chromatic Dances,* the pianist is not only challenged by the complexities of deciphering the score, but is also called upon to execute passages of great technical difficulty. Most important, however, the performer is challenged by the wide range of expressive and emotional demands of this, to quote David Burge, "profoundly human piece of music."

Sunico, Raul Morales. *Selected Philippine Concerti: A Performance Guide.* Ph.D. dissertation, New York University, 1992, 681 p. UM 9306880. The Philippine piano concerti, numbering almost twenty, have been virtually unexplored both in research and performance. Considering the richness and intercultural blend of Philippine music, the country having been under Spanish and American domination for more than 300 years, the piano concerti represent fitting examples of the country's compositional development. This study seeks to explore the stylistic characteristics of Philippine music as reflected in the piano concerti, as well as to provide a performance guide to this particular genre.

Starting with the history of Philippine music from the pre-Spanish era to the period of independence after 1946, this paper includes the published piano concerti written after 1945 in order to examine the compositions supposedly independent of foreign influence. Fifteen works are discussed, including the composer's background, the work's general form and style, and a time-line representation of its architectural shape.

Surdell, Jacob J. *Tonality, Form, and Stylistic Features in Sergei Rachmaninoff's Etudes-Tableaux, Op. 39.* D.M.A. paper, Austin: University of Texas, 1992, 135 p.

Suter, Kristina Jean. *The Four Unpublished Piano Sonatas of Charles T. Griffes: A Performance Edition with Editorial Notes, and a Recording of the Five Piano Sonatas.* D.M.A. paper, College Park: University of Maryland, 1987, 274 p. UM 8808629. This dissertation consists of three parts: a performance edition and editorial notes of the four unpublished piano sonatas of Charles T. Griffes (1884–1920), an accompanying essay, and the recording of all five piano sonatas. The focus of the essay is on the four unpublished works; however, the published *Sonata* of 1917–1919 and the recording are included in the essay to give a complete picture of Griffes's work as a composer of piano sonatas, and references to other piano works are included in order to show stylistic development from the earlier sonatas to the published *Sonata.* Since pianists frequently refer to the single piano sonatas of some of the major American composers (Barber, Carter, Copland, Griffes), this apparent fivefold increase in Griffes's contribution to the genre seems to point toward a thorough reappraisal of Griffes's formative years and the artistic growth that culminated in the *Sonata* of 1917–1919.

Suter is the first to record the unpublished sonatas of this major American composer and has premiered three of the sonatas in public performances. Griffes gave the first performance of the first movement of the *Sonata in F Minor,* A63, in 1905 (Donna R. Anderson, in her compilation of Griffes's complete works, has catalogued the four unpublished piano sonatas by "Anderson" numbers, A63, A64, A65, and A71). The author's recording of the published *Sonata* of 1917–1919 (A35) won the First Place Gold Medal in the 1987 International Piano Recording Competition, Guild Teacher Division. The recordings that accompany the dissertation are available at the Hornbake Library, University of Maryland.

The four unpublished piano sonatas, *Sonata in F Minor,* A63 (1904?), *Sonata in D-Flat Major,* A64 (1909–1910?), *Sonata in D-Flat Major,* A65 (1911?), and *Sonata in F-Sharp Minor,* A71 (1912–1913?), show the influences of various Romantic and late-Romantic composers. Although these same influences are evident in the published *Sonata* of 1917–1919, the stylistic traits of French Impressionist composers are more prominent. Griffes's synthesis of these different influences, plus his own original style, produced five highly virtuosic piano sonatas.

Suwan, Intira T. *Contrasting Interpretations of Chopin's Nocturne, Op. 27, No. 2, and Waltz, Op. 64, No. 2, as Recorded by Four Great Pianists of the Nineteenth Century and Four of the Twentieth Century.* M.A. thesis, Washington, D.C.: American University, 1989, 36 p. UM 1336879. This thesis focuses on different approaches to performing Chopin's *Nocturne,* Op. 27, No. 2, and *Waltz,* Op. 64, No. 2, by great pianists of the nineteenth and twentieth centuries. It shows that in different eras the interpretations of these works have been varied, depending on the pianists' personalities and training, and on the performance practice of their times.

The pianists of the nineteenth century were more flexible with the actual notes in the score; they felt justified in altering the notes and markings. Pianists of the twentieth century are more conservative and follow the composer's directions more strictly. The elements studied in these works include tempo, rubato, ornamentation, and rhythmic and melodic freedom.

Svard, Lois. *Illusion in Selected Keyboard Works of Gyorgy Ligeti.* D.M.A. paper, Baltimore: Johns Hopkins University, Peabody Conservatory of Music, 1991, 158 p. UM 9125561. Some of Ligeti's most interesting rhythmic illusions have occurred in his keyboard works. After an introduction and a biographical summary, the works from 1960 to 1968 are briefly examined in Chapter Two with respect to various rhythmic and harmonic illusions. In-depth analyses of four keyboard works that show a definite progression in the use of illusionistic rhythmic devices make up Chapters Three through Six: *Continuum for Harpsichord,* 1968; *Monument—Selbstportrait—Bewegung* (The Three Pieces for Two Pianos), 1976; *Etudes pour Piano,* 1985; and *Konzert für Klavier und Orchester,* 1985–1988.

Swan, Robert Hathaway. *The Piano Concertos of Saint-Saëns with a*

Detailed Analysis of No. 5, the "Egyptian." D.M.A. paper, Tucson: University of Arizona, 1990, 94 p. UM 9114074. The five concertos of Charles-Camille Saint-Saëns (1835–1921) were the first works in that genre to be written in nineteenth-century France. The composer, a versatile musician of strong intellectual and imaginative power, was one of the great pianists of his era, and his concertos, highly idiomatic for the keyboard, were an important addition to the repertory. They demonstrated coloristic devices not previously employed, and imposed more stringent demands upon virtuoso technique.

Saint-Saëns's style is a blend of traditional and novel elements. An eclectic and a Romantic, he was attracted to melodic and rhythmic patterns of other cultures—particularly the Arabic—and incorporated them judiciously. The most prominent use of such "exoticisms" is found in his *Fifth Piano Concerto,* the "Egyptian." Although this concerto deservedly receives fullest attention, this paper describes and analyzes all five, with emphasis on those distinctive aspects of structure, harmony, rhythm, melody, and orchestration which are the hallmarks of the composer's genius.

An innovator, Saint-Saëns was no less a formalist, who anticipated and influenced the neoclassicism of the early twentieth century. The five piano concertos, a distillation of his finest writing, are works of intrinsic and enduring value.

Taggart, James L. *Franz Joseph Haydn's Keyboard Sonatas: An Untapped Gold Mine.* Lewiston, N.Y.: Edwin Mellen Press, 1988, 119 p. Explores the keyboard sonatas of Haydn from the standpoint of aesthetic appreciation and teaching suitability. Written for all lovers of Haydn, including amateurs, teachers, students of all ages, and concert performers. Uses partly technical language, but not to an excess.

Takenouchi, Aleksei. *Numbers and Proportions in George Crumb's Solo Piano Compositions.* D.M. paper, Evanston, Ill.: Northwestern University, 1987, 277 p. UM 8722558. George Crumb (b. 1928) is one of America's most significant composers and has written major works for various mediums. This paper is strictly devoted to the study of Crumb's solo piano compositions; its aim is to explore the basic principles and means by which Crumb organizes and expresses his musical arguments.

It has been postulated that the music of George Crumb is based on "Golden Section," a proportional system in which a given length is divided in two so that the ratio of the smaller to the larger will equal the ratio of the larger part to the whole. After applying conventional analytical techniques, certain procedural methods were noted; in addition, the pieces were analyzed from a proportional perspective and the results carefully transcribed into a visual architectural system that clearly demonstrates the existence of Golden Section. These findings clarify the relationship between numbers and proportions in Crumb's music and explain why Crumb places certain musical events, dynamics, and other pertinent elements in the positions in which they are located.

In Chapters One and Two, questions and arguments are set: description and explanation of the proportional system known as "Golden Section," and observation and existence of Fibonacci numbers in "Caballito Engro, Donde Llevas tu Jinete Muerto?" from *Madrigals, Book II.*

Chapters Three through Six contain analyses of *Five Pieces for Piano: A Little Suite for Christmas, A.D. 1979; Gnomic Variations;* and *Processional.* Many of the pieces in these collections are based on proportional systems and Golden Section. Chapters Seven and Eight include analysis of *Makrokosmos I and II;* discussion of problems of temporal dimensions and metronome marks; and solutions offered. In Chapter Nine, George Crumb is interviewed by the author. Conclusions are drawn from the findings, and philosophical and aesthetic values of Crumb are discussed in Chapter Ten.

Tanasescu, Dragos, and Grigore Bargauanu. *Lipatti.* Trans. Carola Grindea and Anne Goosens. White Plains, N.Y.: Pro/Am Resources, 1988, 256 p. A study of the legendary Romanian pianist Dinu Lipatti, who died in 1950 at the age of thirty-three. Details his concert career, recording sessions, and interpretative art. Liberal use of letters. Especially interesting are Lipatti's views of contemporaries, including Clara Haskell and Emil von Sauer, and a love-hate review of a Horowitz concert.

Tarasti, Eero. *Heitor Villa-Lobos: The Life and Works, 1887–1959.* Trans. from the Finnish by the author. Jefferson, N.C.: McFarland, 1995, 438 p. A survey of musical history in Latin America and a short biography, but mainly a discussion of the works, with 227 music examples. Bibliography, index.

Tashjian, Rosalie Ann. *Optacon Use in Private Piano Lessons for the*

Blind. M.A. thesis, Fullerton: California State University, 1990, 98 p. UM 1338925. The purpose of this study is to determine whether visually impaired piano students can achieve success with minimal instruction in Optacon music reading. The Optacon is a recent development in electronic technology and education which has affected all types of reading by blind persons.

Six visually impaired persons of various ages participated in this study as private students in piano and theory. The teaching methods utilized the tactile and auditory modalities. This report of the individuals demonstrated that after only two and one-half hours of Optacon training, all of the students were able to read simple melodies with accuracy and speed. The results of this study support the viability of the Optacon as a tool for music reading by the visually impaired. Additional studies need to be conducted using the Optacon as a music reading device to further validate its effectiveness.

Taubman, Dorothy. *Choreography of the Hands: The Work of Dorothy Taubman.* Video cassette. Brookline, Mass.: JTJ Films, Inc., 52 minutes. Taubman works with advanced students, pointing out physical problems and how they affect the performance. She has remarkable perception and can identify problems that most teachers never see. Taubman has helped a number of well-known pianists and many students with physical and musical problems.

———. *Master Class on Franz Liszt's "Paganini (Variations) Grand Etude No. 6 in A Minor."* Video cassette. Amherst, Mass.: JTJ Films, 38 minutes.

———. *Master Class on Frédéric Chopin's "Scherzo in C-sharp Minor,"* Op. 39. Video cassette. Amherst, Mass.: JTJ Films, 40 minutes.

———. *Master Class on Ludwig van Beethoven's "Sonata in F Minor,"* Op. 57 (Appassionata). Video cassette. Amherst, Mass.: JTJ Films, 44 minutes. In all of these videos, Taubman works with students covering interpretative, musical, and physical problems.

———. *Master Class on Ludwig van Beethoven's "32 Variations in C Minor."* Amherst, Mass.: JTJ Films, 46 minutes.

———. *The Taubman Techniques.* Video cassette. Medusa, N.Y.: Taubman Institute. A five-part video series of Taubman's lectures presented by Edna Golandsky, co-founder and associate music director of the Taubman Institute, with a twenty-eight-page addendum by Golandsky, and commentary and segments of master classes by Taubman. Taubman's approach is "based on the principle that correct motion overcomes technical problems and limitations, produces virtuosity and prevents injury. At the same time, correct motion is therapeutic and eliminates injury" (from *The Taubman Institute* brochure, 1995).

Taylor, Harold. *Kentner: A Symposium.* White Plains, N.Y.: Pro/Am Resources, 1987, 88 p. This eightieth-birthday symposium celebrates one of the outstanding pianists of his generation. The articles by Ronald Stevenson and Harold Taylor are outstanding. Louis Kentner's own self-portrait, wise and beautifully written, is rich in his personal recollections of many great musicians.

————. *The Pianist's Talent: A New Approach to Piano Playing Based on the Principles of F. Matthias Alexander and Raymond Thiberge.* London: Kahn & Averill, 1982. New ed., 1994, 112 p. The new edition contains two new chapters and revised bibliography. This book is an interesting approach based on the now fashionable linkage of psychology with performance. The report of the lesser-known Thiberge's teaching is particularly useful.

Taylor, Stephen Andrew. *The Lamento Motif: Metamorphosis in Ligeti's Late Style.* D.M.A. paper, Ithaca: Cornell University, 1994, 176 p. UM 9429314. This essay examines Ligeti's late style (for he has said that this will be his last) by concentrating on four movements which all use the same theme, a chromatically falling lament: the last movement of the *Horn Trio* (1982); the *Sixth Piano Etude,* "Automne à Varsovie" (1985); and the second and third movements of the *Piano Concerto* (1985–1988). These pieces not only let us see how Ligeti uses the same idea in different contexts, but they also provide an overview of Ligeti's late style.

Thibodeau, Michael James. *An Analysis of Selected Piano Works by Sergey Prokofiev Using the Theories of B. L. Yavorsky.* Ph.D. dissertation, Tallahassee: Florida State University, 1993, 287 p. UM 9318528. In this thesis, greater attention to compositional detail has been accomplished by separating the rhythmic and pitch-based elements of Yavorsky's theories in order to more fully develop the latter. Three Prokofiev *Visions Fugitives,* Op. 17, Nos. 5, 10, and 13, and one *Sarcasm,* Op. 22, No. 3, are analyzed by applying Yavorsky's systems, modes, and adaptations of other pitch-based aspects of his theories.

Thomas, Martha Lynn. *Analysis of George Rochberg's "Twelve Bagatelles" and "Nach Bach" for Solo Piano.* D.M.A. paper, Austin: University of Texas, 1987, 198 p. UM 8806449. This paper focuses on two solo piano works by George Rochberg, *Twelve Bagatelles* and *Nach Bach.* Written in 1952 and 1966, respectively, these two works represent different stylistic periods in Rochberg's compositional career. The *Twelve Bagatelles* are Rochberg's first completely serial work and usher in about eleven years of serial composition. Following this period, Rochberg began to use quotations of other composers' music incorporated into an avant-garde style. *Nach Bach,* written in an avant-garde style, quotes from J. S. Bach's *Sixth Keyboard Partita in E minor.* The purpose of this study is to provide an analysis of each of these two works and to compare and contrast their styles.

Thompson, Sidney Jean. *The Piano Works of Norman Dello Joio.* M.M. thesis, Austin: University of Texas, 1962, 115 p.

Thomson, Warren. *Schubert: The Piano Sonatas.* Taren Point, Australia: Alfred Publishing (Australia), 1997, 30 p. The author gives a background to all of the sonatas and analyzes the eleven complete sonatas. The incomplete sonatas are listed. Briefly discussed are Schubert's handling of first movements, second movements, third movements, and finales, and his use of dynamics, rhythm, ornaments, and tempo. Also includes an explanation of terms and a bibliography.

Thorlakson, Paul Jeffrey. *A Performer's Guide to Selected Solo Piano Compositions of Oskar Morawetz.* Louisville: Southern Baptist Theological Seminary, 1995, 98 p. The purpose of the dissertation is to examine how to study, learn, practice, and perform selected solo piano works of Oskar Morawetz with intelligence and musicianship. Three multimovement works, the *Fantasy, Elegy, and Toccata,* the *Suite for Piano,* and the *Contrasting Moods,* were selected for study. A biographical sketch, discussion of general aspects of Morawetz's style, and a summary of his compositions set the context for the study.

Following is an analysis of each of the selected works using the La Rue paradigm of sound, harmony, melody, rhythm, and growth. Performance suggestions are made which grow out of the analysis. A conclusion compares stylistic aspects of the three works along with their performance implications.

Tillard, Françoise. *Fanny Mendelssohn.* Trans. Camille Naish. Portland, Oreg.: Amadeus Press, 1996, 400 p., 33 black-and-white illustrations. The older sister of Felix Mendelssohn, Fanny Mendelssohn-Bartholdy (1805–1847) was a remarkable pianist and composer. In their youth, Fanny and Felix were inseparable friends; they encouraged each other, collaborated in musical endeavors, and received the same education and training from distinguished tutors. But under later pressure to neglect her talents in favor of her brother's, Fanny stifled her career. She married and continued to compose—principally lieder—and organized concerts in her home, which became an integral part of the Berlin musical scene.

   At the age of forty Fanny went against the orders of her father and Felix and published her compositions which, until recently, have remained virtually unknown. This is the first and only authoritative biography of Fanny Mendelssohn. It contains a complete list of her published compositions. There is no doubt about it: this superb musician could have held her own among the greatest if she had not been discouraged from venturing into the professional world.

Timbrell, Charles. *French Pianism: An Historical Perspective.* White Plains, N.Y.: Pro-Am Music Resources, 1992, 312 p. Foreword by Gaby Casadesus. An impressive 150-year overview of the school of French piano playing, including much emphasis on piano pedagogy and interviews with contemporary performers. Includes discography, bibliographical references, and index.

Todd, R. Larry. *Schumann and His World.* Princeton University Press, 1994. Includes bibliographical references and index.

———, ed. *Mendelssohn Studies.* New York: Cambridge University Press, 1992, 261 p. This volume of ten essays presents the most recent trends in Mendelssohn research, covering three broad categories—reception history, historical and critical essays, and case studies of particular compositions. Based on primary sources, including little-known autograph manuscripts and letters of the composer, the volume examines Mendelssohn's historical reception; his relationships with such contemporaries as Franz Liszt, A. B. Marx, Eduard Devrient, and Friedrich Wilhelm IV; and such works as the *Variations sérieuses, Preludes and Fugues,* Op. 35, *Calm Sea and Prosperous Voyage Overture,* and *Reformation Symphony.*

————, ed. *Nineteenth-Century Piano Music.* New York: Schirmer Books, 1990, 426 p. The editor and nine authorities focus on the representative works of eight major composers: Beethoven, Schubert, Weber, Mendelssohn, Chopin, Schumann, Brahms, and Liszt. Two introductory chapters explore the piano in the nineteenth century and performance practices in nineteenth-century piano music. Includes numerous musical examples and an index.

Torok, Debra. *Paul Hindemith's "Ludus Tonalis": Harmonic Fluctuation Analysis and Its Performance Implications.* Ph.D. dissertation, New York University, 1993, 336 p. UM 9411204. This study provides a detailed analysis of the *Ludus Tonalis* that is both visual and descriptive. In order to establish a context for the piece, Hindemith's life, works, writings, and theories are examined. Since the *Ludus Tonalis* is based on Hindemith's controversial theories, the emphasis of existing studies has been on the theoretical rather than interpretative aspects of the work. This study stresses the latter, with analysis integrating both components.

Trechak, Andrew, Jr. *Pianists and Agogic Play: Rhythmic Patterning in the Performance of Chopin's Music in the Early Twentieth Century.* D.M.A. paper, Austin: University of Texas, 1988, 169 p. UM 8909777. Modern pianists tend to view piano playing in the early part of the twentieth century as exaggerated and ruled by caprice. This study seeks to foster a greater respect for the artistic attainments of the Romantic pianists of the early twentieth century by a closer look at their rhythmic style. For the purpose of understanding the rhythmic patterning found in earlier piano playing, sixteen recordings of the Chopin Waltz in C-sharp minor, made during the period 1903–1946, are analyzed and compared. To place the questions raised by the analysis in context, this treatise begins with a brief discussion of the historical questions of tempo modification in performance, looks at the predominant views toward rhythmic freedom during the period under discussion, and examines some of the significant sources for the change in approach that occurred by the middle of the twentieth century.

From detailed observations of the recordings, it was found that the playing was often driven along a philosophy of interpretation that attempted to resist predictability. Nevertheless, rhythmic freedom was bounded by its interaction with the form of a composition, harmonic tensions, and the principle of compensation. This last principle was managed in a manner different from the inhibiting type of compensatory rubato espoused by Matthay. This paradoxical rhythmic style has been described in this treatise by the use of the phrase "agogic play."

It is not attempted in this study to establish a claim that this school represented a thoroughly "authentic" Chopin style. More likely, it represented an amalgamation of various stylistic schools, the Lisztian being paramount. The recordings are an important legacy that provides a storehouse of ideas for the pianist wishing to impart at least a limited amount of agogic flexibility to a performance. In order that this not degenerate into exaggeration or arbitrary distortion for the sake of individuality, the various analyses offer up principles of rhythmic interpretation that help keep agogic play within bounds. It is hoped that they also restore a certain dignity to a school of piano playing often not taken very seriously.

Trice, Patricia Jean. *Gray Thomas Perry, Piano Performer and Pedagogue.* Tallahassee: Florida State University, 1988, 209 p. UM 8812044. Music education research literature indicates that there is a need not only for more biographical studies of well-known music educators from this and recent generations, but also for more studies of those about whom we are unaware. Gray Perry, now in his eighty-ninth year, is an important American piano pedagogue whose contributions to piano teaching and performance seem to be largely unknown outside the community of Florida piano teachers. The purpose of this study, therefore, is to add to existing empirical knowledge in music education by examining the life and teachings of an individual, Gray Perry, to isolate and identify the traits that seem to have contributed to his effectiveness, to establish him as a role model, and to invite others to emulate him.

The procedure is twofold. First, Perry's pedagogical heritage is examined against the historical perspective of trends in piano pedagogy from Ludwig Deppe (1828–1890) to the present. The heritage of velocity from Isidor Philipp, the Leschetisky tradition of tone production acquired from Ethel Leginska and Franklin Cannon, and the pedagogical thoroughness of A. M. Virgil have been linked and combined by Perry into broad-based pedagogical methods. The comparison of Perry's collection of exercises to those of some of his pedagogical ancestors—A. M. Virgil, Malwine Bree, and Marie Prentner—indicates a grasp of pianism that is both eclectic and efficient.

Second, a list of characteristics that can enable teachers to be effective was developed based upon data from a review of literature in education, music education, and piano pedagogy, and the evidence of those characteristics in pedagogues from Leschetisky to the present. Events from Perry's life, statements from former students, activities of past and present students, and anecdotes from the lives of his pedagogical ancestors and contemporaries provide documentation for each characteristic.

Triplett, Robert. *Stage Fright: Letting It Work For You.* Chicago: Nelson-Hall, 1983. Reprint, 1985, 206 p. Triplett, an organist, has written about performance anxiety from a highly personalized vantage point, and has many interesting tips and ideas for coping with stress. One of his especially interesting ideas is that of "making friends" with anxiety, and giving it tangible form to counteract its otherwise vague and frightening qualities.

Tse, Benita Wan-Kuen. *Piano Variations Inspired by Paganini's Twenty-Fourth Caprice from Op. 1.* D.M.A. paper, University of Cincinnati, 1992, 159 p. UM 9232389. Paganini's Twenty-fourth Caprice from Op. 1 has prompted much attention because of its strong, clear, conclusive harmonic basis, and its distinctive repetition of a sixteenth-note figure in the melodic line. The purpose of this thesis is to discuss five subsequent sets of variations for the piano based on this original set of variations, which has aroused such interest on the part of numerous composers. This study includes Liszt's *Grandes etudes de Paganini* No. 6; Busoni's *Paganini-Liszt Thema Mit Variationen, Etuden No. 6: "Eine Transkription-Studie von Ferruccio Busoni"*; Brahms's *Variations on a Theme by Paganini,* Op. 35; Lutosláwski's *Wariacje Na Temat Paganiniego*; and Rachmaninoff's *Rhapsody on a Theme by Paganini,* Op. 43. Each composer's individual style of writing and different approaches to transcription technique are examined. Even within this small group of works there is a good deal of variety in performance medium (solo piano, piano and orchestra, and duo-piano) as well as in the different approaches to the theme that these composers have taken. Furthermore, a fusion of the concert etude and variation form is apparent in these works. The role of the concert etude was to display virtuosity, while variation form provided the means for a composer to expand a work to include a variety of techniques. The thesis begins with an introductory chapter that includes a brief discussion of the origin of the variation form and musical aesthetics of the nineteenth century, followed by a chapter on the historical background of Paganini's Twenty-fourth Caprice and its influence on other composers. Each of the five piano works is then treated in terms of historical background, variation and transcription techniques, and pianistic devices.

Tusing, Susan Marie. *Didactic Solo Piano Works by Alexandre Tansman.* D.M.A. paper, Baton Rouge: Louisiana State University, 1993, 103 p. UM 9405428. This monograph examines the didactic solo piano works of Tansman, focusing primarily on the collections *Pour les enfants* (1934), *Les jeunes au piano* (1951), and *Happy Time* (1960). Following an introductory chapter that briefly outlines Tansman's life and career, Chapter Two provides a discussion of the genres (dances, barcaroles, marches, etudes) and styles (contrapuntal, "blues," ethnic) used by Tansman in his didactic music. Chapter Three focuses on the technical and musical features found in these works. A final chapter summarizes the information in the previous chapters and contains recommendations for making this music more readily available to piano teachers and students.

Unger, Joyce. *Galaxy of Composers.* Published by author, 430 East Vine, Mulvane, KS 67110, 1988, 75 p. This book is a collection of biographical sketches of modern composers of piano educational materials. Includes composers from Hansi Alt to Robert Vandall.

Unrau, Lucia Rochelle. *The Piano Music of Eugene Kurtz.* D.M.A. paper, Austin: University of Texas, 1992, 183 p. UM 9225788. Eugene Kurtz is an American composer who has lived in Paris since 1949. His music is widely performed throughout Europe and the United States. This treatise gives special attention to his five published piano pieces, *Quatre Mouvements, Le Capricorne, Motivations, Animations,* and

Five-Sixteen. Each work is analyzed in depth, with special emphasis on performance aspects.

Uszler, Marienne. *The Well-Tempered Keyboard Teacher.* Foreword by Andre Watts. New York: Schirmer Books, 1990, 447 p. This is a thorough piano pedagogy text designed for piano pedagogy courses. Offers an enormous amount of information on the world of piano teaching. This book may be the finest work on the subject.

Vadala, Kathleen Cooper. *The Concert Works of Jean Absil for Solo Piano: A Performance Tape and Stylistic Analysis.* D.M.A. paper, College Park: University of Maryland, 1986, 132 p. UM 8625751. Jean Absil (1893–1974) was a major figure in the twentieth-century Belgian musical community. His compositions, in a wide range of genres which include orchestral, choral, vocal, and instrumental chamber and solo works, were frequently performed during his lifetime. In his academic career, primarily as a teacher of composition, he attained the respected position of Professor of Fugue at the Royal Conservatory of Brussels where he influenced a succeeding generation of Belgian composers.

The sixteen concert works for solo piano, a recording of which forms the major part of this study, represent the more technically challenging portion of an output which also includes many well-crafted teaching pieces. The concert works include suites of programmatic and genre character pieces, three small-scale sonatinas, and three large single-movement works. Two of the sixteen pieces are written for one hand alone: the *Ballade pour la main gauche seule,* Op. 129, for the left, and *Trois pièces de piano pour la main droite seule,* Op. 32, for the right, the latter in a category almost unique in the literature of the piano.

Absil's music reflects a varied combination of influences. Several of them, including atonality and impressionism, are revealed in a treatise which he authored as an apologia for the new music of the early twentieth century. In *Les postulates de la musique contemporaine* (1937), Absil discusses with great enthusiasm the revitalizing effects of Debussy, Ravel, Stravinsky, and Schoenberg, among others, on the degenerating system of functional harmony represented by the domination of late-nineteenth-century German Romanticism.

Spurred by a sense of discovery and innovation in his study of contemporary music, Absil formulated a well-defined style based on the pervasive use of a vocabulary of selected intervals and chords. Other distinguishing features include great structural clarity enhanced by melodic and harmonic contrast.

Only a small portion of Absil's solo piano music has been recorded, and the only study of Absil's life and works is oriented toward biography and chronology rather than stylistic analysis (Richard De Guide, *Jean Absil, vie et oeuvre* [Brussels: Casterman, 1965]). This project thus represents the first complete recording and systematic consideration of the concert works as a body.

Valenti, Fernando. *A Performer's Guide to the Keyboard Partitas of J. S. Bach.* New Haven: Yale University Press, 1989, 136 p. Valenti answers questions asked him over thirty-five years as a teacher and performer of the partitas.

Vallentine, John Frank. *Proportional Use of Instructional Time and Repertoire Diversity in Relationship to Jury Performance in University Applied Music Lessons.* Ph.D. dissertation, Lexington: University of Kentucky, 1991, 149 p. UM 9132181. The purpose of this investigation is to examine the use of instructional time during private studio instruction in relationship to the temporal proximity of jury examinations. The main area of interest involved the amount of instructional time used during the lessons as it related to: student performance; teacher modeling; simultaneous student performance with teacher modeling; repertoire diversity of scale/technical exercises, etudes, and recital music; teacher talk (on-task); student talk (on-task); non-task student/teacher discussion or activities; and the frequency of correct approvals and disapprovals given by the teacher. Additionally, the differences between performance mediums—brass, woodwinds, strings, voice, and piano—are examined.

Van Cort, Bart. *The English Classical Piano Style and Its Influence on Haydn and Beethoven.* D.M.A. paper, Ithaca: Cornell University, 1993, 212 p. UM 9333288. This study represents an attempt to formulate the differences between the English and Viennese schools of piano building, and the resulting differences in piano playing. An analysis of the style of works written for the English piano leads to the definition of a particular English style of composing which is different from the well-known Viennese Classical style.

The inefficient damping of the English piano led not only to a different basic touch, but also to a greater emphasis on sustained melody, and resulted in a more extensive use of the pedal; the relatively heavy feel of its action and fullness of its tone led to a thicker, more orchestral texture; its lack of brilliance was counteracted by increased activity in the treble; and the way the bass and treble are balanced led to different activity in both hands. For both its technical and musical features, this style may be called the English Classical Piano Style.

Vickers, Laura M. *An Annotated List of Standard Piano Literature for Use in the Christian Church Service.* D.M.A. paper, Norman: University of Oklahoma, 1996. This document annotates 200 pieces from the standard piano repertoire to assist church musicians in the selection of literature for the Christian church service. Representative repertoire includes works from the Baroque, Classical, Romantic, Impressionistic, and Contemporary eras. Repertoire selections cover four levels of difficulty: intermediate, upper intermediate, lower advanced, and advanced. Entries created for the 200 pieces in the database include the following information: title and composer; a brief description of the mood, character, and musical or technical difficulties encountered; level of difficulty; occasion for which the work is suitable; historical era of composition; key, meter, and tempo markings; duration of the work (approximate times are given); and selected editions where the pieces can be located. The user can also reference pieces described in the annotations by three different indexes that are categorized by level of difficulty or historical era. In addition, the document contains background information on the evolution of church music and the role of the piano in the Christian church.

Viljoen, Willem Diederik. *The Ornamentation in the Fitzwilliam Virginal Book with an Introductory Study of Contemporary Practice.* D.Phil., University of Pretoria, South Africa, 1986. This study sets out to examine the ornamentation in the *Fitzwilliam Virginal Book* as representative of sixteenth-century practice. The concept of ornamentation belonging to this period is revealed as an *ars diminutionis,* manifesting itself as *passaggi,* ornaments realized in notes and ornaments indicated by sign. The printed edition of the *FVB* contains many inaccuracies in ornamentation, mainly printer's errors, due to wrong placements and frequency of occurrence, which do not correlate with the manuscript, and stenographic cancellation signs which are printed as ornaments. All of these are corrected and listed, and the original alignment of ornaments on the note stems is also indicated. Examining the use of the written-out ornaments in the *FVB,* one discovers that they are primarily employed as decoration of the individual closes in a cadence, where they occur as diminutions of the notes constituting the cadence. They are also employed inseparably from the *passaggi* as virtuoso decoration. The single- and double-stroke ornament signs in the *FVB* are decorative elements which add brilliance to the music, yet research into their use reveals that they are also employed systematically. The frequency with which they coincide with the pulse unit and the rhythmic pulsation created by it, together with their profusion of concurrence, make these signs a unique phenomenon in late-sixteenth-century ornamentation. The two ornaments also differ in the manner of their use, such as where and on what note values they occur, and in which melodic contexts they are applied. Their realization in note values remains a difficult issue to clarify in the absence of a contemporary explanation. The evidence collated by this study makes it possible, with a fair degree of certainty, to ascertain what they are likely to signify.

Violett, Martha Lynne Watson. *The Solo Piano Music of Xavier Montsalvatge.* D.M.A. paper, Iowa City: University of Iowa, 1990, 313 p. UM 9126370. Xavier Montsalvatge was born in 1912 in the Catalonian city of Gerona, north of Barcelona, Spain. His works for solo piano span his entire career, from his student days to the present. The eight piano compositions are short, but they represent many of the influences and compositional techniques that also appear in other works.

Montsalvatge empathized with the ideals of nationalism and universalism and utilized traditional and twentieth-century techniques. His interest in the folk music from throughout Spain included the habañeras and other influences of the music of the Antilles, the antillanismo. Quotes from folk songs and works of other Spanish composers also represent the influence of nationalism. The piano pieces contain examples of many compositional techniques that were employed for dissonance, such as polytonality, dissonant extended chords, and chromatically moving triads. In addition to a study of each individual piano composition, the thesis contains a summary of the musical climate of twentieth-century Spain and an overview of Montsalvatge's career as a composer. Many details of the study were clarified through letters from Montsalvatge, which are included in an appendix. Corrections to the published editions of three of the works were excerpted from those letters and appear in a separate appendix. Another appendix is a list of Montsalvatge's compositions by category; it was prepared from a study of available scores, secondary sources, and Montsalvatge's communications. The dates of composition, premiere, publication, and other pertinent information are given for each work.

Vogelsang, Kevin Ralph. *The Piano Concertos of Ned Rorem.* D.M.A. paper, University of Cincinnati, 1991, 164 p. UM 9200513. American composer Ned Rorem (b. 1923) has produced three piano concertos: *Concerto No. 2* (1950), *Concerto in Six Movements* (1969), and *Double Concerto* (1979) for cello and piano. An analytic study of these works shows an early adherence to traditional forms and dramatic conventions, an exaggerated language incorporating serial procedures and rhythmic complexities, and a more harmonically accessible, chamber like, and motivically unified style. A melodic orientation prevails throughout, and there is a growing preference for short movements with descriptive titles. This stylistic evolution reflects the "French" aesthetic professed in Rorem's published diaries. The ideals are objectivity, economy, and pleasurable effect.

Von Gunden, Heidi. *The Music of Lou Harrison.* Metuchen, N.J.: Scarecrow Press, 1994. Catalog of compositions; includes discography, bibliographical references, and index.

Wachter, Claire Larue. *American Women Composers and Selected Piano Works Written and/or Published since 1970.* D.M.A. paper, Austin: University of Texas, 1993, 212 p. UM 9400837. The study is divided into four main chapters. Chapters One and Two provide an overview of the role of women composers in American musical life from 1800 to 1970, as well as a consideration of the sociological and political factors affecting their work. Chapter Three narrows the focus to the past twenty years (1970–1990) and looks at thirty-five piano works in order to identify significant compositional trends. Chapter Four narrows the focus again to four solo works that the author believes to be important contributions to the standard piano repertoire. The works discussed in Chapter Four are Judith Zaimont's *Nocturne,* Emma Lou Diemer's *Toccata,* Nancy Van de Vate's *Sonata* (1978), and Barbara Kolb's *Appello.*

Walker, Alan. *Franz Liszt.* Vol. II: *The Weimar Years, 1848–1861.* New York: Knopf, 1989, 625 p. Rev. ed., Ithaca: Cornell University Press, 1993. Bibliographical references. Covers Liszt through his best-known years. Divided into four books: New Beginnings, 1847–1848; Court and Liszt, 1848–1853; The Years of Maturity, 1853–1857; and Gathering Storms, 1857–1861. Each book contains subdivisions. Contains numerous references to unpublished material. Also available in paperback.

————. *Franz Liszt.* Vol III: *The Final Years, 1861–1886.* New York: Knopf, 1996, 594 p. Covers the "tripartite life" when Liszt spent part of each year in Rome, Weimar, and Budapest. He taught much of this time to over 400 students, and for free. Liszt always focused on helping the pianist become his or her own self—no drills, exercises, etc. Detailed analyses of many works are especially helpful. A massively researched and beautifully written volume. All three volumes are by far the finest of all the Liszt biographies.

Walker, Alan, ed. *Living with Liszt from The Diary of Carl Lachmund: An American Pupil of Liszt 1882–1884.* Stuyvesant, N.Y.: Pendragon Press, 1995, 421 p. Walker also annotated this book and wrote a prologue. This is a detailed account of the years during which Lachmund studied with Liszt. Lachmund discusses Liszt's playing for his students, how Liszt taught by parablelike illustration, and Liszt's higher spiritual ideas and ideals. Liszt used few words, but they were very much to the point. He taught by symbolism, gesture, or even grimace. A fascinating document with much idealistic and practical advice for the pianist.

Walker-Hill, Helen. *Piano Music by Black Women Composers.* Westport, Conn.: Greenwood Press, 1992, 143 p. Discusses the solo piano and ensemble works by fifty-five black women composers. Publishers listed plus addresses where unpublished music may be located. Four appendixes: available published piano music, ensemble instrumentation, easy and moderate pieces for teaching, and chronology of surviving piano works before 1920. Includes selected bibliography and selected discography.

Walkinshaw, Jean Margaret. *Improvisatory Aspects of the Keyboard Music of C. P. E. Bach* (1714–1788). Thesis, Seattle: University of Washington, 1972.

Wallace, Elizabeth Ann. *The Effect of War on the Lives and Work of Piano Composers and the Evolution of Compositional Technique in War-Related Piano Pieces from 1849 through the Second World War.* Ph.D. dissertation, Lubbock: Texas Tech University, 1990, 206 p. UM 9104821. Many authors have addressed the poetry, literature, and painting created in response to war. Although music has been included in discussions concerning the effect of war on the arts, there is little said specifically about keyboard works. Since the mid-nineteenth century, coverage of keyboard "battle music" is particularly sparse. This study addresses the effect of war on the lives and works of piano composers during the years from around 1840 through World War II. Primary sources, such as composer's correspondence and diaries, form a major basis for the investigation.

Several war-related compositions are analyzed in this paper. These include works by Robert Schumann, Louis Gottschalk, Theodore La Hache, Claude Debussy, Leo Ornstein, Maurice Ravel, C. F. Malipiero, Sergey Prokofiev, Paul Hindemith, and Walter Stockhoff. Some of the areas examined are the presence of emotional content in the music which seems to reflect the expressed opinions and attitudes of its composer; stylistic traits normally associated with the individual composer which are present or absent in the music; the prevailing spirit toward war on the part of keyboard composers of a particular time period; the changing musical language and expression over time in the battle piece genre; and the general evolution in the use of signature battle devices.

Walton, Peggy Marie. *The Music of Charles Tomlinson Griffes: Harbinger of American Art Music's Transition into the Modern Age.* M.M. thesis, Houston: Rice University, 1988, 159 p. UM 1334886. Charles Tomlinson Griffes heralded a new era of twentieth-century internationalism for American music. Rather than restrict himself to writing American nationalistic or German romantic music like most American composers of his time, Griffes built upon his classical background to write eclectic new music that incorporated ideas from around the world, especially from France, Russia, and the Orient.

This thesis looks at the composer in terms of the musical culture in which he lived. It considers issues which affected American musicians and highlights many of the ways Griffes transcended the stylistic limitations of early-twentieth-century American music. Analyses of the *Piano Sonata* of 1917 and the *Roman Sketches,* Op. 7 reveal Griffes's traditional background, particularly the influence of Liszt, and illustrate Griffes's integration of the forward-looking ideas of Ravel, Scriabin, Schoenberg, and other modern composers, as well as his anticipation of new twentieth-century trends.

Wampler, Cheryl Lee. *The Legacy of European Compositional Techniques in the Piano Music of Domingo Santa Cruz Wilson.* D.M.A. paper, Austin: University of Texas, 1986, 173 p. UM 8705949. This treatise analyzes the utilization of various European compositional techniques by the twentieth-century Chilean composer Domingo Santa Cruz Wilson as they appear in his piano works, and demonstrates how he combines certain aspects of these techniques to create his own personal, original compositional language as a part of his poetic aesthetics.

The first chapter presents a historical overview of the decades immediately preceding Santa Cruz's career. The next two chapters provide biographical details, including his activities in both administrative and artistic realms. The material in these chapters is largely based on the composer's memoirs and on the author's personal interviews with him in Santiago, Chile, between 1983 and 1985. The fourth chapter analyzes Santa Cruz's use of specific European techniques in his piano works, including counterpoint and other neo-Baroque practices, chromatic harmony, thematic transformation, characteristics of French impressionism, various Hispanic features, polytonality, and the use of unordered pitch cells. The fifth chapter demonstrates the eclecticism of his original style and aesthetics. The study reveals that his music shows originality in incorporating all elements of an eclectic technique into a personalized and highly skilled style, unified by his consistently poetic aesthetic position.

Watanabe, Shuko. *Tradition and Synthesis: Influence on the Solo Piano Works of 34 Japanese Composers Surveyed.* D.M.A. paper, College Park: University of Maryland, 1992, 740 p. UM 9234711. The author presents the results of a survey research instrument submitted during 1989 and 1990 to contemporary Japanese composers, all professionally active in the post–World War II era. The thirty-four composers responding are Romei Abe, Hideo Arashino, Sadso Bekku, Hiroshi Hara, Hikaru Hayashi, Masao Honma, Ryuta Ito, Riyoshige Koyama, Yoshimitsu Rurokami, Michio Mamiyo, KikuRo Massumoto, Yori-Aki Matsudaira, Yoritsune Matsudaira, Michiharu Matsunaga, Akira Miyoshi, Hideo Mizokami, Makoto Moroi, Issas

Nagao, Masayuki Nagatomi, Yoshinao Nakada, Teruyuki Noda, Hajime Okumara, Sukehisa Shiba, Makoto Shinohara, Toshiya Sukegawa, Hideaki Susuki, Toru Takemitsu, Masayuki Takenishi, Toraku Takagi, Runio Toda, Hidenori Tokunaga, Akihiro Tsukatini, Renjiro Urata, and Joji Yuasa.

The survey response consists of two parts. Part One includes up-dated biographical information, lists of published, unpublished, and out-of-print solo piano works, and a list of major works. Part Two provides questionnaire answers regarding compositional techniques, influences on styles, reactions to the suggestion of East-West amal-gamation, and views of national identity.

Waters, Ann W. *Factors Affecting Motor Control in the Five-Finger Pitch Pattern Performance of Beginning Pianists.* Ph.D. dissertation, Kent, Ohio: Kent State University, 1991, 164 p. UM 9200540. This study was based on the assumption that descending finger movements in piano performance are influenced by mechanisms inherent in the grasp reflex of the fingers. Accordingly, each finger pattern in piano playing represents an action unit with a spatial-temporal pattern similar to that found in reflexive patterns. The spatial and temporal errors asso-ciated with performance of these action units were investigated by varying barline locations in short musical examples requiring differ-ent sequences of finger movements.

Twenty-seven beginning pianists between the ages of seven and nine each performed twelve musical examples designed by the investiga-tor. Each example was initiated by one of four different finger se-quences (five, four, three, and two fingers) with the right hand. Each example was sixteen beats long and used only quarter notes. Con-secutive white-key pitch patterns in C Major, G Major, D Minor, and A Minor were used with three barline locations: no barlines, 4/4 meter, and 2/4 meter. The audio-taped performances were evaluated for spa-tial (pitch) and temporal (rhythm) performance errors by the investi-gator and two expert judges.

Weaver, Robert E. *The Piano Works of Charles T. Griffes.* M.M. thesis, Austin: University of Texas, 1956, 121 p.

Weber, Stephen Paul. *Principles of Organization in Piano Etudes: An Analytical Study with Application through Original Compositions.* Ph.D. dissertation, Lubbock: Texas Tech University, 1993, 228 p. UM

9416658. This research focuses on figural, motivic, rhythmic, and technical unity in etudes of the nineteenth and twentieth centuries. The document details types, roles, and settings of unifying features in the context of selected works. One of the appendixes for the document is an extensive compilation of technically unified etudes, arranged by categories of technical focus. Over seventy composers and 500 etudes are represented in this appendix.

Weekley, Dallas, and Nancy Arganbright. *The Piano Duet: A Learning Guide.* San Diego, Calif.: Kjos Publishing, 1996, 46 p. Many helpful ideas and sound advice from America's top piano-duet team.

————. *Schubert's Music for Piano—Four Hands: A Comprehensive Guide to Performing and Listening to the Dances, Fantasies, Marches, Polonaises, Sonatas, Variations and Other Duets.* White Plains, N.Y.: Pro/Am Resources, 1989, 148 p. The authors are an outstanding husband-and-wife duo piano team who have devoted some thirty-five years to research on Schubert. This outstanding volume includes biographical background, historical and critical evaluations and analyses of each Schubert piano duet in chronological order, and a chapter on performance problems.

Wemple, Littlepaige. *A Structural and Interpretive Analysis of Selections from the "Poems for Piano" of Vincent Persichetti.* Ed.D. dissertation, New York: Columbia University Teachers College, 1985, 230 p. UM 8602079. Persichetti wrote the *Poems for Piano* during 1939–1941 and used techniques of tertian and quartal harmony. These compositions reflect his skills and craftsmanship in short works of relatively simple design at levels ranging from upper intermediate to advanced. Many of the Poems are accessible to pianists of intermediate ability who might otherwise avoid contemporary music as being too difficult to play. A study of these works offers students and teachers the opportunity to become familiar with the repertoire of a well-known composer, to develop analytical skills for understanding some twentieth-century techniques, i.e., tertian and quartal harmony, and to develop the interpretative skills to perform the *Poems for Piano* as well as other contemporary compositions.

This dissertation presents a structural and interpretative analysis of six of the *Poems for Piano* which can be used for teaching and learning these pieces. Two Poems from each of the three volumes were selected for detailed analysis which included form, underlying harmonic treatment or progression, and salient characteristics of the work as a whole, with an examination of each section in relation to overall structure. Following the analyses are a review of structural and stylistic aspects of the compositions and some implications for further study of twentieth-century music.

Wenger, Faith. *Performing the Early Nineteenth Century Four-Hand Piano Duet.* M.A. thesis, Fresno: California State University, 1992, 123 p. UM 1351886. The four-hand piano duet developed as a popular form of domestic music making during a period of important social and economic change in the late eighteenth and early nineteenth centuries. The present study focuses on the performance of the four-hand works of this period. The research involved a survey of the literature regarding the historical development of the four-hand duet form as well as the performance practices of the period. Two representative four-hand works, the *Fantasy in F minor,* Op. 103 by Franz Schubert, and the *Allegro Brillante,* Op. 92 by Felix Mendelssohn, were chosen for special study. These works were analyzed according to specific performance practice considerations using scores of various publishers, recordings by current artists, current performance practice literature, and historic documents. These works were also performed at a recital of four-hand and duo piano works.

Werner, Warren Kent. *Brahms's Piano Works in Relation to His "Four Periods."* M.M. thesis, Urbana-Champaign: University of Illinois, 1950, 57 p. A list of the periods: 1) 1852–1857: Opp. 1 25; 2) 1857–1865: Opp. 26–40; 3) 1873–1883: Opp. 51–90; and 4) 1884–1892: Opp. 98–120. Gaps between Op. 40 and Op. 51 are represented by vocal music.

Wernli, Lou Ann. *Stylistic Characteristics in the Solo Piano Works of Robert Schumann: Their Function in Performance.* Thesis, Seattle: University of Washington, 1964.

Whang, Un-Yong. *An Analysis of Dello Joio's Chamber Music for Piano and Strings with Performance Suggestions.* Ed.D. dissertation, New York: Columbia University Teachers College, 1986, 261 p. UM

8620420. Norman Dello Joio, a prominent contemporary American composer, wrote for various media. His music belongs to a representative style of our time, neo-Romantic or neo-classical, and utilizes various twentieth-century compositional techniques. Prominent characteristics such as church modes, melodic lines, free uses of quartal and tertian chords, bi-chords, bi-tonality, and rhythmic vitality are combined with the composer's artistic sense of direction and balance in his unique style. Chamber players and instructors should be familiar with literature of this stature which includes these techniques.

An introductory chapter is followed by an overview of his composition and his influences on contemporary music. The four chamber works are then studied in chronological order: *Fantasia on a Gregorian Theme* (piano and violin), *Duo Concertanto* (piano and cello), *Variations and Capriccio,* and *Colloquies* (piano and violin). Rhythmic, melodic, and harmonic elements are discussed as they relate to musical developments. Also included are suggestions for achieving a more musical performance. The last chapter contains a summary of the analyses and educational implications. In these works, Dello Joio's sensitivity in the communicative aspects of ensemble music and his understanding of instruments is manifested. Although the two earlier pieces are not technically demanding, they are effective. The later works require solid skills and musical maturity.

Wheelock, Gretchen A. *Haydn's Ingenious Jesting with Art.* New York: Schirmer Books, 1992, 269 p. The author discusses how Haydn, utilizing the subversive potential of wit in a variety of classical forms, genres, and venues, both supported and challenged the musical conventions of his day. This is a unique critical and historical study of this celebrated aspect of the composer's music and the key role of listeners in its success.

Whiteley, Daniel H. *A Graded List of Solo Piano Sonatas Written by American-Born Composers Between 1950 and 1975.* D.A. paper, Muncie, Ind.: Ball State University, 1986, 118 p. UM 8613031. The purpose of this study is to develop and apply an experimental grading system to sonatas written by American-born composers from 1950 to 1975. Although several authors have addressed the problem of grading or classifying piano music, there are generally no precise criteria provided to substantiate the validity of their systems. The present author discovered some significant and innovative, yet generally neglected piano sonatas.

The grading system in this research was based on the physiological factors affecting the pianist's development. These factors include equality of fingers (finger independence and mobility); passage of the thumb (scales and arpeggios); double-note and polyphonic playing; extensions (stretches between the fingers); and arm rotation (execution of chords and octaves). In addition, since factors such as retuning of the instrument, polyrhythms, and improvisation can make a moderate or intermediate piece into a difficult one, a "special problem" category was added.

Each of the six physiological divisions are assigned a numerical difficulty level from one to ten. The divisions are then averaged and assigned a final "grade" as follows: Easy 1 (E-1) = 1.0–1.9; Easy 2 (E–2) = 2.0–2.9; Moderate 1 (M–1) = 3.0–3.9; Moderate 2 (M–2) = 4.0–4.9; Intermediate 1 (I–1) = 5.0–5.9; Intermediate 2 (I–2) = 6.0–6.9; Difficult 1 (D–1) = 7.0–7.9; Difficult 2 (D–2) = 8.0–8.9; Virtuoso (V) = 9.0.

Eighty-six sonatas were reviewed and graded. These compositions represent a broad selection of works of various degrees of difficulty. By knowing the student's abilities and needs, the piano instructor may use this study to select sonatas that correspond to the appropriate level of attainment.

Of the works reviewed, the majority fall into the Moderate category. This was not an unusual finding in that certain pianistic development is required before being able to play the score. The grading system differs from previous systems in that it provides criteria for the placement of the works into a difficulty rating based on the physiological factors affecting the pianist's development.

Whiteside, Abby. *Abby Whiteside on Piano Playing.* Portland, Oreg.: Amadeus Press, 1997, 384 p. Revolutionary piano teacher Whiteside (1881–1956) influenced numerous American pianists and her ideas remain important today to piano pedagogy. This volume is a reprint of her two out-of-print works *Indispensables of Piano Playing* and *Mastering the Chopin Etudes and Other Essays.*

Whiting, Steven Moore. *To the "New Manner" Born: A Study of Beethoven's Early Variations.* Ph.D. dissertation, Urbana-Champaign: University of Illinois, 1991, 588 p. UM 9136764. In 1802 Beethoven announced to his publisher that he had adopted a "completely new manner" in his two latest sets of piano variations, in token of which he was numbering them among his "greater" musical opera. Given the aesthetic disrepute into which variations had fallen during the latter eighteenth century, Beethoven's declaration is striking, all the more so because he had taken a novel approach to this fashionable genre nearly from the start.

The present study is addressed to the twenty-nine variations sets and movements Beethoven composed by 1800, from the Dressler Variations of 1782 to the Sussmayr Variations of 1799. It argues that he subjected the genre to formal principles rooted in development before leaving Bonn (e.g., WoO 65, WoO 67), that he invested some variations (e.g., WoO 28, WoO 72, WoO 73) with specific dramatic contents by implicit reference to the opera from which the themes were drawn, and that he even shaped certain variation works, *mutatis mutandis*, along lines analogous to sonata form. The dual thematic configuration that marks Op. 35 was present as early as 1790 (WoO 65). The relation in Op. 34 of successive variations by median keys and the closing complex of Adagio and Fugue in Op. 35 were clearly prefigured in 1799 (WoO 76). Beethoven was, so to speak, to the "new manner" born.

Whitmore, Philip J. *Unpremeditated Art: The Cadenza in the Classical Keyboard Concerto.* New York: Oxford University Press, 1991, 248 p. The first book in English devoted to the subject. Illuminating and readable account, essential for students, scholars, and informed performers of the concerto repertory.

Whitton, Jeffrey. *The Art of Practicing the Piano.* London: Stainer & Bell, 1993, 105 p. Drawn from experience by the author. Includes bibliographical references and index.

Whitwell, David, comp. *Mendelssohn: A Self Portrait in His Own Words.* Northridge, Calif.: Winds, 1986, 136 p. Part One: Mendelssohn's Reflection on His Own Music. Part Two: Mendelssohn's View of the World. Part Three: Mendelssohn, A Self-Portrait.

Wicks, Don. *The Family Piano Doctor: A Step-by-Step Guide to the Re-*

pairing, Tuning, and Renovating of the Family Piano. London: Batsford, 1991, 143 p. Includes index.

Widhalm, Patrick Robert. *Robert Casadesus, Composer and His Four Sonatas for Piano.* D.M.A. paper, Kansas City, Mo.: University of Missouri, 1991, 149 p. UM 9126172. The purpose of this dissertation is to explore the salient features of Casadesus's compositions by reviewing a rather limited body of material written on the subject, and to expand on and exemplify these features through a consideration of his four sonatas for piano. The analysis of the sonatas is from the viewpoint of a performer, with the purpose of introducing these works as valid and worthy additions to the twentieth-century repertoire.

Wilder, Pamela Wright. *Sergei Rachmaninoff: Understanding the Composer Through the "Etudes-Tableaux," op. 33.* D.M.A. paper, Tuscaloosa: University of Alabama, 1988, 85 p. UM 8826967. The purpose of this study is to examine the multifaceted musical value of Sergey Rachmaninoff's *Etudes-Tableaux,* Op. 33. The first portion of the document is devoted to cyclic and title implications. Special attention is focused on painter Arnold Böcklin's influence on the works of Rachmaninoff, and especially these *Etudes-Tableaux.* Rachmaninoff's idiomatic approach to composition, as well as performance problems, are discussed. Historical information is given.

   The second major division of the document deals with Rachmaninoff's employment of specific compositional elements which contribute to his musical signature. The elements of melody, rhythm, and harmony are discussed. Next, a study of the secondary elements of transitions, cadenzas, codas, and texture are presented. Finally, the formal structure and its relation to Rachmaninoff's interest in the culminating point is examined. The fact that Rachmaninoff utilized the mathematical formula of the Golden Mean is considered in detail. The use of this formula is the most significant point made in the document. Concluding statements contend that the *Etudes-Tableaux,* Op. 33 are highly representative of Rachmaninoff's mature piano style and should be included as a vital part of the pianist's study of the Rachmaninoff literature.

Wiley-Lippoldt, Adrienne Elizabeth. *A Pedagogical and Performance Anal-*

ysis of the Five Miniature Preludes and Fugues, "Etudes in Tonality," Op. 44, and "Polyrhythms," Op. 50 by Alec Rowley. D.M.A. paper, Norman: University of Oklahoma, 1991, 210 p. UM 9210504. These collections have been selected because they represent the early to late intermediate levels and prepare students to perform music from various style periods. Furthermore, these collections are currently accessible to today's piano teachers and students.

Wilkens, Randall Philip. *Articulation in the Keyboard Music of François Couperin.* D.M.A. paper, Lawrence: University of Kansas, 1990, 181 p. UM 9110935. Few Baroque composers communicate so much about the articulation of their music as does François Couperin. This information is conveyed in his keyboard method, *L'Art de toucher le clavecin* (1716, 1717), and in the abundance of slurs and other markings in his *Pièces de clavecin* (1713, 1716–1717, 1722, 1730). In addition, further clues to articulation in his music are found in a variety of outside sources: writings on keyboard playing by Guillaume-Gabriel Nivers and M. Saint Lambert; treatises on string bowing and wind tonguing by Georg Muffat, Jacques-Martin Hotteterre, and others; and clavecin pieces of Couperin's predecessors Louis Couperin and Jean Henri d'Anglebert. Further insight is gained by examining Couperin's pieces for instruments other than the clavecin, and by comparing his works with those of his contemporaries such as Jean-Philippe Rameau, Louis-Claude Daquin, and Johann Sebastian Bach.

The information provided in these sources makes it possible to approach the subject of Couperin's keyboard articulation from several angles. The first chapter focuses on *L'Art de toucher le clavecin*. In Chapter Two articulation markings in selected orders (1–8, 13, 16, 19, 23, and 27, with samplings from others) of Couperin's *Pièces de clavecin* are examined in order to discover patterns that can be applied to unmarked passages—this is probably the most innovative facet of the entire study. Chapter Three deals with a variety of aspects that may have influenced Couperin's keyboard articulation practice: string bowing, wind tonguing, articulation markings in the keyboard music of Couperin's predecessors, Baroque dance forms, and Couperin's own expression markings. The fourth and final chapter investigates the possible influence of Couperin's keyboard articulation practice on his instrumental chamber music, the keyboard music of his younger contemporaries, and a selection of French-style music by J. S. Bach. The study concludes with a discussion of how Couperin's articulations might be applied to his own *Pièces d'orgue* (1690).

Willett, Thelma Elizabeth. *A Study of Haydn's Piano Sonatas.* M.M. thesis, Urbana-Champaign: University of Illinois, 1946, 74 p. Includes five chapters, conclusion, and two appendixes: I. Form of each movement of the 52 sonatas; and II. Summary of the use of the Rondo (ABACA) form in the Haydn sonatas.

Williams, Adrian. *Portrait of Liszt by Himself and Contemporaries.* New York: Oxford University Press, 1990, 746 p. Williams has put together a kaleidoscope of eyewitness accounts and anecdotes—including many that are likely to be new even to Liszt devotees and specialists—extracted from the diaries, letters, and memoirs of those who knew the great musician as man, pianist, and teacher. The book also presents an absorbing picture of the rich musical and cultural life of nineteenth-century Europe.

Wilson, Marian. *Felix Mendelssohn's Works for Solo Piano and Orchestra: Sources and Composition.* Ph.D. dissertation, Tallahassee: Florida State University, 1993, 510 p. UM 9318530. Felix Mendelssohn's works for solo piano and orchestra are the *A-Minor Concerto* (1822), the *Capriccio brilliant,* Op. 22 (1831–1832), the *Piano Concerto in G Minor,* Op. 25 (1831), the *Rondo brilliant,* Op. 29 (1833–1834), the *Piano Concerto in D Minor,* Op. 40 (1837), and the *Serenade and Allegro giocoso,* Op. 43 (1838). Almost all were composed specifically for Mendelssohn's own performances, and only the *Capriccio brilliant* originated as a solo piano work. Manuscript evidence and contemporary sources suggest that the versions of the *G-Minor Concerto,* the *D-Minor Concerto,* and the *Serenade and Allegro giocoso* which Mendelssohn first performed differed considerably from the eventual published pieces.

Winters, Glenn R. *An Analysis of Sergei Rachmaninoff's Preludes, Opus 23 and Opus 32, and Etudes-Tableaux, Opus 33 and Opus 39.* D.M. paper, Evanston, Ill.: Northwestern University, 1986, 200 p. UM 8703786. Despite the overall rise in critical esteem of the solo piano works of Sergey Rachmaninoff since his death in 1943, the time had not yet come when any but a handful of them could rival the composer's works for piano and orchestra in popularity among pianists and the general public. The purpose of this document is to provide critical examination of a representative body of Rachmaninoff's solo piano music, namely the twenty-three Preludes compromising Op. 23 (1902) and Op. 32 (1910) and the fifteen Etudes-tableaux of Op. 33 (1911) and Op. 39 (1916–1917), with detailed analysis of musical content and a discussion of performance problems and practices.

The main body of the document consists of individual analyses of each composition. Each chapter of analysis is preceded by an introductory chapter serving two purposes: to provide a brief summary of the history of the composition of the music, and to sketch a brief survey of other composers' works in the same genres, relating them to Rachmaninoff's contributions and helping to place the latter in their proper position in the literature.

This overview leads to conclusions by the author that the pieces discussed, viewed as a cross-section of Rachmaninoff's total output, not only document his stylistic development, but display his best qualities, including mastery of small forms, gift for melody, command of the keyboard, compositional craftsmanship, and sincerity of expression. The value of these works as concert and teaching material is roughly equal to the standard piano works of Chopin, Schumann, Brahms, and Liszt in terms of pianistic challenges and musical integrity.

Wise, Herbert Harold. *The Relationship of Pitch Sets to Formal Structure in the Last Six Piano Sonatas of Scriabin.* Ph.D. dissertation, Rochester, N.Y.: University of Rochester, Eastman School of Music, 1987, 317 p. UM 8713023. The purpose of this study is to determine the relationship between pitch sets and musical form in Sonata Nos. 5–10 of Alexander Scriabin. The methodology employed involves the location and identification of significant pitch sets, and the analysis and description of the compositional procedures. The study also includes a survey of the available analytical literature, emphasizing the late works of Scriabin in general and the late sonatas in particular. The study utilizes pitch-class set theoretical principles and terminology. Pitch combinations within melodies, harmonies, and entire textures are identified. Judgments regarding the significance of a pitch set or its worthiness for analytical attention are based on frequency and location of occurrence within the context of musical form.

The study demonstrates that there is a limited number of pitch sets of significance to the musical structure of sonatas. An extraordinary amount of music analyzed is based on one or more of a group of six supersets, including members of scs 8–27, 7–35, 9–10, 8–28, 9–12 and 10–6, of which members of the last five are symmetrical in structure. Each of the Sonata Nos. 5 through 9 is based on one, two, or three supersets. Sonata No. 10 has no superset structure of the type observed in the previous sonatas. The results of the investigation show that the composer preferred the following procedures: intersection, union, difference, literal and abstract halfstep displacement of one pc, symmetrical pcset construction, complementation, and maximal/minimal invariance under transposition.

Sonata Nos. 5 through 10 can be divided into three consecutive pairs based on procedures of set techniques. Sonata Nos. 5 and 6 represent early attempts to deal with a new vocabulary of pitch selection. Sonata Nos. 7 and 8 are the most highly structured, demonstrating intricate set techniques. Sonata Nos. 9 and 10 show a new compositional orientation emerging in which the techniques of superset structure become less important.

Witten, David, ed. *Nineteenth-Century Piano Music: Essays in Performance and Analysis.* New York: Garland Publishing, 1997, 310 p. Nine essays by different writers deal more with analysis than performance. Joel Sheveloff's essay "A Masterpiece from an Inhibition: Quashing the 'Inquisitive Savage'," dealing with Mussorgsky's *Pictures at an Exhibition*, is the most performance oriented. Other essays by Witten, Nicolas Marston, Camilla Cai, Charles Burkhart, John Daverio, Christina Capparelli Gerling, and Antony Hopkins deal with various aspects of works by Beethoven, Felix and Fanny Mendelssohn, Chopin, Schumann, Schubert, Liszt, and Brahms.

Wolfe, Randall N. *The Pianist's Control of Tone Quality.* D.M.A. paper, University of Cincinnati, 1991, 65 p. UM 9200466. The pianist may control only certain variables pertaining to the production of the tone of his or her instrument. Piano tone quality and volume are not independent of one another; the only physical manner in which a pianist can change the timbre of a single tone is to change its volume as well. However, the combination of two or more tones provides the pianist with a means by which constellations of overtones can be mixed. The overlapping of tones and the use of rubato influence the resulting sound as well. The thickness and shape of the soundboard, the hardness of the hammers, and noise from the action and the key mechanism may affect the instrument's tone. The pianist may create tonal differences by the use of the damper pedal and the soft pedal and by varying the time of release of these pedals. Acoustical reflection, reverberation, absorption, refraction, diffraction, and sympathetic vibration may influence the listener's perception of the pianist's tone. Finally, the visual and emotional stimuli which play upon audience members' senses may convince them that the tone which they are hearing is quite different from that which is actually proceeding from the instrument. Although those who would argue that the artist cannot control tone quality without changing the volume of at least one note of a chord are correct on the basis of the experiments with the oscillograph, those who adamantly advocate specific technical methods regarding the proper use of the fingers, arms, wrists, elbows, and shoulders may also have a valid contention because of the visual effects upon the listeners and their hearing mechanisms.

Wood, Patricia A. *The Teaching of Abby Whiteside: Rhythm and Form in Piano Playing.* D.M.A. paper, Columbus: Ohio State University, 1987, 84 p. UM 8726583. Abby Whiteside (1881–1956) was a pioneer in the teaching of piano. She thoroughly investigated the problem of rhythm, how it is related to musical form (phrasing), and, most important, how rhythm and form are created by an emotional reaction to the music. She related rhythm, form, and emotion to the physical act of playing the piano. In her writings, Whiteside discussed rhythm, meter, and form and defined them by creating two new terms: *basic rhythm* and *rhythm of form.* This study clarifies Whiteside's concept of rhythm and form and describes her physical approach for implementing them. Some perspective as to what influenced her thinking is offered by providing a short biography and a discussion of the development of her philosophy. Her "tools for learning" are described and specific musical examples are selected from the piano repertoire and explained in light of her principles. It is concluded that Whiteside proved to be innovative in her study of the relationship between rhythm and form. She understood that emotion was what originated a rhythm, and this she termed *emotional rhythm.* She taught that the musician must use emotion to create an exciting rhythm, which in turn would allow his or her natural coordination to express the music.

Wood, Ruth Ann. *The Piano Sonatas of Erich Wolfgang Korngold.*

D.M.A. paper, Tuscaloosa: University of Alabama, 1991, 72 p. UM 9213860. The purpose of this document is to examine Korngold's three piano sonatas more closely and to show how they illustrate certain characteristic features of his style. The three main subdivisions of this document include a biographical sketch; a structural, melodic, and harmonic analysis of the sonatas; and a conclusion in which the sonatas are briefly compared with other important piano sonatas written in the early part of the twentieth century.

Woolfolk, R. L., and P. M. Lehrer, *Principles and Practice of Stress Management.* New York: Guilford, 1984. A thorough review of basic stress management techniques with extensive references to research literature. The book covers a range of topics including progressive relaxation, meditation, and other techniques of great value to performers. The book assumes some background in psychology, and is most useful as a general reference to acquaint the reader with both clinical techniques and research.

Worman, Regina Marydent. *The Effects and Roles of Unity and Contrast as Implemented by Composer and Performer of Four Different Periods with Special Emphasis on a Variation Set Representative of Handel, Beethoven, Brahms, and Copland.* D.M.A. paper, Tuscaloosa: University of Alabama, 1993, 161 p. UM 9403323. This document surveys four sets of keyboard variations by composers from four contrasting periods of musical composition: Baroque, Classical, Romantic, and Contemporary. The primary works are "The Harmonious Blacksmith" Variations by G. F. Handel from *Suite No. 5 in E Major* (1685–1759), *Thirty-two Variations in C Minor on an Original Theme* by Ludwig van Beethoven (1770–1827), *Variations and Fugue on a Theme by Handel in B-flat Major,* Op. 24 by Johannes Brahms (1833–1897), and *Piano Variations* of Aaron Copland (1900–1990). This document examines a form favored by many composers as a vehicle for unity and contrast, and the discussion focuses on these two elements existing in each set of variations. Whether they coexist or oppose, unity and contrast are crucial to balance within a set and to variety. This document reveals the importance of the roles of composer and performer as they relate to these two elements of music.

Wylie, Roy. *Argentine Folk Elements in the Solo Piano Works of Alberto Ginastera.* D.M.A. paper, Austin: University of Texas, 1986 149 p.

UM 8700322. The treatise examines the early piano works of Alberto Ginastera and how their composition was influenced by the folk music of his native Argentina. The indigenous music of the country is discussed, followed by a biography of Ginastera and a description of how Argentine folk elements were incorporated into his compositions. Emphasis is given to rhythmic, melodic, and programmatic factors of the music itself and to statements made by Ginastera on the purpose of his coming to terms with the music of his native land and how he incorporated it into his compositional style. Further discussion of performance problems in these pieces is provided to help the artist-teacher in the utilization of these works in his repertoire and that of his students.

Wythe, Deborah. *Conrad Graf (1782–1851): Imperial Royal Court Fortepiano Maker in Vienna.* Ph.D dissertation, New York University, 1990, 2 vols., 677 p. UM 9113068. Graf, a Württemberg cabinetmaker, settled in a Viennese suburb in 1798 or 1799. He founded his piano-building business in 1804 and relocated to Vienna proper in 1811. By 1824 Graf's instruments were distinguished enough that he was named fortepiano builder to the court. In 1835 Graf received a gold medal at the Erste Allgemeine österreichische Gewerbs-Producten-Ausstellung, in Vienna. Graf's business, large enough to be considered a factory rather than a workshop, was located at the Mondacheinhana, a Vienna landmark. His status as a property owner, successful businessman, and art collector is noted in many nineteenth-century sources. Included here are a documentary biography and business history; a catalogue raisonné of sixty-one extant instruments; analyses of the instruments; an investigation of Graf's contacts with Beethoven, Chopin, the Schumanns, and Liszt; and the critical reaction to Graf's instruments.

Yampolaky, Carol Jane. *The Solo Jazz Piano Music of Three American Composers: Armando "Chick" Corea, William "Billy" Taylor, Mary Lou Williams: A Performance Tape Project.* D.M.A. paper, College Park: University of Maryland, 1986, 63 p. UM 8625761. This project concerns itself with a performance tape of the original nontranscribed solo jazz piano music of three American composers: Armando "Chick" Corea, William "Billy" Taylor, and Mary Lou Williams. As jazz musicians, these composers are unusual in the sense that some of their keyboard works have been written out, following the procedure used in the traditional classical approach, as opposed to the typical jazz musician's practice of writing only sketches to be improvised upon during performance, and perhaps transcribed from recordings into traditional notation at a later date.

Perhaps surprisingly, there are very few jazz composers who have adopted the traditional approach to composition, and these three composers seem to be the only American composer-performers of note to have contributed in this way. The following list of compositions comprise the most complete catalogue to date of piano music using the traditional procedure of these three composers. 1) Armando "Chick" Corea (b. 1941): *Twenty Children's Songs, Piano Music* series 1–5 (unpublished manuscript). 2) William "Billy" Taylor (b. 1921): *B.T's-D.T's, Beer Barrel Boogie, Big Horn Breakdown, Big Shoe Shuffle, Birdwatcher, Bit of Bedlam, Black Swan Rag, Cool and Caressing, Crazy Oak Cakewalk, Declivity, Different Bells, Early Morning Mambo, Hoghead Shout, Hotfoot Hamfat, Jelly-Bean Boogie, Latin Soul, Lucky Buck Boogie, Midnight Piano, Society Strut, Sounds in the Night, Titoro.* 3) Mary Lou Williams (1910–1981): *Chili Sauce, Deuces Wild.*

The accompanying document focuses attention on biographical data including important influences, accomplishments, aspects of piano style, annotations of some of the works, and a discussion of the relationship of this music to the history of various keyboard styles. Since most of these works are in unedited form, the writer-performer will suggest fingerings where necessary, as well as dynamics, phrasing, and stylistic practices.

Yang, Shu-mei. *Piano Music of Native Chinese Composers, with Particular Focus on the Piano Works since 1950: A Lecture Recital, Together with Three Recitals of Selected Works of J. S. Bach, L. V. Beethoven, S. Prokofiev, F. Chopin, R. Schumann, J. Brahms, M. Ravel, and A. Skryabin.* D.M.A. paper, Denton: University of North Texas, 1988, 68 p. UM 8817065. This document aims at the identification of the sources of influence on the styles of selected twentieth-century Chinese composers. Personal influences are reflected as well as those general influences specific to the different stylistic periods discussed. Most important, however, is the description of the methods by which these composers employ contemporary compositional devices to project musical gestures that are uniquely Chinese elements of culture, and which are fundamentally programmatic and intimately related to the lives of the Chinese people.

The introduction of Western music and musical instruments to China in the early seventeenth century and cultural exchanges with Japan served to gradually westernize the musical environment and training. The establishment of decidedly Western schools was accomplished at the beginning of this century with the founding of Peking University and Shanghai National Conservatory. Music theory was taught, as well as history and composition, but with an emphasis on the practices of the eighteenth and nineteenth centuries. Compositions from this period reflect Western techniques from these eras, with some use of the pentatonic scale.

In the 1930s, nationalism arose, a mirroring of the nineteenth-century European nationalistic trends. This philosophical conception has remained essentially unchanged to the present, as composers have aimed to utilize Western techniques to create artistic works and compositional styles which are uniquely Chinese. The musical works examined are limited to works for piano solo, as it is believed these are often more immediately revealing of compositional technique and stylistic idioms.

Yedra, Velia. *Julian Orbon: Biography and Analytical Study of Toccata for Piano and Partita No. 1 for Harpsichord.* D.M.A. paper, University of Miami, 1986. Chapter One is devoted to a biography of the composer, tracing the events of his life and examining controversial criteria concerning his placement in the history of Cuban music.

Chapter Two outlines the main elements of Orbon's style of composition, citing examples of some of his works. This chapter also provides an introduction to the music of Orbon.

Chapter Three consists of discussion and analysis of two works for keyboard, *Toccata for Piano* (1943) and *Partita No. 1 for Harpsichord* (1963). The detailed study of these two compositions contains a view of the composer's keyboard treatment and a formal analysis of the music, including rhythmic, melodic, and harmonic analysis.

Five appendixes include a chronological synopsis of Orbon's life, a chronological list of his compositions, a classified list of compositions, and a discography, as well as a partial translation into English of *The Cuban Presence in World Music.* A bibliography citing relevant sources of information ends the essay.

Yeomans, David. *Bartók for Piano: A Survey of His Solo Literature.*
Bloomington: Indiana University Press, 1988, 153 p. Each piece is
identified with a Sz. (Szöllösy) number, available editions, timings, difficulty ratings from both a technical and a musical standpoint, translations of the text if the piece derives from folk music, and commentary on Bartók's own performance if the composer recorded it. Where
applicable, background information is included as well as quotes from
Bartók, analyses, performance suggestions and programming, and
suggestions for further study. The finest reference book on the subject.

Young, Barbara G. *The Use of Computer and Keyboard Technology in
Selected Independent Piano Studios.* D.M.A. paper, Norman: University of Oklahoma, 1990. This study was undertaken to determine
how computer and keyboard technology is being employed currently
in selected independent piano studios. Information was sought regarding the types and brands of electronic keyboards, synthesizers,
samplers, and digital pianos being used; the features of these keyboards; and the brands of computers and types of software being used.
The incorporation of computer and keyboard technology into the independent studio curriculum was investigated, including methods of
scheduling and questions of supervision and group teaching. The study
sought to determine teachers' attitudes toward the motivational aspect of this technology, its appropriateness for students at various
levels, and the effects the use of this technology has on the development of expressive musicianship and the acquisition of keyboard skills.
   A review of related literature reveals several categories of information about computer and keyboard technology: philosophical and
theoretical orientation, general introductory information, information sources, hardware, software, and ways of implementing the technology in the independent studio. A survey of independent piano teachers was conducted, and the data regarding their uses of computer and
keyboard technology were analyzed to determine the most frequently
used types of computers, keyboards, and software. Information was
compiled regarding the incorporation of computer and keyboard technology into the studio curriculum, including practical considerations
such as scheduling, fees, and difficulties encountered, and educational
considerations such as creative applications of the technology and the
reasons for using it. Survey respondents identified creative and successful users of computer and keyboard technology, and case studies
were conducted on some of these individuals.

Based on information obtained from the survey and from the case studies, recommendations are made for teachers interested in using computer and keyboard technology, including suggestions for types of computers and keyboard technology, software, and learning experiences. Recommendations for further study are made involving educational, practical, and philosophical aspects of the use of computer and keyboard technology in independent piano studios.

Zaluski, Iwo, and Pamela Zaluski. *The Scottish Autumn of Frederick Chopin.* Edinburgh: John Donald Publishers, 1993, 95 p. Traces Chopin's tour of Scotland in the autumn of 1848 at the invitation of his student Jane Stirling. He was expected to play everywhere, yet he was already dying of tuberculosis before he left Paris. He gave two concerts, one in Edinburgh and one at Glasgow. In October the frail Chopin left for London where he gave the last concert of his life before returning to Paris.

Zerlang, Timothy. *Karol Szymanowski's "Studies," Op. 33: The Demonstration of a New Style.* D.M.A. paper, Stanford University, 1989, 55 p. UM 9011445. In 1918, Karol Szymanowski, aware of the apparent complexity of the piano works composed in his new style, wrote to his publisher defending the pianistic qualities of these middle-period works. The twelve Studies (1916) form a concise presentation of the textures and technical demands that characterize this new style, and they serve as a model for some of Szymanowski's formal strategies. The Studies were conceived as a continuous whole despite their fragmentary appearance; this paper discusses how Szymanowski realized continuity in compositional terms and how the pianist can realize this continuity in performance. Szymanowski's use of the Tactus and his handling of the progression of tonic centers unify the studies without relying on shared thematic material or tonal argument. Within each study the tonic centers are usually expressed as two triads a tritone apart. In moving from study to study, Szymanowski utilizes common tones and their enharmonic equivalents, dominant-tonic progressions, and chromatic motion. His careful notation guides the performer in controlling the temporal elements of these transitions. The studies depend on the whole for the completion of their individual gestures and realize their full impact only when performed in their entirety. A brief survey of other piano works from Szymanowski's middle period, and a discussion of how the studies prepare the pianist for the challenges found in these other works, are included.

Zhang, Shi-Gu. *Chinese and Western Influences Upon Piano Music in China.* D.M.A. paper, Tucson: University of Arizona, 1993, 74 p. UM 9328572. This study chronicles the development of piano music in China through seven representative works. An important aspect of this research is to evaluate how and to what extent the repertoire reflects the diverse influences of Western music, traditional Chinese culture, and Chinese politics. Due to the tumultuous social history of modern China, political factors have dictated and continue to dominate cultural aesthetics in a unique way. At some period, styles closely conformed to the political ideology. When the political climate was freer, however, the composer's creative ideology was allowed to be expressed more openly, and the cultural exchange with the West was freer. Although many Chinese pieces are not of high quality, a number of Chinese composers have successfully devoted themselves to integrating Western musical techniques with their own rich cultural background.

Zilberquit, Mark. *Book of the Piano.* Trans. from the Russian by Yuri S. Shirokov. Neptune City, N.J.: Paganiniana Publications, 1988, 79 p. This illustrated history of the piano contains beautiful prints and concise text.

Zirpoli, Danny Ronald. *An Evaluation of the Work of Jazz Pianist/Composer Dave Brubeck.* Ph.D. dissertation, Gainesville: University of Florida, 1990, 237 p. UM 9106501. The primary purpose of this study is to evaluate the work of jazz pianist and composer Dave Brubeck in order to ascertain the extent of his contributions to the field of jazz. The thrust of the research concentrates on areas related to general biographical information; Brubeck's meter/rhythm experiments; European classical influences; cultural aspects, including sociological factors; compositional output; pedagogical and instructional values; and jazz ambassadorial contributions. Brubeck's relationship with the critics is also probed.

Specific research questions included: 1) To what extent did Brubeck contribute to the development of jazz? 2) To what extent has Brubeck been influential in promoting the cause of jazz? 3) What is the extent of Brubeck's contribution as far as the quantity of music literature is concerned? 4) To what extent might Brubeck's music be utilized in an educational setting?

From the findings, it is evident that Brubeck contributed to the field of jazz in a variety of ways. He contributed to the development of jazz piano by the systematic application of unusual meters, polyrhythms, and polytonality. He expanded the concept of free improvisation within the context of odd meters. Through the integration of classical and jazz elements Brubeck helped to pave the way for other jazz musicians and create new markets for jazz. He also promulgated the cause of jazz and, in so doing, increased intercultural understanding and feelings of goodwill.

Although the focus of the study is on the piano works, selected examples of other genres are also examined. It is concluded that Brubeck's large-scale choral/jazz compositions are a viable contribution to music literature. Pedagogical value in Brubeck's piano compositions and improvisations is evident. It is concluded that a study of his music could benefit both the beginning and advanced jazz student. Recommendations are made to include a study of his music within a curriculum of jazz.

Subject Indexes

Accompanying (includes chamber music)

Allsop, P.
Benestad, F.
Berry, F. A.
Brown, J. W.
Cheny, E. W. III
Christensen, J.
Edel, T.
Fillion, M. M.
Goertzen, V. W.
Gracia, A. L. A.
Hornick, A.
Hukill, C. L.
Karpati, J.
Komlós, K.
Loft, A.

McGowen, J. J.
Millican, B.
Outland, J. J.
Pelley, J. F.
Price, D. N.
Rangel-Ribeiro, V.
Riggs, R. D.
Roe, S.
Rogers, B. J.
Signor, J. F.
Sisman, E. R.
Smallman, B.
Walker-Hill, H.
Whang, U.-Y

Aesthetics

Adams, N.
Alexander, M. J.
Andrews, J. S.
Angilette, E.
Autry, P. E.
Axford, E. C.
Backus, J. P.
Bailey, B.
Becker, P. J.
Berry, R. A.
Bloomquist, W. C., Jr.
Bowling, I. R.
Brechemin, L.
Brink, M. A.
Bruhn, S.
Bruno, S. J.
Burge, D.
Carr, C. I.
Carruthers, G. B.

Cartright, C. S.
Cline, E. T.
Clinton, M. K.
Coleman, D. J.
Cortright, C. S.
Crosby, R. A.
Drake, K.
Dunsby, J.
Dyal, E. I. C.
Englund, V. A.
Fouse, K. L.
Friedburg, R. C.
Fritsch, M. F.
Garcia, S. P.
Gitz, R. J.
Gordon, S.
Gould, G.
Graziano, V.
Guhl, L.

Analysis (also see Biographies Index)

Biographies (also see Analysis Index)

Construction and Design

Editors, Performers, Teachers, and Writers

History and Criticism

Performance Anxiety. Stress and Tension

Performance Technique

Piano Duet

Transcriptions

Two or More Pianos

Bonello, M.
Frieling, R.
Purrone, R. C.

Schults-Berndt, E. D.
Svard, L.
Tse, B. W.-K.

Video Cassettes

Alexander, Dennis
Anatomy of a Piano
Beethoven Piano Concerto No. 1
Brandman, Margaret
Brendel, Alfred
Case, Angeline-Newport
Choreography of the Hands
Complete Chopin Etudes
Concerto!
   Mozart K. 453
   Mozart K. 467
   Mozart K. 216
Conversations with Frances Clark
Cooke, Max
Fink, Seymour
Goldenzweig, Hugo
   Chopin etudes

Gordon, Stewart
Gould, Glenn (2)
Grindea, Carola
Haydon, Sona
Hinson, Maurice
How to Choose a Piano Teacher
Janis, Byron
Lister-Sink, Barbara
Mozart on Tour
Peskanov, Alexander
Nelita True
Ott, Margaret Saunders
Piano
Rachmaninoff Piano Concerto No. 2
Rubinstein, Arthur
Taubman, Dorothy

Composer Index

This index is organized alphabetically by composer. Under each composer's name appear the author(s) of material pertaining to that composer, followed by a listing of the particular compositions discussed (in italics). If no compositions are listed following the author's name, the subject matter is general in nature. The compositions are assumed to be for piano unless otherwise designated (i. e., sonatas means piano sonatas).

Absil, Jean
  Vadala

Agay, Denes
  Andrews

Albéniz, Isaac
  Baytelman
  Redford, *Iberia*
  Sellek-Harrison, *Suite Espanola,*
    Op. 47

Albright, William
  Burge, D.
  Sulton, *5 Chromatic Dances*

Alkan, Charles V.
  Ahn
  Henning, Opp. 35 & 39
  Lopez, Op. 39

D'Anglebert, Jean-Henri
  Maple

Antheil, George
  Fouse

Auric, Georges
  Sitton

Austin, Larry
  Brandenburg, *Sonata Concertante*

Avni, Tzvi
  Espiedra, *Sonata II*

Bacewicz, Grazyna
  Mills

Bach, C. P. E.
  Chay
  Koehler, *Rondos*
  Walkinshaw

Bach, Johann Christian
  Derry, *concertos*
  Kidd
  Roe

Bach, J. S.
  Altschuler, *WTC*
  Andrews
  Badura-Skoda
  Barsalou, *Goldberg Variations*
  Bruhn, *WTC*
  Butt
  Carruthers, *transcriptions*
  Curry
  Ellsworth, *keyboard concertos*
  Forrest, *Preludes*
  Gluckman, *Toccata* BWV 911
  Goldberg, *WTC*
  Groves, S. E.
  Kong, *Chromatic Fantasy & Fugue*
    BWV 903
  Little & Jenne, *dance music*
  Marshall
  Munger
  Pruett, *Chaconne*
  Renwick, *WTC*
  Schulenberg
  Valenti, *Partitas*

Hollander
Hong, Y.-L., etudes
Hudson
Janis (video cassette)
Kallberg
Kang, Y., preludes
Kirk, preludes
Klein, etudes
Kreaky, preludes
Lee, E. Y.-W., etudes
Leikim
Martin, T. N.
McClain
Mitchell
Ott, M. S.
Parkilas, ballades
Rowland, pedal
Rubinstein, Arthur
Samson, ballades
Siepmann
Smith, E. L., mazurkas
Suwan, *Nocturne*, Op. 27/2 and
    Waltz, Op. 64/2
Taubman (video cassette)
Todd
Trechak
Whiteside
Witten
Zaluski

Cimarosa, Domenico
Dettman, *32 Sonatas*

Clark, Thomas
Brandenburg, *Peninsula*

Clementi, Muzio
Hong, Y.-L., *Gradus ad Parnassum*
Komlós, K.

Confrey, Zez
Dossa

Copland, Aaron
Brunelli
McGowan, *Quartet for Piano and
    Strings*

Morris, *Sonata*
Nyquist
Worman, *Variations*

Corea, "Chick" Armando
Yampolaky

Corigliano, John
Simms, *Etude Fantasy* and *Fantasia
    on an Ostinato*

Couperin, François
Wilkens

Cowell, Henry
Fouse
Lichtenwanger

Cramer, J. B.
Ellsworth

Creston, Paul
Brook, *Rhythmicon*
Leach, dances

Crumb, George
Burge, D.
Becker, *Makrokosmos*
Fouse
Jiorle-Nagy, *Makrokosmos*
Takenouchi

Cumming, Richard
Kindall, preludes
Sanchez, preludes

Curran, Alvin
Paul

Czerny, Carl
Maxwell
Sheets, sonatas

Davis, Peter Maxwell
Bowling

Debussy, Claude
Berthiaume, etudes
Bruhn
Chiang, *The Engulfed Cathedral*

Appendix

List of Publishers

Mailing address of publishing houses and other organizations which print or circulate writings discussed in this volume.

Alfred Publishing (Australia) Ltd.
P.O. Box 2355
Taren Point NSW 2229
Australia

Alfred Publishing Co.
16380 Roscoe Blvd.
P.O. Box 10003
Van Nuys, CA 91410-0003

Allans Publishing Pty. Ltd.
Box 364
South Melbourne 3205
Australia

Amadeus Press
133 S.W. Second Ave., Suite 450
Portland, OR 97204-3527

Appian Publications & Recordings
P.O. Box 1, Wark, Hexham
Northumberland NE 48 3EW
United Kingdom

A-R Editions, Inc.
801 Deming Way
Madison, WI 53717

Artmusique Publishing Co.
31 Perry Hill
London SE6 4LF
United Kingdom

Associated University Presses
440 Forsgate Drive
Cranbury, NJ 08512

Baker Book House
Box 6287
Grand Rapids, MI 49516

Batsford
Box 257
North Pomfret, VT 05053

BBC Publications
35 Marylebone High Street
London WIM 4AA
United Kingdom

(BBC) British Broadcasting Corp.
630 Fifth Ave.
New York, NY 10020

Bell Tower
201 East 50th St.
New York, NY 10022

George Braziller, Inc.
60 Madison Ave.
New York, NY 10010

Brookside Press
Box 178-PQ
Jamaica Plain, MA 021308

Brown Composition Systems
128 North Walnut
Bloomington, IN 47404

Cambridge University Press
32 East 57th St.
New York, NY 10022

Carol Publishing Group
120 Enterprise Ave.
Secaucus, NJ 07094

Castillon Press
34 Druidsville Rd.
Liverpool L18 3EW England

Chicago Biographical Center
Box 557755
Chicago, IL 60655

Clarendon Press
see Oxford University Press

Cornell University Press
P.O. Box 250
Ithaca, NY 14851

Creative Arts Book Co.
833 Bancroft Way
Berkeley, CA 94710

Culver Crest Publications
Box 4484
Culver City, CA 90231-4484

Damore Publications
631 South Irene Ave.
Redonda Beach, CA 90277

David Daniel Music Publications
Indiana University Bookstore
Bloomington, IN 47405

Delacorte Press
1540 Broadway
New York, NY 10036-4094

Distinctive Publishing Corp.
Box 17868
Plantation, FL 33318-7868

Doubleday & Co.
245 Park Ave.
New York, NY 10017

John Donald Publishers
138 St. Stephen St.
Edinburgh EH3 5AA
United Kingdom

Edition HAS
P.O. Box 1753
Maryland Heights, MO
63043-0753

Ekay Music
223 Katonah Ave.
Katonah, NY 10536

European American Music Corp.
Box 850
Valley Forge, PA 19482-9985

Facts on File
460 Park Avenue South
New York, NY 10016

Fallen Leaf Press
Box 10034-N
Berkeley, CA 94709

Films for the Humanities & Sciences
P.O. Box 2053
Princeton, NJ 08543-2053

Garland Publishing Co.
136 Madison Ave.
New York, NY 10016

G.I.A. Publications, Inc.
7404 South Mason Ave.
Chicago, IL 60638-9927

Greenwood Press, Inc.
88 Post Road West
P.O. Box 5007
Westport, CT 06881

Grove Press
Grove Atlantic Inc.
841 Broadway, 4th floor
New York, NY 10003-4793

Guilford Publications, Inc.
72 Spring St.
New York, NY 10012
    distributed by Mercedes Book Dis-
    tributors Corp.
    62 Imlay St.
    Brooklyn, NY 11231

Harcourt Brace & Co.
525 B St. Suite 1900
San Diego, CA 92101-4495

Harcourt, Brace & Jovanovich
757 Third Ave.
New York, NY 10164

Harmonie Park Press
23630 Pinewood
Warren, MI 48091

Frederick Harris Music Co.
340 Nagel Drive
Buffalo, NY 14225-4731

Harvard University Press
79 Garden St.
Cambridge, MA 02138

Christopher Helm, Ltd.
35 Bedford Row
London, WC1R4JH
United Kingdom

Hollowbrook Publishing
236 South Third St.
Montrose, CO 81401

Indiana University Press
601 North Morton St.
Bloomington, IN 47404-3797

Information Coordinators, Inc.
1435-37 Randolph St.
Detroit, MI 48226

The Instrumentalist Co.
200 Northfield Road
Northfield, IL 60093

International Piano Archives
University of Maryland
College Park, MD 20742

I.S.A.M.
Brooklyn College
Conservatory of Music
2900 Bedford Ave.
Brooklyn, NY 11210-2889

JTJ Films
27 Pine Grove
Amherst, MA 01002

Kahn & Averill
21 Pennard Mansions
Goldhawk Rd.
London W12 8DL
United Kingdom

Kjos West Music Co.
4382 Jutland Drive
San Diego, CA 92117-0894

Alfred A. Knopf
400 Hahn Rd.
Westminster, MD 21157

Peter Lang Inc.
62 West 45th Street (4th floor)
New York, NY 10036

Hal Leonard Corp.
8112 West Blue Mound Rd.
Milwaukee, WI 53213

Library of Congress
Washington, DC 20540

Little, Brown & Co.
200 West St.
Waltham, MA 02154

London Road Books
535 Ramona St., No. 33
Palo Alto, CA 94301-1710

Longwood Academic
27 South Main St.
Wolfeboro, NH 03894-2069

Robert B. Luce, Inc.
c/o Integrated Distributors Service
195 McGregor St.
Manchester, NH 03101

Lynwood Music
2 Church St.
West Hagley, West Midlands
DY9 ONA
United Kingdom

Macmillan Publishing Co.
866 3rd Ave.
New York, NY 10022
  refer orders to:
  Front & Brown Sts.
  Riverside, NJ 08370

Magnamusic-Baton
  now MMB
3526 Washington Ave.
St. Louis, MO 63103-1019

Manduca Music Publications
P.O. Box 10550
Portland, ME 04104

Marik Publishing
10622 North Blaney Ave.
Cupertino, CA 95014-6039

McFarland & Co.
Box 611
Jefferson, NC 28640

Media for the Arts
Newport, RI 02840

Mellon Press
Box 450
Lewiston, NY 14092

Music Sources
1000 The Alameda
Berkeley, CA 94707

Thomas Nelson Publishers
Box 14100
Nelson Place at Elmhill Pike
Nashville, TN 37214-1000

Nelson-Hall Publishers
111 North Canal St.
Chicago, IL 60606

Northeastern University Press
360 Huntington Ave.
Boston, MA 02115

W. W. Norton Co.
500 Fifth Ave.
New York, NY 10110

Novello & Co., Ltd.
Borough Green, Sevenoaks
Kent TN15 8DT
United Kingdom

Oberon Press
Suite 400
350 Spark
Ottawa, Canada K1R 758

Oxford University Press
16-00 Pollitt Drive
Fair Lawn, NJ 07410

Paganiniana Publications, Inc.
Box 427
Neptune City, NJ 07410

Pendragon Press
RR 1, Box 159
Stuyvesant, NY 12173-9720

Penerbit Muzikal
11900 Bayan Lepas
Penang, Malaysia

C. F. Peters Corp.
373 Park Ave. South
New York, NY 10016

Philips Classics
Polygram Classics
Worldwide Plaza
825 Eighth Ave.
New York, NY 10019

Popular Culture
Box 1839
Ann Arbor, MI 48106

Theodore Presser
Presser Place
Bryn Mawr, PA 19010

Princeton University Press
41 William St.
Princeton, NJ 08540

Pro/Am Music Resources, Inc.
63 Prospect St.
White Plains, NY 10606

Random House, Inc.
201 East 50th St.
New York, NY 10022

Andrew Rupert Publishing
17 Windmill St.
Valletta, Malta

San Francisco Press
Box 6800
San Francisco, CA 94101-6800

SH Productions
6151 Paseo Blvd
Kansas City, MO 64110

Scarecrow Press
15200 NBN Way
P.O. Box 191
Blue Ridge Summit, PA 17214-0191

Schirmer Books
see Simon & Schuster Macmillan

Simon & Schuster Macmillan
1633 Broadway
New York, NY 10019

Stainer & Bell, Ltd.
82 High Rd.
East Finchley
London N2 9PW
United Kingdom

Stanford University Press
Stanford, CA 94305-2235

The Taubman Institute
Medusa, NY 12120

Teacher's Pet Productions
Box 3783
Spokane, WA 99202-3783

Texas A&M University Press
College Station, TX 77843-4354

Gordon V. Thompson Music
29 Birch Ave.
Toronto, Ont. M4V 1E2
Canada

UMI Research Press
300 North Zeeb Rd.
Ann Arbor, MI 48106

University Microfilms
300 North Zeeb Rd.
Ann Arbor, MI 48106

University of Chicago Press
5801 Ellis Ave. 4th Floor
Chicago, IL 60637

University of North Texas Press
Drawer C
College Station, TX 77843-4354

University Press of America
4720 Boston Way
Lanham, MD 20706-9990

Vantage Press
516 West 34th St.
New York, NY 10001

Warner Brothers Music Australia
1 Cassins Ave.
North Sydney, Australia
NSW 2060

Willis Music Co.
7380 Industrial Rd.
Florence, KY 41042

Winds
Box 513
Northridge, CA 91328

Xin Hua Ma Publishing
Box 50202
Pasadena, CA 91115-0202

Yale University Press
302 Temple St.
New Haven, CT 06520

For books that have recently gone out of print, try:

United States

Steven's Bookshop
Corner North and Main
P.O. Box 71
Wake Forest, NC 27587

Books on File
Dept. MY 67
Union City, NJ 07087

United Kingdom

Blackwell's Music Shop
38 Holeywell St.
Oxford OX1 3SW
United Kingdom

Europe (other than United Kingdom)

Otto Harrassowitz
P.O. Box 2929
D-6200 Wiesbaden
Germany

MAURICE HINSON is Senior Professor of Piano
at the Southern Baptist Theological Seminary in
Louisville, Kentucky. His many publications include
the classic *Guide to the Pianist's Repertoire*.